Holger Norgaard
Jan. 1975

£10

£4.50

The English Language
in Modern Times
(since 1400)

The English Language

in Modern Times (since 1400)

by MARGARET SCHLAUCH

Professor of English Philology
University of Warsaw

PWN — Polish Scientific Publishers, Warszawa

Oxford University Press, London

First Edition 1959
Reprinted 1962, 1964, 1965, 1967, 1973

CONTENTS

PREFACE

In presenting the second edition of this textbook I should like to express my thanks for the corrections and suggestions that have come to me by way of reviews and private correspondence. Basic errors, both typographical and factual, have I trust been properly dealt with. However, it has not been possible to deal with or even include reference to many of the individual problems and special studies mentioned by the reviewers. All of them are no doubt valuable and significant. But in the first place, I do not here have at my disposal the materials essential for a discussion of some of the topics proposed (for instance, Canadian or Australian English, interesting as these are). In the second place, I have tried to keep in mind the needs of undergraduate students at a Polish university, most of whom are specializing in literary, not linguistic research. They require philological aid primarily for the better understanding of literary texts included on their reading lists. Even for linguists proper I have done little more than indicate the general trends and the major studies which would guide them towards further investigation. Special articles are cited by way of example or because they give useful bibliography; there is no pretense to exhaustiveness.

Recent important studies, unavailable when I concluded the first edition of this book (March, 1958), suggest revisions not as yet undertaken, for reasons of time and technique. For instance, B. Trnka, "A Phonemic Aspect of the Great Vowel Shift", in *Mélanges de linguistique et de philologie F. Mossé in memoriam* (Paris, 1959), proposes a neat correlation of quantity and tenseness of vowels which should be carefully considered in any treatment of the subject. The chapter on American dialects by R. I. McDavid, Jr., in W. N. Francis, *The Structure of American English* (New York, 1958), should be read as supplement to my brief discussion. The whole question of Middle English dialects is now being subjected to rigorous scrutiny by Angus McIntosh (Edinburgh) and others. The results will probably lead to a basic revision of the pioneer work by Whitehall, Moore and Meech (1935), upon which I have chiefly relied. Current work on Modern English dialects will also, in due course, render obsolete my discussion of that subject, based on materials and analyses of the never-to-be-forgotten Joseph Wright. In the meantime, I can only hope that the present outline, sketchy as it is, may continue for some time to serve the interests of the students and general readers for whom it was intended.

Margaret Schlauch

Warsaw, February 1964

ACKNOWLEDGEMENTS

Grateful acknowledgement is herewith made to the following for permission to use and quote from material already appearing in print: to Harcourt, Brace and Co. (New York) for the quotation from Jean Stafford's *Boston Adventure* and to Random House (New York) for the one taken from William Faulkner's *The Old Man*, both of these appearing in the text of ch. 8; also to the following for excerpts appearing in the Appendix: to Sir Alexander Gray for his translation of Heine's "Still ist die Nacht" and to Sydney Goodsir Smith for his poems "Sweet Womankind" and "A Bairn Sick"; to Hugh MacDiarmid for the excerpts from his "Second Hymn to Lenin"; to Faber and Faber (London) for the shortened extract from A. G. Street's *Harvest by Lamplight*; to Macmillan and Co. (London) and also to Mrs. Stephens for the passage from James Stephens' *The Crock of Gold*; to Barrows Dunham and his publishers, Little, Brown and Co. (Boston) for the recorded speech of a Negro taken from *Giant in Chains*; to Lars Lawrence for the passage from *Morning Noon and Night*; to Charles Scribner's Sons (New York) for the extract from Ring Lardner's "You Know Me Al"; to The Bodley Head (London) for the extract from the *Ulysses* of James Joyce; and to Messrs Monro, Pennefather and Co., solicitors (London), representing the estate of James Joyce, for the one taken from *Finnegans Wake*.

ABBREVIATIONS

AN: Anglo-Norman
Ant. and Cl.: *Antony and Cleopatra*
arch.: archaic
As You L.: *As You Like It*
Boeth.: Chaucer's translation of Boethius
  De Consolatione Philosophiae
Ch.: Chaucer
Cock.: Cockney
colloq.: colloquial
Coriol.: *Coriolanus*
CT: Chaucer's *Canterbury Tales*
Cymb.: *Cymbeline*
D: dative
dial.: dialect
Dor.: dialect of Dorset
EETS: Early English Text Society
  —ES: Extra Series
  —OS: Original Series
ELH: *English Literary History*
EMdl: East Midland
euph.: euphemism
Every Man In: *Every Man in his Humour*
Every Man Out: *Every Man Out of his*
  Humour
expl.: expletive
fem.: feminine
Fr.: French
Gael.: Gaelic
Gesta Rom.: *Gesta Romanorum*
Gul.: Gullah
Haml.: *Hamlet*
impers.: impersonal construction
Ir.: Irish; Anglo-Irish
Jul. Caes.: *Julius Caesar*

Macb.: *Macbeth*
masc.: masculine
ME: Middle English
Meas. for Meas.: *Measure for Measure*
Mel.: Chaucer's *Melibeus*
Mer. of Ven.: *Merchant of Venice*
Merry Wives: *The Merry Wives of Windsor*
ModE: Modern English
ModScots: Modern Scots
MScots: Middle Scots
n.: noun
naut.: nautical term
NED: *New English Dictionary*
neut.: neuter
Nth: Northern dialects
O: object
OE: Old English
OFr: Old French
ON: Old Norse
OScand: Old Scandinavian
Oth.: *Othello*
P: predicate
Pard. T.: Chaucer's Pardoner's Tale
Parl. F.: Chaucer's *Parlement of Fowles*
part.: participle
perf.: perfect
pl., plur.: plural
pret.: preterite
Prol.: Prologue to Chaucer's *Canterbury*
  Tales
pron.: pronunciation
S: subject
Sc.: Scots; modern Scottish
sg., sing.: singular

Sh.: Shakespeare

sl.: slang (including cant and jargon)

Sp.: Spanish

Sth: Southern dialects

Temp.: Shakespeare's *Tempest*

Tim. of Ath.: *Timon of Athens*

Tr. and Cr.: Chaucer's *Troilus and Criseyde*; also Shakespeare's *Troilus and Cressida*

US: United States; also dialects of the United States

V: verb

var.: variant

vb: verb

vulg.: vulgar

WBT: Chaucer's Wife of Bath's Tale

Wint. Tale: *A Winter's Tale*

WMdl: West Midland

PHONETIC SYMBOLS

Vowels

[i:] as in English *feel* (but without the off-glide [j])

[i] as in French *fini*

[ɨ] a high central vowel, lax and unrounded, between [i] and [u]

[ɪ] as in English *fit*

[i̯] the "short *i*" of Shakespeare's time (see ch. 3, sec. 5)

[e:] as in German *See*; indicated in ME as *ē*

[e] the same, shortened

[ę] as in English *set*

[ę:] the long vowel in *stale* of Shakespeare's time

[ɛ:] as in French *père*; indicated in ME as *ę̄*

[æ] as in English *hat*

[æ:] the same, lengthened

[a] as in French *là*

[a:] the same, lengthened

[ɑ] as in French *pas*

[ɑ:] as in English *father*

[ɒ] as in English *not*

[ɒ:] as in English *naught*

[ɔ] and [ɔ:] the "cardinal vowels" corresponding to the last two, in higher back position

[o] as in French *dos*

[o:] the same, lengthened, as in German *Lohn*

[u:] as in English *fool* (but without the off-glide [w])

[u] as in French *foule*

[u̯] the "short *u*" of Shakespeare's time

[ʊ] as in English *full*

[ʌ] as in English *cut* (conservative pronunciation)

[ə] as in the first syllable of *about*

[ɜ:] as in English *bird*

[y:] as in German *kühn*

[y] as in French *bu*

Consonants

[θ] as in English *thin*

[ð] as in English *this*

[j] as in English *yet*

[ç] as in German *nicht*

[χ] as in German *Nacht*, Scotch *loch*

[γ] as in German (dialectal) *fragen* or OE ʒ in *daʒum*

[ŋ] as in English *song*

[ʃ] as in English *shall*

[ʒ] as in English *pleasure*, French *joie*

[w] as in English *way*

[ʍ] the same, voiceless

[ɹ] untrilled *r*

[l̩], [m̩], etc., indicate syllabic consonants

[l̥], [m̥], etc., indicate voiceless consonants

LIST OF MAPS

Reprinted from Fernand Mossé, *A Handbook of Middle English*, tr. by James A. Walker (for Mossé's source see Whitehall, Moore and Meech, *Middle English Dialect Characteristics*, Michigan 1935):

Reprinted from Hans Galinsky, *Die Sprache des Amerikaners*, II:

Reprinted from Hans Kurath and others: *Linguistic Atlas of the United States*, I, (New England), p. 30, chart 8:

CHAPTER I

FORMATION OF THE NATIONAL LANGUAGE:
14th CENTURY BACKGROUNDS

1. A DEFINITION OF PERIODS

The task of delimiting significant periods in any kind of social history is difficult at best; perhaps most difficult of all in the case of linguistic history. Here the changes which transform any given language from one phase to another must of necessity be gradual, though they do not by any means occur at the same rate in all historical situations. Under normal circumstances the differences between the speech of one generation and the next are in an absolute sense very slight, even when relatively speaking they are most rapid. It is only after they have been accumulated over a span of several generations that they become obviously perceptible. This is particularly true of the transformations affecting the structure of a language, its method of organising words and phrases into sentences. It is also true, however, of the general mode of uttering the characteristic individual sounds (phonemes) of a specific language. Even transformations in vocabulary, which of all changes are on the whole most easily accomplished, do not take place with complete abruptness.

These general observations may be readily illustrated from the history of the English language. In the Middle Ages it passed through one period, from 1066 to about 1200, when it was exposed to influences causing relatively swift changes of all sorts. It was, as is well known, subjected to political conquest from the outside; it was officially submerged for a time, at least with respect to the activities of the administrative governing powers; it was thus brought into close contact with an alien tongue on its native soil. One might have expected a prompt and large-scale influx of foreign loans into English. Nevertheless — although means of communication must have been established very quickly between the new feudal overlords and the masses of the people — the internal transformation of English in this period appears to have been only very slightly accelerated. The tendencies to shifted pronunciation and to simplified linguistic structure which found realisation in the 150 years after 1066 were already clearly operating in Late Old English. They were manifestations of inner forces, inner laws of growth in the language. Even the borrowing of French words, a more facile and external process of change, remained slow until after 1200.[1] Only in the course of the latter 13th century, when English was already quite well established as a medium of general communication, did French loan words begin to multiply strikingly. Their influx did not essentially modify English syntax, however, and they had but a slight influence on native pronunciation, though they did affect English versification to a certain extent.

The reasons for the slow tempo of change are obvious. Each generation begins to master humanity's accumulated knowledge, its skills and arts, by learning directly from its older contemporaries. Spoken language is an intimate, essential part of the heritage and at the same time the chief medium of learning and instruction. As that medium is passed on it may at the same time be modified; but modification beyond a certain point would defeat the primary purpose of communication between the generations.

Hence the extreme gradualness of linguistic change, even at its most rapid, and hence also the difficulty in choosing boundaries between periods in the history of a language.

In the case of English, however, there are some fairly strong reasons why the decades just before and just after 1400 A. D. may well be taken as a starting point for a history of the language in modern times. The reasons for such a choice have to do with a number of factors. Some of them are internal to the language, some external

---

[1] It was usual in older handbooks to exaggerate the speed of transformation of English after 1066, and also to exaggerate the gap dividing the native speakers from the French settlers on English soil. While it is true that the highest circles of royalty and aristocracy retained the Norman dialect of French and for several generations held aloof from English, intercommunication began early on the lower levels, where English held complete sway. The administration of justice, the conduct of manor economy and church affairs was in English or Latin, not French, in the 11th and 12th centuries. See G. E. Woodbine, "The Language of English Law," *Speculum*, XVIII (1943), 395—436.

to it. Chief among the internal ones was a set of changes in vowel pronunciation, carried out soon after the turning point of the century, which constituted the first step in a fundamental transformation of the English phonemic system.

So far as accented vowels were concerned, what happened was primarily a change in quality, the beginning of a very extensive shift which occupied several centuries and in a sense is still going on. So far as the unaccented ones were concerned, what happened was the complete loss of final unaccented -e [ə] sounds, which had been very numerous in the terminations of words as spoken a century earlier (ca. 1300). In the interval these final -e's had been reduced gradually in quantity and in distinctness of articulation. The final change to zero was accomplished by the beginning of the 15th century, as the scansion of verse indicates. For these internal reasons, therefore, a dividing line placed about the year 1400 has meaning in the history of the English language.

It may be remarked at the same time that this division cor- . responds in a very real way to a meaningful one in literary history. The year 1400 witnessed the death of Geoffrey Chaucer, incomparably the greatest of a group of distinguished poets who had flourished late in the 14th century in England. The group included John Gower (who outlived Chaucer for but a few years) and the authors of such poems as *Piers Plowman* and *The Pearl* and *Sir Gawain and the Green Knight*. In the next generation the followers of Chaucer and the others, though they numbered among them men of talent, were imitators rather than creators. At their technical best they still fell far behind their pre-decessors in their linguistic skill, to say nothing of their gift of imagination. It is quite possible, as has been suggested, that the internal linguistic changes of the period increased the technical difficulties besetting 15th-century poets, and thus partly explain their inferior performance. The changes in language were at least enough to make more difficult a fluent and pleasing imitation of Chaucer's musical effects: the kind of thing his epigones most zealously aimed to achieve in the next generation.

There were also certain extra-linguistic factors of decisive importance in shaping the English language about this time, and these reinforced the ones operating from within. Briefly, these were factors of an economic and political nature which favoured the emergence of a single, generally accepted national language out of the multiple contrasting local dialects of the feudal period. Though external in a certain sense they played an essential role in English linguistic history.

2. External Tendencies Favouring Linguistic Unity

During the earlier centuries of the Middle Ages, the feudal system had not only tended to preserve regional dialects but in many ways had actually tended to accentuate their separateness and multiply their number. The Midland area, for instance, seems to have become more diversified linguistically than had been the old Mercian kingdom occupying approximately the same territory (at least, so far as we can judge from surviving written texts). In the pre-Conquest centuries, it will be recalled, the pressure of political events during the Scandinavian invasions had fostered a kind of unity in military cooperation and also in cultural relations among the separate Anglo-Saxon kingdoms then existing. The alliances among them were loose ones, to be sure, lacking the force of amalgamation which can arise only from a single large-scale national economy with a single political system of administration. Nevertheless the military and political leadership of Wessex in relationship to Kent and Mercia was so heightened by the educational and literary activities of King Alfred that West Saxon assumed something of the role of a literary *koinē* familiar in other kingdoms.[2]

The feudal system of the 11th century, with its sharpening of linguistic boundaries, meant in effect a regression from the late Old English tendencies towards unity. That Anglo-Saxon England was already showing trends towards a native feudalism does not change the historical fact that the feudalism actually realised was built on the Norman pattern, being introduced by the Normans. It was already well developed when it was introduced.

After 1066, the country as a whole was transformed, politically and administratively, into a typical concatenation of vassals' holdings, each leading an all but exclusive economic life, each centred on a local power, each separated from others by a series of local regulations: tolls and taxes and fixed prices, rules controlling the residence and employment of outsiders, all of which ensured a high degree of economic

---

[2] This *koinē* was itself marked by Anglian and Mercian traits due to the presence of Northern writers and scribes in the Southwest. Some of these alien traits in written texts were probably due to transcription from lost originals composed elsewhere. For recent discussion of this situation see Kenneth Sisam, "Dialect Origins of the Earlier Old English Verse," ch. 8 in his *Studies in the History of Old English Literature* (Oxford, 1953).

autarky. Culturally, the individual villages, market towns and castles were more or less separate units, especially in the first century after the Conquest, to an extent which it is hard for a modern student to realise. Linguistically, this entailed the development of local dialects for purposes of local administration and also of entertainment.

As a consequence the poetic literature and the official records of the various shires in England were until the latter 14th century composed in distinct regional dialects. Students of Middle English literature are at once made aware that the earliest saints' lives of the 12th century (the so-called "Katherine Group") were composed in the West Midland and show affinities with late West Saxon style. They are no less aware that *Cursor Mundi* belongs to the North, that Orm wrote his *Ormulum* in the East Midlands, that the author of *Pearl* came from the West Midlands, and that Dan Michael —that ponderous moralist— could have written nowhere but in Kent. The regional literature produced in England up to and including the 14th century was often very distinguished. By the end of that period, however, its heyday was past. The dialects of the provinces were yielding place to that of London, the city which had become both the political and administrative centre of the country and by far its most important focus of trade.

In the earlier Middle Ages London had boasted of no such prominence. It had gained its first relative importance when Edward the Confessor, last but one of the Anglo-Saxon kings, had transferred thither from Winchester the seat of his government. It was a government which, though loosely coordinated and easily shaken by rebellions and invasions, already claimed to represent England as a whole. Now it was the Norman kings who tried to weld medieval England into a political and administrative unity within the insecure framework of the feudal system, likewise using London as a centre. They too encountered perennial resistance from powerful baronial families. Nevertheless, throughout the rebellions and internal warfare of the medieval centuries, London maintained and steadily strengthened its position.

It was the growth of an internal market, expanding constantly towards economic unity within the national sphere, which gave solidity to the position of London and ensured the triumph of its speech as a basis for a generally accepted national language. Without the rise of market towns, the extension of trade beyond the confines of local boundaries, and the development of large-scale trade in wool with the continent (in which London far outdistanced all the other East-coast cities), there would have been no foundation for the kind of national political unity which in turn facilitated the rise of a single national language.

The process was of course an uneven one, interrupted, accelerated or retarded from time to time by political upheavals, military campaigns, visitations of pestilence and so on. The general outline is however clear and consistent.

The middle class of the towns, the traders together with the artisans, apprentices and others whom we may roughly classify as "plebeians," played a leading part in this transformation. Nowhere was city life more stimulating than in London, whither came both visitors and permanent residents from other parts of the country. Linguistically speaking, the population was already a rather mixed one in the latter 14th century because of the continuing influx of new residents, both domestic and foreign. The latter group included such diverse elements as Flemish weavers, Italian bankers and French prisoners-of-war. Since the royal court resided here, upper-class social life added prestige to the dialect spoken in the streets of the capital city.

True enough, the English court itself was at the end of the 14th century still bilingual, preferring French to English in much of its social activity. But the native speech had already become current and even popular among some of the loftiest members of the court group. This fact is attested by the extraordinary success of Geoffrey Chaucer's writings, for which he received pay and patronage from members of the royal family.[3] During his lifetime the English language won its major victories in the administrative life of the country. In 1362 Parliament was opened in English for the first time; in the same year English was accepted as the official language of the law courts.[4] Such events do not mean that French and Latin at once disappeared

---

[3] Besides the evidence of his own dedications and the official documents rewarding him for his services, we have an illumination in one of the manuscripts of his *Troilus and Criseyde*, showing the poet reading aloud that masterpiece of vernacular narrative before a company that included King Richard II, his Queen Anne of Bohemia, his mother Joan of Kent (widow of the Black Prince) and representatives of the highest aristocracy. On these identifications see Margaret Galway, "The Troilus Frontispiece," *Modern Language Review*, XLIV (1949), 161—77.

[4] Friedrich Kluge, *Geschichte der englischen Sprache*, reprinted from Paul's *Grundriss der germanischen Philologie* (Strassburg, 1890), pp. 950 ff.

from official life. As a matter of fact they continued to be used; but from this time onward the success of English was assured.

The original native dialect of official London, as represented by the oldest documents, was a form of the Southwestern literary language or *koinē* inherited from Old English. The language of the medieval capital was however largely shaped by the East Midland dialect, and this influence early became the prevalent one in writing as well as speaking. By the 14th century, London English was practically identical with that of the East Midlands, though a certain number of traits distinguished it from its closest neighbours, the local dialects of Middlesex and Westminster.[5] There are a number of marked Anglian features observable in certain word-forms adopted into London speech, such as the unbroken vowel of *old* (from Anglian *ald* rather than Southern *eald*) and the unpalatalised consonants of *give, gate* (instead of *yive, yate*), which testify to strong dialectal influence from the Northeast.

In confirming the establishment of London English as a specific literary standard for the rest of the country, Chaucer's writings themselves exercised a certain influence. His artistic eminence was generously recognised during his own life-time; his admirers and imitators perpetuated many of his usages and mannerisms during the ensuing period. Nevertheless it would be a mistake to argue (as was formerly done) that Chaucer's creative work was a sole or even a primary factor in the achievement of an English national language.[6] Rather, his work and his preeminence were vastly facilitated by the underlying historical forces at work in his age. It is no accident that the brilliant author or authors commonly referred to as "the *Pearl*-poet" did not succeed in founding a permanent school of literature in the West Midland dialect. Chaucer's position in the capital was far more auspi-

---

[5] For instance, the Middlesex dialect preferred short *e* where the City pronunciation favoured *a* for the sound descended from OE æ, whether "broken" by palatalisation or modified to *ea* in certain positions (before *r* or *l* plus a consonant, etc.). The fluctuating usage is reflected in the discrepancy today between spelling and pronunciation of some place names, e. g. the River Thames pronounced [temz] and Pall Mall when pronounced [pelmel]. See Lorenz Morsbach, *Der Ursprung der neuenglischen Schriftsprache* (Heilbronn, 1888); Ernst Dölle, *Zur Sprache Londons vor Chaucer* (Göttingen, 1913); Barbara Mackenzie, *The Early London Dialect* (Oxford, 1928).

[6] See Albert C. Baugh, *A History of the English Language* (New York, 2nd ed., 1959), pp. 184–87, for a discussion of the situation

cious, not only for his worldly success but for his contemporary reputation. The field in which Chaucer's example did exercise a recognisable linguistic influence was restricted to the poetic diction of his imitators.

For one thing, it can be established that Chaucer inclined to some slight archaisms in usage, perhaps for aesthetic reasons such as the requirements of metre, as compared with the current speech of London in his time. It is likely, for instance, that the typical unaccented final -e [ə] of Middle English was more frequently suppressed in ordinary conversation than is the case in Chaucer's verse, where scansion indicates that it was normally (though not universally) retained except before a word beginning with a vowel.[7]

Moreover, Chaucer drew upon dialect forms with a freedom which may well have been exceptional. He introduced Southern expressions more frequently than appears to have been normal in the average non-literary documents of the period (e. g., *ich* for *I*, *yiven* for the current Anglian *given*, occasional Kentish forms such as *lest* for the normal Midland *list*, which is an *i*-umlaut of *lust*). His knowledge of other dialects is also revealed in his adaptation of them for purposes of literary characterisation, as when the two students in his Reeve's Tale talk a convincing North-country dialect, or when Harry Bailly betrays his origin by a sprinkling of Southern forms in his speech. Part of Chaucer's linguistic variety was due to the needs of artistic creation, part no doubt to personal choice, and part to the conditions of his environment which made so broad a choice possible.

3. A Review of Chaucer's Phonology

Because of this wide variety and the fluctuations in his usage, Chaucer's language is from some points of view not the best point of departure, perhaps, for a history of modern English. On the other hand, Chaucer's type of speech is the form of Middle English best known to students of the period; it was looked upon as a kind of

---

[7] The following discussions contain bibliographies pertinent to the problem: Ruth Buchanan McJimsey, *Chaucer's Irregular -e* (New York: King's Crown Press, 1942); J. G. Southworth, "Chaucer's Final -e in Rhyme," *PMLA*, LXII (1947), 910—35; E. Talbot Donaldson, "Chaucer's Final -e," *ibid.*, LXIII (1948), 1101—24. This discussion deals mainly with -e at the ends of lines, where its articulation is disputable. The situation is clearer for final -e within the line.

model in the age following his, and therefore there is good reason for using it as an initial standard of reference.

The vowels in Chaucer's language were subdivided into long and short. This we know in part by their later behaviour, for the ones we call long have in general diphthongised in modern times, while the short ones have remained relatively stable. There are additional historical reasons which justify the differentiation between the two groups.

A. The unrounded long vowels were as follows: $\bar{\imath}$ [i:], $\bar{e}$ [e:], $\bar{e}$ [ɛ:], $\bar{a}$ [a:]. They appear thus. [8]

$\bar{\imath}$ [i:], written in the MSS. as *i*, *y*, sometimes *ii* or *ij*, in words like: *my*, *mine*; *finden*, *child* (with lengthening in the last two before a liquid or a nasal plus a homorganic voiced stop).

$\bar{e}$ closed [e:], usually written *e* in open syllables and *ee* in closed ones, as in: *depe*, *deme*, *leef*, *me*, *feld*. Words which had a vowel derived from OE $\bar{æ}$ corresponding to West Germanic $\bar{a}$ (Mod. Ger.: *Tat*, *Saat*, etc.) existed in ME in dialectal forms: the Southwestern had open long $\bar{e}$ [ɛ:], while the Anglian had a closed $\bar{e}$ [e:]. Chaucer, it appears from his rimes, used both. It is to be noted that *e* long or short tended to be lowered before *r*, as in early ME *dǣre* from *dēor*, or in *lernen*, but the lowered pronunciation did not often prevail.

$\bar{e}$ open [ɛ:], likewise written *e* and *ee*, but in some dialects not normally riming with words having the closed vowel $\bar{e}$. Choice of

---

[8] The precise quality of some of these long vowels is of course in doubt, and authorities differ in their interpretation of them. Some assume that long $\bar{a}$ had the back position of *a* in modern German *Vater*, rather than the value of *a* in French *là*. Some like Albert Marckwardt in his *Introduction to the English Language* (New York: Oxford University Press, 1942) assume that open $\bar{e}$ was as low as [æ:] instead of [ɛ:]. The discussion by Bernhard ten Brink and Friedrich Kluge, *The Language and Metre of Chaucer* (London, 1901) may be compared with more recent analyses in Markwardt, *op. cit.*, and Fernand Mossé, *Manuel de l'Anglais du Moyen Age* (Paris, 1949), tr. J. A. Walker (Baltimore: Johns Hopkins Press, 1952). Much valuable information on late ME pronunciation is contained in the recent exhaustive study by E. J. Dobson, *English Pronunciation 1500—1700* (Oxford, 1957), in two volumes. Compare also Helge Kökeritz, *A Guide to Chaucer's Pronunciation* (Stockholm, 1954), which differs from Markwardt in matters of detail, especially in unaccented words.

dialectal forms in the London area obscured this distinction. Examples of the open vowel in Southwest: dẹẹf (from OE dēaf), dẹẹl
(from OE dǣl). When final, however, the vowel derived from OE ǣ
was closed, as in see < OE sǣ. Further examples of open ẹ: brẹken
(< OE brecan with lengthening and lowering of the vowel in an
open syllable); also dẹde < OE dǣd in the Anglian dialect which
Chaucer also drew upon.

Notice that a phonemic distinction between open and closed long
ē [e:] / [ɛ:] is assumed for some dialects but not for all. Where it
exists it is established by the contrasting treatment of bẹn < bēon:
bẹn < bēan; lẹẹf < lēof: lẹẹf < lēaf. In Chaucer's dialect the distinction
was obscured by the choices of forms available to him.

ā [a:], written a or aa in words like made, laat. In most native words,
Chaucer's long ā is due to lengthening of an original short a in an
open syllable, before certain consonant combinations, or in monosyllables in consequence of loss of a following consonant. When
Chaucer is imitating the Northen dialect (see below, sec. 5), he
substitutes the characteristic long ā, retained from OE, for the long
open ǭ [ɔ:] which his own dialect had developed in place of it in
words like twǭ (Northern twā). Recent studies have convincingly
demonstrated that ME ā had a front quality: that is, its pronunciation was [a:], not [ɑ:], as is sometimes stated. In the light of
later history we may assume that a positional variant (allophone)
appeared for [a:] before w and perhaps after it also in words like
gnawen, warm.

B. The rounded long vowels were ǖ [y:], ū [u:], ọ̄ [o:] and ǭ [ɔ:]

ü [y:] was preserved still in French loan words like fortune, vertu,
music. These later changed the vowel to [iu].

ū [u:], written ou and ow, as in hous, mowth. In such words it was
original; but it was also lengthened from a short u when followed
by a liquid or nasal plus homorganic voiced stop, e. g., founden.

ọ̄ closed [o:], written o and oo, as in blood.

ǭ open [ɔ:], also written o and oo, as in stone, foon (meaning foes).
The chief source of this sound was OE long ā, preserved in ME
only in Northern dialects (see above under ā). This OE ā is sometimes due to lengthening, as in cold from an early Anglian form
cāld (with unbroken vowel).

Note that a fluctuation between ọ̄ and ǭ appears in words where OE
ā was preceded by w, as in wo, two.

It is noteworthy that in Chaucer's language a number of monosyllabic words today unaccented were still pronounced with long final vowels: *tǭ, frǭ* (< *frā*), *thē*. The quantity can often be established by rime. This would indicate that the contrast between accented and unaccented syllables was less conspicuous than in modern English.

C. The short vowels of Chaucer's dialect differ less than do the long ones from those we use today, but they were tenser and their points of articulation were higher than with the corresponding modern sounds. The most striking difference is to be observed in the short *u*-sound, which in the 14th century (and for some time thereafter) had at least in some areas the quality of [ʊ], being not yet slackened and lowered to [ʌ]. We may assume nevertheless that the lowering process had already begun at some time in the later Middle Ages, and affected both *i* and *u* especially.

i, written indifferently as *i* or *y*, appears in words like: *sitten, byt, spirit.*[9]

e, normally written *e* in all positions, as in *men, bed,* and in the accented syllables of *helpe, setten.* A positional variant of the character of [ɛ] appeared before *r*; this is attested by fluctuating forms like: *derk* and *dark, clerk* and *clark.* In French loan words an open variant appeared before doubled consonants, e. g.: *dette, dressen.*

a, as in *at, hadde.* The value was almost certainly [a].

ü or short [y] appeared (but may well have been unrounded before 1400) in French loan words such as *humble.* The rounding was probably preserved longer after palatal consonants, as in *just.*

u, as in *up, lust,* in native English words.

o, probably with the value of cardinal [ɔ], as in *lot, dog, song, horn.*

In addition to these, the neutral vowel [ə] often appeared finally in unaccented syllables. As has been pointed out, it was a sound very characteristic for the rhythm of Chaucer's verse. It represents a levelling of several OE unaccented short vowels into a single neutral sound. It was also to be found in the final syllables of many French loan words: e. g., *divine, service,* both of which were normally trisyllabic. Chaucer habitually elided this final vowel before words beginning with

---

[9] On the lax quality of *i* even in ME see Dobson, *op. cit.,* p. 569 f. It is indicated by spellings of *sperit* for *spirit,* etc.

a vowel, and at times he appears to have suppressed it even before those beginning with a consonant. For this reason we conclude that final -*e* had all but disappeared in colloquial speech before 1400. Poetic usage is for understandable reasons nearly always more conservative than informal prose discourse.

In the pronunciation of long and short vowels within Chaucer's dialect, certain tendencies could be observed which were to affect the later history of standard English. Besides the fluctuations in forms already mentioned, and the continuing reduction of unstressed syllables, there was for instance a tendency to shorten originally long vowels if they appeared before certain heavy consonant combinations. Thus *wisdōm* was in time reduced to *wisdom* ['wizdəm], modern ['wɪzdm]; *gōdsib* had become *godsibb* (Mod E *gossip*) already in OE. The long vowels in certain weak verbs adding the preterite suffix -*de*/-*te* directly to the root were shortened on the same principle: *grētte* > *grette*, *drǣdde* > *dradde* ("dreaded"), etc. But the operation of analogy with verbs having a suffix -*ed* without shortening gave rise to alternate forms like *drēmed*, *plēded* beside *dremte, pledde,* and some of these double preterite forms survive to the present day (modern *dreamed* beside *dreamt,* etc.).

In the same way, the lengthening of *e, o* and *a* in open syllables of Chaucer's dialect affected the inflected cases of some nouns which still kept the short vowel in a nominative singular, if that formed a closed syllable. Thus *staf* was short, but the genitive singular and the plural forms were *staves* with the normally lengthened vowels. Here too analogy could operate and produce two alternate forms; in the 16th century both *staffs* and *staves* appear.

In the vocalism of late ME there appeared an incipient tendency to lower short *i* and *u* in open syllables to *e* and *o*. This testifies to their already somewhat relaxed quality in such positions. Thus OE *wicu* became *wēke* (modern *week*); OE *wudu* became *wood* (later shortened again); and Chaucer and others have forms like *note* and *bok* for *nut* and *buck*. This tendency did not, however, cause decisive changes in many words. The most pervasive tendency was the dual one towards lengthening accented middle-position vowels in open syllables, and towards shortening long ones in closed syllables (both with certain limitations).

D. The diphthongs appearing in Chaucer's language came from several sources. In the native language they were frequently derived from OE simple vowels when followed by velar and palatal spirants [χ, γ, ç, j]. These consonants had vocalised and contributed the second

element in the formation of new diphthongs. In French words the
original diphthongs like [ei], [ai], [ɔi], [au] and [yi] were taken over
and assimilated to English pronunciation. A number were simplified
in Anglo-Norman speech before the loans took place:[10] for instance
fruit (from Latin *fructus* with the consonant vocalised before *t*). Other
words preserved the diphthong or but slightly modified it: e. g., *point*,
AN *puint* (from Latin *punctus*). Diphthongs of various origins may be
summarised briefly as follows:

ai [ai] had several origins. It came from:
   Earlier ME *ei* from OE *e* + ȝ pronounced [ej], later as a pure
      diphthong; in later ME this became [ai] and fell together
      with original [ai] (see below): e. g., *wey*, later *way*.
   Earlier ME [ai] from OE æȝ, pronounced [aj], later as a pure
      diphthong; as in *dai, day*. Rimes of words˙ like˙ *wey*: *day*
      establish the identity of sound. (Notice that the modern
      diphthong [ei] is due to a much later development.)
   ON *ei* and *ey*, taken over unchanged at first and later shifted to
      [ai] along with the native diphthongs: e. g., *steik* "steak" and
      ey "island."
   AN ẹi [ɛi], a diphthong of several origins including earlier French
      ai and *ei* as well as *a* or *e* followed by a palatalised and later
      vocalised consonant: e. g., *pay, fey* "faith," *preyse* "praise,"
      fait "deed," *feyne* "feign," *assaille, vicaire* (< Latin *vicarius*).
      Notice that AN and continental Norman French had *ei* in
      a number of words where Parisian French had *oi*. Both forms
      were sometimes borrowed into English, thus giving rise to
      doublets such as *reial* : *royal, convey* : *convoy*.

au [au] appeared in both native English words and in French loan
   words.[11] It came from:
   OE *a* + ȝ (original, non-palatalised ȝ which later vocalised com-
      pletely) as in *drawen* < OE *draȝan*.
   OE *a* before [χ], [χt] with the velar sound still preserved, as in
      sauh, lauhte.
   OE *a* + *w* as in *clawe* < OE *clawu*.

---

[10] Johann Vising, *Anglo-Norman Language and Literature* (London,
1923), pp. 29 ff.

[11] E. E. Wardale, *An Introduction to Middle English* (London, 1937),
p. 54. The chronology of this change is obscured by the orthography,
which does not clearly distinguish between *u* and *w*.

OFr *au* borrowed direct, as in *cause.*

OFr *au* < *a + l* vocalised in the same syllable, as in (*p*)*saume* "psalm."

AN *a* before a nasal consonant as in *straunge, chaumbre.*

ou [ou] had two main sources:

    OE *o + ʒ* (original, non-palatalised *ʒ*) where the velar consonant vocalised completely, as in *lowe* < *lāʒe* (<ON *lāgr*); or *o + ʒ* where the velar was still preserved in modified form after -*u*-, as in *souhte, bough.*

    OE *ŏ + w*, or *ā + w* which became *ǫ + w* South of the Humber. Examples are *blowen* < *blōwan, knowen* < *cnāwan.* There may well have been a distinction between higher and lower first elements of the ME diphthongs, according as the OE had *ō* or *ā* before the *w.*

oi, probably spoken [ɔi], was a diphthong mostly taken over from French, where it had several origins. Old French *oi* and *ui* appear side by side in various dialects, with AN at first preferring *ui*, which very generally became *oi* in ME loans. (Traces of the *ui* -diphthong, as distinct from *oi*, are found as late as the 16th century in English.) The Vulgar Latin sources of *oi* may be exemplified in the following words: *joy* < *gaudiu(m)*; *cloistre* < *claustru(m)*; *point* or *puint* < *punctu(m)*;[12] *voice* < *voce*; *Troye* < *Troia* (a learned word); also *royal* < *reial* < *regale* (see above under the diphthong [ai] < [ei]). In *fruit*, already mentioned, the original diphthong has been simplified in English.

eu appeared in relatively few words. The native English forms derive it from earlier *e + w* as in *fewe*; in the French loan words it has several origins: *nevew* "*nephew,*" *lewté* (contracted from *leauté*) "*loyalty.*"

iu was also rare, but appeared in *spiwen* (*spew*), *stiward* (*steward*), etc.

E. The consonants of Chaucer's dialect, of whatever origin, may be presented in simplified form in the following chart:

---

[12] On *oint* < *u* before *nkt*, see М. В. Сергиевский, *История Француского Языка* (Moscow, 1947), p. 48. On AN in general see J. Vising, *op. cit.*, and Louis Emil Menger, *The Anglo-Norman Dialect: A Manual of its Phonology and Morphology* (New York: Columbia University Press, 1904).

Labials   p b   m   w   ʍ (hw?)
Labio-dentals   f   v
Dentals and   θ . ð
  post-dentals   t d   tʃ[13] dʒ[13] r l   n
                                     ʃ   ʒ
                                s   z

Palatals   ç   j
Velars   k g χ   ŋ

In general, the spelling of Chaucer's consonants is less ambiguous than that of the vowels and diphthongs, but there are nevertheless a number of inadequacies in the medieval system of orthography as represented in the best manuscripts of about 1400. These are the most important:

v is often written as *u*, the two characters being interchangeable. Similarly, *w* appears as either *uu* or *vv*.

th is used to represent both voiceless [θ] and voiced [ð].

h is used to represent both [ç] and [χ] as well as an initial aspirate as in *home*. See below under *gh*.

j stands for either a semi-vowel or a consonant. In origin it was an ornamental variation of the letter *i*, especially when preceded by another *i* as in the occasional spelling *ij* to indicate long *i*. The semi-vowel value of *j* is usually represented in ME by *y* (sometimes by *i*) as in *yiven, yaf* or *iaf*. On *j* to represent [dʒ] see below.

wh appears as the continuation of OE *hw*. Its phonetic status is in some doubt. In Chaucer it may have been merely a voiceless *w* [ʍ], but in the North at least it appears to have been something like [χw], if we may judge from the regular spellings like *qwh, quh, qu*.

sh, sch and ss are written for [ʃ]; the variations are mostly scribal. Examples are: *fish, fiss, schal*.[13a]

[ʒ] had no specific symbol; its existence in words like *pleasure* is surmised by comparison with ModE.

ch is the usual representation of initial [tʃ], both Germanic and Romance, as in *chepe, chaste*. Medially the same sound may appear as *tch* and *cch*: *catchen, cacchen*.

---

[13] Since each of these two combinations functions as a single phoneme, some text-books represent them by single symbols such as [č] for [tʃ] and [ž] for [dʒ].

[13a] For details see H. M. Flasdieck in *Anglia*, LXXVI (1958), 339—410.

[dʒ] (or ž, in the transcription of some text-books) was written *j, dg,*
   and *gg*: *judgen* or *juggen.*

ng   is the spelling for [ŋg]; the sound [ŋ] appeared in fact only before
   the velars *k* and *g*, and was there always written *n.*

gh   and h represented [χ], as in *though, thouhte*: actually, an allophone
   of [ç].

It is noteworthy that forms which in ModE possess voiced consonants because of lack of sentence stress, e. g., *was, of, the, that,* were
probably still spoken with enough stress to preserve them as voiceless.
Some consonant combinations which have since been simplified still
retained full values, as in *gnawen, knell* and *knif.* It is to be assumed
also that *r* was a strongly trilled sound, and was still clearly pronounced in positions within words where ModE has lost it: finally, that
is, and after vowels. In the combination *wr*, the *w* was still heard.

Some of the consonants listed above are merely variants of neighbouring ones, due to variations in phonetic environment. Thus the
palatal spirant [ç] appears to be limited to an environment of front
vowels, while the velar spirant [χ] (its voiced counterpart [γ] being
already eliminated in Chaucer's dialect) was limited to a position after
back vowels. Therefore we may reduce two historically distinct sounds —
[ç] and [χ] — to a single phoneme /χ/ subject to positional variations.
The velar nasal [ŋ] had been historically no more than a positional
variant of [n], occurring before the gutturals [k] and [g]. In words
like *sing, singing*, the final *-g* was probably still heard. Phonemically
therefore it would be possible to use a single symbol /n/ to transcribe
both nasals [n] and [ŋ], and thus to write /sing/, /singing/. But in
the ensuing period of early ModE, final [g] following a velar nasal
was surely lost. Thereupon the contrast between [n] and [ŋ] became
the only trait distinguishing such word-pairs as *sin : sing, fan : fang*, etc.
Since the contrast was shortly to become an essential one, it is useful
to recognise it in transcribing Chaucer's language also.

Middle English possessed a certain tendency to unvoice final consonants. This is reflected in the spelling of some words, such as
gossip from OE *gōdsibb.* Though it did not become a generally effective
principle (as it has in modern German), the tendency was strong
enough to fortify and preserve voicelessness in final consonants which
have since become voiced because of lack of sentence stress, as has been
pointed out above on this page.

Lengthened consonants existed in ME. They represented a basis
for contrasts in speech rhythm not always involving lexical contrasts;

they were moreover not limited to the geminated groups of OE. There
is evidence that in early ME all non-final consonants following accented
short vowels were somewhat prolonged, in rhythmical contrast to those
following long vowels. As a consequence, two different types of syllables approximated to a single unit of time: those containing a short
vowel plus two consonants or a doubled single one, and those containing a long vowel plus a single consonant. Thus *grettest, lippes,
beddes* approximated *lǫres* and *wordes* in metrical value. Lengthening
does not, according to the orthography, appear in final position (thus
al, bed are written beside *alle* and *beddes*).

In the well-known orthographical experiment of Orm in the *Ormulum* (late 12th century), doubled consonants are written consistently
after accented short vowels as a kind of diacritical sign, and they are
non-phonemic in function. At the same time there is some reason to
suppose that Orm heard such consonants as relatively long (though
probably not so long as OE geminated consonants). The treatment of
long consonants in the several dialects is connected with the extent
to which vowels were lengthened in open syllables. In the North
and Northern Midland, that lengthening seems to have affected all
vowels quite generally, and hence a distinction between long and short
vowels could replace that between single and double consonants. In
the South Midland and South (including Chaucer's dialect), on the
other hand, *i* and *u* were not usually lengthened in open syllables, and
after these vowels a distinction between long and short consonants thus
continued to have phonemic significance.[14] Though their scope was

---

[14] On the general problem —which is a complicated one— of the
interrelation between long (or double) consonants and vowel lengthening
see the important article by Hans Kurath, "The Loss of Long Consonants and the Rise of Voiced Fricatives in Middle English," *Language*, XXXII (1956), 435—45. Authorities have differed in their
interpretations of Orm's doubled consonants; confusion has arisen
because no effort had been made before Kurath's study to define their
phonemic as opposed to their phonetic significance. See Richard Jordan, *Handbuch der mittelenglischen Grammatik* (Heidelberg, 2nd ed.,
1934), pp. 37 and 143—45 for a statement of the thesis that Orm's
doubling reflects actual prolongation in speaking. Whether the poet was
indicating native speech practice accurately or was in part conditioned
in his very listening by the influence of classical metrics is another
question. The latter thesis is advanced by H. H. Glunz, *Die Literar-
ästhetik des europäischen Mittelalters* (Bochum—Langendreer, 1937),

much reduced in 14th-century London, the prevalent and generally consistent scribal usage in many native words would indicate their survival in accented syllables when non-final.[15]

F. Accentuation of polysyllables in Chaucer's dialect is another aspect of contemporary speech rhythm, and one that concerns his versification. In dealing with the incidence of tonic accent we are on fairly sure ground, for Chaucer's total work shows careful regard for a basic pattern of lines equal in syllable count and similar in the alternation of stressed with unstressed syllables. Doubtful lines or those showing occasional deviations for variety may therefore be interpreted against a background of an easily established normal usage. Inductively it is not difficult to establish certain leading principles in relation to accentuation.

Native English words were in general accented as in OE, according to principles which have survived with very little modification into ModE. That is to say: simple words maintained their accent on the first (root) syllable throughout all inflections (*wīf, wīfes*); nominal compounds formed of two elements maintained it also on the first syllable (*'plowman, 'outlaw, 'out-ryders*), except that certain prefixes like *be-, un-, for-* and *mis-* never took the accent (*for'giveness, un'happy, mis'deed, be'hest*). Verbal compounds generally had the accent on the root syllable (*to'hewen, for'geten, be'ginnen, under'taken*). A perceptible secondary accent fell on some syllables which today have none, for instance the *-ing* ending of verbal nouns. Thus *swevening(e)* could rime with *thing(e)*. In some compounded forms a certain elasticity of accent was possible, as for instance in the word for "to answer" which could be either *'answeren* or (as usually in Chaucer) *an'sweren*.

Words borrowed from the French had an accentual system still very close to that of their origin, but many shifts were occurring and the scansion of verse reveals considerable fluctuation. Disyllables ending in a vowel other than [ə] quite generally had the accent on the first

---

pp. 311—29. See also K. Sisam, *Studies*, pp. 188 ff. In any event Orm's pedantic zeal for consistency is a factor to be reckoned with; cf. René Huchon, *Histoire de la langue anglaise*, II (Paris, 1930), p. 85.

[15] Their existence is assumed by Markwardt when he transcribes passages of Chaucer in his *Introduction to the English Language*. Mossé, *op. cit.*, does not discuss the significance of doubled consonants, nor does Brunner in his *Die englische Sprache*, 2 vols. (Halle a/S., 1950—51). The aspect of the problem bearing on rhythm and versification still awaits definitive treatment.

syllable, but in many cases either syllable could receive it: thus *'citee* beside *ci'tee*, *'virtue* beside *vir'tue*. Disyllables ending in a consonant prevailingly though not always had the accent on the second syllable: *tre'tys, mis'chief* (but also *'mischief*).

In French words of three or more syllables there was a marked secondary accent, sometimes even two of them, as well as primary one. The alternation of stressed and unstressed syllables fell readily into an iambic-trochaic rhythm: *'reve`rence*, (four syllables), *a'bomi-`naci`oun* (or *a'bomi`naci'oun*). From the elasticity of accentuation in Romance words, as well as the rhythmic conspicuousness of secondarily stressed syllables, we may conclude that the quality of vowels in syllables today unaccented was at this time still relatively clear. In quantity too these syllables were closer to their original values, not yet having undergone the widespread reduction and syncopation to which they were exposed in the course of the ensuing century and a half.[16] This conservation of values may be compared with the phenomena of vowel length and consonantal voicelessness in unaccented native words, as already noticed.

An experimental transcription of some Chaucerian lines as the poet may have spoken them will illustrate the principles just summarised. The speaker in this excerpt is Pandarus, giving some good advice to his friend the ardent young lover Troilus:

> "My deere frend, if I have don for the
> In any cas, God wot, it is me lief;
> And am as glad as man may of it be,
> God help me so; but tak it nat a-grief
> That I shal seyn: be war of this meschief,
> 5 That, there as thow now brought art in thy blisse,
> That thow thiself ne cause it nat to misse.
>
> "For of fortunes sharpe adversitee
> The worste kynde of infortune is this,
> A man to han ben in prosperitee,
> 10 And it remembren, whan it passed is.
> Th'art wis ynough, forthi do nat amys:
> Be naught to rakel, theigh thow sitte warme;
> For if thow be, certeyn, it wol the harme."

---

[16] For an exhaustive study of this problem see A. J. Bliss, "Vowel-Quantity in Middle English Borrowings from Anglo-Norman," *Archi-*

In transcription:

mi: de:rə fre:nd if i: hav(ə) do:n for θe:
in ani: ka:s gɔd wɔ:t it is me: le:f
and am as glad as man mai ɔf it be:
gɔd help me: sɔ: but tak it nat ə'gre:f
θat i: ʃal sain be: war ɔf θis mis'tʃe:f
5 θat θɛ:r as θu: nu: brouχt art in θi: blis:ə
θat θu: θi:self ne kauz it nat to: mis:ə

for ɔf for'ty:nəs ʃarp ad'vɛrsi'te:
θe wurstə ki:nd ɔf 'infor'ty:n is θis
a man to: han be:n in prɔs'pɛri'te:
10 and it rə'membrən ʍan it pas:əd is
θart wi:s i'nɔuχ forθi: do: nat ə'mis
be: nauχt to: rakəl θaiç θu: sit:ə warmə
for if θu: be: sɛr'tain it wɔl θe: harmə

Troilus and Criseyde, III, 1618 ff.

Here Criseyde laments her imminent departure from Troy:

"Allas!" quod she, "out of this regioun
I, woful wrecche and infortuned wight,
And born in corsed constellacioun,
Moot goon, and thus departen fro my knyght.
5 Wo worth, allas! that ilke dayes light
On which I saugh hym first with eyen tweyne,
That causeth me, and ich hym, al this peyne!"

aT:as kwɔd ʃe: u:t ɔf θis 're:dʒi'u:n
i: wɔ:ful wretʃ and 'infor'ty:nəd wiçt
and born in kursəd 'konste'lasi'u:n
mo:t gɔ:n and θus də'partən frɔ: mi: kniçt
5 wɔ: wurθ al:as θat ilkə daiəs liçt
ɔn ʍitʃ i: sauχ him first wiθ aiən twainə
θat kauzəθ me: and itʃ him al θis painə

Ibid., IV, 743 ff.

vum Linguisticum, IV (1952), 121—47 and V (1953), 22—47, with an
index of words discussed. These articles throw retrospective light on
quantity relations in the Norman French dialect spoken in England.

4. A REVIEW OF CHAUCER'S MORPHOLOGY

The inflectional forms to be found in Chaucer are in general those of the Southeast Midlands. Being a resident of London, with its varied population, the poet heard, adopted and used a number of occasional forms which came from outside that territory, as was also the case with the forms appearing in his phonological patterns.

The nouns were in effect grouped in no more than two declensions, the strong and the weak, and of these two the former was by far the larger. The latter consisted of but a small and diminishing group of words. Most nouns of the various OE strong declensions had been attracted to the morphology of the first (masculine strong) declension, which was now simplified to an *-es* ending for the genitive singular, a zero suffix for all other singular cases, and an *-es* ending for all cases of the plural. Feminine strong ō-stem nouns, the *u*-stem and *i*-stem nouns of all genders, also fell into this category. Thus:

Sing. Nom. & Acc.	fish	hūs	world	son = [sun]
Gen.	fishes	hūses	worldes	sonnes
Plur. All cases	fishes	hūses	worldes	sonnes

Some feminine nouns, and those belonging to the old minor declension, still occasionally show a genitive singular without *-es*, as in: *lady grace, the sonne upriste, my fader soule*.

Weak nouns represent a new minor declension in Chaucer's language, and even here the signs of attraction to the strong declension are clearly apparent.

Sing. Nom. & Acc.	ox	eye
Gen.	oxen	eyes
Plur. All cases	oxen	eyen, also eyes

The pronouns reflect a certain dialectal diversity:

Sing. 1st Per.   Ī (ich), mīn(e), mē   Pl. wē, ūr(e), ūs
      2nd Per.   thou, thīn(e), thee   yē, your(e), you
      3rd Per.
          Masc.   he, his, him
          Fem.   she, hir(e), hir(e)   Pl. thei, their (here), hem (them)
          Neut.   hit, his, hit

Adjectives had both strong and weak forms, but the differences were but slight. The strong forms had no inflection in the singular and terminated in -e in the plural: e. g., Sing. *good, strong*; Plur. *goode, stronge.* The weak adjectives had -e throughout, as did strong ones which possessed final -e as part of the uninflected form: e. g., *able, feeble.*

Verbs were divided into strong and weak, as in OE, but the number of strong verbs had decreased since a number of them had been transferred to the weak conjugation. At the same time the number of weak verbs was further increased by the large group borrowed from the French, since almost every verb taken over from this source was made weak. (The case of *strive-strove-striven* from *estriver* is exceptional.) The strong verbs maintained their distinctions by classes as these had been established in OE, except for the vowel changes and levellings which had occurred since the Conquest. The following examples represent the seven traditional classes of the surviving strong verbs:

Class I	drīven	drǫf [drɔːf]	driven	driven
II	clēven	clę̄f [clɛːf]	clǭven [ɔː]	clǭven [ɔː][17]
III	bīnden	bǫnd, bānd[18]	būnden	būnden
	melten	malt	multen	molten
IV	bę̄ren[17]	bar	Sth bę̄ren [ɛː]	bǭren [ɔː][17]
			Mdl bēren [eː]	
V	trę̄den[17]	trad	Sth trę̄den [ɛː]	trę̄den
			Mdl trēden [eː]	
VI	fāran	fǫr	fǭren	fāren
VII	lēten [eː]	lēt [eː]	lētten [eː]	lētten [eː]
	hǫlden [ɔː]	hēld [eː]	hēlden [eː]	hǫlden [ɔː]

Weak verbs had a suffix -(e)de for the past tense. The shorter form was modified to -te after voiceless consonants. The ending for the perfect passive participle was the same except for the absence of a final -e. Thus we find the following typical inflections:

---

[17] Vowels like *e* and *o* when lengthened in open syllables had open quality. See Margaret M. Roseborough, *An Outline of Middle English Grammar* (London, 1937), p. 73.

[18] Lengthening is here assumed because of position before -*nd*. Not so Roseborough, *loc. cit.*

luven	luvede	(y)-luved [19]
dēmen	dēmde	„ dēmed
setten	sette	„ set(t)
casten (< ON kasta)	cast(t)e	„ cast
waiten (< AN guaiter)	waitede	„ waited

The conjugation of the verb in Chaucer was normally that of the East Midlands:

		Singular	Plural	Singular	Plural
Present	1.	bīnde	bīnden	drīve	drīven
	2.	bīndest	„	{drīvest, drifst	„
	3.	bint, bīndeth	„	drīveth	„
Preterite	1.	bǫnd	būnden	drǫf	driven
	2.	bǫndest	„	drǫfst	„
	3.	bǫnd	„	drǫf	„
Infinitive		bīnde(n)		drīve(n)	
Pres. Part.		bīndende, bīnding(e)		drīvende, drīving(e)	
Subjunctive: Pres.		bīnde	bīnde(n)	drīve	drīve(n)
Pret.		bǫnde	būnde(n)	drǫve	drive(n)

It is to be noted that in verbal roots ending with a dental consonant, there was usually a contraction of the third person singular -*eth*,

---

[19] The prefix *y*- comes from OE ȝe, Germanic ȝa- as in Gothic, which originally had a meaning of togetherness and completion. It became in a sense a sign of perfective aspect, though it was not at first limited to the perfect passive participle. Some OE verbs had the prefix throughout their entire system. An exhaustive study of the extinction of the prefix has been made by Herbert Pilch, "Der Untergang des Präverbs ȝe- im Englischen", *Anglia*, LXXIII (1955), 37—64. This article throws light on the mechanics of the loss, considered from the phonetic point of view.

resulting in loss of a syllable. Thus: *bindeth* > *bint, slideth* > *slitt, rideth* > *ritt,* etc. The same endings occurred throughout in the corresponding forms of weak verbs. These did not, of course, show the interior vowel change called apophony or ablaut, but some of them (e. g., *sellen, solde, y-sold*) had secondary vowel changes due to Germanic umlaut.

A group of preterite-present verbs existed in ME, continuing the development of the ones that had become established in OE. These verbs, it will be remembered, had a present tense system which followed the pattern, both in ablaut and in endings, of the preterite tense of strong verbs, classes one to six. Examples in OE were: *wāt, sceal, mǣʒ, mōt,* etc. After these preterite forms had been shifted (in prehistoric times) to take over the functions of the present tense, new preterites were created for them on the model of the weak conjugation: *wiste, sceolde, meahte, mōste,* etc. The ME forms represent a regular development: *wǫt, wiste; shal, shulde; may, mihte; moot, mōste,* etc. In their use they did not coincide entirely with that of the modern auxiliaries. For example, the conjugations of *shall* and *will* had not yet been fixed in the pattern of grammatical meanings now attached to them.

5. OTHER MIDDLE ENGLISH DIALECTS

At the end of the 14th century the local dialects of English still possessed, as has been remarked, a certain authority and literary prestige. In the period to come they were to lose their social importance except in Scotland, a special case which will later be discussed in detail. The English local dialects nevertheless continued to exist, and they appear sporadically in literary texts from the Middle Ages to modern times. For this reason it is desirable to present a short outline of their leading traits as they appeared in the 14th century. The scheme given below will form a basis of comparison with later developments.

For convenience' sake it has been customary to divide the area of ME dialects into three main parts, Northern, Midland and Southern. Of these, two are further subdivided: Midland into East and West, and Southern also into East and West. In the Midland area, the most important texts written in the West are actually Northwestern, and those of the Southeast area are Kentish. The situation is in reality somewhat more complicated than the conventional divisions would indicate, for some of the isoglosses cut across more than one of the major divisions of territory.

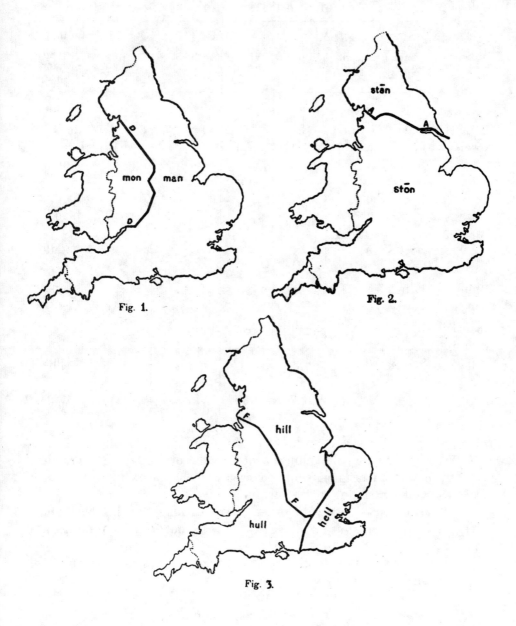

Fig. 1 The distribution of a/o before nasals; Fig. 2 The development of OE ā in
ME dialects;   Fig. 3 The development of OE y in ME dialects

Vowels and Diphthongs[20]

	Old Engl. WSax.	Middle Engl. Nth.	EMdl.	WMdl.	Sth. W.	Kt.	Mod. Engl. Examples
Accented simple vowels	ў	ĭ	ĭ	ў̃ [1]	ȳ̃ [1]	ĕ	fill, mice
	æ̅₁ [2]	ē [e:]	ę̄ [e:]	ę̄ [ɛ:]	ę̄ [ɛ:]	ę [e:]	deed
	æ̅₂ [2]	ę [ɛ:]	ę [ɛ:]	ȩ̄ [ɛ:]	ę̄ [ɛ:]	e [e:]	lead
	ā [a:]	ā [a:] [3]	ǭ [ɔ:]	{ā [a:] / ǭ [ɔ:]}	ǭ [ɔ:]	ǭ [ɔ:]	stone
	ō	ui [y¹] or [u¹]? [4]	ō	ō	ō	ō	food, blood
	a + nasal	a	a, o,	o	a,o	a	handle
Diphthongs	ēa [æ:a]	ę̄ [ɛ:]	ę̄ [ɛ:]	ę̄ [ɛ:]	ę̄ [ɛ:]	[iæ:] [5]	bean
	ēo	ę̄ [e:]	ę̄ [e:]	ę̄ [e:]	ȫ [6] > [e:]	ȫ [6] > [e:]	be
Unaccented non-final	-e-	-i-, -e-	-e- [ə]	{-e-[ə] [7] / -u-[ʌ]}	-e- [ə]	-e- [ə]	wishes
Unaccented final	e, a, u, o	(zero)	-e [ə]	-e [ə]	-e [ə]	-e [ə]	hope

Notes on the Vowel Chart:

[1] Written *u* under the influence of French orthographical practice.

[2] OE æ̅ was an original simple vowel which appears in Gothic as *ē*; æ̅₂ < Gmc. *ai* followed by umlaut.

[3] Often written *ai*. As with other Northern long vowels, the letter *i* serves in such cases as a diacritical mark, not the sign of a true diphthong.

[4] In this instance the letter *i* appears to have represented an off-glide.

[5] Written *ya, ia, ea*.

[6] Written *eo*; the rounding antedates the 14th century.

[7] Final -[ə] is usually written -*e*, as is non-final [ə] in most dialects. But in WMdl. the spelling of the latter alternates between *e* and *u*; the quality of the latter is not clear, but it was probably a lowered central vowel.

[20] For general descriptions see Mary S. Serjeantson, *Distribution of Dialect Characters in Middle English* (Amsterdam, 1924), and also the

Consonants

WSax	Nth.	EMdl.	WMdl.	SthW.	Kt.	ModE. examples
f (initial)	f	f	f	f, v[1]	v	foes, fine
ċ [tʃ] < k palatalised	k, also ch [tʃ]	ch [tʃ]	k, ch [tʃ]	ch [tʃ]	ch [tʃ]	kirk / church
ʒ̇ [j] < g palatalised	g, also ʒ̇ [j]	g, also [j]	g	[j]	[j]	give
hw	quh=[kʷ] or [χʷ]	wh [ʍ]	quh=[kʷ] or [χʷ],wh	wh[ʍ]	wh [ʍ]	who
s (initial)	s	s	s	z	z	see, sum
sċ [ʃ] < sk palatalised	sk[2] also sh[ʃ]	sh [ʃ]	sk, sh	sh [ʃ]	sh [ʃ]	skirt / shirt

Notes:

[1] Spelling fluctuates in Layamon and other texts of the Southwest.
[2] This appears as *s* when initial in words not receiving sentence accent, e.g., *sal* < **skal* corresponds to Sth. *shal*. Forms in *sk-* are often Scandinavian doublets of Southern words from OE.

The predominance of unpalatalised consonants in the North is partly due to the retention of such sounds from prehistorical OE, and partly due to the great influx of Scandinavian loan words which also retained unpalatalised Germanic consonants. In fact, the numerical frequency of Scandinavian forms may have exercised a conservative

---

convenient scheme given by M. M. Roseborough, *op. cit.*, here summarised with slight modifications. For a more detailed picture of the complicated dialect situation consult H. Whitehall, Samuel Moore and Sanford Meech, *Middle English Dialect Characteristics and Dialect Boundaries*, published in *Essays and Studies in English and Comparative Literature* (University of Michigan, 1935). Cf. also the dialect maps given by Mossé, which are based on this study.

influence on the native phonology. On the other hand Southern
English, especially in the East, shared tendencies operating in Low
German dialects across the Channel. In both areas initial *s* and *f* were
voiced to *z* and *v* respectively. The tendency affected words borrowed
from French at a sufficiently early date. The voicing was most consistently recorded in Kentish texts. Those written in the more westerly
areas fluctuate in the spelling for these sounds. It is difficult therefore
to determine whether a distinction existed between *vaire* < OE *fægere*
and *vaire* < OFr meaning "fur trimming." [21] The impulse towards the
voicing of these initial consonants appears to have radiated with
diminishing effect in a westerly, then in a northwesterly direction.
Intervocalically, of course, *f* and *s* had already become regularly voiced
in OE (e. g., *lufu, wīfa*), so that in this position original *f* and *v*
represented a single phoneme, and *s* and *z* (written *s*) another. French
borrowings have restored the phonemic significance of contrast between
voiceless and voiced consonants in this position, as in: *wafer* versus
waver, face versus *phase*. The role played by long consonants in the
dialects has already been discussed (sec. 4).

Morphological indices of dialect are most conspicuous in verbal
forms. The following paradigm may be contrasted with Chaucer's
East Midland forms:

	Nth.	WMdl.	Sth. & Kt.
Pres. Sing. 1.	bīnde, -es, -is	bīnde	bīnde
2.	bīndis, -es	bīndest, -es	bīndest
3.	bīndis, -es	bīndeth, -es	bīndeth
Plur. 1—3	bīndis, -es	bīnden, -es, -us, -un	bīndeth
Pres. Part.	bīndand	bīndend, -and, -ind; *later* bīnding	bīndind(e)

In addition, certain pronoun forms were specialised in the various
dialects:

---

[21] The problem of the phonemic distinctions in an interdialectal
survey is too complicated for schematic presentation. On this subject
see James Sledd in *Language*, XXXI (1955), 318 ff. On the OE antecedents see the helpful article by David De Camp, *ibid.*, XXXIV
(1958), 232—44.

	OE	Nth.	EMdl.	WMdl.	SthW.	Kt.
Singular						
Nom.	hio "she"	scho	sche	scho	heo,he	heo,he
	heo	ȝho	he,ho	ho,hui	ho,hui	
	hie			hue	hi	hi
Plural						
Nom.	heo,hie	thai,they	thai,they	thai,they	hi,heo	hi,hy
			he,hi	heo	here	
Gen.	hire	thair	hyr,here	hor,hur	hor,hure	hare,hire
			theyr,her	here	here	
Dat.[1]	him	thaym	hem,them	hem,hom	hem,ham	hem,ham
	heom	theym		heom	hom	

Note to chart

[1] The forms which sprang from the OE and ON datives later assumed the function of accusatives as well.

As may readily be seen, the Scandinavian forms of the plural were earliest adopted in the North and thence spread southwards. They

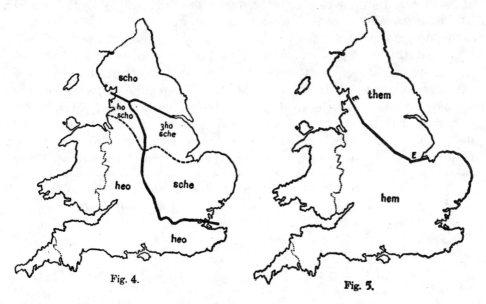

Fig. 4 The distribution of feminine pronoun forms; Fig. 5 The distribution of plural pronoun forms in ME

were still unknown in the Southern districts in the 14th century, but within the next hundred years they spread to all shires. When London adopted them, their acceptance elsewhere was rapid. In rural Southern districts however the Anglo-Saxon forms with initial *h*-persisted much longer than in the cities. The feminine pronoun *sche/scho* also originated in the Northern regions and spread southwards.[22]

In the light of these standard tests for dialect, it is interesting to observe with what care Chaucer reproduced the traits of the dialects he introduced into his work. His "good ear," as it has been called,[23] picked up salient traits of the varied speech about him (see above, sec. 3), not only in respect to regional dialects but also to personal idiosyncrasies of speakers' styles in handling language. The latter included variations in syntax, choice of words, structure of sentences, and nuances of style. These are matters of a different category, about which a few words of comment are now in order.

6. Syntax and Sentence Structure

The operation of phonological decay, analogical shifts and resultant drastic reduction in the number of ME inflections resulted, obviously, in an enormous simplification of syntactic patterns. As multiplicity of forms was reduced to simplicity, many grammatical categories ceased to be overt and became covert. Gender was one of them. In OE, a highly inflected definite article (originally a demonstrative) had signalised the gender of substantives with which it necessarily agreed. The grouping of nouns in declensions was in part correlated with the category of gender. In ME, however, the manifold forms of the definite article were levelled to a single form, namely *the*, often abbreviated to *th'* before a word beginning with a vowel. The various declensions were reduced (with a few exceptions), as we have seen, to a single one with only two case-number forms. In native words

---

[22] The origin of this form is a matter of debate. For recent discussion see E. Dieth, "Hips: A Geographical Contribution to the 'she' Puzzle," *English Studies*, XXXVI (1955), 209—17. See also K. Brunner, *Die englische Sprache*, II, p. 100.

[23] Thus Dorothy Everett, "Chaucer's Good Ear," in her *Essays on Middle English Literature* (Oxford, 1955), pp. 139—48. Ruth Bradley, "The Use of Cockney Dialect by Chaucer," *Quarterly Journal of Speech*, XXIX (1943), 74—76, points to evidence that Chaucer noted and made use of the characteristic omission of initial *h*.

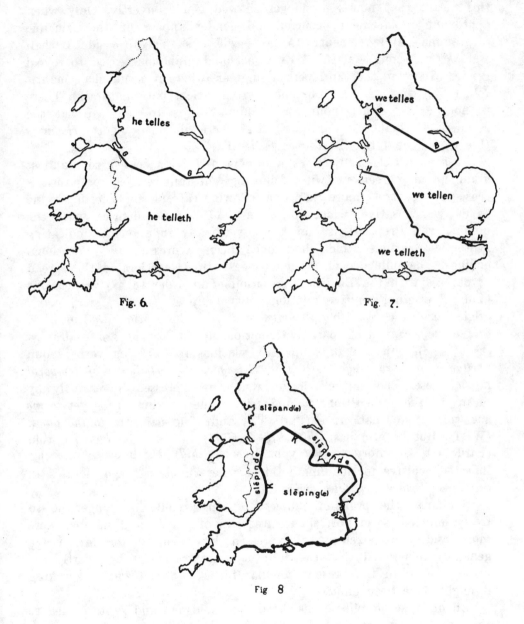

Fig. 6 The ME dialect endings of the third singular present of verbs; Fig. 7 The same for plural forms; Fig. 8 The present participle forms

this meant that nouns no longer showed gender overtly. Only when a pronoun replacement occurred did gender appear on the principle of grammatical agreement: "A good wif was ther of beside Bathe,/ But *she* was somdel deef..." Even personal pronouns ceased to reveal gender except in the third person singular, where it assumed a semantic role purely (i. e., it was no longer grammatical but "natural"). There is nothing in either noun or pronoun forms to tell us that the revellers of Chaucer's Pardoner's Tale were all men: "Thise *riotoures* thre of whiche I telle... And as *they* sat..."

Just as articles, adjectives and demonstratives ceased to manifest grammatical agreement with following substantives, so prepositions ceased to "control" more than one following case (a single form serving as dative-accusative, which for nouns had become identical with the nominative). Prepositions now took over many functions of indicating syntactic relations which had once been expressed by inflectional endings. The influence of French usage with *de* accelerated the spread of phrases with the English preposition *of* in order to express various kinds of original genitive relations: ownership (*the voys of every man*), origin (*hem of Grece, kyng Priamus of Troye*), description (*God of Love, boot of my connynge*), partitive relationship (*o lore of two contraries, ech of hem*), objective or subjective relationship following verbal noun (*writynge of oure tonge, lovyng of Criseyde, the betydynge of temporal thinges*), etc. The dative relation was also expressed increasingly by means of the prepositions *to* and *for*. Chaucer writes: But yet *to me* she will not do that grace (Pard. T.); and... he gaf him *to the quene* (WBT). But he also has: *this sely Troilus* was wo; it was *me* told (Pard. T.); God foryeve *you* your trespas (*ibid*). He likewise uses an inflected genitive for inanimate things where modern usage dictates an *of*-phrase: *beddes feet, tales ende*.

Similarly, the pronoun subjects of verbs could no longer be so freely omitted as in OE, since categories of person and number were more and more exclusively expressed by them. Later ME usage generally demanded that the subject of a verb must be overtly expressed, even in the present singular forms, where formally speaking it might have been omitted.

All of these simplifications, both morphological and syntatic, led to the establishment of a relatively fixed and restricted word order, which more and more took over the function of indicating grammatical relations within the sentence. The sequence actor → action → (receiver or complement, if any) began to be established as normal, though inversions were employed more often than in modern English. Head position in a sentence was increasingly assumed to indicate grammatical function as subject of its main verb. But original datives could still stand at the beginning, especially with impersonal verbs. They were retained there, without prepositions, in a considerable number of instances. Direct objects could also be transposed to head position.

In the absence of inflectional endings, such transpositions sometimes resulted in ambiguity. The sentence: *Him wants* (or *lacks,* or *needs*) *wit,* shows clearly, still, that the verb is a third person singular impersonal form, without expressed subject (*hit, it*), and preceded by a dative-accusative pronoun. The construction is not so clear if a noun replaces the pronoun: *The man wants* wit; or, in the plural: *The men wants* wit. Under the influence of prevailing word order, there was created an expectation of agreement between *men* and *want(s)* or *want(eth)*. This led to the syntactic reorganisation of such impersonal constructions and their transformation into personal ones. The sentences became: *He wants* (*lacks, needs*) wit, and: *The men want* wit, etc. Such shifts affected other impersonal verbs such as *think* (< OE þyncan, þyncean, "to seem"), *stand* (in the sense of "to be"). *Me stands* awe of him — eventually became: *I stand* in awe of him; while *methinks* survived as an archaic stereotype (cf. Hamlet's *methinks* I see my father).[24]

As part of the trend to a fixed word order, modifiers were relegated to a position very close to the words or groups of words modified. In general there was a tendency to place single-word modifiers before nouns, and multiple-word modifiers after them (*the good man,* but *the man in the moon*). French influence, however, led to postposition of single modifiers in certain traditional expressions, especially those connected with the law (*the lords spiritual, the blood royal*). The usual position for adverbial modifiers was after the verb, but phrases as well as single words were rather more freely placed before it than today: he *for his disport* is went into the feeldes (Mel.); *out of the chambre* he wente (*Tr. and Cr.*). The inversion sometimes is clearly intended to increase emphasis: for stylistic reasons: And *gladly* wolde he lerne and *gladly* teche (*CT*, Prol.).

---

[24] Hans Marchand, "The Syntactic Change from Inflectional to Word Order System and some Effects of this Change on the Relation 'Verb to Object,' in English," *Anglia*, LXX (1951), 70—89. This article traces the shifting from impersonal to personal constructions, with datives in head position converted into nominatives, from late OE through ME to ModE.

In general late ME word order still preserved a certain freedom since lost. In both elaborate literary writing and in simpler colloquial speech, either the object or the predicate modifier of the subject could be placed in leading position for emphasis. The direct object could be inserted between inflected auxiliary and main verb, and in the subordinate clauses the inflected part of the verb could be delayed, as was habitual in OE, to end position. Chaucer writes: and *suretee* wol I han... *thy body* for to yelden (WBT); *the whiche vyce* he hidde (*ibid.*); if ich *it* wiste (*Tr. and Cr.*); sin *al my wo* thou wost (*ibid.*); Right as the fresshe, rede rose newe/ *Ayen the sommer-sonne coloured* is (*Parl. F.*). This order resembles that of Modern German.

Complex sentences, including those used to express indirect speech, were organised in late ME very much as in ModE. That is to say, many constructions that had originally been paratactic or only partially (and awkwardly) hypotactic, were now increasingly subordinated as modifiers of a main clause. [25] Adverbial clauses, especially temporal and conditional ones, were early given subordinate status, as in the lines of Troilus addressed to the moon: Ywis, *whan thou art horned newe/* I shal be glad, *if al the world be trewe*. On the other hand certain other constructions which are today subordinate were often coordinate and appositional in ME. This different status appears especially in the case of adjectival clauses, as if we should say in ModE: That house is built on sand; it will not last, instead of: The house *which is built on sand* will not last. Notice however that even in the first version modern English intonation would indicate subordination; so also in Chaucer's: Tak water of that welle and wassh his tonge,/ *And* it is hool anon (*CT*, C 356 f.), where the *and* clearly connects with a preceding implied conditional statement.

---

[25] See Leon Kellner, *Historical Outlines of English Syntax* (London, 1892), pp. 51 ff. This book has value as a pioneer attempt, unfortunately not adequately followed up and developed by later writers, to analyse the rise and elaboration of subordinate clauses. It suffers obviously from a failure to take into account suprasegmental morphemes such as intonation and types of juncture between segments of sentences. For instance, Kellner considers the two clauses of: Sow well, reap well (p. 52) as completely paratactic, whereas the intonational pattern of spoken English is capable of indicating that the first clause is a subordinate (conditional) modifier of the second. For a brief survey of types of subordinate clauses in ME see Mossé, *op. cit.* In their analysis of Chaucer's language, Ten Brink and Kluge have no section devoted to syntax and sentence structure.

Adjectival clauses too show traces of earlier parataxis, which leads to pleonastic use of pronouns when the subordination is not complete, as if we should say: *That man* — I saw *him* yesterday and he was wearing a dark suit; or *The man* I saw yesterday, *he* was wearing a dark suit; or *The man* I saw yesterday, *that man* was wearing a dark suit. Instead, ModE prefers: *The man (whom)* I saw yesterday was wearing a dark suit (the *whom* being optional). In Chaucer we find: And *I, of whom* the sighte... was dirked... *I* wax al abaysshed (Boeth. tr., i, pr. 1); *The which schrewes* whan hem list to usen hir strength, *they* rejoyssen hem... (*ibid.,* i, m. 5); *A knyght* ther was... *that* fro the tyme that he first bigan/ To riden out, *he* loved chivalrie... (*CT,* Prol., 43 f.). On the other hand, omission of the relative pronoun gives rise to what Jespersen has called contact clauses. The effect is elliptical, as in the line: With hym ther was a Plowman, was his brother (*ibid.,* 529).

In the treatment of reported discourse, which involves a special type of noun clause, ME had not yet achieved a sharp distinction between direct and indirect constructions. It was still possible to shift from the one to the other. Direct reporting would take the following form: And I said: Youre opinioun is goode. Indirect is found thus: And I said (that) his opinioun was goode, with that congruence of tense between main and subordinate clauses which is typical of modern English. But mixed forms and shifts from direct to indirect discourse are also found in both the 14th and 15th centuries. For instance, the connective *that*, which later came to serve as signal of indirect speech only, was at times prefixed to direct speech also: He sayd... *that* "to an euyll owre hath your lady so madde."[26]

The use of various types of sentence structure available for various literary effects is a question of style. Chaucer mastered a wide range of these, extending from simple, uncomplicated ones, often distinctly colloquial, to long periodic statements with many modifiers. There are numerous signs that Chaucer distinguished levels in structural usages, assigning them appropriately to various types of speakers. He employs contrasting sentence types —those with loose constructions, complicated subordination, periodic effects and anacoluthon— according to the requirements of context. Thus he demonstrates the variety of structural devices which were at his disposal in the language of his time, waiting to be put to the use of stylistic effects in literature. A rich but unlettered artisan, the carpenter of the Miller's Tale, speaks of seeing the burial on that very day of someone who had been alive and

---

[26] Caxton, as quoted by Kellner, *op. cit.,* p. 59.

working the week before. In trying to express the time relations he produces a sentence of life-like confusion: [27]

> A 3429   I saugh to-day a cors yborn to chirche
>   That now, on Monday last I saugh hym wirche.
>
>   (Today I saw a corpse being borne to church,
>   That just now, Monday last, I saw him at work.)

When he makes persons in the upper classes of society talk informally, Chaucer frequently puts into their mouths also the loosely constructed, even slightly dislocated type of sentence which may arise occasionally among trained speakers in moments of relaxation. There are numerous examples of this syntactic style in the discourse of Pandarus in *Troilus and Criseyde*. On the other hand, when these same characters express themselves in more exalted style, at moments of serious reflection or elevated feeling, their sentences usually become at once more complicated, more tightly organised, and also more strictly logical.

The general medieval doctrine about style, as purveyed in Latin handbooks of rhetoric, distinguished three levels of discourse: lofty, medium, and lowly (*stylus altus, medius* and *humilis*). Several jesting references by Chaucer show that he was quite familiar with this doctrine. It was inherited from classical antiquity, but the Middle Ages somewhat modified it in attempting to correlate the three styles with three levels in society such as (1) courtiers (*curiales*), (2) citizens or burghers (*civiles*), and (3) simple countrymen (*rurales*). The three were supposed to be distinguished by differing prose rhythms as well as differing choice of words and grammatical traits. [28] In actual practice

---

[27] On the subject of Chaucer's colloquial English see M. Schlauch in *PMLA*, LXVII (1952), 1103—16; also Michio Masui, "The Speech of Chaucer", *Anglica* (Hiroshima University, Japan), No. 5 (Jan., 1954), 105—17. Quotations from Chaucer unless otherwise noted follow the edition of F. N. Robinson (Boston, 1957).

[28] For a survey of medieval rhetorical theory, including the problem of levels of discourse, see Charles Sears Baldwin, *Medieval Rhetoric and Poetic* (New York, 1928). John of Garland, also called Johannes Anglicus, was one of those who correlated style with social position: see his *Poetria*, ed. G. Mari, *Romanische Forschungen*, XIII (1902), 883—965. Bibliographical references are given by M. Schlauch, "Chaucer's Prose Rhythms," *PMLA*, LXV (1950), 568—89.

however few writers made any effort to catch and record any speech except that on the formal level associated with courtly circles. John Gower, the *Pearl*-poet, the 14th-century romancers and preachers are alike in confining themselves to dialogues of a formal sort. Even where simple persons appear, their language has been passed through a kind of literary screening to eliminate dialect, colloquialisms and vulgarisms. Except for Chaucer, we have little material reflecting genuine popular speech in the 14th century. Chaucer's contribution in this sphere is one of the many marks of his exceptional genius.

CHAPTER II

FORMATION OF THE NATIONAL LANGUAGE CONTINUED: 15th AND EARLY 16th CENTURIES

1. GENERAL CHARACTERISTICS OF THE PERIOD

In respect to its cultural history, as well as its social and economic development, the 15th century in England is often curtly labelled a mere "period of transition." Accordingly, it is not infrequently dismissed by text-book writers with rather scant attention. This is to a certain extent understandable when attention is concentrated on literary history primarily. The century separating the brilliant age of Chaucer from the still more dazzling period of the Tudors appears by comparison undistinguished. The achievements of Lydgate and Hoccleve, Malory and Caxton —significant though they were from many points of view— can scarcely be mentioned in the same breath with those of Chaucer and the *Pearl*-poet on the one hand, or with those of even the minor pre-Shakespearean lyricists and dramatists on the other.

For linguistic history the label "period of transition" has far less meaning. All centuries have the characteristics of such periods; the question is merely one of relative tempo. As it happens, however, the internal transformations affecting the English language were occurring in the 15th century at an unusually rapid rate, slow as they may have been in an absolute sense as compared with many other changes affecting social life. Hence the 15th century, of inferior importance to the literary historian, is of exceptional interest to the student of language. If it has attracted less research activity than its predecessors and successors, this is partly because of limitations in the type of material available for analysis. It is regrettable, for instance, that aside from a restricted number of popular religious plays in verse, and the files of family correspondence like the Pastons', we have rather little non-formal composition which would provide a clue to the colloquial speech of the time. What evidence does exist concerning non-formal types of discourse has as yet received insufficient attention from linguists as opposed to literary historians.

In the 15th century the role of French as a spoken language seems to have been reduced practically to zero. Ability to speak French became an acquired skill in the aristocracy and elsewhere, and by the end of the century handbooks for the learning of French became a widely saleable item. They were used by merchants wishing to conduct business with France and Belgium.[1]

In the same period education spread as never before until it included the lower ranks of the gentry, merchants, and even artisans in the towns. Literacy meant contact with written texts in English which now normally if not universally embodied the standard speech of London. Latin continued to be the primary language of learning and instruction, while English remained ancillary to it in the schools. Nevertheless the vernacular was itself affected by the wider knowledge of Latin imparted to laymen. No longer was literacy a sign of the clerical estate alone. Government secretaries and civil servants were now quite frequently laymen: for instance, the poet Hoccleve or Occleve, Chaucer's great admirer, who held a post in the office of the Privy Seal and who like his master devoted his leisure time to writing. Bookkeepers, accountants and merchants' secretaries were needed increasingly, and these too were laymen. Education itself was passing out of the hands of the clergy, as various guilds, communities and private patrons organised and endowed instruction outside of the church. Teachers at such schools were sometimes laymen by stipulation. Tutors in private families were likewise chosen from the ranks of laymen as well as the clergy, though the latter continued to exercise a widespread educational influence still both in homes and institutions.

One result of the dissemination of education is the effort made by many persons in groups hitherto cut off from literary expression to write original verse. A notorious example is the zealous but uninspired Harry Lovelich, a skinner of London, who on the urging of the mayor produced long-winded doggerel romances about King Arthur and his knights. Less pretentious and often more successful efforts were made by anonymous writers in various parts of the country who collected anthologies and themselves composed occasional pieces of verse to be

---

[1] Caxton's Dialogues in French and English were designed, he tells us, for those who wished "to take on honde marchandises fro one land to another." See Baugh, *A History of the English Language*, p. 182.

added to them.[2] Most of these efforts were however distinctly imitative. Almost all were composed under the influence of 14th-century models, especially of Chaucer. Therefore their testimony is not entirely reliable even for questions of syllable counting and accentuation, where scansion normally offers a fairly reliable guide. Uncertainties and inconsistencies in usage would seem to indicate that some of these amateur poets wrote visually by one system (an outmoded one) while speaking by another. There are numerous lines of 15th-century verse, indeed, which defy scansion by any system. Nevertheless among the best-known, such as Lydgate, the percentage of rough lines will be found to be not as high as the severer modern critics have claimed, once it is realised that accentuation of Romance words was still not fully established in today's pattern, and that a considerable number of these words still had movable stress in versification.

At the end of the century the invention of printing still further facilitated the spread of vernacular learning among lay circles. William Caxton, the pioneer printer, took his function as educator seriously. His moral and didactic preoccupations are reflected in the introductions composed for the texts he edited and translated. He was aware, too, of his responsibilities in helping to regularise and establish preferred forms in the emerging national language. His orthographical practice, for one thing, became a norm which has lasted with surprisingly little change into modern times. Some of the idiosyncrasies of his spelling, like the use of *gh* to indicate non-palatalised *g* in such words as *ghost, ghoos* for "goose," were in turn affected by Flemish practice, which he came to know during his sojourn in Bruges. Faced with conflicting dialect forms for the same word, Caxton admitted that he was disturbed. He disapproved of such variety, attributing it naively to the variable English temperament: "For we englysshe men been borne under the domynacyon of the mone, whiche is never stedfaste, but euer waverynge..." He deplored the fact that "that comyn englysshe that is spoken in one shyre varyeth from a nother." To illustrate the situation, he cited the now famous anecdote of some merchants who, seeking refreshment in the countryside, asked a good wife for "eggys." She replied that she didn't know any French. Neither did the merchant, as it happened, so he became angry; but his companion stepped

---

[2] See Rossell Hope Robbins, "The Findern Anthology," *PMLA*, LXIX (1954), 610—42, for a description of a manuscript collection which is indicative of such writing and gathering of materials. Pertinent also is the study of Humphrey Newton by Robbins, *ibid.*, LXV (1950), 249—81.

forward and asked for "eyren." "Then the good wyf sayd that she understood hym wel. Loo, what sholde a man in thyse dayes now wryte, egges or eyren?" asks Caxton, plaintively.[3] His double profession of printer and translator made him unusually eager to have a single standard recognised for printed books. Though he would not have expressed the matter in those terms, he was actually advocating a single national language for England.

Caxton's publication of outstanding poetic masterpieces of the 14th century, chiefly Chaucer's, had an effect on the diction of poetry and belles-lettres generally. The delight in these works was shared by a growing number of cultivated readers by the first decades of the Tudor age. The tendency to imitate was further strengthened, thanks to the wider circulation of printed copies of the *Canterbury Tales,* *Troilus and Criseyde,* romances and allegories by Lydgate and others. The vogue of Chaucer's poetic diction may be traced continuously through the 15th century down into the work of Spenser at the end of the 16th.

2. PHONOLOGICAL CHANGES IN STANDARD (LONDON) ENGLISH

A. A reader of 15th-century verse will notice at once that final *-e* of ME is by this time regularly unpronounced, both before initial consonants and vowels of the next words. This loss of *-e* is obviously realised apart from the qualitative changes also occurring at the time. An anonymous translation of part of the *Romance of the Rose* (fragment C, formerly attributed to Chaucer) shows clearly the reduction of final [ə] to zero in the early transitional period. The dots under *-e*'s indicate that they are not pronounced:

> 5811 Whannę Lovę haddę told hem his ententę
> The baronagę to councel wentę.
> In many sentences they fillę
> And dyversęly they seidę hir willę.

If an occasional *-e* is demanded here and there by scansion, we may assume that it was preserved as a literary archaism.

---

[3] Caxton, Preface to the *Eneydos* (1490), as edited by M. T. Culley and F. J. Furnivall, EETS, ES, No. 57 (1890).

In medial unstressed syllables, the -[ə]- between consonants persisted longer. In the 15th century it is in general practice dropped only in the neighbourhood of liquids and nasals, as in the word *appalled* in the following lines from Lydgate's *Fall of Princes*:

> iv, 1646 Law haddę perisshęd naddę be writyng;
> Our feith appallęd, ner vertu of scripturę;
> For al religioun and ordrę of lyuyng
> Taketh ther exemplę by doctryn of lettrurę.

The accentual status of other syllables is less clear, but such lines as these illustrate the reduction of stress on the suffixes in French words, and on -*ing* of English verbal nouns. An awkward amount of elision, syncope and slurring is sometimes necessary to make such lines by Lydgate and his contemporaries conform to the pattern of octosyllabic couplets. An exhaustive study of metrical practice at the time would probably reveal that they often permitted two or more unaccented syllables to intervene between those accented. Hence it is difficult to determine the precise status of those not receiving main stress.

B. The long vowels of ME at this time began a general and long-continued shift which led, eventually, to a complete transformation of the English vocalic system.[4] The first to be affected were the ones in middle tongue position both front and back: namely *ē* [e:] and *ō* [o:]. These two were moved up to the highest positions, [i:] and [u:] respectively, in all environments (even before *r*). Thus the verbs *see* and *do* were now pronounced [si:] and [du:], approximately as in

---

[4] General descriptions, though differing in details, are given in Jordan, *Handbuch*; Brunner, *Englische Sprache*; Karl Luick, *Historische Grammatik der englischen Sprache*, II (Leipzig, 1929); Henry Cecil Wyld, *A Short History of English* (London, 1926). Valuable material deduced from current orthography is to be found in Asta Kihlbom, *A Contribution to the Study of Fifteenth Century English* (Uppsala, 1926) and Constance Davies, *English Pronunciation from the Fifteenth to the Eighteenth Century* (London, 1934). Both of these make extensive use of family correspondence of the period, but the results should be checked with other studies, especially Dobson's.

ModE (but without off-glides). The adverb *here* is often written *hier*, indicating the fronted vowel, and spellings like *whiel* for *wheel*, *kipe* for *keep*, etc., also reflect the change. There are signs of an early tendency to shorten long *ū* from *ō* in spellings like *blud* for *blood*, *fluddes* for *floods*. Some words with [e:] or even [ɛ:] in late ME which began to move forward at an early date, fell together with words having original long *ī* [i:], and eventually developed diphthongs (see below). In this way *frere* and *brere*, Anglo-Norman words, shifted to *frīr* and *brīr*, modern *friar* [fraiə] and *briar* [braiə].

But most of the newly created high vowels did not fall together with original long *ī* and *ū*, because these sounds were themselves already in the process of a kind of internal splitting which was to produce new diphthongs in their stead. At first the two internal elements must have been almost identical except that the first was more open and lower than the second: [ïi] and [u̟u].[5] The process probably did not go very far in the 15th century, but it sufficed to make the old long *ī* and *ū* sounds phonemically distinct from the new ones raised from original long *ē* and *ō*.

In certain positions original long *ū* did not undergo internal breaking: that is, after the labial semivowel *w*, as in *wound* (the noun); also before other labials, as in *room*, *droop*. Obviously the labial consonants tended to conserve the tight lip-rounding of *ū*. There were however inconsistencies due to dialectal variations and analogical leveling, as in the past tense of the verb *wind*, written *wound*, which today has a diphthong [waund]. Romance words with accented [u:] were subject to incipient diphthongisation with the rest, e. g. in *couch*, *vouch*.

ME long *ā* [a:] began a gradual rise to a higher fronted position. In the 15th century it may well have reached the stage of [æ:], though hardly of [ɛ:], since it did not fall together with ME original open *ę̄* [ɛ:]. Meantime this original open *ę̄* began about 1500 to be written *ea* fairly consistently, as an indication of its open quality and its contrast with the original closed long *ẹ̄*, now pronounced [i:]. The long open *ǭ* [ɔ:] showed little sign of change in this period.

---

[5] There are spellings like *heyff* for *hithe*, etc., interpreted by some (e. g., Luick) as indicating a pronunciation [əi]; inverted spellings like *voyne* for *vine* also occur, showing an approximation of original long *ī* to the original diphthong *oi*. Cf. also *poynted* for *painted*, recorded by Davies.

A simple scheme with examples will give a graphical summary of the first stage in the shift of long vowels:

Modern Examples: Modern Examples:

wife   ịi ↙ i: u: ↘ ụu   house

see   e: o: do

leaf, seed   ε: ɔ: stone, hope[6]

make   æ:

                                              ↖ a:

Notice that after the raising of closed long $\bar{e}$ and $\dot{o}$ it must be assumed that these earlier sounds were then lacking in the language. Subsequently however the raising of open $\bar{e}$ and $\underset{\,}{o}$ —each from several sources— replaced the missing sounds in the above scheme. In addition, loan words from French provided a secondary source for them.

C. ME diphthongs, we have seen, had two main sources: OE simple vowels followed by vocalised consonants (as in *day, dawn*), and French diphthongs, whether original (as in *joy, convey*) or secondarily developed (as in *faute, straunge*). Both of these types were affected by the general shift observable in the simple vowels.

eu from *ew* in *trew* (< *trēowe*) became [iu] and fell together with the [iu] derived from OFr [y:], as in *pure, virtue*. Thus the plural noun *mews*, "gulls," from EMidl *mewes*, became homonymous with the French loan word *muse*.

ευ as in *few* < *fēawe* also became [iu].

ai from various sources was raised and simplified to [æ:]. Its later history coincides with that of the contemporary [æ:] out of ME [a:] in open syllables. In this way the pair *made* : *maid* became homonymic in the 15th century. Simplification of the diphthong is indicated by spellings like: *feth, daly* and *frad* for: *faith, daily* and *afraid*.

---

[6] The short *o* lengthened in an open syllable was open in quality; see ch. 1, n. 17, and Oliver F. Emerson, *A Middle English Reader* (New York, 1927), Introduction. The precise quality of ME *o* after lengthening is not however entirely clear. See Dobson, *op. cit.*, p. 674 and 576.

au in Romance words simplified to [æ:] before labials, as in *sauve* for *save*, and in *chaumbre* for *chamber*. Before other sounds the pronunciation seems to have fluctuated. Forms like *daunce* and *dance* existed side by side about 1400, and the later development was uneven in specific cases: cf. ModE *dance* beside *haunt*.

au in Germanic words, derived from *a + w*, remained a diphthong for a time, as in *law* and *saw*; simplification occurred later to [ɔ:] by way of [ɔu].

ɔi, ui in French words were widely levelled to [ɔi], but still distinguished by some speakers. There are signs of an approximation to a diphthong resembling [ai], as indicated in spellings such as: *vayage, alay, pyson*, for: *voyage, alloy* and *poison*.

ou representing either [ou], or [ɔu] from OE *ā + w*, as in *sowle, knowen*, simplified (probably towards the end of this period) to [ɔ:], which later shared in the development of original [ɔ:] from OE *ā*. The same simplification affected *ou* from *o* plus [χ].

In summary, the development of diphthongs may be presented thus:

Diphthongs

Modern Examples: Modern Examples:

```
true      eu  )                 ( ou < o + w           flow
few       ɛu  } > iu      ɔ: <  ( ou < OE ā + w        know
pure ü = [y:] )                 ɔi < OFr ɔi remained   joy
                                      (approx. ai?)

day       ai > æ:
```

au < Gmc   a + w remained; later > ɔ: law
au < OFr   au + labial > later æ: save
au < OFr   au + non-labial > later a:, au   dance, haunt

D. ME shortened accented vowels underwent very little change. The high vowels *i* and *u* had an open lax quality carried over from late ME, but in certain positions they kept high articulation. Phonetically the variation ranged between [i] and [ɪ], [ʊ] and [ʌ]. The distinction was not phonemic. The two phonemes in question may be represented as /i̧/ and /u̧/ respectively.[7] Short *e* had a relatively

---

[7] Wyld, *Short History*, p. 184, quotes 15th-century instances of lowered short *u*, but they remain infrequent in this period. There are also cases of short *i* lowered to *e* in open syllables: *lemon* from *limon*, *wedowe* for *widow*; rarely however in closed syllables.

high articulation, as is indicated by frequent spellings of *i* for *e*. Short *a* was a front vowel, but its value was still [a], not yet [æ]. Before nasals, the vowel *a* often prevailed over *o* [ɔ], which Chaucer had frequently used. Thus *hand* was established as the standard form rather than *hond*, and in such words the short quantity prevailed despite the presence of the lengthening combination -*nd*. These shortened forms originated in the North and Northeast Midland and spread to London. But Caxton still wrote *hond, lond,* and the like, quite frequently, and ModE has the *o* in words like: *long, song.*

In several instances, vowels were affected by neighbouring consonants. Short *e* was raised especially often before *l* and *n*, as is indicated by spellings such as *till, insincible* for *tell, insensible.* As previously, *r* continued to exert a retracting influence, as is seen in forms like *clark* beside *clerk, hartely* beside *hertely.* Rounding of *a* after *w* (also *kw* spelled *qu*) began in the 15th or 16th century, but was not accepted in educated speech before the 17th century. Before *l* a back glide developed which produced diphthongs in combination with *a* and *o*. The result of the former combination, [au], eventually became [ɔ:], as in *all, fall,* together with the diphthong [au] produced by *a* + *w* as in *claw.* In words where the *l* after *o* was itself followed by a consonant it regularly disappeared: *yolk, folk.* A glide also began to appear before post-vocalic *r* as this consonant weakened. This had a front quality, as is attested by the later history of words like *fear, fire, fare.* In Scotland, however, no such glide appeared before *r*, which remained strongly articulated. A *u*-glide before *l* is attested in Scotland by later forms like *auld, cauld* for *old, cold*; this did not appear in London speech.

E. In unaccented syllables, the surviving vowels continued the tendency to reduction. The central vowel was usually though not always lost, as has been said previously, in inflectional endings and other unstressed syllables when it was found in the neighbourhood of liquids and nasals: *hours, sadles* (for *saddles*) and *flowers* (scanned as one syllable), etc. Elsewhere it was still preserved, as in the verbal suffix -*ed* when not following a liquid or a nasal. The use of -*i*- for normal -[ə]- (spelled -*e*-) is regarded as a sign of Northern influence. This -*i*- is to be found in Caxton's inflections of nouns (the plural forms *stedis, renkys,* etc.[8]), and also appears in London texts of the

---

[8] Helmut Wiencke, *Die Sprache Caxtons,* Kölner anglistische Arbeiten, XI (1930), gives a partial account of the fluctuations between *i*

early 16th century. Unaccented monosyllabic words ending in vowels, including prepositions and articles like ModE *to*, *the*, had lost in quantity by 1500, but words with greater sentence stress, like the adverb *too*, preserved it fully. Reduction of vowels in the unstressed and secondarily stressed syllables of Romance words, e. g., *opinion*, must have begun at this time also.

F. Consonants were on the whole very stable, but a few underwent modification in the 15th century. To this period may be assigned the simplification of ME lengthened consonants. With the use of printing there began the more or less consistent practice of doubling consonants in spelling, in order to indicate preceding short vowels before a suffix beginning with a vowel: *maddest* (superlative adjective) in contrast to *madest* (second person singular of *made*). Many other conventions associated with the spelling of modern consonants were also established in the first decades of printing.

The most conspicuous consonant change was total loss in certain positions, usually by simplification before other consonants. Spellings like *fust* for *first*, and *akoded* for *accorded*, as well as inverted spellings like *arnswer* for *answer*, reflect the weakening of *r* in such positions.[9] The spelling *husbon* for *husband* illustrates likewise a tendency to simplify final combinations. There are also such forms as: *wod* for *would*, *worll* for *world*, *behaf* for *behalf*, *handull* for *handfull*. The more important consonant changes may be summarised briefly:

Dentals. The voiced stop [d] became the spirant [ð] by way of [dð] before unaccented -er [ər], as in *mother* < *moder*, *gather* < *gader*, *weather* < *weder*. During the 15th century probably, there began the voicing of initial voiceless fricatives in unaccented words like *the* and *this*. An unhistorical -t appeared at the end of three prepositions indicating position: *betwixt, amongst, against*; also in the conjunctive adverb *whilst*. In all of them there were factors of meaning involved, for the words concerned were thus assimilated to the pattern of the word *next* (by origin a superlative from OE *nēah* meaning *near*). This change

---

and *e* in suffixes. Colet, Lupset and others have sporadic forms like *semith, preceptis, lernyd,* etc., in the early 16th century. See Dobson, *op. cit.* pp. 915—17.

[9] Gösta Langenfelt, *Select Studies in Colloquial English of the Late Middle Ages* (Lund, 1933), pp. 46 ff.; partly based on E. Zachrisson, *The Pronunciation of English Vowels*, 1400—1700 (Göteborg 1913).

is therefore an example of morphemic analogy, not simple phonemic development.

The dentals *t* and *d* when followed by [j] began the palatalisation which eventually produced [tʃ] and [dʒ]. How far the process had gone by 1500 or thereabouts, it is hard to say. Spellings like *reselush-ons* for *resolutions, sogers* beside *soudeours* (for *soldiers*) indicate that it was in process, but early in the 16th century we find forms like *lecter* for *lecture*,[10] and throughout the 18th century conservative pronunciation kept unpalatalised *t* in words like *nature* and *creature*. (See ch. 5, sec. 2). Such spellings also indicate that unaccented [ju] was often pronounced [ə].

Sibilants. Like *t* and *d*, the sounds *s* and *z* also palatalised before [i] and [j], thus producing the sounds [ʃ] and [ʒ] respectively in words like *sugar, confession* and *measure*. The voicing of final *-s* in unaccented words like *is, was*, and in the unaccented suffix *-es*, presumably began in this period. It is difficult to determine how far it had advanced by the middle of the 16th century, however, since a rime like *bliss : is* may have been permitted at that time when it was not perfect.

It is to be noted that Southern dialects, including that of London, retained [ʃ] < original *sk-* in unaccented words, while the Scots dialect simplified the sound to *s* in such cases. Thus the London forms *shal, should* are represented in Scotland by *sal, suld*.

Liquids. The pronunciation of non-initial *l* must have had a quasi-vocalic character, for it disappeared between back vowels and labial or velar consonants. In some instances the result was a simple vowel (e. g., in *half*); in others, a *u*-diphthong had already been formed before the *l* was lost (e. g., *walk*). In the Scottish dialect final *-l* was also lost after back vowels: *fu'* appears in early modern texts for *full*, etc.

The liquid *r* also shows signs of weakening when in non-initial position; cf. the spellings *fust* for *first*, etc. already cit[?] l.

Palatals and velars. In the original combination [iχt], the [χ] had long since palatalised to [ç] which now further developed into [j], eventually producing a simple long vowel before the dental. Thus *might, night* were already being pronounced with [iːt] early in the 15th century,

----

[10] John Tayler, the English ambassador in France, writes to Cardinal Wolsey in 1526 about a "lecter" given in Greek. See John Archer Gee, *The Life and Works of Thomas Lupset* (Yale University Press, 1928), p. 126.

and the vowel underwent diphthongisation along with original long *ī*. The voiced palatal spirant also vocalised to *-i* after front vowels, as in the suffix *y < -iȝ*, for instance in adjectives like *mighty, weighty*. Here as in the suffix *-ly* the result was a long *-ī* which already existed in Chaucer's time. Evidence of 16th-century rimes from Skelton to Shakespeare (and even later) shows that these final long vowels shared in at least the incipient tendency to diphthongise, precisely as in the case of long *ī* in accented syllables.

The unpalatalised spirant [χ], preserved after back vowels in ME, vocalised as *u* before a following consonant. The resultant diphthongs developed normally into ModE, as in *caught, daughter*. Outside of London, the Northwest Midland and Northumbrian dialects retained [χ] in this position.

When final, [χ] generally became [f] or was lost as in the modern standard pronunciation of *rough, enough, plough*; but in Scotland as well as parts of Northern England (Cumberland and Lancashire) the velar persisted, as in the contemporary Scots forms *rouch, eneuch, dwerch*. There is also evidence that conservative speakers of standard English in London preserved some sort of velar spirant throughout the 16th century.

The voiced velar spirant [γ] of early ME had already vocalised and produced lengthened vowels or diphthongs. (See above, sec. 2C).

Initial *k* and *g* were retained before *n*, but the articulation was modified, perhaps towards the substitution of voiceless *n* [n̥] for the initial velar.[11] Thus *know* and *gnaw* became either [n̥nou], [n̥nau] or [hnou], [hnau].

Analogously, final *-g* after [ŋ] (written *ng*, pronounced [ŋg]) was also weakened and eventually lost. Thus *long* and *sing* became [lɔŋ] and [siŋ] respectively, though probably not universally until the 16th century.

In the competition of dialect forms, a number of Anglian words with initial *k-* and *g-* replaced Southern doublets with palatalised consonants which had previously been current in London speech. Forms like *give, gate, care* prevailed over *yive, yate, chare*; but many of the palatal forms also survived.

---

[11] Northern dialects provide evidence that a dental was sometimes substituted for the initial guttural, thus yielding *tnow* for *know*. See Helge Kökeritz in *Language*, XXI (1945), 77–86; also Dobson, *op. cit.*, p. 976 f.

3. THE MORPHOLOGY AND SYNTAX OF LONDON ENGLISH

Most of the morphological changes in the 15th century were due simply to the operation of the sound changes just described. Among these, the loss of final -*e* [ə] had the greatest effect on inflections in general. It caused the complete extinction of adjectival inflections, both strong and weak. Many adverbs originally marked solely by an unstressed final -*e* now·lost this suffix and thus became indistinguishable from adjectives. In the 15th century, for instance, it was possible to say *He is late come home* (for *lately*). Today we say: *He came home late*; but *He has lately arrived*. A number of the suffixless adverbs survive in ModE in special locutions including some colloquialisms: *hard by, fast shut, drive slow, mighty proud.*[12] It was probably the levelling of so many adjectives with adverbs which led to the extension of the suffix -*ly* as a typical sign of the adverb. This suffix was used to create adverbs out of nouns also in some cases: *traitourly, housewifely, proportionly*. Even today, however, many dialects (e. g., Anglo-Irish) prefer the uninflected adverbial forms.

In nominal inflections the strong, originally masculine ending -*es* was now universal except for the small group of surviving weak nouns left from ME. Archaising poets from the 15th to the end of the 16th century, as late as Spenser, kept forms like *eyne* for *eyes*. These are not however typical of the more popular writers. Syncopation of the -*es* ending is found (see above, sec. 2E), after liquids and nasals; elsewhere too in stereotyped phrases like: for *Godds* love. The ME genitive cases without -(*e*)*s* still appear from time to time in the 15th century: e. g., of jantill strene *of fadir syde and of modir syde* (Malory); and we also find the uninflected neuter plural: *all thynge shoulde be done* (Malory).

The verbal inflections represent for the most part a continuation and standardisation of the conjugation as found in Chaucer. Here also certain archaisms were kept artificially alive in poetry, for instance the -*en* ending for the infinitive as late as Spenser. Strong verbs surviving into the 15th century underwent the regular vowel changes already indicated. Some showed a fluctuation of forms under the influence of the weak conjugation. Thus *hewe* had either *hewe* or *hewed* in the past tense; *cleven* had either *clave* or *clefte*; *berste*, either *brast* or *breste*; while *growed* appeared beside *grew* for the past tense of *grow*. Some verbs like *leap* were absorbed entirely into the weak conjugation. The present participle ending in -*ing* became universal in standard

---

[12] On this see Brunner, *op. cit.*, II, pp. 53 ff.

English of the 15th century. One noteworthy deviation from the
Chaucerian conjugation of verbs was the analogical restoration of full
forms in place of the contracted third person present of verbs ending
in dental consonants. We now find *rideth, bindeth,* etc., instead of
Chaucer's *rit* and *bint*. In this same third person singular present, the
ending *-es*, of Northern origin, was gaining ground, but *-eth* was still
common.

Before 1500 there is as yet little sign of the expanded use of certain
auxiliary verbs, notably *do* and *be,* which is so characteristic of ModE.
The verb *do* was already being employed as a substitute for other
verbs, to avoid repetition as well as in the sense of "to cause, to
order" something to be done: Therefore *do* as I bade [thee] *do* (*Gesta
Rom.*)[13] But the characteristic modern functions of *to do* in relation
to questions and negative statements first began to be prevalent in
the ensuing century. There are instances in Malory of the verb *to be*
functioning as an auxiliary to express continuous action, but such cases
are still sporadic.

The personal pronouns may be thus summarised from the standard
usage of Malory and Caxton:[14]

	1st Person	2nd Person	3rd Person		
Nom.	I	thou, thow	he	she	it, hit
Gen.	my, myn(e)	thy, thyn(e)	his	her, hers	his
Dat.-Acc.	me	the(e)	hym	hyr	it, hyt
					(hym)

Nom.	we	ye	they
Gen.	our(e), ours	your(e), yours	their(e), her
Dat.-Acc.	us	you, yow	them, hem

The feminine form *she*, it will be noticed, had become general, but
plural oblique forms with initial *h-* instead of *th-* still appeared. The
feminine dative-accusative *hyr* eventually became identical with the
genitive *her*. The neuter pronoun had as yet no distinctive genitive,

---

[13] Citations from the *Gesta Romanorum* follow the edition by S. J. H.
Herrtage, EETS, ES, No. 33 (1879), and those from Malory are taken
from the edition of his *Works* by E. Vinaver (Oxford University Press,
1947), unless otherwise noted.

[14] C. S. Baldwin, *The Inflections and Syntax of the* Morte d'Arthur
of Sir Thomas Malory (Boston, 1894).

but still retained the form *his*, identical with the masculine. The disjunctive possessives marked by final -*s*, as in: The plan is *ours/ yours/ theirs*, had already appeared in the 14th century, and they became extended in usage thereafter.

Relative pronouns were not standardised in their present-day inflections in either the 15th or the 16th century. The extension of the interrogative pronouns *who* and *which* to perform relative functions had not yet occurred, and there was considerable fluctuation in the forms employed: *that, the which, which* being used for persons as well as things. Similarly, the emphatic-reflexive pronoun had not yet been regularly associated with the suffix -*self* (-*selves*) which is today an essential part of it.

In the syntax of pronouns there are a number of differences from ModE usage. For one thing, inanimate objects are occasionally referred to still by masculine or feminine pronouns: e. g., the sonne in *here* clereness (*Gesta Rom.*). These may well be instances of faint personification rather than survivals of grammatical gender.[15] The case of the pronoun to be used in predication after the verb *to be* was not yet fixed in today's patterns. Chaucer, it will be remembered, had used the construction *It am I* (cf. OE *Ic hit eom*), with the neuter pronoun serving as predicate complement. But the prevailing habits of word order usually placed the subject first, and this convention caused a reorientation in the construction. As a result the pronoun began to function as subject, drawing the verb into agreement with it. Hence we now find constructions like: *Hit is I* (*Gesta Rom.*). The settling of word order into the modern pattern also affected the interpretation of dative pronouns placed before verbs in head position of sentences with impersonal verbs. Nevertheless many of the original datives were retained as such: *them happed* to be, instead of: *it happened to them* to be, or, as ModE would prefer: *they happened* to be. In such phrases the impersonal *it* is often omitted; occasionally (but not often) a personal pronoun subject is also unexpressed. Caxton exemplifies a rather awkward shift from personal to impersonal construction, with omission of *it*, when he writes: *I*, sitting in my studye, ... *happened that* to my hand came a lytyl book (Preface to the *Eneydos*). Among the syntactic features connected with pronouns there may be noted a certain lack of strictness (by our standards) in matters of agreement. For instance, the plural pronoun *they* is sometimes made to refer to the singulars *each* and *every*, as often in contemporary colloquial English. The

---

[15] S. Moore, "Grammatical and Natural Gender in Middle English," *PMLA*, XXXV (1921), 79—103, is the authoritative investigation.

distributive role of these two demonstratives readily suggests plurality: *every* woman þat tooke an oþer man ..., þei shuld be put to perpetuell prison (*Gesta Rom.*).

The extension of plural pronouns of the second person to apply to the singular number had implications of a social nature. Beginning in this transitional period, the plurals *ye, you, your* were applied more and more generally to single individuals (for instance in the *Paston Letters*). This occurred not only in situations implying formality and respect, but also in informal relations. Later a single form *you* discharged the functions of both the nominative and dative-accusative cases. The adoption of *you* for both numbers eliminated both the need and the means for expressing social distinctions grammatically, as has been the case in a number of Modern European languages. Though some tendencies toward such nuancing may be detected in the late medieval distribution of *thou* and *ye* for the singular, the distinction never became a rigid one.[16]

In the syntax of the adverb the most conspicuous feature, from the point of view of the modern student, is the doubling of negatives and of degrees of comparison. It was still possible and in fact habitual in the 15th century to say as Caxton did: *Nothing* will please them *no* time; but after 1500 the elimination of extra negatives was rapid, and by Shakespeare's age single negatives only were favoured in standard speech. Double negation exists to this day in many dialects, however. The adverbial superlative *most* was tautologically prefixed to an adjectival or adverbial superlative in expressions like: *most noblest knight*. A similar doubling occurred in the comparative degree, with *more* preceding adjectives and adverbs ending with the usual suffix -*er*. Such grammatical tautology persisted down to Shakespeare's day.

The syntax of verbs offers several points requiring brief mention here.[17] Besides the somewhat more restricted role then played by auxiliaries, as already stated, the syntax of two of them, namely *to be* and *to have,* marked a distinction no longer made today in re-

---

[16] Norman Nathan, "Pronouns of Address in the Friar's Tale," *Modern Language Quarterly*, XVII (1956), 39—42, finds that nuances of intimacy, contempt, etc., are still to be found in Chaucer's use of *thou* as opposed to *ye,* conforming to the general principle defined by Skeat in his edition of Chaucer's *Works*, V, p. 175.

[17] A more detailed discussion will be given in connection with the verbal system at the end of the 16th century. During two centuries that system changed little, whereas syntactic usage had become rather more clearly established.

lation to the formation of the perfect tense. As in older English, *have* was generally restricted to transitive verbs (e. g., they *have cloven* it in two), while *be* expressed the perfect tense relationships of intransitive verbs of motion (e. g., *he is come*; *it is risen*), very much as in modern German. The distinction is still to be found in Biblical English of the early 17th century (ch. 4, sec. 1). The historical syntax of direct objects appearing after the transitive perfect tense forms is sometimes illuminated by the word order. In these constructions, the verb *to have* was not always a simple auxiliary, a purely formal indicator of time and aspect relations; it began with the "notional"[18] sense of holding, possessing, retaining. Thus the sentence *Thou haste þi lif savid* (*Gesta Rom.*) may be understood as having still something of the sense: As yet you *hold your life* in your own hands— *saved*. This may be compared with the historical syntax of Modern French: *Il l'a sauvée* (referring to a feminine noun).

Tense sequence involving perfect tense relations was as in ModE: The chorle *was gladde* that he this birdde *hadde take* (Lydgate); So when they *were assemblyd* there, / He *roose* hym up (Lydgate). Sometimes, however, the time anterior to that of a past main verb was also expressed by a simple past: And when that I *came* before her presence, / Unto the ground I *dyd knele* adowne (Stephen Hawes, *Pastime of Pleasure*).

Numerical concord between verbs and their subjects does not always appear to be strictly observed in texts of the 15th century and after. That is to say, there are instances in non-colloquial writers where plural verbs follow singular subjects, and the reverse. Malory writes: *trees and erbys burgenyth*; *lovers callyth* to their mynde; *men spekith* of our loue. Such forms may well be explained however as survivals of Southern plural inflections, while occasional verbs in -*es* having plural subjects may indicate Northern influence.

The subjunctive mood of verbs was still widely employed in the 15th century and continued to be syntactically important throughout the Renaissance period. Usage required it in clauses following main verbs expressing doubt, contingency and conditions, as well as other clauses where modern English has simple indicative, now using special auxiliaries to convey the semantic distinction from factual statements. Thus: they deeme *we be not ensuryd* (*Paston Let.*); I can not leave

---

[18] Modern grammarians sometimes speak of the main verb, as opposed to its auxiliaries, as the notional verb. See for instance George O. Curme, *Principles and Practice of English Grammar* (New York, 1947), following Jespersen's terminology.

thus without *it be* a gret displeasure to Godde (*ibid.*) The increasing
use of auxiliaries to replace subjunctive constructions can already be
noticed, however, in the less formal texts of 15th-century English.

Infinitives, participles and verbal nouns appeared in sentence constructions very much as in ModE, though there were differences in
matters of detail. The insertion or omission of the preposition *to* as
a sign of infinitive construction was not yet standardised. Some finite
verbs which today are followed by an infinitive without *to* did not then
show suppression of that preposition, and the reverse was also true.
Malory could say: Sir Launcelot made sir Lavayne *to arme* hym; but
one could also say: I beseche God *comfort* us (*Paston Let.*), —though
this may be a subjunctive. Some authors habitually used *for to* instead
of *to* as a sign of an infinitive construction; others avoided the duplication; still others fluctuated.

Both present participles and verbal nouns were by this time marked
by the suffix *-ing*. The syntax of both was still rather fluid. Here
particularly we have to reckon with the influence of Latin syntax
on English, even before the age of More and Erasmus, but the extent
of that influence is not easily calculated. The use of participles in the
formation of absolute constructions will be discussed in the next
section.

Connectives such as prepositions and conjunctions play an important
part in signalising and indeed in making possible various kinds of
complex structural relations in a sentence. Only when a certain body
of words or phrases has become specialised as indicators of abstract
relationships, does it become · possible to organise sentences whose
members show various ranks of subordination. The connective words
often originated as independent terms with very concrete meanings,
and their relegation to a more abstract function was not a sudden
development, as the history of the separate Indo-European languages
clearly testifies. In the 15th century English already possessed a large
number of such connectives, most of which had achieved their specialised abstract function in the earliest period of the language. But
not all of them were as yet conventionally fixed as to form and
meaning. One could say either *who, which* or *the which* in referring to
people; either *because* or *for because*; *why* or *for why*; *when* or *the time
that*; *if* or *if that*. The chronology of standardisation has yet to be
investigated in detail. In any event it is clear that a recognised
technique of grammatical subordination was an essential pre-condition
for that development of the complex sentence structures in which the
writers of the English Renaissance found delight in the 16th century.
The 15th century had itself inherited such a technique, though its

finer points were not yet established. A discussion of subordinating
connectives thus leads directly to problems of sentence structure, which
in turn involve problems of literary style.

4. SENTENCE STRUCTURE AND STYLE

Even the literary writers of the 15th century, to say nothing of
the popular, informal ones, betray a certain awkwardness and hesitation
when they are faced with the task of building complex sentences.
Such traits are due to the lack of a controlling pattern of usage in
these matters: that is to say, an accepted standard for the emerging
national language.

Relative clauses were not as yet smoothly and easily attached to
the substantives they modified, especially if some sort of parenthetical
phrase intervened. The incomplete adaptation of interrogative pronouns
to relative functioning increased the confusion, for some writers used
the which for all numbers and genders, some used *which* for all, while
others were beginning to use *who(m)*, *whose* for persons, reserving *which*
for animals and things. The demonstrative *that* had also been drawn
into the same function as relative conjunction before the 15th century,
but as an uninflected form it was often followed by a reinforcing
(pleonastic) personal pronoun which we today find superfluous when
it is introduced in non-standard speech: The boy *that* yesterday *he*
broke his leg... There are many instances of incomplete subordination,
repetitious wording and shifting of construction from coordination to
subordination, not only among unskilled writers but also among those
like Malory and Caxton who possessed talent, experience, and a concern
for style. Some examples will illustrate the types of relative pronouns
employed, and some of the structural difficulties connected with them:

> the Damsell of the Lake *that* hyght Nynyve, *whych* wedded the
> good knyght sir Pelleas (both *which* and *that* used for a person;
> Malory)
>
> quene Gwenyver, *for whom* I make mencion (*who* used for a person,
> *ibid.*)
>
> he *that* smites, *he* shall be smitten (*that* with pleonastic personal
> pronoun; *Towneley Mysteries,* quoted by Kellner)
>
> Now turne we unto sire Lamorak *that* upon a day *he* took a lytel
> barget (the same pleonasm; Malory)
>
> *of whom* may not well be recounted the valyaunce *of him* (*of
> whom* instead of *whose,* followed by pleonastic phrase; Caxton, *Charles
> the Grete* as cited by Kellner)

his wif was a strompet, *and which* purveith.... that hire husbond
shuld be ded (*which* used for a person and preceded by pleonastic
and; *Gesta Rom.*)

There was also the possibility, sanctioned by tradition, of attaching
adjectival relative clauses asyndetically to the main one: there be many
men spekith of our love (Malory).

Conjunctions introducing temporal adverbial clauses were fairly well
established and the clauses themselves were clearly related to the main
statements of sentences. One matter of detail varied somewhat from
modern speech habits. There was a stereotyped correlation of *when...
then,* which today would appear redundant, especially in short sentences.
For instance: And so *whan* she herde how the quene was greved for
the dethe of sir Patryse, *than* she told hit openly (Malory). In sentences
where the clause following *when* is a long one, on the other hand, the
than still has a valid stylistic function as a signal of the shift (or
return) to the main clause. As with relative pronouns, adverbial
connectives are also frequently reinforced by *that*, producing combinations like *when that, if that, lest that,* etc. Several types of adverbial
subordination appear in the following sentence from Malory:

So *whan* trumpettis blew unto the fylde and kynge Arthur was
sette on hyght uppon a chafflet to beholde *who* did beste (but, *as* the
Freynshe booke seyth, the kynge wold nat suffir sir Gawayne to go
frome hym, *for* never had sir Gawayne the bettir and [= if] sir
Launcenlot were in the fylde, and many tymes was sir Gawayne
rebuked *so whan* sir Launcelot was in the fylde in ony justis
dysgysed), *than* som of the kyngis... were that tyme turned to be
uppon the syde of kynge Arthur (p. 1069).

Here the correlation of *when... then* appears essential to clarify the
sentence structure, but the phrase *that time* is a redundant recapitu-
lation of *then*. Such instances as this reveal the stylistic importance
of adverbial constructions in the sentence.

The handling of indirect discourse presented a special problem. The
connective word *that*, genetically identical with the demonstrative
pronoun, was the usual sign that the ensuing noun clause would report
an utterance indirectly, as in ModE: He said *that* he had finished the
work. (The original sense was: He said *that*: i. e., he had finished the
work.) Modern English convention, in contrast to Polish, for instance,
requires that an anterior time relation must be indicated by the tense
sequence; in this case, that the act of finishing was already completed

before the act of speaking. Indirect speech also requires, of course, a consistent change in the persons of the subject pronouns and their predicates. In the 15th century such distinctions were already habitual but not yet observed with entire regularity. Authors sometimes slipped back into direct speech almost immediately after announcing indirect by means of the connective *that*. The reverse could also occur, as when Malory shifts at once from direct to indirect discourse: "Sir," he sayde, *he saw* nothyng but watirs wap and wawys wanne.

In summary it may be said that 15th-century writing shows a wide range of preferences in matters of sentence structure, extending from the artlessly simple to the fairly complicated. The latter type often reveals incomplete stylistic (and even grammatical) mastery. The early popular drama, though cast in verse form, presumably reflects fairly accurately the habits of colloquial English in these matters. It represents a body of linguistic material of exceptional importance for the history of non-courtly, non-formal style. Here, as might be expected, parataxis is the prevailing type of sentence structure. The subordinated elements have to do chiefly with time sequences and simple conditions introduced by the conjunction *if*. The *Paston Letters* illustrate the epistolary style of persons without literary ambition, but endowed with a certain unpretentious eloquence in depicting the events of daily life among members of the landed gentry. Fairly complex syntactic relations of sentence parts appear in the *Letters* from time to time, and the writers on the whole extricate themselves from them creditably, if not always with stylistic finesse. In *The Book of Margery Kempe* we have the record of an illiterate woman's hysterical religious experiences, dictated to her priest and set down with, no doubt, a certain amount of editing on his part. The sentence structure is not what we should regard today as strikingly naive. It may well have been modified by him in the act of transmission, but behind the written words it is sometimes possible to detect the simple discourse of uneducated speakers, especially when fragments of conversation are set down in direct speech.

Among the more formal writers there are also some who typically avoid elaborate hypotaxis and show a certain lack of skill in handling even its simpler forms. The sentences of these writers make much use of simple coordinated statements and simple modifiers, repetitions, redundant pronouns and tautologies. Malory is such a writer. His descriptive passages tend to coordination of clauses where we should today choose subordination, but on the other hand his dignity of style is inextricably bound up with the straightforwardness of his linguistic structure, and no one who appreciates the savour of his prose can wish that he had adopted a more complicated organisation of sentences. Even where Malory adopts subordination, it is apt to be simple and rather repetitious, as when he writes:

> But   the kyng of Irelond his name was sir Marhalte, that was fadir unto the good knyght sir Marhalte that sir Trystram slew; and he had the speache, that sir Trystram myghte hyre (p. 729).

The sentence is reorganised in the process of being formulated. There is a false start, so to speak, with the *kyng of Irelond*; then the construction is shifted to *name* as the leading term, with *the kyng* now made subordinate. Today we should begin: The name of the King of Ireland was... , though the looser construction exists in colloquial speech:

Caxton, Malory's editor, was more experimental in his approach to sentence structure, but he was also less sure of himself, if we may judge by his style. In his writing we come upon evidences of that imperfectly assimilated Latin influence which is the mark of more sophisticated composition in the 15th century. When such writers essay an imitation of classical style, they rely chiefly on two or three grammatical devices in order to achieve the desired effect.

The first device is an imitation of the Latin ablative absolute construction, which had already been adapted in OE as a dative absolute. It was now perforce expressed as a nominative absolute because of the wide loss of inflectional endings during the intervening centuries. Thus Lydgate begins a long sentence having *King Priam* as its subject with the absolute construction: *the sorwe aswaged* (*Troy Book*, l. 479 ff.). Similarly Caxton writes: But *wel consydered the facyon of this paynym and of this cristen man,* there was grete loyalte & curtoyse bytwene them (*Charles the Grete*).

The second main device used was the insertion of rather long modifiers, such as participial or clausal constructions after the subject, thus interrupting the normally close sequence between it and the predicate. In the opening stanza of *The Churl and the Bird,* Lydgate exemplifies a clausal interruption which is not very smoothly handled:

> Problemys of olde likenesse and figures,
> Whiche proved been fructuous of sentence,
> And hath auctorite grownded in scriptures,
> By resemblances of nobille apparence,
> Withe moralitees concluding of prudence,
> Like as the Bibylle rehersithe by writing,
> How trees somtyme chase hemself a kyng.[18a]

[18a] As printed by Neilson and Webster; see reference on p. 242.

Here the predicate of *problemys*, delayed until the last line but one, appears to be *rehersithe*; but the construction remains in some doubt since *like as* could function either as a preposition or a conjunction. Adverbial interruptions may have the same effect, especially when they appear in inverted position.

Inversion of sentence parts was in fact a third conspicuous technique employed to obtain periodic effects. The parts concerned may be either short or long. Some prose examples are:

> þat in holi scripture is noon of þese now rehercid gouernauncis groundid or witnessid or ensaumplid by eny persoon expressli, lo, y proue þus... (Reginald Pecock, *The Repressour*, I, 19).

> Also ful ofte, whanne a man comeþ to chirche & wole be remembrid vpon such now seid þingis, his heed is feble for labour or studie bifore had or for siknes or for age (*ibid.*, I, 11).

> Whan hyt cam on the morn the grekes by the conduyte of Eneas and of Anthenor that were open traytours vnto theyr Cyte and also to theyr kynge and lord, cam and entrid in to the palays of ylyon where they fonde no deffence (Caxton, *Recuyell of the Histories of Troye*).

Such departure from normal word order could be elaborated to achieve oratorical effects. Putting long subordinate elements of the sentence in head position created suspense because of the delay of the essential statement to the end. Lydgate occasionally permits himself such elaborate periodicity (e. g., *Troy Book*, 11. 203 ff.), but neither he nor any of the other pre-Tudor poets tries the effect very often. Shorter inversions for emphasis are on the other hand frequently encountered in both verse and prose.

Because the conventions of English sentence structure were not yet precisely laid down, and the relations within the longer units were not always clear, various extra words were sometimes required as signals to remind a listener or reader of their basic structure. If for instance a subject was separated from its predicate by a' number of modifiers, a repeated reference to the subject might be necessary in order to recall it to attention before passing to the predicate. A recapitulatory pronoun was useful after interrupting modifiers of the subject, as in this prose sentence which recalls Chaucer's usage:

> Amonge these thynges the prynces that were yet in troye/ Whan they sawe that the kynge had so fowle and shamefully trayted with

the grekes *they* wente oute of troye and toke theyr men with them
(Caxton, *Recuyell*).

The same doubling of a pronoun for its distant appositionary noun
still occurs in verse, as in these lines of Skelton (early 16th century):
Thus *I*, Colin Clout,/ As I go about,/ And wandering as I walk,/
I hear the people talk. Both recapitulating and otherwise repetitive
pronouns were also freely used, much more frequently than today,
when there was no interrupting modifier: My pen *it* is unable,/ My
hand *it* is unstable (Skelton, *Philip Sparrow*).

Experimentation towards the realisation of a literary prose style
was still uncertain in respect to vocabulary as well as sentence structure.[19] There were those who inclined to a free borrowing of Latin
words, which tended to keep learned writing far removed from everyday speech. There were a few, like Reginald Pecock, who strenuously
rejected the importation of Latin words, and attempted to form
English equivalents, so far as possible, by compounding native Germanic
elements— even when their sentences were incongruously constructed
on the model of Latin periods. Thus Pecock creates words like *inleding*
for *introduction, endal* for *final, undernyming* for *reproaching.* If he was
striving for simplicity, he spoils the effect by multiplying synonyms
and organising his sentences cumbersomely, at times almost to the
point of incoherence. Caxton also writes synonyms in pairs, sometimes
in groups, when he is translating, in an anxious effort (as it would
seem) to convey all requisite shades of meaning for one word of the
original.[20] The contemporary admiration for Chaucer's poetry strengthened a vogue for decorative vocabulary, extending into the 16th century. The Chaucerian terms most favoured by courtly writers were the
polysyllables taken directly or indirectly from Latin. Excessive use of
them produced a style called aureate (that is, gilded), which was later
condemned as ink-horn writing. Before the Tudor age, however, this
fashion was for the most part limited to verse, and it was less exaggerated among the English than the Scottish poets.

---

[19] On this subject see George Philip Krapp, *The Rise of English
Literary Prose* (New York, 1915).

[20] Ernst Leisi, *Die tautologischen Wortpaare in Caxton's "Eneydos,"*
Zürich diss. (Cambridge, U. S. A., 1947), concludes that no single theory
(a translator's needs, a desire to imitate or instruct, influence of sound
effects, etc.) will explain all cases of double terms in Caxton, but he
notes that these are especially frequent in emphatic positions. The
affective element appears to have been the strongest factor.

5. THE SCOTTISH LITERARY LANGUAGE

After Chaucer's death in 1400, an important school of writers carried on his literary tradition in the North and adapted it to meet the requirements of native inspiration. The dialect of medieval Scotland developed further towards a national language, for the region was politically separate until the early 17th century, resisting attempts at subjugation by the English in a series of wars. Political alliances with France were followed by cultural influences which are reflected, among other things, in numerous French loan words which were taken over into Scots in the late Middle Ages. The earlier heritage from the Danish language remained very conspicuous in Scotland, and there was also a certain infiltration of Celtic. All of these elements gave a variegated colour to the Scottish literary language, distinguishing it from the English.

Scottish poets of the 15th and early 16th century wrote in two contrasting styles: a fairly simple one in rather realistic vein, drawing freely on the local native vocabulary, and an artificial style decorated with the learned terms of aureate diction. In both instances the phonology and grammatical structure were faithful to the tradition of the Northern dialect as preserved in Middle Scots.

This underwent relatively few changes, at least in the written form, between the 14th and the 16th century. In the former period Scots had anticipated late Middle English in carrying through certain sound changes such as the loss of final unaccented -e [ə], and in the raising of long closed $\bar{e}$ and $\bar{o}$ to higher positions. (See ch. 1, sec. 5.) After these shifts, however, a period of stabilisation seems to have followed, and the Northern language became the more conservative of the two. Among the sounds preserved in the North were: long $\bar{u}$ and probably also long $\bar{\imath}$, which did not show the Southern tendency towards breaking; also long $\bar{a}$, which was not fronted to [æ:] as in the dialect of London.[21] The velar spirant [χ] and its palatal variant [ç], both lost in the South, were here preserved. As previously, a written letter i, having no value in pronunciation, was used orthographically to indicate a simple long vowel: *mair* for *mār*, etc.

In late Middle Scots, the morphology continued to differ conspicuously from that of London English, and in much the same way

---

[21] On the possibility of an off-glide after long $\bar{u}$, see vowel chart in ch. 1, sec. 5. The long $\bar{a}$ may have been slightly raised in this period, but the change was not as marked as in the South. The spelling gives no indication of it.

as previously. The verbal conjugation still had -is as the normal suffix for all persons and numbers of the present tense: *I, thou, he, we, ye, thai keipis* (= *keeps* or *keep*). Weak verbs still had the suffix -*it* rather than -*ed* for both past tense and perfect passive participle: *knokkit, proceidit, sugerit*. The vocalism of these endings reflects the Northern preference, already mentioned, since the front vowel *i* appears here instead of *e* or [ə] in unaccented syllables. The same vowel appears in the inflectional -*is* for the genitive singular and for all plural endings of strong nouns: *thoughtis, lufaris*. The present participle active of verbs is still -*and*. A number of pronouns have specifically Scottish forms: *quhilk, quha* for *which, who*; *thai* and *thir* for *these*, etc. Numerous traits, therefore, make easy the identification of a text of Scottish provenience in the post-Chaucerian period.

Among the writers who employed the more artificial or aureate diction of the Scottish Chaucerian school were King James I (1395—1437) in his *Kingis Quair* (*The King's Book*); Robert Henryson (1425—1500?), author of *The Testament of Cressid*; William Dunbar (1460—1520?), and Gavin Douglas (1475—1522), who translated the *Aeneid* into Scots. But several of these poets, especially Henryson and Dunbar, were also masters of a vigorous and homely style, which they perfected for the realistic portrayal of life among poor and simple people. A strong vein of satire is perceptible in their more realistic writing, as for instance in the *Fables* of Henryson and the burlesques of Dunbar. Sir David Lindsay (1490—1555) reached a high point of native satire, singularly independent of the artificiality often attendant upon learning, in his play *Ane Satyre of the Thrie Estaits*. The work has dual interest as an important philological document and an even more important instance of social history mirrored in art. The vocabulary of this play, along with its morphology and syntax, offers a rich field for the study of the Scottish linguistic heritage in the early 15th century.

CHAPTER III

THE LITERARY LANGUAGE IN THE 16th CENTURY:
ITS WORDS AND ITS SOUNDS

1. ATTITUDES TO THE ENGLISH LANGUAGE

Caxton's pioneer labours as a printer were directly connected, as we have seen, with his experimental efforts to shape English prose into a worthy medium of literary expression. It was a task concerning which he felt many doubts and hesitations. His questionings as to the intrinsic value of English for any sort of literary usage were as a matter of fact widely shared, and sentiments like his continued to be expressed frequently throughout the first part of the 16th century. They extended to English verse as well as English prose, and this, inconsistently enough, despite the tributes of profound veneration still being paid to Chaucer, and the recognition of poetic achievements by men like Skelton, Wyatt and Surrey in the early Tudor period. Skelton himself speaks thus of his native language through a character who is obviously his mouthpiece:

> Our natural tongue is rude
> And hard to be ennewed
> With polished termes lusty;
> Our language is so rusty,
> So cankered, and so full
> Of frowards, and so dull,
> That if I would apply
> To write ornately,
> I wot not where to find
> Terms to serve my mynd.[1]

It was particularly when comparing the resources of English with those of Latin and Greek that writers were moved to make remarks

---

[1] From "Philip Sparrow" by John Skelton, *Complete Works*, ed. Philip Henderson (London, 1948), p. 82.

unfavourable to the vernacular. The range of humanistic studies increased rapidly after Caxton's day, and these studies engendered a certain mistrust of English. They even cancelled temporarily much of the prestige acquired by the language in the 14th and 15th centuries. This was due to the understandable admiration and enthusiasm felt for the great works of classical antiquity but recently recovered in Western Europe. The corresponding mistrust of the vernacular appeared especially among translators of classical works into English. Arthur Golding, well known for his rendering of Ovid's *Metamorphoses*, speaks in another work (1564) of "this my rude translation voyd of ornate termes and eloquent endityng." [2] William Barkar, translator of Xenophon's life of King Cyrus of Persia (ca. 1560), remarks in his Preface:

> And although herin I haue a goodly occasion to commend the writer, that in the moste eloquent and excellent tong hath written moste purelie, yet bycause it carieth the matter whole into another tongue, and keepeth his own fines [i. e., observes its own limits] still in his owne tongue, and our grosse tongue is a rude and a barren tong, when it is compared with so florishinge and plentifull a tongue, I wil passe ouer this praise...[3]

Roger Ascham explained in his *Toxophilus* (1545) that he wrote English only because he wanted to be read by gentlemen and yeomen without knowledge of the classics; otherwise Latin would have been easier for them and better for his prestige:

> And as for the Latin or greke tonge, euery thyng is so excellently done in them, that none can do better: In the Englysh tonge contrary, euery thinge in a maner so meanly, bothe for the matter and handelynge, that no man can do worse.[4]

William Adlington, who Englished *The Golden Ass* of Apuleius (1566), spoke deprecatingly of the result as "beyng now barbarously and

---

[2] *The Histories of Trogus Pompeius*, translated into English by Arthur Golding (1564), cited by Richard Foster Jones, *The Triumph of the English Language* (Stanford University Press, 1953), p. 20.

[3] William Barkar, Preface to *The Bookes of Xenophon*, cited by Jones, *op. cit.*, p. 23.

[4] Roger Ascham, Preface to *Toxophilus*, in *The English Works*, ed. by William A. Wright (Cambridge University Press, 1904); cited by Jones, *op. cit.*, p. 14.

simply framed in our Englishe tongue." Like sentiments are repeated
many times in the first three-quarters of the century.

When these critics speak of English as a barbarous language they
refer specifically to its lack of rhetorical discipline, as compared with
Latin and Greek. Eloquence was the quality which they prized,
apparently; and eloquence was what some of them set out to realise
for the English vernacular under the tutelage of classical models. The
very term "barbarous" was understood by some to mean merely:
lacking in oratorical effect. The upsurge of classical studies in the
age of humanism brought with it a particular devotion to the theory
and practice of oratory. The foundation for such studies was supplied
by the recently published works of Aristotle, Quintilian, Cicero (the
discussions of orators and oratory, as distinguished from the pseudo-
Ciceronian *Rhetoric* current in the Middle Ages), and others. Moreover,
the political life of the Renaissance gave occasion for political
oratory in the ancient use of the term, as opposed to the medieval
type of eloquence which had been largely restricted to preaching
and moral admonition.[5] The ability to compose and deliver Latin
speeches in classical style yielded both honour and worldly success
as rewards: at first in the Italian city-states, later at the courts
of Northern European rulers. Typical of the Renaissance attitude was
the admiration accorded by all of Florence to the orator-professor
Giovanni Lignano, praised by Chaucer (Prologue to the Clerk's Tale)
for his great eloquence. The same attitude is reflected in a statement
written to the Bishop of Chichester by Aeneas Sylvius Piccolomini
on the importance of both oratory and epistolary skill: "Great is
eloquence; nothing so much rules the world. Political action is the
result of persuasion; his opinion prevails with the people who best
knows how to persuade them."[6] As Sir Thomas Elyot remarked in
his *Boke Named the Gouernour* (1531):

> The utilitie that a noble man shall haue by redyng these oratours
> [i. e., Demosthenes, Isocrates and Cicero] is, that, whan he shall
> happe to reason in counsaile, or shall speke in great audience, or to

---

[5] See J. W. H. Atkins, *English Literary Criticism: The Renascence*
(London, 2nd ed., 1951), ch. 2; Elizabeth J. Sweeting, *Early Tudor
Criticism, Literary and Linguistic* (Oxford, 1940), ch. 6, especially p. 108.

[6] Cited by Lewis Einstein, *The Italian Renaissance in England* (New
York: Columbia University Press, 1902), p. 9 and by M. Creighton,
The Early Renaissance in England (Cambridge, 1895), p. 19. The letter
was written in 1444.

strange ambassadours of great princes, he shall not be constrayned
to speake wordes sodeyne and disordered, but shal bestowe them
aptly and in their places.[7]

It is reported that Thomas Lupset, a teacher of both Latin and
Greek at Oxford, won especial praise by calling attention to the
rhetorical figures in Cicero's orations.[8] The vogue for Ciceronian eloquence led to downright absurdities which Erasmus ridiculed in his
well-known dialogue *Ciceronianus*.

The direct result of these intensified studies was a reestablishment
of classical standards in the writing of dead languages. Greek studies
were introduced into England by those pioneering scholars Grocyn,
Linacre and Latimer, beginning in the 1490's, and they were carried
forward by Colet, More and Lupset, with inspiration and aid from
the distinguished visitor Erasmus. Since one objective of a classical
education in the early Tudor period was to have students imitate
the ancients as closely as possible, the emphasis in grammar and
rhetoric was placed, even more than previously, on preceptive or
normative instruction. Significant is the title of Linacre's work, *De
Emendenda Structura Latini Sermonis,* which reflects the eagerness to
get away from medieval Latin and substitute the classical form as
the standard. By their example the humanists led a revolt against
the pretentious and obscure coinages of aureate Latin; indirectly, therefore, against those of aureate English.

Despite the humanists' concentration upon ancient languages, however,
there were a number of social factors operating at the time which
tended to elevate the importance of the vernacular as an instrument
of education. For one thing, the English Reformation brought about
a secularisation of teaching which removed it from the exclusive
domain of a Latin-speaking clergy and put it into the hands of wider
groups in the community. The movement for secular instruction had
already become strong in the 15th century: gentlemen and members
of the upper nobility organised classes and tutors for their children
apart from the church, and merchants, guildsmen and other middle-
class groups endowed schools which were staffed by laymen, the
clergy being excluded from some by specification.[9] Secular teaching

---

[7] Elyot, *The Boke Named the Gouernour,* Bk. i, ch. 11; ed. Foster
Watson (Everyman's Library, reprint of 1937), p. 42.

[8] Lupset, *Works,* ed. J. A. Gee, p. 96.

[9] Clara P. McMahon, *Education in Fifteenth-Century England* (Johns
Hopkins University Press, 1947).

6

naturally weakened the exclusive position of Latin as a medium of instruction. Moreover, the triumphant movement for translation of the Bible into English brought a heightened prestige to the vernacular. Both Erasmus and More commended Biblical translations into English, provided only that they were made with careful accuracy. Others expressed a like desire for wide dissemination of the Bible in English so that it would become (as we should say today) a means of democratic religious education. Tyndale (died 1536) declared that he could bring it about that a boy following the plow would know more of the Scriptures than many a learned bishop. He noted that Greek and Hebrew are closer to English than to Latin in word order and sentence structure, and he replied with some sharpness to the traducers of English:

> Seynt Hierom [Jerome] also translated the bible in to his mother tonge. Why may not we also? They wil saye it can not be translated in to our tonge, it is so rude. It is not so rude as they ar false lyers (from *The Obedience of a Christen Man,* 1528).

The writer of an anonymous tract (1539) claimed with satisfaction that Bible reading in English had supplanted the earlier vogue for romances of chivalry:

> Englishmen have now in hand in every church and place, almost every man the Holy Bible and New Testament in their mother tonge instead of the old fabulous and fantastical books of the Table Round, Launcelot du Lac & c., and such other, whose unpure filth and vain fabulosity the light of God has abolished utterly.[10]

Thus there was very wide agreement on the desirability of translating the Bible. Differences of opinion arose however concerning the vocabulary and style to be employed. Here the basic split between purists and innovators (see below, sec. 3) came to the surface.

Throughout the early Tudor period, the primary purpose of language teaching was and remained the achievement of a good Latin (or Greek) style. This was the end envisaged by handbooks of grammar and rhetoric, and discussions of educational methods in general. But it would be a mistake to assume, as has sometimes been done, that skill in using English was a matter of indifference in the schools of Tudor

---

[10] The citations from Tyndale and from the anonymous tract are given by Sweeting, *op. cit.*, pp. 30 and 40 respectively.

England. Though the English language was not taught as a separate subject in the grammar schools, it was cultivated with some care in relation to the secondary art of translation. The improved mastery of Latin was expected to bring about an improvement in the use of the vernacular. As early as 1483 the author of a text on translating phrases from Terence into English (probably the schoolmaster John Anwykyll) had urged students to master his book in order to express themselves better in English as well as Latin.[11] The translator of Cicero's *De Officiis*, Nicholas Grimald, suggested in his preface the care with which such a task should be carried out:

> For allthough an English man hath his mother toung; & can talk apace as he lerned of his dame: yet it is one thing to title tattle, I wott not how, or to chatter like a iaye: & an other, to bestowe his wordes wisely, orderly, plesantly and pythiely.[12]

Roger Ascham's well-known system of "double translation" —that is, having pupils put Latin texts into English and then back again into Latin without consulting the original— not only emphasised the unique qualities of the classical authors being studied, but also made students aware of English as a medium, and encouraged them to achieve a conscious mastery of its resources.[13] In this way progress was made towards realising in English that polished eloquence which critics of the language demanded. Some exercises in translation even called attention to the phraseology of informal, colloquial English, for instance in the rendering of Latin comedies into the vernacular. Nicholas Udall, head of Eton and author of a Plautine comedy in English (*Ralph Roister Doister*, ca. 1550?) pointed out in his *Floures for Latine Speaking* how Latin idioms and expletives might be handled in native speech: "Ita me dij ament honestus est. As god helpe me

---

[11] The reference to Anwykyll's *Vulgaria Quaedam abs Terencio in Anglicam Linguam Traducta* is taken from a valuable article by William Nelson, "The Teaching of English in Tudor Grammar Schools," *Studies in Philology*, XLIX (1952), 119—43.

[12] Cited by Nelson, *loc. cit.*, p. 124, from the 1553 ed. of Grimald's translation of Cicero. See also Veré L. Rubel, *Poetic Diction in the English Renaissance* (New York: Modern Language Association of America, 1941), p. 83.

[13] Roger Ascham, *The Scholemaster*, ed. W. A. Wright in *The English Works*; see n. 4.

it is a goodly feloe; or (as we vse commonly to speake) as I shall be saued; or, as I trust to be saued, it is a goodly feloe." In the same spirit Richard Bernard later gave lists of equivalents in his *Terence in English* (1598): "Perij. I am vndone; my ioy is past in this world; my good daies are at an end; I am a man of another world: I am quite cast away; I am but dead; God haue mercy vpon mee; woe is me; out alas; ah weladay."[14]

The Tudor handbooks of rhetoric published in English were not all designed for use in the schools exclusively. They reached wide circles of readers outside of institutions of education. They thus contributed a broad basis to the shaping of literary English and helped further to establish its value and dignity as an artistic medium of expression. A pioneer text was Leonard Cox's *Arte or Crafte of Rhetoryke* (first published about 1530). After it the most famous text book was Thomas Wilson's *Arte of Rhetorique* (1553 and 1560), written for the general reader. It follows traditional models but it consistently applies ancient doctrines to the vernacular and it illustrates these by original examples and imagined situations that are specifically English.[15] Richard Sherry's two books on rhetoric (*A Treatise of Schemes and Tropes*, 1550 and *A Treatise of the Figures of Grammer and Rhetorike*, 1555), were designed to aid in the appreciation rather than the practice of eloquence by English students. The author is one of those who argued that eloquence could be realised in the native tongue. Others who contributed to rhetorical studies were P. Rainolde with his *Foundations of Rhetoric* (1563), H. Peacham with his *Garden of Eloquence* (1577), and A. Fraunce with his *Arcadian Rhetorike* (1584, with many illustrations drawn from Sidney's well-known *Arcadia*).

These various influences in humanistic education brought about a complete vindication of English by the last decades of the 16th century. By this time, too, the achievements of creative writers in verse and prose had vindicated it incontrovertibly in practice. Though some still

---

[14] The examples from Udall and Bernard are both given by Nelson, *loc. cit.*, p. 137 f.

[15] Leonard Cox, *The Arte or Crafte of Rhetorique,* ed. Frederick Ives Carpenter (University of Chicago Press, 1899); Thomas Wilson, *The Arte of Rhetorique,* ed. G. H. Mair (Oxford, 1909). For discussion, see Atkins, *op. cit.*, pp. 74 ff. and Jones, *op. cit.*, p. 186. On the entire rhetorical tradition in English learning see the detailed study by Wilbur Samuel Howell, *Logic and Rhetoric in England, 1500—1700* (Princeton University Press, 1956).

held to the opinion that the language was rude and barbarous,[16] the newer and more prevalent attitude was expressed by Richard Mulcaster, the teacher of Edmund Spenser, who wrote books to aid in the establishment of a standard orthography (see below, sec. 4). His famous passage in defense of English, which appeared in his textbook *The First Part of the Elementarie* (1582), deserves to be quoted once more at this point:

I take this present period of our English tung to be the verie height therof, bycause I find it so excellentlie well fined [i. e., refined], both for the bodie of the tung it self, and for the customarie writing thereof, as either foren workmanship can give it glosse, or as homewrought han[d]ling can give it grace. When the age of our peple, which now use the tung so well, is dead and departed there will another succede, and with the peple the tung will alter and change. Which change in the full harvest thereof maie prove comparable to this, but sure for this which we now use, it semeth even now to be at the best for substance, and the bravest for circumstance, and whatsoever shall becom of the English state, the English tung cannot prove fairer, then it is at this daie, if it maie please our learned sort to esteme so of it, and to bestow their travell [i. e., labour] upon such a subject, so capable of ornament, so proper to themselves, and the more to be honored, bycause it is their own.[17]

2. THE SOCIAL AND CULTURAL ENVIRONMENT

There were many influences outside of rhetorical studies which affected the English language in a general way during the 16th century. These were factors of a broad social character, and they had to do chiefly with vocabulary, pronunciation and usage in relation to the accepted standard.

The changes in the class structure of England, continuing the tendencies already apparent in the 15th century, affected the linguistic situation precisely at the time when the standard form of the national

---

[16] George Pettie speaks with some impatience of this opinion in his book on *Civile Conversation* (1586), quoted by Baugh, *History of the English Language*, p. 249.

[17] See Baugh, *History*, pp. 245 f.; also Jones, *op. cit.*, pp. 192—94.

language was being definitively established. An expanding, newly enriched middle class was deriving fortunes from the wool trade, from
shipping and (later on) from the colonies recently acquired in the New
World. It was mastering new techniques in navigation and in early
types of manufacture. Though some fortunes were as quickly lost as
won in the fierce competition among merchant capitalists, others were
consolidated, and many of the successful families were now able to
buy out the remnants of feudal nobility, replacing them in the roles
of courtiers, statesmen and patrons of literature. The sons and daughters
of the new aristocracy, together with the children of untitled wealthy
families, took part in the education and cultural interests stimulated
by humanism. There was a market for classical education in England
such as had not been dreamed of in the Middle Ages. The atmosphere
was favourable to extensive literary expression centred in the national
capital, with theatres, court shows and above all the printing presses
stimulating the use of language arts for entertainment.

Nor was it only the noble and the wealthy courtiers and the professional writers who wished to improve their mastery of English as
a tool of expression. Though rhetoric proper made its appeal primarily
to members of the privileged classes, the general study of English also
attracted many newly literate members of the lower orders such as
traders, craftsmen, clerks and many others. Edward Coote, author of
The English Schoolmaster (1596) was by the end of the century appealing
to these social groups with an exhortation to improve their mastery
of the language for practical reasons:

> I am now therefore to direct my speech unto the unskilful, which
> desire to make use of it for their own private benefit, and to such
> men and women of Trade, as Tailors, Weavers, shop keepers,
> Sempsters and such others, as have undertaken the charge of teaching
> others.... [For] if thou take diligent pains in [this book] but 4 days,
> thou shalt learn very many profitable things that thou never
> knewest;... thou shalt teach thy Scholars with better accommodation
> and profit, than any other (not following this order) teacheth, and
> thou mayest sit on thy shop board, at thy Loom, or at thy Needle,
> and never hinder thy work to hear thy Scholars, after once thou
> hast made this little book familiar to thee.[18]

Such appeals to wide circles of English working people must have
found a corresponding echo, otherwise it would be difficult to under-

---

[18] Nelson, *loc. cit.*, p. 142.

stand the comic presentation by Shakespeare and others of affected
rhetorical exercises being carried out among the youth of country
districts by pedants like the famous Holofernes of *Love's Labour's Lost*.
Thomas Wilson, in his *Arte of Rhetorique*, tells amusing anecdotes about
half-educated townsmen who tried to imitate the artificially cultured
style of certain courtiers and scholars, with the result that they fell
into comic distortions and malapropisms. A town mayor wishing to
speak like a fine learned man is said to have addressed a vagabond
or "runnegate fellowe" in these words: "Thou ingrame and vacation
[ingrate and vagabond?] knaue, if I take thee any more within the
circumcision of my dampnation: I will so corrupt thee, that all other
vacation knaues shall take ilsample by thee." Another, asking for
a loan of money from a gentleman, spoke thus: "I pray you sir be
so good vnto me, as forbeare this halfe yeres rent. For so help me
God and halidome, we are so taken on with contrary Bishops, with
reuiues, and with Southsides to the King, that all our money is cleane
gone." The good man meant to say "contributions, reliefs and sub-
sidies," Wilson explains. "And thus we see," he continues, "that poore
simple men are much troubled, and talke oftentimes they knowe not
what for lacke of wit, and want of Latine and French, whereof many
of our strange wordes full often are deriued." [19]. The anonymous
collection *A Hundred Merry Tales* (1525) tells about an Oxford student
delighting in ornate English who asked his cobbler in these refined
terms to pick out a design on his shoes according to the latest fashion:
"I pray the set me .ii. tryanglys and .ii. semy cercles vppon my sub-
pedytals & I shall gyue the for thy labor." No wonder the craftsman
replied: "Syr youre eloquence passith myne intelligence," but if he
were too often exposed to such harangues he too might well have
tried to become "eloquent". [20]

From these anecdotes of the earlier 16th century, whether founded
on fact or not, it is but a short distance to Shakespeare's delightful
use of malapropisms in the mouths of Bully Bottom, Launcelot Gobbo
and Dogberry. Their mistakes and the laughter attendant upon them
alike indicate the breadth of interest in matters of language.

Another aspect of England's social transformations may well have
had a profound effect on the emerging standard, an effect which however

[19] Thomas Wilson, *The Arte of Rhetorique*, anecdotes from Bk. iii
on Elocution.

[20] Tale No. 8 in *A Hundred Merry Tales* as edited by H. Oesterley,
Shakespeare's Jest Book (London, 1866), p. 17.

it is today difficult to trace. We know that the enclosure of farm lands
and their transformation into sheep-runs for private landlords, the
depopulation of villages, the closing down of monasteries and the
dissolution of feudal households under Henry VIII had uprooted and
cast adrift a large number of people. From stably located and relatively
secure members of society they had been transformed into vagabonds
wandering about the countryside. They were not only made homeless
and workless; they were also subject to severe punishment by the
state for being so. These vagabonds, sometimes popularly called
"vacabones," gravitated towards the large cities, especially to London,
earning a doubtful living by begging, cheating, and transitory employment. Gathered in the metropolis, these people —at least, those
who became citizens of its underworld— developed a jargon of their
own which has been in part recorded for us by Robert Copland (in
his poem, *The Highway to the Spitalhouse,* ca. 1520), and later by
Robert Greene in his pamphlets about "conny-catchers" or city swindlers
in the 1580's. Certain of their special words and phrases have thus
been preserved. But it is not so easy to surmise how the pronunciation,
intonation and general phraseology of the larger cities may have been
affected by the influx of declassed countrymen from many parts of
England, besides Ireland and Wales. As Ferdinand Brunot remarks
about a similar shift of working people in 16th-century France, the
linguistic results are a matter of conjecture.[21] A contemporary English
description of vagabonds and their ways tells of the pretexts given
by them for wandering about so far from home. "Others there bee,"
says the author, "that walke sturdely about the country, and [each]
faineth to seke a brother or kinsman of his... they wyll cary a cirtificate
or pasport about them from som Iusticer of the peace, with his hand
and seale vnto the same, how hée [the bearer] hath bene whipped
and punished for a vacabonde" (and presumably must therefore hurry
home again).[22] Irishmen, says the same author (p. 44) avoid interrogation by pretending they do not speak English. Others carry forged
papers dated from distant parts of the country and stating that they

---

[21] F. Brunot, *Histoire de la langue française,* VII (Paris, 1926),
pp. 188 ff.

[22] Thomas Harman, *A Caueat or Warening for Common Cursetors
Vulgarely Called Vagabones,* ed. F. J. Furnivall, EETS, ES, No. 9 (1869,
1898, 1937), p. 37. Notice the colloquial style of this report, marked
by shifts of number from plural to singular and back to plural.

had to emigrate because their homes had been destroyed by fire: "They will neuer begge in that Shiere where their losses (as they say) was [sic]" (p. 61).

The mobility of English workers in the 16th century was the chief social factor, besides the expansion of education, which affected the language. Other social changes had a more limited bearing on the situation. The discovery of the New World, the increased trade and cultural exchange with neighbouring countries and with those of the Mediterranean area, enriched the language with new words and new turns of expression. The achievements of navigation as an applied science, the enormous advances in geographical knowledge, the new lore of the heavens and the earth inspired a popular interest in science. Books and reports of discoveries were composed for various types of readers. While the most technical works, designed for specialists, were still done in Latin, the popular demand led to more and more writing in English. The first experiments were made in the forging of a concise, objective, reasoned style for scientific writings in the vernacular. At the turn of the century Francis Bacon elevated this new type of composition in English to distinguished heights, though he too chose to write some of his most serious works in Latin.

Interest and pride in the English language was reinforced, at least for a special group of studious persons, by the beginnings of a scholarly interest in the language originally spoken by the Germanic (Anglo-Saxon) inhabitants of the island before 1066. There were several motives which led to the cultivation of Old English studies. Writers on jurisprudence and legal theory needed it, and so did antiquarians, historians, and those amateur scholars who in the Tudor age began to produce descriptions of separate counties of England. The religious controversies of the ages also gave a motive for investigating the history of the medieval English church in its earliest phases. Old English texts were read by polemicists debating the issue of Protestantism versus Catholicism, and later by literary critics debating the relative worth of ancient and modern languages.[23] The issues at stake were not primarily concerned with language for its own sake, but they enhanced interest in it and helped to deepen the current knowledge of English and to add to its prestige.

---

[23] See Jones, *op. cit.*, chs. 7 and 8; Eleanor Adams, *Old English Scholarship in England from 1566—1800,* Yale Studies in English, LV (1917); Rosemond Tuve, "Ancients, Moderns, and Saxons," *ELH* (= *English Literary History*), VI (1939), 165—90.

3. The English Vocabulary in the Earlier Renaissance

The English language received loan words from many sources during
the age of humanism and the early Renaissance. The new influx of
loans can not be compared quantitatively with that which occurred
in the Middle Ages from French and Latin. It came from more various
sources, taking less from each, but it thus added very considerably
to the diversification of the native vocabulary. The newer elements
were absorbed by direct contact with foreign countries, through trade,
colonisation and travel for pleasure, more often than through purely
learned channels. It is interesting, too, to observe the fields of interest
and activity represented, which include trade and military science, the
arts and social relations. Words adopted in the Tudor age usually
underwent the subsequent sound changes of English. Sometimes a word
already borrowed in ME was taken over afresh, and maintained a pronunciation closer to that of ModFr. Thus ModE *turquoise* represents
a renewed borrowing of a word previously current in ME as *turkis*;
while *genteel* (later with a differentiated meaning of its own) has the
same relationship to the older loanword *gentle*.

Among typical classes of French words taken over in the 16th century[24] were military terms such as *trophy, pioneer* (originally meaning
a foot soldier; the word is a lengthened form of *pawn*, first recorded
1369, which like Spanish *peon* comes from Latin *pedo*), *pilot, corsair,
sally* and *volley* (the last two with anglicised final syllables), *colonel*
(with its later pronunciation as *coronel* due to dissimilation) and *rendez-
vous* (recorded in the military sense in 1591). Some of the later Tudor
and Stuart loans from French military science, like the last one
mentioned, have preserved traits of French pronunciation such as final
accentuation or the continental quality of vowels. Some of these are:
cartouche, parole, rencontre, dragoon and *platoon* (earlier 17th century).
The artistic and cultural ties with France brought such words as *scene*
(recorded 1541), *rondeau* (already known in the form *rondel*), *grotesque*
and *hautboy* (1575), also *vase, vogue* and *esprit*.

Italian loans like the French represented several spheres of activity,
but especially interesting are the ones connected with music and
architecture. Many borrowings were no doubt due to English travellers
in Italy, a country so widely admired and often visited that the

---

[24] These word lists are based on the material given by Mary S. Serjeantson, *A History of Foreign Words in English* (London, 1935), sup-
plemented by others taken directly from the *NED*.

"Italianate Englishman" became a subject of home satire on the part of writers like Ascham. The cultural debt is reflected in architectural terms like *cupola, cornice, fresco, frieze* (from Italian *fregio,* 1563), *pedestal, citadel, piazza* (a cognate of English *place* and German *Platz*), *stucco* and *belvedere*; also musical terms like *fugue* (directly from *fuga,* despite the French orthography), *canto, canzone, madrigal, viol da gamba* and others. The borrowings in music have continued, of course, into recent times. Maritime trade and commerce yielded *traffic, contraband, frigate* and *citron.* Especial interest attaches to the word *argosy* from *ragusa,* originally meaning a ship of Ragusa. Perhaps the initial meta-thesis was expedited by associations with the classical Argonauts? A miscellaneous group of words indicates contact with Italian social life. These include: *artisan, podesta, magnifico, signor, gondola, carnival, cavalcade, bandit.* The word *seraglio* originally came from *serraglio,* an enclosure of palisades; by confusion with the like-sounding Turkish *seräi,* applied to the emperor's palace in Constantinople, it came to mean a harem. The French form *serail* is likewise current in English (as also in German: compare Mozart's *Die Entführung aus dem Serail*).

Spanish loans include a number which have to do with relations in polite society, such as *don, infanta, señora, grandee, punctilio* and *hidalgo.* This last word is a contracted form of *hijo de algo,* "son of something" (that is, an important person, not a "son of nothing"). War and trade brought words like *real* and *peso* (coins), *sherry, renegade, galleon, armada, casque, bilbo* (from Bilbao), *sombrero* (from *sombra,* a shade) and *comrade* (first recorded 1591; from *camarada,* meaning a room-sharer, derived from Latin *camera*). Spanish colonialism brought some special terms like *Negro, mestizo, mulatto* and *peon,* besides a considerable list of those originating in New World languages (see below) but transmitted through Spanish.

The Low Countries, including modern Holland and Belgium, began to supply English with nautical and military terms as early as the 15th century: *buoy* (from *boje,* recorded 1466), *hoist, bulwark* (also known in a later French form as *boulevard*), *groove* (a dug-out), *deck, orlop* (the lowest deck of a vessel, from *overloop,* a run-over or a cov-ering). These were augmented in the 16th century by: *dock, rove* (cognate with German *rauben,* to rob or to be a pirate), *yacht* (Dutch *jacht,* 1557), *smuggler, stoker, freebooter* (Dutch *vrijbuiter,* a pirate) *filibuster* (indirectly from the same word, put passed through Spanish and there modified to *filibustero,* with dissimilation), *waggon, uproar* (from *oproer,* cognate with German *Aufruhr;* not at all connected with English *roar* < OE *rārian*), *beleaguer* (from *belegeren*) and *forlorn hope* (recorded 1539 and derived from Dutch *verloren hoop,* a lost troop or "heap" of soldiers; not connected genetically with English *hope*). As the Low Countries developed into a colonising nation with a fleet and foreign trade rivaling England's, the loans continued to be made in the 17th century: *sloop, cruise, smack, yawl, onslaught* and *furlough* (from *verloof*) are typical. Terms of social import include familiar ones like *burgher, burgomaster, mannikin, younker, minx* (a pejorative neuter derived from *mensch*) and *kermesse* (from *kerk-misse*). There are also terms connected with handiwork such as *snip, ravel* and *split*. The 17th century added other words of this type, including several closely associated with the art of painting, in which the Low Countries enjoyed preeminence: *sketch* (from Dutch *schets*, ultimately derived from Italian *schizzo*), *stipple* and *easel* (first recorded in 1654; borrowed from Dutch *ezel* corresponding to German *Esel*).

The discovery and exploration of the New World resulted in the importation of a whole cluster of native terms from North and South America, often through Spanish. Haitian *batata* produced *potato* by way of Spanish *patata*; *tobacco* and *cacique* arrived by the same route. Peruvian *nanas* became *ananas* (today displaced by *pineapple*). The Carib language gave *hammock, hurricane* (from *hurricán*, an evil spirit of wind), *papaw* (the name of a fruit) and *cannibal*, also through Spanish. The Mexican language of the Aztecs sent into English the familiar terms *chocolate* and *tomato* (from *chocolatl* and *tomatl*), but that was not until the 17th century. Words connected with the life of North American Indians also appeared after 1600: *wigwam, tomahawk, squaw, wampum, tepee*.

Classical Greek made a special contribution to English in connection with the study of grammar and rhetoric. Humanistic writers like Linacre took pains to furnish lists of technical expressions in their original Greek forms, together with definitions in Latin and examples taken from classical texts. Thus in the sixth book of his "Figures of Construction" Linacre defines *hyperbaton* as a deviation from normal order of words or clauses and he identifies five types of it:[25] *anastrophe* (with a meaning different from that given to it in rhetoric proper), *hysterologia, tmesis, synchysis* and *parenthesis*. Some terms he gives in Greek characters, as for instance these illustrating types of modification in sounds:

μετάθεσις: transmutatio uel ut Donatus Immutatio;
πλεονασμός: quæ est adiectio;
ἀναδίπλωσις: reduplicatio;
διαίρεσις: diuisio, hæc est syllabæ distractio.

---

[25] Linacre, *De Emendenda Structura* (1545 ed.), p. 481: "Cum ordo legitimus dictionum clausularum mutatur, Hyperbaton Grammaticis dicitur."

As the reference to Donatus indicates, the humanists did not cease to use grammars already known as Latin textbooks of the Middle Ages.[26] What they added was direct reference to Greek authorities as well, together with a wide range of illustrative citations, many from works but recently recovered.

Far more original was the treatment of rhetorical terminology by George Puttenham. His *Arte of English Poesie* was probably first drafted about 1569 though not registered for publication until 1588.[27] Instead of adopting the Greek terms mechanically and then putting into English the traditional definitions, Puttenham often coined equivalents of his own: sometimes by paraphrase, sometimes by a rendering of the separate Greek elements by means of English equivalents (a process known as loan translation), and sometimes by a metaphorical substitution. His comments are often pithy, apt and original; the examples he composed to warn against artificiality are sometimes quite diverting.

Greek Term	Puttenham's Equivalent	Type of Treatment
antistrophe	counter turn	loan translation
anaphora	report	loan translation
antiphrasis	broad flout [i. e., flat contradiction]	metaphor
asyndeton	loose language; [lacking in] good band or coupling	explanation
climax	marching figure	metaphor
epizeuxis	underlay or cuckoo spell	synonym and metaphor
hyperbole	over-reacher	loan translation
parenthesis	insertour	synonym
pleonasmus	surplusage or too full speech	synonym with explanation

A typical complete definition is the one given by Puttenham for *hysteron proteron*: "when ye misplace your words or clauses and set that before which should be behind, & *e conuerso*, we call it in English prouerbe, the cart before the horse, the Greeks call it Histeron proteron we name it Preposterous...." As an example he offers: "My dame that bred me vp and bare me in her wombe" (p. 169).

---

[26] On these see R. H. Robins, *Ancient and Mediaeval Grammatical Theory in Europe* (London, 1951), ch. 3.

[27] George Puttenham, *The Arte of English Poesie*, ed. Gladys Doidge Willock and Alice Walker (Cambridge University Press, 1936).

The addition of so many loan words from various sources, ancient and modern, evoked sentiments of alarm among certain writers. The attitude towards neologisms was in fact connected with literary problems such as the choice of a proper vocabulary for Biblical translations and for the composition of original verse. The proponents of an elaborate, decorative style continued the tradition of aureate English from the 15th century and often combined Latin derivatives with archaic native words kept in limited circulation by the vogue for Chaucer's poetry. To a certain extent, then (though not exclusively), the predilection for recondite terms was a medieval inheritance.

A vigorous resistance developed in the 16th century against aureate diction or ink-horn terms, as they were called. These were condemned by the purists, who believed that English should resist the intrusion of foreign expressions. In translating the Bible into English, Sir John Cheke (ca. 1550) went very far in order to avoid the Greek or Latin words which Wycliff (ca. 1380) and Tyndale (1534) had carried over into English. For *centurion* Cheke used *hundreder*; for *parables* (*similitudes* in Tyndale) he used *biwords*; for *apostle, fro-sent,* and so on. His principle was that "our own tung shold be written cleane and pure, vnmixt and vnmangled with borrowing of other tunges,"[28] — a quite impossible requirement (if understood literally) in view of past English history, and one which Cheke himself interpreted to mean: Keep the language pure of unnecessary borrowings. The passion of antiquarian students for Old English also led some of them to condemn the use of French and Latin words and to reproach Chaucer, Gower and others for too extensive importations from these sources.[29] Less vehemently, Thomas Wilson and Roger Ascham opposed excessive borrowing, though they admitted that it was desirable when English offers no adequate native expression. Wilson's advice was that:

Among all other lessons this should first be learned, that wee neuer affect any straunge ynkehorne termes, but to speake as is commonly receiued: neither seeking to be ouer fine, nor yet liuing ouer-carelesse, using our speeche as most men doe, and ordering our wittes as the fewest haue done. Some seeke so far for outlandish

---

[28] From a letter by Cheke to Sir Thomas Hoby, printed in the latter's translation of Castiglione's *Courtier* (1561); see Jones, *op. cit.*, p. 102.

[29] Thus Robert Verstegan in his *Restitution of Decayed Intelligence* (1605). See T. Mersand, *Chaucer's Romance Vocabulary* (New York, 1937), ch. 1.

English, that they forget altogether their mothers language. And I
dare sweare this, if some of their mothers were aliue, thei were not
able to tell what they say....[30]

In his *Toxophilus* Ascham complained that "Many English writers...
vsinge straunge wordes as latin, french and Italian, do make thinges
darke and harde"; but he did not condemn justified borrowing, only
what Puttenham called *soriasmus* or the "mingletangle" of indiscriminate
loans. His advice was temperate: "He that wyll wryte well in any
tongue, muste folowe thys councel of Aristotle, to speake as the common people do, to thinke as wise men do: and so shoulde euery
man vunderstand hym, and the iudgement of wyse men alowe hym."[31]

4. THE ORTHOGRAPHY OF THE 16TH CENTURY

With the widespread fresh interest in other aspects of English, it
is no wonder that writers also began at this time to look at traditional
spelling with a new attention. By the latter part of the 16th century,
pronunciation had deviated still further from spelling than in Caxton's
day, and yet people still wrote more or less according to medieval
norms. To add to the confusion, enthusiasts for classical languages had
tampered with words long since naturalised from Greek and Latin, in
a misguided attempt to make them look more like their originals — or
what those originals were imagined to have been. For instance, ME
dette and *doute,* both taken over from the French, were provided with
"silent" *b*'s and became *debt* and *doubt*, though the pronunciation remained unchanged; *vittles* (a plural based on OFr *vitaille*) masqueraded
as *victuals*; *rime* (from OFr *rime*, or perhaps OE *riman* to count) was
transfigured into *rhyme* under Greek influence; *saume* reappeared as
psalm, and ME *eilond, ilond* was changed to look like *isle* (based on
French *île* from *insula*). Pseudo-learned spellings actually became the
basis of new pronunciations, as when the French-derived *autor* was
spelled with an unhistorical *h* after the *t* (presumably to make it look
more like a Greek word, which it was not), and was in time pronounced with [θ] for the original [t]. Similarly, the ME *faute* (from

---

[30] Wilson, *Arte of Rhetorique*, Mair ed., p. 172; see J. M. Berdan,
Early Tudor Poetry (New York, 1920), p. 141 f.

[31] Ascham, *Toxophilus* in *English' Works* ed. W. A. Wright; cf.
Berdan, *op. cit.*, p. 144.

a late Latin *fallita later contracted to *fal'ta, with consequent vocalising of l) was redressed as fault, and the l has duly been restored in pronunciation. Finally, Romance loan words were erroneously made to look Germanic when the levelling of sounds had obliterated certain distinctions between them. In this way delite (from OFr delit as noun and deliter or deleiter as verb) was written delight. Similarly, sprite and spite sometimes appeared as spright and spight. The written language was full of irrationalities and inconsistencies which caused a number of serious writers to agitate for a reform of English orthography.[32]

Among these was Sir John Cheke, who adopted a fairly consistent and sensible method of spelling in his Biblical translation. To indicate a long vowel in a closed syllable he hit upon the device —also used in modern Dutch and Flemish— of simply doubling the written vowel: taak, haat, maad for take, hate, made. When the vowel represented ME long $\bar{\imath}$ (then breaking into a diphthong), he like the medieval scribes of the Low Countries made the second of the two i's into a j, thus giving mijn, tijm for our mine and time. He frequently doubled a consonant to show that a preceding vowel was short. Cheke dispensed with final "silent" -e (which in his system was no longer needed to show length of vowels in closed syllables), and he used the character y exclusively to represent [θ] and [ð], now spelled th. Though his system was not consistently phonetic, it represented a creditable effort to improve upon the current usage, as this specimen will indicate:

On a tijm ye souer went forth to soow, and whil he was in soowing summ fel bi ye wais sijd, and ye birds cam and devoured it. and somm fel in stooni places, wheer it had not much earth, and it cam up bi and bi, becaus it had no depth in th'earth, and when ye sonn was risen it was burnt up, and bicause it had no root it dried up.

Other writers in the 16th century devoted serious attention to the reform of English orthography. Their contribution to our knowledge of contemporary pronunciation has been on the whole underestimated until the recent exhaustive study by E. J. Dobson (see ch. 1, n. 9). Among the pioneers who analysed orthography in relation to pronunciation, an outstanding place is occupied by John Hart, author of an Orthographie of English (1568) and A Methode or Comfortable Beginning for All Vnlearned (1570), who wrote with a clear conception of a standard

---

[32] On this general subject see Eberhard Buchmann, Der Einfluss des Schriftbildes auf die Aussprache des Neuenglischen (Breslau, 1940).

national speech in mind. In it, he said, "the generall flower of all English countrie speaches are chosen and used" by cultivated circles of the capital city. Greater attention was attracted by William Bullokar, who set forth a proposal for spelling reform in his *Booke at Large for the Amendment of Orthographie for English Speech* (1581), and followed this up with other works. In general Bullokar retained the conventional alphabet as basic, but he attempted by means of many detailed modifiers —accents, dots, hooks and the like— to distinguish various sounds or variants of single sounds associated with single letters. These symbols of his were regarded as too complicated, however, to win general favour.[33]

More conservative were the reforms proposed by Richard Mulcaster in his *Elementarie* (1582) and by Alexander Gil in his *Logonomia* (1619 and 1621). Mulcaster's work was widely known.[34] It advocated a consistent standard usage based on tradition but did not try to do more than approximate a phonetic alphabet. A strictly accurate one, Mulcaster apparently thought, would cost teachers and pupils too great an effort of readjustment. He tried to dispense with letters which served no function at all, such as the extra *t* in *putt* for *put*; he regularised the use of final "mute" *-e* to indicate length in a preceding vowel, as in *hope* versus *hop*, and he urged that a letter or digraph once adopted for a given sound should regularly be employed to represent it in all environments except where well-established custom might intervene. For consistency he recommended *fear* and *dear* on the model of *hear*, but he permitted *where, here* and *there* (though they rimed with the former words) as being justified by usage. Not all of Mulcaster's proposals were followed. Nevertheless he did much towards putting order into English orthography and establishing it in the form prevalent today. Alexander Gil, less famous than Mulcaster, perhaps, was a very acute observer and he gives particularly valuable testimony concerning nuances of current speech, including affectations which he attributes to fashionable ladies and their associates.

The orthoepists of the 16th century, even the most skilful and consistent of them, lacked phonetic training, of course. Some of their

---

[33] The problem of 16th-century orthography is discussed by Baugh, *History*, ch. 8. The selection from Cheke's Bible, cited above, is quoted from his appendix, p. 486 f. For a detailed account of these spelling reformers see Dobson, *English Pronunciation*, I.

[34] The *Elementarie* of Mulcaster has been edited by E. T. Campagnac (Oxford, 1925); for discussion see Baugh, *op. cit.*, pp. 253—56; Dobson, *op. cit.*, I, pp. 117—28. On Gil see Dobson, *ibid.*, pp. 131—55.

theories and practices seem to us both unclear and inconsistent. Nevertheless, when adequately analysed, they furnish valuable evidence for
the state of 16th-century pronunciation. Further evidence is provided
by the rimes of the poets, which form a check on the orthography
(though we must allow for the fact that probably not all rimes were
perfect ones). Puns and word-plays give additional clues. These stylistic
devices had become very fashionable in the writing of Shakespeare's
time, both in prose and verse. In connection with them too we have
to remember that the puns may not always depend on perfect homonyms, for humour and poetic "conceit" do not demand a strict co-
incidence of sound.[35] Nevertheless we can project a fairly reliable scheme
for the sounds of late 16th-century English as it may have been heard in
the theatre and court, on the basis of these various types of evidence.

Detailed studies making use of rimes, puns and orthography have
recently[36] shown that the evolving standard English of about 1600 was
not just a regular, consistent development from the heritage of Chaucer's standard court language as modified by the incipient vowel and
consonant shifts of the 15th century. For the social reasons already
mentioned (sec. 2), Southern England, especially London, was subject
to many linguistic influences from without. The types of pronunciation
current in educated circles were more varied than they are today. Any
specific "standard" vowel might well be the result —not of a regular
evolution out of the 15th-century standard— but of a sudden vogue,
a displacement or an abrupt importation from another dialect. Failure
to understand the complex social factors affecting 16th-century speech
has led some scholars to simplify phenomena inadvisably in a search
for simple "sound laws" explaining the pattern of most ModE vowels.

---

[35] A "conceit" in the 16th and 17th centuries meant an elaborate
figure of speech, often depending on word-play and far-fetched similar-
ities or esoteric allusions.

[36] Among the latest studies two are outstanding: Helge Kökeritz,
Shakespeare's Pronunciation (Yale University Press, 1953) and Dobson,
op. cit. Among earlier ones the following are useful: R. E. Zachrisson,
Pronunciation of English Vowels, 1400—1700; H. C. Wyld, *A History of
Modern Colloquial English* (London, 1920); also Luick, *Historische Grammatik*, II; but this survey especially is one that too often assumes
regular developments of the standard vowels throughout, not allowing
for irregularities due to the competition among various acceptable
forms, preferences due to fashion, and the variegated dialectal influences operating in London as a result of large-scale emigration from
the country side.

Besides the laws there were also conflicting tendencies and vogues.
A complete description is not easily formulated in a short space, in
view of the various and sometimes conflicting sources of our evidence.
But detailed research on Shakespeare's rimes and puns, taken in connection with the evidence from 16th- and early 17th-century orthoepists, has aided in the reconstruction of a typical (if not by any
means universal) London pronunciation of the time. So far as Shakespeare's own speech is concerned, it must be remembered that part of
the evidence for it is debatable. Shakespeare may well have carried
over idiosyncrasies of the Warwickshire dialect into his literary works.
Moreover, the cultured speech of his day was less unified, less subject
to strict standards than it was to become later on, especially in the
18th century, when schoolmasters and lexicographers assumed the role
of arbiters of correctness. In the period about the year 1600 there were
still a number of possibilities of choice among equally "correct" forms,
because conservative and advanced pronunciations could be heard side
by side, as well as competing dialect forms and even vulgarisms which
were beginning to be accepted.

5. THE PRONUNCIATION OF SHAKESPEARE'S TIME

A. A simplified scheme of the basic vowel scheme at this time may
be thus attempted:[37]

Examples	Front		Back	Examples
he, seem	i:		(i)u:	pure, new, moon
it, bit	i̧		u̧	pull, blood; cut *
stale, steal, rain, seal	ȩ:		o:	stone, know, gold
bed	ȩ	ɔ:		claw
hare, fair	ɛ: + r	ɒ: < ɔ: / ɒ < ɔ		off, frost, fort / hot, not
hat, marry	æ/a			
bath, dance, warm, "desart"	æ:/a:			

[37] This scheme is less complicated than the one proposed by Kökeritz, *op. cit.*, p. 340. Divergences are due in part to elimination of
special variants, in part to dissenting evidence offered by Dobson.

Middle Vowels

ə as in about

3 + r as in bird, verse, cur

[*ʌ as in cut (mostly after 1650)]

There is some difference of opinion among specialists concerning individual sounds listed above.[37] It is generally assumed that short *i* had the value of [ɪ] despite rimes in which this vowel is paired with words apparently (not certainly in all cases) having [i:]. In some positions, on the other hand, for instance before -*ng*, short *i* had a higher articulation. Short *u*, though lower than [u:], seems not to have been relaxed from [ʊ] to [ʌ] in general usage until the latter 17th century. Both pronunciations may well have been current in Shakespeare's time. The symbols *i̯* and *u̯* in the above chart are used once more to indicate fluctuations in pronunciation between tense and lax articulation, subsumed under a single phoneme in each case.[38]

The precise position of long *ē* from three sources (ME *ā*, *ai* and *ę̄* not appearing before *r*) is a matter of dispute. Recent studies show that by the 16th century it had reached the position of a long *ę̄* of open quality, somewhat higher than ME *ę̄*, and was already passing into closed *ē* by the early 17th century. We follow Kökeritz in representing this sound as *ę̄*. But the situation with regard to its status was not simple. Not only did more conservative and more advanced pronunciations exist side by side, but there were also alternate forms of the same word due to currency of more than one dialect form in London. Frequent puns like *steal: stale, tale: tail,* and *reason: raisin* indicate that Shakespeare still used long open *ę̄* in both pairs of words. At the same time there is evidence that for words like: *steal, leaf,* etc., there were alternate pronunciations in which the ME long open *ę̄* had already been replaced by the modern [i:]. This latter sound, as most authorities now agree, was the result not so much of gradual phonetic evolution as of direct transfer from "advanced," even "vulgar" speakers to those

---

[38] The lowering of *i* and *u* to [ɪ] and [ʊ] may be traced back to late ME and it is clearly attested in descriptions by foreign observers as well as native orthoepists. Rimes of short and long *u*, as in the series *come: tomb: doom,* indicate the preservation of this [ʊ], which Dobson thinks prevailed quite generally until about 1600, if not longer. On the evidence for the retention of [i] beside [ɪ] see H. Whitehall, "The Historical Status of Modern English [ɪ]," *Language,* XVI (1940), 104—24.

in more conservative circles like the court. In a few words (for instance, *great, break, steak*) the more archaic pronunciation has been the one to persist into ModE. The London English of Shakespeare's time must have had pronunciation-doublets for words with ME long open *ẹ̄*: [liːf] beside [lẹːf] for *leaf*, etc. When *r* followed *ẹ̄*, the effect was to lower the vowel somewhat and to conserve it at the stage of [ɛː] while it was elsewhere being raised.

Concomitantly with the tendency to raise ME *ẹ̄*, the ME long open *ǫ* was undergoing the same process. By the early 16th century this latter vowel had already reached closed [oː] in words like: *stone, home,* etc.; before *r* it may have been retained at [ɔː] or been raised and lowered again in the 18th century. In some dialects there is evidence that ME *ǫ* went as far as [uː], with a shortened variant [ʊ].[39] The new closed [oː] of standard English fell together with the long *ō* monophthongised from *ou* as in *know*. Original [au] as in *claw, law,* took the place vacated by the now shifted original [ɔː], and a new [ɔː] also developed from short *o* before [f, θ, s], and the consonant *r*, which was beginning to be untrilled: *off, moth, loss, forth.*

Among the short vowels, short *a* was fronted to [æ] during the 16th century unless affected by neighbouring sounds (it was lengthened before [f, θ, s, ns], and lowered before *r*); *o* became more relaxed and open. It may well have survived as [ɔ] in some types of speech and have been lowered to [ɒ], even [ɑ] in others.[40] The precise quality of Shakespeare's pronunciation is in doubt. Some satirical writers ridicule as an affectation the pronunciation of *stop* and *lord* as *stap* and *lard.* Following traditional practice, we shall subsume these variations under the single transcription [ɔ]. The ME short vowels *i, e, u* became [ɜ] before *r*, and as the *r* became untrilled and began to disappear, the vowel lengthened.

B. The diphthongs current at this time were as follows:

əi (perhaps [ɪi]) from ME long *ī*, e. g. *ride, my*
əu (perhaps [ʌu]) „   „   „   *ū*, e. g. *house, now*

---

[39] ModE (*n*)*one, nothing, struck* may thus be explained as dialect forms. Cf. Chaucer's occasional rime *doom: home* (Monk's Tale, 3123 f., cited by Kökeritz, p. 33).

[40] Luick assumed that [ɔ] > [ɐ] generally in the 17th century, and was later rounded to [ɔ] again in the 18th. But see Dobson, p. 578 n.

ɔi   from ME *oi* and *ui*, e. g. *joy, point* (but [ui] also remained,
     and [ʌi] or [əi] appeared after labials, e. g. in *boil,
     poison,* etc.)
iu, later (17th century) [ju:], from ME [y:], [eu] and [ɛu],
     e. g. *pure, grew, few*

The development of ME *oi* and *ui* in this period presents some difficulties. Along with the [ɔi] to be expected from the earlier tendency
to level these two, there were surviving pronunciations of original [ui].
Moreover, the similarity of [ɔi] to [əi] led to a close approximation
if not to complete levelling, as is indicated by puns like *line: loin,*
and rimes like *join: sign.* Since modern standard pronunciation now
clearly distinguishes the diphthongs of these word pairs, the coalescence
of [ɔi] and [əi] under the latter pronunciation can not have been
complete for all speakers. The establishment of [ɔi] for ME *oi* as
preferred form (latter 18th century) must have been in large part due to
the conservative influence of the standard orthography, which was
a factor of great importance among schoolmasters of that period.
However, they could hardly have been so successful if survivals of
the older diphthong had not been widely current. A variant pronunciation [ɒi] is attested in Shakespeare for words like: *boy, alloy.*
Estimation of the extent of its currency is difficult, however, and for
the purposes of a brief description it may be ignored.
     The ME diphthong *au* had become a simple vowel [ɔ:] by the
16th century. It was now merely relaxed in articulation in words like:
claw, law, etc. But in some Romance words where *au* had developed
before *m* or *n* (as in *chamber, dance, vaunt*), there were several alternate pronunciations possible: an occasional [e:] existed beside [ɔ:] and
an [a:] or [æ:] which later became [ɑ:]. The three words cited illustrate
the three possible developments. As for the ME diphthong *ou* of various
origins, it had developed by way of [ɔʊ] and [ɔ:] to [o:], coinciding
with [o:] from [ɔ:] of other origins. Examples are: *bowl, gold, soul.*

     C. Reduced vowels appeared as a result of loss of accent on syl-
lables with original full vowels, whether long or short, or as a result
of lack of sentence stress on an entire word. Thus words like *the* and
to, which normally lack sentence stress, reduced the final [i:] and [u:]
to a neutral [ə], as is indicated by frequent elisions. The usual
unstressed pronunciation of *the* and *to* was therefore [ðə] and [tə],
though [ði] and [tu] were preserved under emphasis. The neutral [ə]
appeared for various earlier short vowels lacking accent: [əz] for *as,*

[bət] beside [bʌt] for *but*, [əv] beside [ɔv] for *of*. It was also frequent as an unaccented vowel in polysyllables: [ˈglɔːrjəs] or [ˈgloːrjəs] for *glorious*, [ˈtɔrənt] for *torrent*. The replacement of [ə] by [i̯] was by now quite general in inflectional endings such as *-ed, -es* (see ch. 2, sec. 2E).

In relatively conspicuous suffixes which however normally lacked primary accent there was some choice of vowel lengths and qualities. Where secondary stress was still preserved, the vowel developed as in stressed syllables, but in some cases a single word existed in two forms, both with and without the secondary stress. Thus the final *-y* in *alchemy* and the *-ly* ending of adverbs sometimes rimed with *eye* [əi], but on other occasions it clearly had the value of short *i* [i̯]. Diphthongs were preserved in variants of unaccented *-y, -ly* as late as the 18th century, at least for the purposes of rime based on conservative speech. Short *i* appeared in unaccented syllables with a distribution corresponding very much to today's. The neutral [ə] was often completely lost near liquid consonants as the orthography of the time indicates: *mock'ry, temp'rately, desp'rate*, etc. The *-ed* suffix of weak verbs was subject to reduction in such vicinity: *barr'd, fell'd*, etc., but versification shows that there was a certain latitude of choice for poets in these cases.

D. The consonants and their influence have already been touched upon in the above short account of the vowels. It will be convenient to recapitulate at this point the main instances of consonantal influence on vowels, which caused the development of some new phonemes out of the variants (allophones) of the 15th century.

By the influence of following *r*:	Examples:
[ε:] developed from ME *a, ai* before *r*	fare, fair
[a:] developed from ME *a* as an alternate of *e* before *r*	far[41], serve, clerk, dark
[ɜ:] developed from ME *i, e* and *u* before *r*	bird, verse, cur
[ɔ:] developed from early ModE [o:], also [ɔ] and [u], alternately [o:], [u:]	mourn, court, ford, door; but also poor, moor (after labials)

---

[41] Note the phonemic contrast in *fare: far*. Both vowels were now long, but they differed in quality. The vowel of *far* had been lowered from original *e* before *r*.

By influence of following [f, θ, s, ns]:

[æ:] and [a:] from ME *a* by 1600   calf, dance, ask,
                                          bath[42]

[æ:], also [e:] and [ɔ:] from ME *au* before   dance, haunt,
    m, n in Romance words   chamber

By influence of initial *w*:

[a] tended to rounded articulation, but   war, warm (rimes
    [ɔ] was not yet generally accepted   with harm)[43]

Some of these changes, it will be observed, involved lengthening as well as changes in quality. There were besides some new instances of shortening, probably due to the neighbourhood of certain consonants. Under conditions that are not entirely clear, the originally long vowels of certain one-syllable words ending in consonants were at this time being shortened: for instance, *deaf, head, blood, good*. Shakespeare rimes *east*: *breast* and *deal*: *knell*. The shortening is conspicuous before dentals but is not limited to their environment. On the other hand, 15th-century [u:] from ME [o:] was preserved from shortening near labial consonants: *food, move, moon*, etc. (but not always; cf. ModE *glove* from ME *glōve*).

In general, the consonants appearing in Shakespeare's language are in no way strikingly different from those of London English in the preceding century. The *r*, though now in the process of being untrilled to [ɹ], was still pronounced where it had appeared in ME. The un-trilling of *r* and its trend to vocalisation was accompanied by the development of a preceding glide-vowel [ə], which has survived to the

---

[42] The mechanics of this change have been investigated in detail by Wiktor Jassem, "Regular Changes of Vocalic Quantity in Early New English," *Biuletyn Polskiego Towarzystwa Językoznawczego*, Zeszyt XII (1953), 149—78. Jassem correlates the lengthening of vowels due to reduction and later loss of *r* with the lengthening before [f, θ, s]. This analysis is illuminating for the understanding of general trends in the vocalic system.

[43] Wiktor Jassem, *Fonetyka Angielska* (Warsaw, 1954), p. 85, argues as does H. C. Wyld that the fronted [æ] appeared after *w* also, rather than [a] or —as Kökeritz supposes— a modified [ɑ]. But see the comment by A. Reszkiewicz, *Kwartalnik Neofilologiczny*, II (1955), p. 149, and Dobson, *op. cit.*, p. 716 f. The rime *warm*: *harm* may not have been perfect, but it was no doubt closer than it is today.

present in words like: *hear, hair, hour, poor.* It does not appear after the lower vowels in words like: *carry, glory, shore, far.* Initial *k* and *g* before *n* were being modified, and though still heard as [χ], [h] and voiceless [n̥], were in the process of being lost. The final *g* after [ŋ] was preserved throughout most of the 16th century, but it was lost in the early 17th century. Thus [ŋ] became a separate phoneme, no longer merely a conditioned variant of [n]. Besides, the suffix *-ing* (now [iŋ]) had in many dialects been replaced by [in], the form preferred, as it would seem, by Shakespeare. This in turn may sometimes have been reduced to syllabic [n̩]. The late ME change of final [χ] to [f] in words like: *laugh, enough, dwarf,* etc., was at this time being gradually accepted.

With the loss of ME [ə] or [i] in many unstressed syllables, assimilation often occurred between the consonants thus brought into juxtaposition: *clipp'd,* for instance, was pronounced as [klipt], and *scarfed* as [ska:ɹft].

The consonants of unstressed words were subject to continued weakening. We may assume that the originally voiceless initial *th* [θ] was now completely voiced to [ð] in words like: *the, this, that*; while [z] had long since replaced [s] in *is* and *was.* The pronouns *he, his, him, her,* etc., often appeared without their initial consonants, as the orthography and scanned elisions indicate. In fact, there is reason to assume that Shakespeare habitually used pronominal forms without initial *h,* especially in passages designed for less formal, colloquial delivery. On the other hand he still retained [hw] or a voiceless [w̥] in the relative and interrogative pronouns *who* and *which,* and the adverb *where.*

E. The accentuation of polysyllables in Shakespeare's time differed somewhat from that of ModE. A strong secondary stress was still kept on some on syllables which today lack it. This is revealed by the scansion of verse and also by the rimes indicating diphthongs where we have short lowered vowels today: for instance in the adverbial suffix *-ly* and the noun suffix *-ity* riming with *eye,* as already mentioned. French loan words often showed a fluctuation of accentual usage, as when *confíscate* alternates with *cónfiscate,* or *cháracter* with *charácter,* or *cómplete* with *compléte.* The influence of Germanic accentuation operated generally to throw stress forward to the first syllable of loan words. Thus we have *áccess, súrvey, chástise, púrsuit, cónjure* and many others. Some of these, it will be observed, have thrown the accent back again to the end in modern times. But many disyllabic verbs borrowed from the French kept their accent on the final syllable: *maintáin, rebél, survéy*, etc., possibly under the influence of iambic verb-forms in English due to the presence of unstressed prefixes: *aríse forgét, belíeve*, etc. In this way dual forms of a number of loan-words arose, iambic for verbs and trochaic for nouns: *prój́ect* (n.) and *projéct* (v.), *rébel* (n.) and *rebél* (v.). Shakespeare has examples of this semantic-syntactic role of accentuation to distinguish nouns from verbs:[44]

Shall in these *cónfines* with a monarch's voice... *Julius Caesar,*
III. i, 272
But now I am cabin'd, cribb'd, *confín'd*, bound in... *Macbeth,*
III. iv, 24

The status of cultured London speech at the end of the 16th century may be exemplified by a reconstruction of one of Shakespeare's sonnets in phonetic transcription.

Sonnet XVII

Who will believe my verse in time to come,
If it were fill'd with your most high deserts?
Though yet, heaven knows, it is but as a tomb
Which hides your life, and shows not half your parts.
5 If I could write the beauty of your eyes,
And in fresh numbers number all your graces,
The age to come would say, This poet lies;
Such heavenly touches ne'er touch'd earthly faces.
So should my papers, yellow'd with their age,
10 Be scorned, like old men of less truth than tongue;
And your true rights be term'd a poet's rage,
And stretched metre of an antique song:
But were some child of yours alive that time,
You should live twice; — in it, and in my rime.

hu: wɪl biˈliːv məi vɜːɹs ɪn təim tə kʉm
ɪf ɪt weːɹ fɪld wɪθ juːɹ moːst həi dɪˈzaːɹts
ðoː jɛt hɛvn noːz ɪt ɪz bət æz ə tuːm
hwɪtʃ həidz juːɹ ləif ən ʃoːz nɔt hæːf juːɹ paːɹts
5 ɪf əi kʉd ɹəit ðə ˈbiuːtɪ əv juːɹ əiz

---

44 On the accentuation of Romance loan-words see especially W. Franz, *Shakespeare-Grammatik* (Heidelberg, 1939).

ənd ịn fɹẹʃ nųmbəɹz nụmbəɹ ɔːl juːɹ gɹẹːsịz
ðẹːdӡ tə kụm wụd sẹː ðịs poːət ləiz
sụtʃ hẹvnlị tụtʃịz neːɹ tụtʃt ɜːɹθlị fẹːsịz
soː ʃụd məi 'pẹːpəɹz 'jẹloːd wịθ ðɛːr ẹːdӡ

10 biː skɔːɹnd ləik oːld mẹn əv lẹs tɹuːθ ðæn tụŋ
ən juːɹ tɹu ɹəits biː tɜːɹmd ə poːəts rẹːdӡ
ən stɹẹtʃịd miːtəɹ əv ən 'æntịk *sɔŋ   *or [sụŋ]?
bụt weːɹ sụm tʃəild əv juːɹz ə'ləiv ðæt təim
juː ʃụd lịv twəis ịn ịt ənd ịn məi ɹəim

CHAPTER IV

GRAMMATICAL STRUCTURE AND STYLE IN THE LATER RENAISSANCE

1. GRAMMATICAL FORMS AND CONSTRUCTIONS: NON-VERBAL

The grammatical forms and constructions appearing in the diversified literary texts of the 16th and earlier 17th centuries are themselves extremely diversified. Hence it is almost impossible to give a simple and unified description of them. The task would be relatively simple, to be sure, if we were to choose only those literary works composed specifically for an intellectual audience, for their authors were men trained in the forms and usages of classical grammar, and the English they wrote was shaped, almost unconsciously we may assume, towards patterns of correctness like those set down for the Latin language. As they knew it from classical texts, that language had a very consistent and logical code of relations. Under its influence, questions of English inflection, grammatical agreement and sentence structure were handled more or less consistently by the more learned writers over a long period extending from the age of Humanism to the Commonwealth. The standards of correctness assumed by John Milton in his English prose writing will not be found to be very different from those assumed by Thomas More in his, although certain usages had of course been modified in the interval, and certain constructions of the 16th century had become archaic or had been completely dropped by the latter 17th. Later the drive towards consistency increase   while the structure became markedly simpler.

When the survey of grammatical usages is extended to embrace all sorts of writing, from tragedies to comedies, from sermons to popular satire and *novelle*, the situation becomes more complicated. Pamphleteers set themselves the task of gathering and using the locutions of the less educated speakers of English, including derelict members of the underworld. Writers of comedies strove to reproduce the colloquial language of popular, non-courtly elements in their audiences. On these informal levels of discourse there was a fairly wide range of choice in accidence and syntactic usage. A single author like Shakespeare or Ben Jonson will reveal variations in practice according to the type and level of the discourse (see below, sec. 5). Therefore any description of usages in these matters ought properly to be accompanied by many qualifications. In a short account we can only indicate in a general way the range of forms and constructions appearing in the typical literary compositions of the age. Some of the constructions would be inadmissible today, but although these are conspicuous, they are by no means in the majority.

The simplest manner of presentation will be to call attention to those usages which differ from the modern.

Nouns show an inflectional scheme which is almost without exception identical with today's. An interesting variation appears in the treatment of abstract nouns, which in ModE normally have no plural, except by way of personification. Today an abstraction is regarded as indivisible; the plural of *information* is not *informations* but *pieces of information*. In Shakespeare's time, however, the plural was regularly used in a distributive sense: We'll make our *leisures* to attend on yours (*Mer. of Ven.*, I. i);[1] your better *wisdoms* (*Haml.*, I, ii); break not your sleeps for that (*ibid.*, IV, vi).[2]

The genitive singular of nouns had developed regularly from the ME ending -(*e*)*s*. For masculine nouns however a periphrastic form appeared, at least in print, with an enclitic pronoun *his* functioning instead of -(*e*)*s*, for instance: *Mars his* armour for: the armour *of Mars*, or *Mars's* armour. The origin of this construction is in doubt.[3]

---

[1] For convenience, all citations from Shakespeare are taken from the edition of the *Complete Works* in one volume edited by W. J. Craig (Oxford University Press, imprint of 1954). This edition is based on the First Folio of 1623, but the spelling is modernised and emendations are included. Where variant readings are important, these are noted in the citations given.

[2] On ModE usage with respect to abstract nouns, see among others Max Deutschbein, *System der neuenglischen Syntax* (Leipzig, 1931), p. 178 f.

[3] W. Franz, *Shakespeare-Grammatik*, looks upon this as a genuine native construction comparable to: *Mrs. Smith, her son* is at home (al-

Although grammatical gender had disappeared, pronoun references sometimes indicate that a few regularly neuter nouns were endowed with a new masculine or feminine gender through a kind of personification, perhaps under the influence of Latin categories. Hamlet says to Horatio:

> Since my dear soul was mistress of her choice,
> And could of men distinguish, *her* election
> Hath seal'd thee for *herself*.   (III, ii)

In *The Tempest* Gonzalo says to his companions: You would lift the moon out of *her* sphere, if *she* would continue in it... without changing (II, i). Here the Latin nouns *anima* and *luna* may have affected the pronoun references. The same is true of feminine references for the names of countries, as when Deloney writes: Englands valor [*sic*] was more than *her* wealth (*Thomas of Reading*).[4]

The pronoun forms were still not completely settled. Among those of the personal inflection, *hit* still appeared in the 16th century for the neuter gender, with genitive *his* and dative *him*. For the second person, the general form *you/ye* in both singular and plural seems to have gained acceptance more rapidly in upper class groups (aristocracy and wealthy middle class) than elsewhere.[5] The less formal writing of the time reveals the existence of unstressed forms for various pronouns: *'a* [ə] is written for *he* by Shakespeare; *'em* appears for *them* *'t* for *it* in contractions like *'tis*, and so on. Dialect passages in the comedies testify to a survival of the old Southern form *ich* for *I*. It was familiar in contractions like *cham* for *I am* and *chill* for *I will* (e. g., Jonson's *Tale of a Tub, passim*).

The construction of pronoun forms in the sentences of formal prose was relatively strict, following the patterns familiar in modern prescriptive grammars. But in the more elastic usage of the drama, many

---

though this implies different intonation, and it is questionable whether *Mars, his armour* would normally have been written *Mars his* armour). E. A. Abbot, *A Shakespeare Grammar* (London, 1877) dismissed the usage as a simple mistake in orthography. Brunner connects it with a possessive dative construction, *Die engl. Sprache*, II, p. 28.

[4] Thoms, *Early English Prose Romances,* ed. E. A. Baker (London, n. d.), p. 446.

[5] See Franz, *op. cit.*

deviations may be found, as the following examples from Shakespeare will indicate:

'Tis better *thee* without than *he* within   (*Macb.*, III, iii)
Praise *him* that got thee, *she* that gave thee suck   (*Tr. and Cr.*, II, iii)
...between my good man and *he*   (*Merry Wives*, III, ii)
But *she*, I can hook to me   (*Wint. T.*, II, iii)
you have seen Cassio and *she* together   (*Oth.*, IV, ii)[6]

Some of these deviations from strict usage arise when the pronoun is separated from the grammatical form (verb or preposition) controlling it. Such a separation permits the speaker to forget or modify the structure upon which he first embarked. Thus the example from *Othello* is understandable because the uninflected noun *Cassio* intervenes between the verb and the inflected pronoun object. If the order were reversed, Othello would hardly say: seen *she* and Cassio, even in the most informal conversation; nor would a phrase like: between *he* and my good man be likely even in a broad comedy like *The Merry Wives*. Ellipsis and shifts in construction account for colloquialisms in construction like the one from the *Winter's Tale*, which is the equivalent of: As far as *she* is concerned, or: *She* is the sort who... In addition, it has been pointed out by Jespersen that factors of euphony may have dictated the choice of the oblique for the nominative case, or the reverse: the line cited from *Macbeth* gains force by its echo of identical vowel sounds in *thee*: *he*. Finally, the oblique case is still preferred to the nominative in certain absolute and fragmentary constructions where the pronoun is not joined to the verb, as in Cleopatra's question: Is she as tall as *me*? (*Ant. and Cl.*, III, iii), or in contemporary exclamations like: What? *Me* dance?[7]

A curious example of deviation from modern habits of speech appears in the employment of what we may call a generic singular pronoun of indefinite reference. A plural noun may be followed by a singular pronoun referring to it, when the former designates a group of people. In such cases the singular pronoun stands for a generic representative of the group. The usage is not unknown in ME:

---

[6] Thus the first folio, but it is corrected to: and *her* in the Oxford ed., following Pope and others.

[7] On the factor of euphony, see Abbott, *Shakespeare Grammar*, p. 139 f.; Otto Jespersen, *A Modern English Grammar*, Part VII: *Syntax* (Copenhagen and London, 1949), pp. 262 ff.

> For if there come to an abey   to pore *men* or thre
> And aske of hem helpe   par seinte charité,
> Unnethe wole any don *his* ernde   other ʒong or old,
> But late *him* coure ther al day   in hunger and in cold.[8]

Here the plural noun *men* is referred to later as *his* in the third line
and *him* in the fourth. We find the same sort of substitution of
a generic singular for an expected plural in popular literature dealing
with types of persons· in the nether world: tricksters, vagabonds and
the like. Descriptions of these types frequently begin with a plural
noun and then shift to a singular pronoun in reference. An early
example is to be found in Copland's *Hye Way to the Spitall-House*:

> 724 *They* that dooth to other folkes good dede,
>   And hath themselfe of other folke more nede,
>   And quencheth the fyre of another place,
>   And leueth *his* owne, that is in wors cace,
>   Whan it is brent, and woteth not where to lye:
>   To the spyttell than must *he* nedes hye.

Here the shift from plural to singular may have been aided by the
ambiguity of the verb form in *-eth*, which in the South might have
been either singular or plural. But the same sort of shift is to be
found elsewhere, quite frequently. Robert Greene, in the *Second Part
of Conny-Catching*, speaks thus of thieves who use a long-handled hook
in robbing: they let it out and hook or curb whatsoever is loose and
within reach, and then *he* conueies it to the warp (that is, to his
accomplice, p. 48). John Awdeley, describing the practices of sturdy
vagabonds in the 16th century, habitually slips over from a plural noun
to a generic singular pronoun: These kynde of deceyuing Vacabondes
haue other practises... and when *he* hath agreed of the price, *he* sayeth.
Similarly Thomas Harman writes: to one man that goeth abroad, there
are at the least two women,· which neuer make it straunge when they
be called, although *she* neuer knew him before. — Sometimes on the
other hand the shift is from singular to plural, as also exemplified in

---

[8] A poem of about 1315 A. D. on the hard times under Edward II.
Published by Thomas Wright, *Political Songs* (London, 1839), stanza 22.
Reprinted by А. И. Смирницкий, *Хрестоматия по истории англий-
ского языка* (Москва, 1953), p. 49.

Harman: some yong Marchant man... whose friendes hath geuen them a stock of money...[9]

Finally, among the looser constructions of personal pronouns we find two pleonasms already sanctioned by tradition (see ch. 2, sec. 4). These are: an anticipatory pronoun doubling for a following noun in the same construction, or a reprise construction. A shift of case construction may occur with either of these pronoun-noun pairs, especially in informal writing. Shakespeare has: my lord, *she and that friar*, I saw *them* at the prison (*Meas. for Meas.*, V, i); and : *He* that retires, I'll take *him* for a Volsce (*Coriol.*, I, v). Both of these show incongruity in case construction.

The repeated pleonastic pronoun was used colloquially to gain emphasis as in Ben Jonson's: I scorn it *I*, so *I* do (*Every Man In*, I, i), or: another, *he* cries souldier (*ibid.* IV, i). Reprise constructions (called resumptions by Partridge[10]) in formal discourse employed the appositional pronoun to recall a noun separated from its verb by a long series of interrupting modifiers. Thus Shakespeare's Ulysses speaks of Achilles as the *proud lord*, and then in the fifth line following returns to him by means of an appositional *he* with repeated auxiliary:

> Shall the *proud lord*
> That bastes his arrogance with his own seam,
> And never suffers matter of the world
> Enter his thoughts, save such as do resolve
> And ruminate himself, shall *he* be worshipp'd
> Of that we hold an idol more than he?
>
> (*Tr. and Cr.*, II, iii)

The anticipatory *it* in apposition with a noun clause or an infinitive was of course sanctioned in the most formal English: Is *it* not monstrous that this player here ... Could force his soul... (*Haml.*, II, ii).

---

[9] Robert Greene, *The Second Part of Conny-Catching*, 1592 (London: Bodley Head Reprint, 1923), p. 48; Awdeley, *Fraternitye*, p. 11; Harman, *Caueat*, pp. 41 and 7. (For reference see ch. 3, n. 22.) Shifting from a plural to a generic singular is also to be found occasionally in more learned writers. Leonard Cox says that the demonstrative oration, "wherein *persones* are lauded/ is an historycall exposycyon of all *his* lyfe in order," *Arte of Rhethoryke*, ed. Carpenter, p. 57.

[10] A. C. Partridge, *Studies in the Syntax of Ben Jonson's Plays* (Cambridge, 1953). See also his *Accidence of Ben Jonson's Plays, Masques and Entertainments* (1953). Statements about Jonson's usage are indebted to these two studies.

8

The interrogative and relative pronoun forms were also, like the personal ones, handled with considerable freedom in stage dialogues. Of the former, it may be said that the oblique case could be either *who* or *whom*, almost indifferently, as in Hamlet's elliptical question: Between *who*? (II, ii), and Orlando's complete one: *Who* ambles time withal? (*As You L.*, III, ii: a construction here several times repeated). As with the personal pronouns, a crossing of constructions, often due to a parenthetical remark, may lead to a confusion of cases, for instance in the lines: The mariners... *who*, with a charm join'd to their suffer'd labour, I have left asleep (*Temp.*, I, iii). Jonson was somewhat stricter than Shakespeare in his treatment of *who* / *whom* as disjunctive interrogative pronoun appearing in head position apart from the verb. But he too permits *who* in head position when the governing word is a distant preposition: *Who* would you speak with? (*Alchemist*, IV, ii); I see *who* he laughed at (*Every Man In*, I, ii). An uninflected relative pronoun, giving no overt clue to its construction, may lead to a shift in agreement, as in Shakespeare's lines: 'tis your graces / *That* from my mutest conscience to my tongue / *Charms* this report out (*Cymb.*, I, vi).

Not only *who* and *which* but also other relative pronouns were still loosely expressed with duplication of forms, as in the 15th century. Thus we find not only *the which* but even *the which that,* for persons as well as things, and in the genitive case, *that his* as well as *whose*: A wight *that... his* every step hath left the stamp (*Every Man In*, F version, I, iii). Relative pronouns were frequently omitted as in ME and ModE, thus producing asyndetic contact clauses: see the last line in the quotation given above from *Troilus and Cressida*, p. 99.

Reflexive, indefinite and emphatic pronouns were not as yet fixed in the schemes familiar today, but the differences were not striking. Among the forms then accepted which have since disappeared from the language were: an uninflected plural of *other* (e. g., those *other* came); the simple forms *who, what* for *whoever, whatever*; reflexive forms lacking the suffix *-self* (e. g., he clothed *him* hastily). Though these deviations from modern usage give a special flavour to Tudor and early Stuart English, they do not signify any very important difference in structure.

Adjectives and **adverbs** were in many cases less consistently distinguished than today. That is to say, the suffix *-ly* was less generally used as a sign of adverbial function. Adverbs originally distinguished from cognate adjectives by the suffix *-e* had long since been made identical with them. Shakespeare and his contemporaries quite freely used Romance as well as Germanic adverbs lacking the typical suffix, in phrases like: *wondrous* strange, *seeming* virtuous queen, *noble* spoken, and so on. The use of *more* and *most* in degrees of comparison was still (as previously) not yet fixed according to precise rules. Periphrastic comparison may appear instead of a suffix with monosyllables (*most vile, most brave*), and polysyllables may employ the suffixes *-er* and *-est*. The choice between periphrasis and suffixation in verse was no doubt sometimes conditioned by rhythms. The same factor (or else rhetorical emphasis) may have determined the choice of double comparatives and superlatives, which were still current: This was the *most unkindest* cut of all (*Jul. Caes.*, III, ii). Regularising of the usages was to occur in the latter 17th and the 18th centuries.[11] The double negative still appears sporadically in the latter 16th century and lingers into the 17th: No king can govern, *nor no* god please (Dryden).

2. Verbal Forms and Constructions

The verb forms and their sentence functions reveal some of the most striking deviations from our present standard usage. In discussing them it is particularly difficult to maintain the traditional separation of morphology or accidence from syntax.[12]

Concerning the principal parts of verbs and the general division of conjugations into strong and weak, it may be said briefly that the transfer of verbs from the former conjugation to the latter continued steadily. It has been estimated[13] that about 30 verbs were lost to the strong conjugation in the 16th and 17th centuries. Among the surviving strong verbs, there was a perceptible tendency to level preterite and past participle forms into one, as in Shakespeare's: are *broke* (*Meas. for Meas.*, II, iv) and: have *spoke* (*Mer. of Ven.*, IV, i); have *chose* (*Coriol.*, II, iii). The *-en* ending of strong past participles was lost in some instances, but not universally. We find forms like: is *forgot*, is *writ* (*Haml.*, III, ii), but also: (*be*)*gotten*. The *-ed* ending of weak verbs was still frequently syllabic, as versification shows, in formal if not informal speech. The same ending was sometimes omitted from the past participle of weak verbs derived from Latin ones with the suffix *-ate* (itself originally a sign of the past participle). The omission reflected a knowledge of Latin morphology.

---

[11] Ben Jonson in his *Grammar*, Bk. II, ch. 4, recognised the possibility of using double comparatives and superlatives; he compared these pleonasms to the multiple adverbial particles in Greek which were used for emphasis. See Partridge, *Jonson's Accidence*, pp. 106 ff.

[12] See ch. 8, n. 28.

[13] Brunner, *Die engl. Sprache*, II, p. 182.

Shakespeare writes: minds are *dedicate* (*Meas. for Meas.*, II, ii); was *fatigate* (*Coriol.*, I, ii).

In the third person singular of verbs in the present tense, the fluctuation between -*es* and -*eth* no longer has any dialectal significance. (See ch. 1, sec. 5.) In the third person plural, however, the situation is more complicated. Here we find a zero ending in most cases, but also occasionally -*es* and -*eth* also. When one of the two latter appears, the reason may be: (1) that the form chosen was acceptable in general colloquial speech; (2) that it represented a restricted dialect (-*es* for the North and -*eth* for the South); or (3) that it simply resulted from a syntactic confusion on the part of the individual writer. Shakespeare has: My old *bones aches* (*Temp.*, III, iii, corrected in many modern editions) in a prose passage, and in verse the line: On chaliced *flowers that lies* (*Cymb.*, II, iii), where the choice of an -*es* form may have been dictated in part by the needs of rime. Robert Greene, in the preface to his first tract on the sharp practices of the underworld,[14] writes: my ripe *daies cals*; and later: the three *knaues comes*. Here the -*es* forms in the plural may be regarded as evidence of Northern dialect influence still affecting Southern English. On the other hand, when Greene and others have expressions like: how *doth* all our good friends, this verbal form may likewise be regarded as a survival of a Southern plural ending. At the same time Greene also writes: how *fare* all our friends, which is the more usual form (both examples in his pamphlet on *Cosenage*). We deduce that the Southern verbal inflection had a limited currency in London speech of the time.

In some cases the choice of forms may well have been due to a dislocation of the sentence, and the question becomes one of syntax. In a complex sentence probably not clearly thought through, Greene writes: the villanous *vipers*, ...being outcasts from God, vipers of the world, and an excremental reuersion of sin, *doth* consent (*Cosenage*). Here the form *doth* may simply be a shift to the singular resulting from the intervention of modifiers and appositional expressions between subject and predicate. Similarly, ambiguous relative pronouns may cause a shift in agreement, as in Copland's line: These be *they that* dayly *walkes* and *jettes* (*Hye Waye*, 1. 317), or: For all *estates that* thyder *was* comyng.[15] But in the following lines from the *Hye Waye*, Copland's shift of person from second to third has no such justification, nor need we assume that

---

[14] Robert Greene, *A Notable Discovery of Cosenage*, 1591 (London: Bodley Head reprint, 1923), pp. 7 and 25.

[15] Robert Copland, *Jyl of Breyntfords Testament*, privately printed by F. J. Furnivall (London, 1871), l. 16.

the form *biddeth* was actually a generally acceptable alternate for the normal *biddest*:

> 44 "Copland," quod he, "art thou a-thyrst,
> And *byddeth* me a-fore the to drynke?"

In some instances, particularly in the latter 16th century, unexpected or unusual forms are to be regarded as individual writers' slips and idiosyncrasies, rather than as testimony to a widespread habit of speech. Thus we may interpret the reading in *Julius Caesar*: The *posture* of your blows *are* yet unknown (V, i). The unorthodox agreement is natural in rapid dialogue, but would hardly occur in a learned text.

The system of verbal auxiliaries was also diversified and still unsettled as compared with today's. Within the period being discussed there was a marked expansion in the auxiliary use of the verb *to do*.[16] It began to assume four main functions:

(a) To emphasise the message conveyed by the main or "notional" verb (to use Jespersen's term), as in Othello's lines: Perdition catch my soul But I *do love* thee! (III, iii), and Orlando's: I *do desire* we may be better strangers (*As You L.*, IV, ii). This appears to have been the first semantic area of expansion (see Brunner, *Die engl. Sprache* II, p. 300).

(b) To delay the notional verb to a later position in the sentence, especially in negative statements. Shakespeare has: I *do not like* her name (*As You L.*, III, ii), but also: I *like not* that (*Oth.*, III, ii), with the notional verb directly after the subject.

(c) To formulate questions. The forms of *do* thus permit inversion in word order and yet keep the subject in its normal position preceding the notional verb. Here too Shakespeare's usage in the prose dialogues of his comedies, probably typical of good colloquial speech of the time, may be seen to fluctuate. Rosalind's rapid interrogation of her cousin Celia includes such questions as: What *said he*? How *looked he*? Wherein *went he*? But also: *Did he ask* for me? *Doth he know* that I am in this forest? (*As You L.*, III, ii). When no interrogative word

---

[16] The precise historical reasons for this development are not entirely clear. The verb *do* appeared in earlier English as a substitute for another verb, and in special phrases meaning "to cause to be performed" also, but its uses became multiple and complex beginning in the 16th century. Analogous but not necessarily influential was the development of Welsh *gwneuther* meaning "to make, to do," which also functioned as an auxiliary.

introduces a question, and when both subject and object are nouns, the function of *do* becomes important in avoiding ambiguity between nominative and accusative constructions. For instance, the question: *Loves the king* the queen? is ambiguous, whereas *Does the king love* the queen? is not. With questions involving pronouns the problem of ambiguity does not arise, but these too have been attracted into the *do*-pattern in ModE.

(d) To substitute for a notional verb previously introduced. This function was already familiar in Chaucer. An example from Shakespeare is the line spoken by Octavius to Brutus: Not that we love words better, as you *do* (*Jul. Caes.*, V, i).[17]

The choice of a construction with *do* or without it was of course sometimes dictated by the needs of verse rhythm. Even in prose — especially oratorical prose, but apparently elsewhere as well — the *do*-constructions may have been favoured at times to obtain a desired cadence of speech.[18]

Other auxiliaries were extending or specialising their scope along with *do*. The verb *to be* began to be used to express an aspect of continuous action for the notional verb. The result was in the end the creation of an entire verbal inflection called the continuous or progressive conjugation in modern grammars. Shakespeare offers fairly numerous examples of this conjugational system: the same pulpit whereto I *am going* (*Jul. Caes.*, III, i); we *are* still *handling* our ewes (*As You L.*, III, ii); our thane *is coming* (*Macb.*, I, iv). While this function of *to be* was just beginning to expand, another one was contracting: namely the function of an auxiliary forming the perfect tenses with intransitive verbs of motion, analogous to the use of *to have* with transitive ones. Shakespeare still uses *to be* frequently in such locutions: *Is* Banquo *gone?* (*Macb.*,

---

[17] Other functions were performed by *do* as auxiliary, for instance a distinction between present and past tenses in words like *put, cast,* etc. For a detailed discussion of the entire problem see B. Trnka, *On the Syntax of the English Verb from Caxton to Dryden,* Travaux du Cercle Linguistique de Prague, III (1930); also A. Ellegård, *The Auxiliary Do: The Establishment and Regulation of its Use in English,* Göteborg Studies in English, II (Stockholm, 1953), as well as the earlier study by Victor Engblom, *On the Origin and Early Development of the Auxiliary Do,* in Lund Studies in English, VI (1938).

[18] The factor of rhythm is emphasised by Torsten Dahl, *Linguistic Studies in Some Elizabethan Writings,* II: *The Auxiliary Do,* [Aarhus] *Acta Linguistica,* XXVIII, No. 1 (1956).

III, ii); I would the friends we miss *were* safe *arrived* (*ibid.*, V, vii). While the auxiliary *have* was steadily taking over the perfective function everywhere in popular speech during the 17th and 18th century, formal religious prose remained strikingly conservative in this respect. The reason is that the Authorised Version of the Bible (1611) consistently preferred the more archaic treatment of intransitive verbs in the perfect tenses, and this in turn affected sermons and other types of solemn discourse (see ch. 5, sec. 1).

The auxiliaries *shall* and *will* were moving into the rather complex patterns of modern usage, but the formulation of rules and the strict observance of them belong to the latter 17th century. Meanings of futurity and desire overlap in *will, would*; of futurity and obligation in *shall, should*; and there were other nuances of meaning as well. Probability and doubt are expressed in clauses like: this *should be* the place (*Tim. of Ath.*, V, iii); though hell itself *should gape* (*Haml.*, I, ii). Habitual action is expressed by *will, would*: foul deeds *will rise* (*ibid.*, I, ii); and there are still other functions discharged by this pair of auxiliaries.

The remaining auxiliaries like *may, can, ought,* which are widely employed in ModE, had a somewhat more restricted currency in the 16th and 17th centuries. This was because the subjunctive mood still functioned then to indicate a number of relations which the auxiliaries have since taken over. The subjunctive appeared in dependent clauses associated with verbs suggesting contingency, desire, command, concession, etc. Reported speech put into the subjunctive may suggest doubt; notice the contrast implied in Othello's statement: I think my wife *be* honest and I think she *is* not (III, iii). Other illustrations are:

Note if your lady *strain*   (*ibid.*, *loc. cit.*)
'tis fit that Cassio *have* his place   (*ibid.*, *loc. cit.*)
'Tis a shrewd doubt, though it *be* but a dream   (*ibid.*, *loc. cit.*)
I'll cross it, though it *blast* me (*Haml.*, I, i)
See whe'r Brutus *be* alive or dead (*Jul. Caes.*, V, v)

When *if*-clauses expressed a possibility, either indicative or subjunctive might appear:

If thou *art* privy to thy country's fate   (*Haml.*, I, i)
If thou *hast* nature in thee, bear it not   (*ibid.*, I, v)
If music *be* the food of love, play on   (*Twelfth N.*, I, i)
if none *appear* (*K. Lear*, V, iii); if again this apparition *come*

(Haml., I, i)

Conditions contrary to fact are regularly in the subjunctive: if my heart *were* in your hand (*Oth.,* III, iii); if a man *were* porter of hell-gate (*Macb.,* II, iii).

Parts of speech were often unconventionally handled in Elizabethan English. A shifting back and forth from verbal use to nominal, from no-minal to adjectival, and so on, reflects a stylistic freedom eschewed during the later classical period. Similar to it was the freedom mani-fested in word formation, whether by the creation of compounds, as in Shakespeare's *heaven-kissing* hill, or by the unconventional attaching of prefixes and suffixes, as in such words as *unpeople* for *depopulate,* and *enskied* for *exalted.*[19] The shifting of grammatical categories was facilitated, of course, by the loss of inflections in late ME. Rarely by now did any overt sign indicate the part of speech to which any word normally belonged. Shakespeare exemplifies more often than most the ready transfer of parts of speech; and what he was doing boldly, others also did with greater caution. He uses a noun as a verb in expressions like: how might she *tongue* me (*Meas. for Meas.,* IV, iv), and: he *pageants* us (*Tr. and Cr.,* I, iii); also an adjective as a verb: the grief *violenteth* (*ibid.,* IV, iv), or a noun as an adjective: my *salad* days / When I was green in judgment (*Ant. and Cl.,* I, v). Moreover, normally intransitive verbs may appear as transitive: [this] *dances* my rapt heart (i. e., causes it to dance, *Coriol.,* IV, v), and: he meant to *quail* ...the orb (*Ant. and Cl.,* V, ii). At the same time, Shakespeare was aware that such linguistic practices could easily become ridiculous. He burlesques them in the broken speech of Hugh Evans, a Welsh character in *The Merry Wives of Windsor,* whose imperfect diction is also made comically pretentious: I will *description* the matter to you; can you *affection* the 'oman? (I, i).

3. The Beginnings of English Lexicography

The free treatment of parts of speech is but one symptom of an exploratory attitude to language and its techniques characteristic of the later Renaissance in England. The archaising school of poetry, represented by Edmund Spenser, stimulated curiosity about older words, and the influx of new terms from other languages (see ch. 3, sec. 3) called attention to the variety of the contemporary vocabulary. It is not surprising therefore that the systematic study of that vocabulary had its beginnings in the same period.

---

[19] For definitions of these and other terms in Shakespeare, see Alex-ander Schmidt, *Shakespeare-Lexicon* (Berlin and Leipzig, 1923).

Linguistic studies in the Middle Ages had not been aided by complete lexical registers for the tongues concerned, not even for Latin. Only rare and difficult words were usually explained, or synonyms for them were given in the vernacular, in marginal or interlinear notes of individual manuscripts. Such jottings, called glosses, were sometimes listed separately as a kind of appendix to a difficult text. Complete interlinear translations also existed. These aids did not always follow the alphabetic order, however, and each was usually attached to a particular text.

The first step towards more systematic presentation was the setting up of word-lists for students' aid, independent of specific texts. Such an aid for schoolboys was the *Promptorium Parvulorum,* a non-alphabetical English-Latin word-list written about 1440 and published by Caxton's successor Pynson in 1499. Caxton himself had previously published (1480?) some French-English vocabularies and conversations to aid merchants and other travelers abroad. Wynkyn de Worde and Sir Thomas Elyot also did Latin-English lists. In the mid-16th century these works were superseded by others more closely resembling modern alphabetical dictionaries, but in all of them the purpose served was the mastery of some foreign language, not a better understanding of the native. Such books included John Vernon's trilingual *Dictionarium* (1552) in Latin, English and French; John Withal's *Short Dictionarie for Yonge Beginners* (1553) in English and Latin, and Richard Huloet's *Abecedarium* (1552) also in English and Latin.[20] This last work contained about 26,000 English words in alphabetical order, followed by the Latin equivalents. Huloet appears to have used a French work by Stephanus, *Dictionaire François-latin* (1549), besides earlier lists of synonyms and explanations, both Latin-Latin and Latin-English. He included illustrative phrases as well as definitions. The *Abecedarium* was revised by John Higgins in 1572 and published as Huloet's *Dictionarie.* At the same time, vocabularies for students of Italian and Spanish appeared: Florio's *Firste Fruites* (1578) and Stepney's *Spanish Schoolemaster* (1591).

The pioneer dictionary of English terms explained in English was Robert Cawdrey's *Table Alphabeticall* (1604).[21] This made no pretensions

---

[20] On these early works, see DeWitt T. Starnes, "Richard Huloet's Abecedarium: A Study in English-Latin Lexicography," *Studies in Philology*, XLVIII (1951), 717—37.

[21] The present discussion of this work and its successors is based on DeWitt Starnes and Gertrude Noyes, *The English Dictionary from Cawdrey to Johnson* (Chapel Hill: University of North Carolina Press, 1946).

to completeness, however. It was limited to rare, difficult words and ones borrowed from foreign languages. Cawdrey, interestingly enough, did not have school-boys in mind as the public expected to benefit primarily from the information he offered. Rather, he was addressing the newly educated women of the Renaissance, now eager for further knowledge. The alphabetical list was offered, he said, "with the interpretation thereof by plaine English words, gathered for the benefit & helpe of Ladies, Gentlewomen, or any other unskilfull persons." Cawdrey's debt to earlier bilingual dictionaries is apparent.

John Bullokar, who is to be distinguished from the Bullokar mentioned (ch. 3, sec. 4), contributed *An English Expositor* (1616) which like Cawdrey's had the restricted aim of "teaching the interpretation of the hardest words used in our language." The same limitation appears in the work of Henry Cockeram. His *English Dictionarie* (1623) divided its list of strange and difficult terms into several parts, each alphabetically arranged; the "vulgar" words were for instance separated from the more "refined and elegant" ones. The public he aimed at was apparently broader than Cawdrey's. Among the social groups mentioned are "as well Ladies and Gentlewomen, Schollers, Clarkes, Merchants, as also Strangers of any Nation" who might wish to perfect themselves "in reading, writing and speaking." The usefulness of Cockeram's *Dictionarie* to such groups of people was increased by the inclusion of names from classical mythology, which played so large a part in the literary allusions of the time.

Later writers in the 17th century built on the first pioneer works, while expanding them through the addition of new areas of terminology. Thomas Blount, the author of a *Glossographia* (1656) was a lawyer, and while he made use of various Latin and English dictionaries that had preceded his, he also expanded his material by drawing on a French legal glossary, Rastelle's *Termes de la Ley*. He gave etymologies, and also acknowledged his debt to his predecessors in many if not all instances. Two years later, John Milton's nephew Edward Phillips produced his *New World of Words* (1658), with 11,000 entries. It was indebted to many predecessors, including learned Latin works of the 16th century which indexed geographical, historical, mythological and other terms. Phillips did not always acknowledge his debts nor use them intelligently. Blount expressed his indignation at the mechanical lifting practised by Phillips, in a diatribe entitled *A World of Errors*. Nevertheless, Phillips's *New World* went through a number of later editions. It was used as a foundation for the *English Dictionary* of Elisha Coles, a schoolmaster (1670), who abbreviated what Phillips had given but also expanded it by including words in dialect and cant. A Latin work by Stephen

Skinner, *Etymologicon Linguae Anglicanae* (1671), stressed the origins of English words from various languages, including not only French and Latin but also Anglo-Saxon and what he called "Teutonic." That is to say, Skinner gave analogous forms in Dutch and other Germanic languages. His work was used in turn by an anonymous writer in *Gazophylacium Anglicanum* (1689). Thus considerable foundation work was done in the 17th century, leading up to the lexicographers who were the immediate sources and models for Dr. Samuel Johnson in the 18th.

In a less systematic way, meantime, certain writers were beginning to investigate the special jargons of the underworld created by mass unemployment in England. The dispossessed folk who had become sturdy beggars roaming the countryside, or thieves and tricksters inhabiting the nether parts of cities, had developed vocabularies of their own. Their purpose was in part to evade understanding by the authorities of the law. Writers describing the life of the underworld introduced some of these special terms into their own work, sometimes in a haphazard way, sometimes in the form of short lists with explanations. Copland's *Hye Waye to the Spital-House* offered no glossary, though it included such curious words as:

bewpere, 1. 497: accomplice, good companion. See *NED* s. v. *beau père*

cove, 11. 1046 f.: man, person; from the Gypsy. See Partridge.[22]

feng, 1. 1049: to steal; an alternate form of *fang* in ME.

frydge, 1. 394: to move restlessly about, to fidget, according to the *NED,* which suggests onomatopoetic origin. But the sense indicates: to beg, from OE *frycgean?*

mychers, 1. 141: "Those be *mychers* that lyue in trewandyse" (truancy).Cf. *micher* in 1 *Henry IV*, II, iv, and *miching* in *Haml.*, III, ii. The *NED* relates *micher,* a secret or petty thief, to the verb *miche* derived from OFr *muchier, mucier,* meaning to hide, to skulk, to lurk.

rogers, 11. 392 and 410: begging rogues who pretend to be poor scholars. Partridge, citing Copland as authority, relates this to the word *rogue*; but cf. also the name *Roger.*

sapyent, 1. 432: a quack who pretends to be a physician; from Latin *sapiens.*

tomblyng cast, 1. 372, i. e., *tumbling cast*; *to make a t. c.*: a metaphor for the act of being hanged.

---

[22] Eric Partridge, *A Dictionary of Slang and Unconventional English* (London, 1937).

It will be seen that these expressions come from many different sources. Some of them died out of currency, others like *cove* have persisted until the present.

Here and there in his conny-catching pamphlets Robert Greene introduced short lists of underworld terms. They were grouped together according to the practices dealt with, not in the order of the alphabet. Here are a few examples, slightly revised (for Greene gives his definitions first, his terms last:

> *bong, boung*: a purse. The term *bung-nipper* for cutpurse persisted into the 18th century (Partridge).
> *cuttle-boung*: a knife used in cutting the strings of a purse.
> *foin :* pickpocket. Partridge cites Greene as sole authority for this.
> *rutter*: "he that maketh the fray," i. e., provokes a planned quarrel.
> *shels*: "the monie." Special use of the ordinary word *shell?* Partridge does not give this noun, but only the verb derived from the noun, in the sense of: to strip, to hand out, etc.
> *smoaking*: "spying of him" (i. e., the victim). Partridge gives only later meanings of the 17th and 18th centuries: to ridicule or affront. The meaning of detection may not be connected with Standard English *to smoke* from OE *smoca*, but with a derivative of OE *smācian*, to flatter or seduce.
> *verser*: "he that plaieth the game; he that bringeth him [the victim] in."

A short list of names for various types of neglectful apprentices was appended by Awdeley to his *Fraternitye of Vacabondes*, but the elegance of the terms, often derived from Latin, makes them suspect as representatives of genuine underworld cant:

> *Cory fauell* is he, that wyl lye in his bed, and cory [i e., curry] the bed bordes on which he lyeth in steade of his horse. — Cf. *curry favel* in the *NED*. The expression comes ultimately from the French *Roman de Fauvel* (ca. 1310).
> *Greene Winchard* is he, that when his hose is broken and hange[s] out at his shoes, he will put them into his shooes againe with a stick, but he wyll not amend them.
> *Nunquam*, is he that when his Maister sendeth him on his errand he wil not haue done it in halfe an hour or lesse.

Harman also appended to his *Caueat* an alphabetical list of various types of rogues (but without definitions), and a non-alphabetical list of general terms in the "leud, lousey language of these lewtering Luskes and lasy Lorrels," with synonyms by way of explanation. Some typical examples are:

> *autem*: a church; origin unknown. Partridge implausibly suggests: from *anthem*.
>
> *bene*: good; *benshyp*: very good.
>
> *bowse*: to drink. Cf. ModE *booze, bouse,* from Middle Dutch *busen, bousen*.
>
> *cante*: to speak. Probably an alternant form of *chant*, in Northern French dialect, ultimately from Latin *cantare*.
>
> *dup the gyger*: to open the door. Partridge surmises that *dup* is derived from *do open* (not *do up*); *gyger*, the same as *jigger*, has no certain origin.
>
> *gan*: a mouth; probably from Welsh *geneu, ganau*, says Partridge. But cf. also Icelandic *gana*, to gape.
>
> *gentry cofes ken*: a noble or gentleman's house.
>
> *harmans*: the stocks. Cf. *harman*, presumably derived from *hard man*.
>
> *lightmans*: the day. Cf. *darkmans*, the night.
>
> *mort, morte*: girl or woman; origin unknown (*NED*). Qualifying terms are used: e. g., *autem morte,* married woman, analogous to *autem cove*, married man. (In this combination, Partridge suggests that *autem* is derived from *altham,* a doubtful word meaning wife. But the derivation from *autem* meaning church seems to be easier and just as plausible.)
>
> *Rome*: in various compounds, with the sense of fine or superior. E. g.: *Rome bouse*: wine; *Rome morte*: the Queen; *Rome ville*: London.

As may be seen, the etymologies of most of these words are fairly clear. They show very varied origins for the jargon of London's derelicts in the late 16th century.

Writers like William Harrison in his *Description of England* (prefixed to Holinshed's *Chronicle*, 1586 edition), the author of the anonymous *Groundeworke of Conny-Catching* (1592), and Thomas Dekker in his *Belman of London* (1608), plagiarised Harman's terminology, together with his information. Their zeal in doing so testifies to an eager if not yet scientific interest in the language of the underworld of London.

4. SENTENCE STRUCTURE IN COLLOQUIAL AND POPULAR STYLE

Medieval rhetoric had distinguished, as we noticed (ch. 1, sec. 6, p. 36), three levels of style according to speakers and situations: the lofty, the medium, and the lowly. The third, as the Latin terms *stylus rusticus* or *humilis* indicate, was supposed to be associated with the lowest level in society. Classical examples of it were furnished by comically stupid countrymen or by slaves and servants appearing in comedies and satiric tales. But even these spoke a stylised language, rather than the accurately recorded discourse of the third social stratum.

Something of the medieval distinction based on social levels is still reflected in Renaissance theory, but the practice of the drama shows a broader and more elastic conception of levels of discourse. There were in fact many of these between the extremes of high and lowly. The medieval class division as a basis for division of styles became invalid when the spread of rhetorical teachings began to reach country folk previously illiterate. It is true that the newly educated mastered literary doctrine only imperfectly. Comedies of the latter 16th and early 17th centuries reveal however that it did somehow affect such people as village schoolmasters, clerks, and judges' assistants. Otherwise we can not readily understand the comic meaning for Elizabethan audiences of Miles Metaphor in Jonson's *Tale of a Tub*, or of Holofernes in Shakespeare's *Love's Labour's Lost*. It was recognised, moreover, that one and the same personage might under differing circumstances speak in different ways. Hamlet's verse soliloquies may be said to correspond to the traditional *stylus altus*, while his prose conversations —for instance with Horatio, or with Rosencrantz and Guildenstern— are in the plainer yet still dignified *stylus medius*. For both of these levels we have abundant literary materials.

What is more difficult, at least in the early modern period, is to obtain literary examples which accurately reflect not only the vocabulary but also the grammatical usage and the sentence structure of the third level. With the Elizabethan period these materials begin to multiply. They are represented by some passages in the comedies first of all, and to a certain extent by the realistic and satiric *novelle* printed, together with prose redactions of old romances, for the entertainment of the lower classes. Some of the realistic descriptions of vagabondage already cited are also valuable. All of these texts are no doubt stylised to a greater or lesser degree, but passages of conversation often give some indication of the nature of living speech. It must be admitted that some of the best of the informal prose tales are translated or imitated from foreign models: for instance, a collection called *The Deceit of Women* (1560), which drew from the French *Cent Nouvelles nouvelles* (15th century) for most of its best tales, and a *novella* called *Frederick of Jennen* (ca. 1560), an analogue of the plot of *Cymbeline*, which was translated from a Flemish *volksbuch*. Even when translated or imitated, however, these texts indicate the kind of thing that was at least considered to be (whether or not it actually was) a reflection of informal English discourse. It will be worth while to observe how all of these various sources handled sentence elements in dialogue and simple narrative.

The general ordering of sentences on the colloquial level is here as elsewhere —but with more consistency— the placement of modifiers near the expressions modified. Single words precede, and phrases or clauses normally follow, what is to be thus restricted. Mrs. Quickly, who represents Shakespeare's closest approximation to untutored informal English, organises the essential parts of her sentences and their shorter modifiers in orthodox fashion. The typical order is SVO or SVP, sometimes amplified to SVDO (that is, subject-verb-dative-object) as when she says: I will bar no honest man my house, nor no cheater (2 *Henry IV*, II, iv). Inversions are simple, and they leave no doubt of the basic construction, as in: Cheater, call you him? (*loc. cit.*), with the order PVSO for the more usual VSOP. A typical sentence with short modifiers clearly distributed is Mrs. Quickly's description of the death of Falstaff:

So a' bade me lay more clothes on his feet: I put my hand into the bed and felt them, and they were as cold as any stone; then I felt to his knees, and so upward, and upward, and all was as cold as any stone (*Henry V*, II, iv).

Thus also with the sentences of colloquial speech elsewhere. The minor elements are seldom ambiguously or abnormally placed.

It is in the organisation of larger sentence units such as clauses that colloquial speech shows its characteristic traits. One of the most obvious of these is a preference for parataxis, sometimes for a very loose variety with asyndeton, as opposed to hypotaxis. A formal writer would have reorganised the following sentences so as to subordinate some of the elements to others:

A Kitchen Mortes is a Gyrle, she is brought at her full age to the Vpright man to be broken (Awdeley, *Fraternitye*, p. 5).— There is one of these Autem Mortes, she is now a widow, of fyfty yeres old; her name is Alice Milson; she goeth about with a couple of great boyes, the youngest of them is fast vpon xx. yeares of age (Harman, *Caueat*, p. 67).

These are examples of that successive order —the adding of details in equal rank, without subordination— which one writer on syntax has found typical of naive speech.[23] A loose successive order may also appear

---

[23] Wilhelm Havers, *Handbuch der erklärenden Syntax* (Heidelberg, 1931), speaks of the trait as "das sukzessive Denken."

when the units are hypotactic, but each dependent clause is attached to another in a step-like series. An example from nursery literature is the fable about the cat that chased the mouse that nibbled the sack that lay in the house that Jack built. An example from 16th-century popular fiction is:

> I am here come... to complaine on this false marchaunt that standeth here with the thre Jewels that be myne... that he hath gotten by thefte whiche is openly knowen before your grace by what maner of craft he came by them (*Frederick of Jennen*).

Loosely organised colloquial versions of reported speech prefer coordinate statements in series, punctuated by short interruptions like: *I said, said I*, while the sentence wanders on formlessly. Mrs. Quickly's speech on swaggerers (see Appendix) is a life-like example. Predominantly loose sentences may have a few elements subordinated, however:

> And whan that he came afore his house he sawe that there was yet lyght in it and knocked at the doore, and hys wyfe went with a brome and swept the house, and she asked who was there, and he sayd: I am he thy husband, and she sayd thou art not my husband for my husband is not in the towne (*Deceit of Women*).

In unskilled informal discourse, a hypotactic construction is sometimes begun but not carried through, or it is shifted to parataxis, or is left dangling with nothing to modify. A crossing of constructions underlies many of these lapses in sentence organisation. Here, for instance, the subject of a clause (i. e., *Virgilius*) is left without a verb because of a shift from hypotaxis to parataxis:

> Here may ye se how the mayster Virgilius that was so wise and so crafty in all thinges: and yet was deceyued of a woman (*Deceit of Women*).

The introduction of a present participle which is a modifier of the subject may be made parallel to the verb by the insertion of an unexpected conjunction *and*, thus suddenly converting a dependent into a coordinate construction:

> But in the ende they so vse the matter that both the young man leeseth his part, and, as it seemeth to him, they leesing theirs also, and so maketh as though they would fal together by the eares with this fingerer (Awdeley, *Fraternitye*, p. 9).

In the following sentence there is a similar construction of participle and finite verb in ill-assorted parallelism, together with a shift from personal to impersonal construction:

> This simple man, beholding him wel, and saw he was of taule personage with a good quarter staffe in his hand, it much pitied him, as he sayd, to se him want... (Harman, *Caueat*, p. 42).

Here a shift from personal to impersonal point of view leaves the originally announced subject without a predicate:

> his wyfe beyng a fayre young gentlewoman, the which laye alone, it fortuned vpon a time there cames [*read*: came] a yonge proper gentylman the whych wooed her (*Deceit of Women*); these when they practise there pylferinge, it is all by night (Awdeley, *Fraternitye*, p. 34).

Still another type of shift places an infinitive in coordination with a finite verb: he hard his wyfe say suche wordes and begon for to chyde hym so (*Deceit of Women*).

It is the insertion of long modifiers after the subject that most commonly causes disorganisation of the sentence, which as a result does not always achieve predication. An unskilled writer's efforts to achieve a literary style may betray him into anacoluthon:

> This glimmering Morte [a female beggar who enters a house on the pretext of asking for a light] repayringe to an Ine in the sayde towne where dwelt a wydow of fyftie wynter olde of good welth; but she had an vnthryftye sonne...: this amerous man be holding [*sic*] with ardente eyes thys glymmeringe glauncer, was presentlye pyteouslye persed to the hart, and lewdly longed to be clothed vnder her lyuerye (Harman, *Caueat*, p. 61).

The alliterative phrases reveal the effort to rise to a higher stylistic level, but the structure goes awry when the presumptive subject *glimmering Morte* is abandoned, only to reappear later in non-appositive construction as *glymmeringe glauncer* in an accusative construction after the participle *beholding*.

Somewhat different from this type of anacoluthon is the breaking off of sentences well begun, because of some psychological factor such as wandering attention or lapse of memory or self-interruption. Whereas pseudo-literary anacoluthon may masquerade as a long complex sentence, intricately organised, these fragmentary ones make no such pretension.

9

Shakespeare's Nurse in *Romeo and Juliet* exemplifies the latter type. Her uncompleted comparison is typical of colloquial ModE (e. g., I've just had the most wonderful time—!):

> Well, sir; my mistress is the sweetest lady— Lord! Lord!— when 'twas a little prating thing,— O! there's a nobleman in town, one Paris, that would fain lay knife aboard.... (II, iv).

It is remarkable that Shakespeare seldom uses even this restricted type of anacoluthon —better perhaps called fragmentary discourse— to depict the speech of his lower-class characters. In general these persons speak in quite coherent sentences, whether long or short. The linguistic devices associated by Shakespeare with *stylus humilis* (*rusticus*) for comic effect are rather malapropisms (as with Mrs. Quickly and Bottom), or deliberate burlesque of formal discourse (as when the First Gravedigger in *Hamlet* employs legal-scholastic language in discussing suicide).

   In extreme cases of anacoluthon, as some of the above examples indicate, no predicate may appear for the subject, and there may be no main clause at all, as here where the condition remains suspended in the air:

> therefore if it please your grace to do so much for me that this false marchaunt and traitour may suffre death as ye knowe well that he hath deserued and none other wise (*Frederick of Jennen*).

   Informal, colloquial prose writing is not to be thought of, however, as a mere tissue of crossed or shifted constructions, alternating with monotonous paratactic clauses. It can also attain clarity of statement and vivid, forceful effects in narrative or description by the unpretentious handling of simple types of sentences. Harman's *Caueat*, already cited more than once, contains some anecdotes admirably told in sustained third style. Dislocations of structure may be present, but they are minor ones. There may be a shift from indirect discourse to direct, or vice versa, in popular tales, but it is often quite smoothly made:

> she vp and tolde him what was fortuned, and how she had put her husband in the male [chest] and shewed hym that all thinges was well and therefore (sayd she) ye shal remayne thys night by me, and kepe my husbandes place (*Deceit of Women*, a tale based on a French original).

The passing over from indirect to direct speech in mid-discourse may in fact become a recognised pattern in the literary recording of colloquial conversation, as is abundantly testified in the best and most realistic of the Icelandic family sagas (recorded in the 13th and 14th centuries).

Many of the patterns of simple colloquial speech could be illustrated similarly from popular poetry, especially the ballads. Here there is always the question, however, of the extent to which the arrangement of sentence parts has been affected by the demands of meter and rime. The prose documents are therefore a better guide, though it must be admitted that these too are shaped to a greater or less degree by existing literary habits and models.

5. Sentence Structure in Formal Discourse

Formal composition made use, in general, of two types of sentence structure. The simpler (corresponding roughly to the medieval *stylus medius*) avoided very complex organisation of sentence parts, but insisted on having them conform to a unified pattern, without shifts, crossings or anacolutha. Writers representative of this middle style used simple sentences while avoiding jargon, neologisms and shifted constructions. Though they were cultured writers, they showed a certain affinity to the style of popular verse and prose. In some of his best work Sir Thomas Wyatt uses the middle style in a manner entirely removed from artificiality and decorative additions. It is in fact indistinguishable from the third or popular style except perhaps in its concentration of form, its consistent avoidance of loose constructions: [24]

> Forget not yet the tried intent
> Of such a truth as I have meant,
> My great travail so gladly spent,
>   Forget not yet.

In such composition the distinction from the third style may be said to be negative rather than positive: while adhering to a "correct" morphology and vocabulary, the authors avoid elaborate constructions in general, and when they do use them, they avoid the pitfalls of crossed syntax or anacoluthon.

The most formal writing often had intricate sentence structure, usually modelled on the Latin. A few of its devices may be surveyed here.

---

[24] For texts see the edition by Kenneth Muir, *Collected Poems of Sir Thomas Wyatt* (Harvard University Press, 1949). The lines here cited from poem no. 130 have been modernised as to orthography.

A series of parallel constructions (nominal appositions, participles, clauses, infinitives, etc.) might be used to build up impressive sentence units which attained something of the weight of Latin style by English means. The speech of Brutus in *Julius Caesar* (III, ii) is an excellent example of the unadorned but still dignified middle style. It is composed almost entirely of parallel shorter sentence units which reinforce the balanced logic which is characteristic of the speaker: As Caesar loved me, I weep for him; as he was fortunate, I rejoice at it; as he was valiant, I honour him; but, as he was ambitious, I slew him. The triple repetition of *as he was...* reinforces the parallelism by anaphora. Francis Bacon also uses balanced sentence elements and parallel constructions in series. Describing the four causes which led to the vogue for rhetoric he says:

> the admiration of ancient Authors, the hate of the Schoolemen, the exact studie of Languages, and the efficacie of Preaching did bring in an affectionate studie of eloquence and copie of speach, which then began to flourish.[25]

Here we have a series of modified nouns forming a compound subject of the verb *did bring*. Bacon's essays are full of such aphoristic parallelisms. Sometimes they have quite simple structures, as when nouns and adjectives are balanced: ... the French are wiser than they seem, and the Spaniards seem wiser than they are (Essay 26, *Of Seeming Wise*). Or simple infinitives and substantives may be balanced: To choose time is to save time; and an unseasonable motion is but beating the air (Essay 25, *Of Dispatch*). Another example: ...to speak agreeably to him with whom we deal is more than to speak in good words or good order (Essay 32, *Of Discourse*). John Lyly likewise leaned heavily on the coordination of parts in parallel construction, but he elaborated the elements of his sentences more intricately, and underscored their relations by decorative devices such as alliteration (both simple and interlinked), classical allusions and metaphors.

The formal style at its most elaborate strove to attain effects of periodicity comparable to those of Latin sentence structure. The means used were: the introduction of absolutes and dependent sentence parts at the beginning (that is, out of normal positron), and the interruption of subject-predicate or predicate-complement sequence by the insertion of parenthetical statements (such as a set of participles or clauses),

---

[25] Francis Bacon, *The Advancement of Learning*, as quoted by J. E. Spingarn, *Critical Essays of the Seventeenth Century*, I (Oxford, 1908), p. 2.

modified vocatives and other extended qualifiers. Upon completion of
the essential statement, the sentence might also be rounded out by an
additional segment loosely added, which served to compensate rhyth-
mically for the heaping up of an unwieldy number of clauses at the
beginning. An early 16th-century example of rather inflated style in
imitation of the Latin is the Proheme to Sir Thomas Elyot's *Book Named
the Governour* (1531), dedicated to King Henry VIII. It may be compared
with Caxton's efforts along the same lines (Appendix to ch. 2, no. 4).

> I late consideringe (moste excellent prince and myne onely redoughted
> soueraigne lorde) my duetie that I owe to my naturall contray with
> my faythe also of aliegeaunce and othe, wherewith I am double bounden
> unto your maiestie, more ouer thaccompt that I haue to rendre for
> that one litle talent deliuered to me to employe (as I suppose) to the
> increase of vertue, I am (as god iuge me) violently stered to deuulgate
> or sette fourth some part of my studie, trustynge therby tacquite
> me of my dueties to god, your hyghnesse, and this my contray.
> Wherfore takinge comfort and boldnesse, partly of your graces moste
> beneuolent inclination towarde the uniuersall weale of your subiectes,
> partly inflamed with zele, I haue nowe enterprised to describe in oure
> vulgare tunge the fourme of a iuste publicke weale: whiche mater
> I haue gathered as well of the sayenges of moste noble autours (grekes
> and latynes) as by myne owne experience, I beinge continually trayned
> in some dayly affaires of the publicke weale of this your noble realme
> all moste from my chyldhode.[26]

In the first sentence the subject is put forward at the beginning but
is immediately interrupted by a vocative and a present participle with
two objects, each one elaborately modified. The subject is then repeated,
once more briefly interrupted by a parenthetical statement, and then
the verb is allowed to appear with its complementary infinitive. But
there is loosely attached at the end a final participial construction which
permits the sentence to decline to a graceful conclusion: a prepositional
phrase with triple object. The second sentence begins with a long participial construction which looks forward to the subject it modifies. The
predicate follows here without delay, but again there is an extension
by means of a loosely appended apposition (which mater... undertaking)
and a nominative absolute construction (I beinge... trayned). These
devices are a fair sample of the ones used by imitators of Latin structure

---

[26] Sir Thomas Elyot, *The Boke named the Gouernoure*, ed. Foster
Watson (London: Everyman's Library, reprint of 1937), Proheme.

from Elyot to Milton. In some instances, as in Sir Philip Sidney's *Arcadia*, the heaping up of clauses, phrases, parentheses and absolutes reached monstrous proportions. (See example in the Appendix.) It resulted in a travesty of both Latin and English.

Not all of the learned writers, however, went to extremes of the inflated style for serious writing. Some who had recourse to it in their flattering dedications —like Elyot himself— adopted a simpler form of discourse in their texts proper. Others wrote flamboyantly, it would appear, out of pure linguistic playfulness. Still others, like Roger Ascham, maintained a consistent discretion in their imitation of Latin structures. Some writers turned from a decorated formal style to a more popular one according to theme and occasion. It has been demonstrated, for instance, that Thomas Nashe learned how to replace artificiality by ease and vigour of style from the Puritan "Marprelate" tracts[27] which he was employed to answer. The interplay of influences may be observed in many other writers as well.

It was the drama which called for the widest range of serious styles, obviously. Within the area of his highest manner, Shakespeare shows an extraordinary versatility in the technique of sentence structure. It is one of the marks of his mastery that he habitually marshalled very complex sentences so that in almost all cases they continued forward with an easy flow. In the course of the most intricate speeches, the grammatical structure is not allowed to get out of hand, despite inversions and parentheses. In *Othello*, Iago studs his speech with such planned breaks, finely calculated to augment his hearer's painful suspense:

> I do beseech you,
> Though I perchance am vicious in my guess, —
> As, I confess, it is my nature's plague
> To spy into abuses, and oft my jealousy
> Shapes faults that are not, — that your wisdom yet,
> From one that so imperfectly conceits,
> Would take no notice, not build yourself a trouble
> Out of his scattering and unsure observance.

> III, iii

---

[27] A series of anonymous pamphlets attacking Church of England policies from the dissenters' point of view. They have been edited by William Pierce, *The Marprelate Tracts* (London, 1911). On the influence exercised upon Nashe, see Travis L. Summersgill in *Studies in Philology*, XLVIII (1956), 145—60.

Sometimes a noun or pronoun is repeated so that the basic construction may be recalled after interruptions. Sometimes a statement is designedly broken off unfinished, as if by a rush of strong feeling. This is the rhetorical figure of aposiopesis, artfully used by Iachimo in his speech to Imogen, replying to her question: Why do you pity me?

> That others do,
> I was about to say, enjoy your— But
> It is an office of the gods to venge it,
> Not mine to speak on 't.
>
> *Cymbeline,* I, vi

These deviations from strictly completed structure, occurring in formal discourse, are obviously very different from the rambling repetitions, the loose pleonasms and unfinished statements of third-level speech as exemplified in Juliet's nurse.

With Shakespeare, complex structure is essentially related to the dramatic situation as well as the speakers' mood and character. An example is to be found in Hamlet's long speech near the beginning of Act II, Scene ii (see Appendix). He starts to say: So, oft it chances in particular men That...; he becomes involved in a series of inverted modifiers which delay completion of the clause for six lines; and so he allows himself to break off and repeat the introduction to the main dependent clause, and thereafter he proceeds to the conclusion of the sentence with some further interruptions. The periodic effect in the structure corresponds to the suspense in the dramatic mood, for the lines are spoken by an obviously tense Hamlet, distracted by the consciousness that his father's ghost may appear at any moment. The listener, concentrating on the intricate form as well as the meaning of the long sentence, reacts with heightened effect to the abrupt breaking off of the last one. In such speeches, the unusual constructions and the impressive words of Latin origin are unostentatiously introduced and made to harmonise with the context; they are not applied from outside as external decoration, in the manner of less accomplished writers.

On the other hand, a majestically simple style, relying chiefly on Anglo-Saxon words in uncomplex syntax, is adopted by Shakespeare in situations where this is the appropriate medium of expression. An illustrative passage will be found in the famous soliloquy of Macbeth beginning: Tomorrow, and tomorrow, and tomorrow (V, v; see Appendix). Syntactic analysis of both types of discourse in Shakespeare, the complex and the simple, will reveal some of the technical foundations of his supremely great art.

CHAPTER V

THE LATTER 17th AND THE 18th CENTURIES

1. SOCIAL AND CULTURAL TRENDS AFFECTING LANGUAGE

The period of about a century and a half between the bourgeois revolution in England (1642—60) and the outbreak of the great bourgeois French Revolution (1789) embraced many changes and developments which directly affected all of English culture in general. To a certain extent —though gradually and much less obviously— they were reflected in the history of the English language. In a brief account like the present it is not necessary to trace the steps by which the emergent middle class of rich traders and early manufacturers at first allied themselves for a short time with royal absolutism and later revolted against it when a conflict of interests developed between them. The misery of the lower classes, including artisans, declassed farmers and simple workers, had by the early 17th century reached an explosive point. An alliance became possible between the anti-royal wealthy bourgeoisie and these other elements, in order to cast off the remaining burdens of feudalism which now hampered all of these disparate groups to a greater or less degree.[1] The conflict of the social groups within the Cromwellian forces has been elucidated by Marxist and other historians. It was a conflict of left-wing elements like the Levellers and Diggers against the more conservative propertied adherents of Presbyterianism. After the restoration of the monarchy in 1660, an abortive attempt by the Stuarts to revert to absolutism was followed by the decisive victory of the wealthy middle class (1688). This last event opens the period of relative stability for the middle class, lasting throughout the 18th century. It is true that that

---

[1] For a general account see Christopher Hill, *The Good Old Cause* (London, 1949), tr. as *Rewolucja Angielska 1640 r.* (Warsaw, 1951); on theoretical aspects of the struggle see Perez Zagorin, *A History of Political Thought in the English Revolution* (London, 1954).

same class allied itself with and continued to make use of court and aristocracy, but the leadership had now definitely changed hands and the tone of culture was modified accordingly.

The new class alignments and the political structure founded on a long-enduring Whig supremacy resulted in profound changes in the cultural life of England. They may be traced in the plastic arts, fashions in clothes and literary styles; less obviously but still with some clarity in language and attitudes to language. The general tendency, for a multitude of reasons, was towards esteem for rules and regularity; towards a desire to discipline the media of expression, whether these were artistic, literary or linguistic. It is no accident that the vogue for strict form and classical models became dominant during the period when grammarians set themselves the task of regularising the structure of the English language on the basis of logical standards.

Of course there were contradictory tendencies operating in the 17th century and continuing into the 18th. Flamboyance and over-decoration marked certain styles in art, especially those most closely connected with the restored monarchy. But even the courtly styles of dress, entertainment and speech, despite their passion for decoration, stressed the values springing from a formal restraint and "decorum" so characteristic of what we call neo-classical literature. The middle class way of living at the same time also stressed values of order and restraint on a different level and for different reasons, with overtones of sobriety and self-discipline which were a heritage from the period of the Commonwealth. More and more writers who set the tone in polite letters were men (and women too) who came from the middle class, and they unconsciously propagated its ideals of propriety in their handling of language and their setting forth of its structure in handbooks of grammar and rhetoric. It was not only the literary forms, imitated from ancient Roman models, which qualified the age as Augustan, but also the treatment of language and the theories propounded about its use.

In comparison with the age of Shakespeare, the neo-classical period discouraged variety and free choice in grammar, in the choice of words and their pronunciation. It craved rules and welcomed the edicts of those who laid them down.[2]

The influence of classical learning on the English literary language continued to be strong, but it somewhat changed its nature. Whereas

---

[2] Sterling Andrus Leonard, *The Doctrine of Correctness in English Usage,* University of Wisconsin *Studies,* No. 25 (Madison, 1929). See also Ivan Poldauf, *On the History of Some Problems of English Grammar before 1800* (Prague, 1948).

the admiration for classical, especially Ciceronian Latin, had fostered the writing of very complex sentences in the 16th century, the trend now was towards greater fluency and simplicity, with a more moderate imitation of Latin constructions and idioms. Classical scholarship reached new heights in the age of Milton and Pope, and its influence was more widely felt than before. Schools and tutors were widely extending the foundations of cultured literacy in well-to-do families. The vogue for rhetoric in the preceding age bore its fruit now in the heightened awareness of style among even greater numbers of writers.

Furthermore, a knowledge of Hebrew was now frequently included in the equipment of amateur as well as professional scholars. With the constant spread of education and the increasing dissemination of printed books, these cultural influences affected wide sections of the literate public. They indirectly affected many persons who themselves knew no Latin, Greek or Hebrew.

One of the achievements of early 17th-century scholarship in England was the translation of the Bible into English (1611) by a commission of scholars appointed under King James I. The translators worked directly from the Hebrew text for the Old Testament and from the Greek for the New, while checking their work with previous translations. The outcome of their labours was not merely a sounder and more accurate version than any which had preceded it in English. It was also a document that entered into the mainstream of the people's lives, since the revolutionary struggle against absolutism and surviving feudalism, the struggle against the Stuart monarchy, was expressed in religious terms to a great extent. The soldiers of the Commonwealth drew inspiration from the relatively simpler (at least less rigidly stratified) society portrayed by the Old Testament stories of patriarchs and judges in Israel, and the severe Puritan morality —a form of middle-class reaction against extravagance in state and church officialdom— was readily expressed in Biblical terms. Thus a translation of the Bible done under the patronage of a Stuart monarch reached out to the masses of the people and became a rallying force in the very struggle which defeated the Stuarts in the end. The language used in the King James Version was conservative to begin with, both in vocabulary and grammatical forms (see below, sec. 5). As time passed, the discrepancy between it and the spoken language increased. Archaic diction was also associated with religious usage in sermons and the Book of Common Prayer. The role played by the various Protestant churches in 17th-century public life was immeasurably important. They helped to introduce a wealth of Biblical allusions, metaphors and turns of idiomatic expression into the heritage of the English language.

The rise of experimental science and the rationalist trend in philosophy, both of them of course socially conditioned, contributed a strong additional influence reinforcing the tendency to regularity in language. It was a period when science was calling attention to problems of learned vocabulary by turning to Latin and Greek for the creation of new terms. At the same time, the decline and final loss of Latin as a medium for communication in the learned world led to interest in projects for artificial universal languages, fixed and adapted to the uses of science and philosophy, which (it was thought) could surmount the limitations of the historical vernacular languages. Isaac Newton was one of those who interested themselves in the creation of such a language. Orderliness and fixed perfection were values primarily esteemed by the projectors of such linguistic systems.[3]

Versification too, which contributes valuable evidence of English pronunciation and speech rhythms in any age, now became regular as never before. A strict counting of syllables, a careful attention to the alternation of stressed and unstressed ones, marked the theory and practice of most English prosody from the Restoration to the Romantic period. At a time when correctness was so dominant an ideal, writers discussing problems of language were mostly preoccupied with the establishment of what was "right" as opposed to "wrong" usage, both rather narrowly conceived. Nevertheless it is possible to surmise, partly with the aid of their very strictures, what most people were actually saying in both informal and formal discourse.

2. The Evidence for Pronunciation in the 18th Century

As changes in pronunciation continued their gradual course, orthography was left still farther in the rear of usage as an index of English spoken sounds. The discrepancy was noticed by writers of the 17th and 18th centuries, but it was often misinterpreted by them as a sign of

---

[3] Richard F. Jones, "Science and Language in England of the Mid--Seventeenth Century," *Journal of English and Germanic Philology*, XXXI (1932), 315 ff. reprinted in *The Seventeenth Century* (Stanford University, 1951). On Newton's project, R. W. V. Elliott, "Isaac Newton's 'Of an Universal Language," *Modern Language Review*, LII (1957), 1—18. On the attempts by John Wilkins, John Amos Comenius and others to create a symbolic language for philosophy, see Benjamin DeMott, "Comenius and the Real Character in England, *PMLA*, LXX (1955), 1068—81.

deterioration from some earlier, ideal state. The role of linguistic change was not comprehended as we view it today. Milton, for instance, considered such change to be a result of "corrupt pronunciation" by the lower classes, and of their habit of writing words "falsely."[4] What struck many observers in the ensuing century was a tendency to slur and elide unaccented words and syllables. The trend was not a new one, of course, though some members of fashionable society may have exaggerated it to a mannerism. The prosody of Elizabethan drama already reveals it as operating in the 16th century; we can even deduce the habitual elision of some syllables which have since been re-adopted in informal as well as formal speech, such as *t' (h)is* for *to his*. In 17th-century comedies the contractions of informal slurred speech are orthographically indicated. In the comedies of William Congreve the pronoun *it* is reduced to *'t* in locutions like *'t had, don't* (for *done it) to't, for't*, etc.; *do* is reduced to *d'* in *d' ye* (for *do ye*) and *how d'ee* (for *how do ye*); *not* reduced to *n't*, and so on. Dryden and Samuel Butler write forms like: *t' enjoy, th' had*, (for *they had*), *sh' inherits*. In some unaccented words the loss of intervocalic *-v-* led to contraction and loss of a syllable: *o'er, e'er*— forms that are eschewed today even in poetry. Writers of formal verse generally indicated contracted syllables by the use of apostrophes, in order to make clear the regularity of their scansion: thus preterite tense forms like *flay'd, drudg'd, distress't*, and polysyllables like *presbyt'ry, murm'ring, conqu'ror*, where syncopation had occurred near liquid consonants.

Purists were disturbed by this favouring of contractions, and even more offended by the vogue for clipped forms observable in the colloquial speech of fashionable society. Jonathan Swift called attention to it in an indignant communication to *The Tatler* (No. 230, in 1710). Here he offered as sample of what should be avoided an imaginary gossiping letter written by a young man about town, in which *pozz* appears for *positive, plenipo's* for *plenipotentiaries, rep* for *reputation, mob* (today accepted) for *mobile vulgus*, and *phizz* for *physiognomy*, besides a number of the usual reduced forms of unaccented words, of which Swift also disapproved. Though the debate on the propriety of these forms was, as we see it now, conducted on the basis of rather artificial assumptions, it gives valuable evidence on the state of actual usage.

The naive orthography of non-literary writers supplies further clues for the traits of informal upper-class speech, though such aberrations

---

[4] Joshua H. Neuman, "Milton's Prose Vocabularly," *PMLA*, LX (1945), 102—20. The citation comes from Milton's *Artis Logicae Plenior Institutio* (1672).

are not easy to evaluate in linguistic terms. Ladies in fashionable society
with but sketchy education were capable of the following spellings:

> nor indeed cane I now dow [do] it without blushin
> wriet to the Duek in his be holfe [behalf]
> ablig [oblige] me in this
> you have won [one] thing for your comfort.[5]

Rimes in poetry are also an indication of pronunciation, probably
a fairly accurate one in view of the general passion for regularity then
prevailing, though we must be cautious about assuming that all rimes
were perfect even in the 18th century. Many words then paired at the
ends of couplets, now no longer possessing identical vowel sounds, must
have represented quite acceptable rimes in the Augustan age. A few
couplets will illustrate sufficiently the fact that such rimes of the late
17th and the 18th century are now obviously imperfect. The vowels
given in brackets represent a reconstruction of the probable pronunciation
of the time.

> In contemplation of whose ugly scars   [a:]
> They curst the memory of civil wars.   [a:]
>   Dryden, *Absalom and Achitophel*

> Whom, when their home-bred honesty is lost [ɔ:]
> We disembrogue on some far Indian coast.   [ɔ:] or [o:]
>   Dryden, *Hind and Panther*

> While expletives their feeble aid do join,   [ai]
> And ten slow words oft creep in one dull line. [ai]
>   Pope, *Essay on Criticism*

> Stretch'd on the shelly shore, he first surveys [e:]
> The flouncing herd ascending from the seas.   [e:]
>   Pope, Homer's *Odyssey*

> For what but social guilt the friend endears? [ɛ:] before[ɪ]
> Who shares Orgilio's crimes, his fortune shares. [ɛ:] before[ɪ]
>   S. Johnson, *London: A Satire*

---

[5] Letters by Ann Cecil (1708) and Lady Stafford, quoted by Constance Davies, *English Pronunciation,* pp. 142 and 147.

> Let such raise palaces, and manors buy,   [ai]
> Collect a tax, or farm a lottery.   [ai]
>
> Johnson, *ibid*.

The last couplet would also have been rimed with a diphthong in the 16th century (see p. 89). But notice in contrast with it another rime by the same author:

> By numbers here from shame or censure free, [i:]
> All crimes are safe, but hated poverty.   [i:]
>
> (*ibid*.)

Apparently —and this impression is confirmed by observation of many other poets in the 17th and 18th centuries— there was a choice of pronunciations for the last vowel in suffixes like -*ity*, -*y*, -*ite*, -*ice*, etc.[6] Other pronunciations fluctuated also, and certain liberties were no doubt permitted, for instance in pairing vowels which differed only slightly in quality or length. For instance:

> What though a paltry hare he rashly kill'd   [i]
> That cross'd the furrows while he plowed the field? [i:]
>
> John Gay, *A Tragi-Comi-Pastoral Farce*

> Some frolic drunkard, reeling from a feast   [e:]
> Provokes a broil, and stabs you for a jest.   [e]
>
> Johnson, *London*

A final source of information, especially in the 18th century, comes from schoolmasters' handbooks on orthography, which make constant reference to "correct" versus "incorrect" pronunciation, together with the diacritical marks and respellings used in dictionaries. These aimed at the indication of accents, the quantity and (though none too clearly) the quality of vowels.[7] The injunctions by school-masters and lexico-

---

[6] Bernard Mandeville, in *The Fable of the Bees* (London, ed. of 1732), has rimes like *supply*: *vanity*; *high*: *honesty*; *avarice*: *vice*; *by*: *salary*; but also: *misery*: *ye*: *family*.

[7] These problems are discussed by Esther Sheldon, "Pronouncing Systems in Eighteenth-Century Dictionaries," *Language*, XXII (1946), 27 ff.

graphers are not self-consistent, to be sure. There are many signs of prejudice, of sporadic dialect influence, and above all of an *a priori* assumption —stronger than in the preceding period— that an approximation of "spelling pronunciation" is itself desirable. Nevertheless the normative statements of these two groups of people furnish a very useful body of evidence for our reconstruction of standard speech.[8]

3. THE STANDARD PRONUNCIATION RECONSTRUCTED

The main development of vowels already described in connection with the 15th and 16th centuries continued throughout the two following. That is to say, the upward shift in position was continued in respect to the vowels lower than original ME long *ī* and *ū*, while these latter now completed their evolution into the ModE diphthongs [ai] and [au] respectively. Thus the final forms of original *ī* and *ū* balanced the upward trend of other vowels by providing newly lowered positions in the first elements of the diphthongs.

A. Long vowels. By the middle of the 18th century the long vowels had developed still farther towards their present status. The disappearance of -*r* (now untrilled) when final and before other consonants was by this time far advanced, and the lengthening of preceding vowels was normal. The quality of the resulting vowel was in some instances different according as the -*r* was or was not followed by another consonant (compare *hare* : *hart*; *care* : *card*). Normal developments of long or lengthened vowels can not readily be presented on a single chart together with the many important instances of developments conditioned by neighbouring sounds. The following simplified scheme will attempt

---

[8] An example is given by James Buchanan, a school-master of Scottish origin who in the mid-18th century wrote a number of text-books on grammar and pronunciation. Among the latter was his *Essay towards Establishing a Standard for an Elegant and Uniform Pronunciation* (1766). It has been used by Elisabeth Meyer in her study, *Der englische Lautbestand in der zweiten Hälfte des 18. Jahrhunderts nach James Buchanan* (Berlin diss., 1940). The findings of this study have been used in the present discussion.

to indicate only the fundamental pattern achieved, in relation to ME origins:

Examples: Examples:

my,   ai←-ME i: via əi   ME u: via əu→au   now
join   ͺME ɔi, ui

see,   i:←ME e: ME o:-→u: food, poor
here   ↘ ʊ   book

great,   ⎰ɛ: ME ɔ: → o: stone
stale,   e: ←ME ⎨a: ɔ:+r   more, board,⁹
day, fair   ⎱ai   floor

bare, hare   ɛ:←-- ME a+r   ME ou ⎱   thought,
                                    ME au ⎰ → ɔ: law, chalk
clerk, "sarve"   (ME e+r)   ⎫
arm   ME a(:)+r   ⎬ ME w+a(:)   war, warm
half, bath, pass ME a(:)+f, θ, s   ⎭
                                        ɑ: ↙

Note: Changes of limited scope are indicated by broken lines.

The most important and most general of the above changes may be thus simply stated, if we ignore the influence of conditioning sounds:

ai < ME ī   au < ME ū
i: < ME ę̄   u: < ME ǭ
e: < ME ā, ę̄, ai   ɔ: < ME ou, au

More special and complex changes call for some detailed comments.

The continuation of ME long closed ǭ showed a marked diversification by the mid-18th century. In only one group of words having this original vowel did the later forms preserve the sound indicated as normal on the above chart. That group includes several types: *moon, spoon, food* (here a labial consonant precedes the vowel); *rood* (an archaic word); but also *soon, brood, tooth,* etc. In another group of words the vowel was

⁹ The [ɔ:] here indicated is of several origins: ME ǭ and ǫ before *r*, and ME short *o* lengthened before *r*. For details see Wilhelm Horn and Martin Lehnert, *Laut und Leben: Englische Lautgeschichte der neueren Zeit,* I (Berlin, 1954), pp. 489 ff.

shortened and later became identical in its history with original short *u*. Examples are: *blood, done, mother*. There is a third, intermediate group which preserved a high-back vowel like the original early ModE [u:] until late in the 18th century, and then shortened it to [ʊ] too late to have its share in the reduction affecting the second group. Examples are: *book, good*. The lack of conformity in the history of long *ū* from ME long *ō* is due, no doubt, to a choice of diverse dialect forms, to special influences and fashions now hard to trace. Scattered exceptional cases in other words with long vowels present similar problems. The word *uncouth*, for instance, preserves a ME long *ū* instead of the expected diphthong [au] because it has been taken into standard English relatively late, in a Northern form.

The group represented by ME *a* lengthened and modified in quality before special consonants and groups of consonants has a complicated history.[10] In words which had early ModE short *a* [æ] before strong voiceless fricatives like [s], [f] and [θ], with or without a following stop or a preceding *n*, the vowel was both lengthened and lowered by the latter 17th century. The result was ModE [ɑ:] in words like: *pass, fast, path* and *dance*. The Shakespearean equivalent, it will be remembered, had been the short front vowel [æ] then being lengthened to [æ:]. The change in quality preserved the phonemic contrast in word pairs like *pass: pace*, for *pace* was being pronounced with a similar though not identical vowel —[ẹ:] or [ɛ:]— at the beginning of this period. The older pronunciation of *pass*, etc., with [æ:] or [æ] is still preserved in most American dialects. Fluctuation still persists in many words today: in *mass, morass, paragraph, quaff*, etc.

In the mean time, a number of long and short vowels, including [æ], had been affected by a following *r*. But this tendency did not operate everywhere and at all times with equal effect, as is indicated for instance by the simultaneous existence of doublets going back to ME, like: *person* beside *parson, servant* beside *sarvant*, etc. To this previous influence

---

[10] See the detailed article by Wiktor Jassem, "Regular Changes of Vocalic Quantity in Early New English," as referred to, ch. 3, n. 42. The author emphasises the role of phonemic contrast as a factor conditioning and explaining certain specialised developments otherwise appearing to be erratic. The tendency to a preservation of symmetry and contrast in the total vocalic system is another factor which throws light on general developments and seeming exceptions. On this problem see André Martinet, "Function, Structure and Sound Change," *Word*, VIII (1952), 1—32 and "Concerning the Preservation of Useful Features," *ibid.*, IX (1953), 1—11.

there was added in the 17th and 18th centuries the weakening and
eventual vocalising of *r* except in pre-vocalic position. Before its disappearance there had usually developed between it and the preceding
vowel an *ə*-sound which survived in the case of words like: *here, fire,
poor*. It disappeared, however, or failed to develop, after the lower
vowels [a:] and [ɔ:], as in: *car, cart, floor*. The long *ā* which developed
through loss of following *r* was a new phoneme, not a conditioned
variant, as can be established by contrasting pairs of words like *cart:
caught* (the latter having [ɔ:] from an original diphthong), and *far : fare*
(the latter having [ɛ:ə] from an earlier lengthened ME *a* in an open
syllable), and *far : fair* (the latter having [ɛ:ə] from a ME diphthong [ai]).

In short, two sound changes of the period under discussion produced
a long vowel [ɑ:], with phonemic status, in ModE, which had not existed
in Shakespeare's time: namely the modification of *a* occurring before
[s, f, θ], alone or with a following stop, and the loss of -*r* after *a*, with
a resultant later lengthening and lowering. An [ɑ(:)] which apparently
had developed after *w* was in this period shifted to [ɔ(:)] as in: *warm,
watch, squash*.

Meantime the lengthening of ME short *o* [ɔ] (preserved short in closed
syllables) had been completed before [s, f, θ] alone or followed by
a stop (see chart, p. 130), and to a limited extent before *r*. The result
was the vowel sound [ɔ:] in words like *loss, soft*, and (eventually) *fort*.
Conservative schoolmasters like Buchanan still indicated the short
vowel in the mid-18th century, however. There is evidence too for
a higher pronunciation of long *ō* before *r* as [o:] or [o:ə], a pronunciation
still preserved in Southern dialects of the United States. In words like
hall and *law*, ME *a* developed into a sound like that resulting from ME
aw; hence something like [ɔ:], by the end of the 18th century.[11] An
au-diphthong had developed from *a* before *l* alone or if followed by
a dental or velar: *fall, halt, chalk*. But before a labial the *l* itself was
lost: *half, calm*, etc.

The treatment of long vowels in the late 17th and the 18th centuries
presents a number of special cases in addition to the ones just discussed.

The normal [i:] from ME [e:] was not subject to change at this time,
but there was fluctuation in the treatment of this vowel in foreign words.
Thus we find the spelling *obleedg'd* for *obliged* in the early 18th century,
and spelling books indicate [i:] or its shortened form in words like:
china, elegiac, satiety. On the other hand, they give the Anglicised diphthong
in words like: *cylinder, lizard* and *minatory*, where ModE has a short

---

[11] Jassem, *op. cit.*, p. 161, surmises that the sound was [ɒ]/[ɒ:]; see
also Dobson, *op. cit.*, II, pp. 782 ff.

vowel *i*; and they vary in their treatment of words like: *primer, finance.* Samuel Johnson rimes *submit* with *parasite.* It has already been noted that [i:] alternates with [ai] in the final syllable of words like *lottery.*

The long closed *ẹ̄* which resulted from ME long open *ę* was shortened in some words like *deaf,* and especially before dental consonants: *breath, death, head.* This change occurred before the final raising of long closed *ẹ̄* to [i:], which caused it to fall together with ME *ē* about the end of the 18th century. The alternate forms with long vowels persisted for some time, however. The word *friend* already had a short vowel, sometimes represented in the spelling *frind.* Shortened forms apparently existed in words like: *freak, heathen, reach,* and there was a choice of forms for words like: *break, steak, great.*

The early ModE long *ū* from *ọ̄* and other sources (e. g., *floor, court*) was lowered before *r*, first to *ǭ* and later to [ɔ:], but various stages of this development have been perpetuated in contemporary English. The original *ū* has been maintained in some words, especially near labial consonants (*poor, moor*);[12] the *ō*-stage is preserved in some dialects even before *r*, as for instance in Southern American, while the final stage of [ɔ:] appears in most ModE words whether the vowel was originally *ū, ō, ǭ* or *o* lengthened: *court, floor, lore, corn.* In the 18th century there was apparently some latitude of choice still. When Johnson rimes *shore: poor*, the quality of both vowels is in some doubt.

The long closed *ọ̄* which normally developed from ME long open *ǭ* was sporadically shortened. Thus *o* instead of *ō* is occasionally reported in words like: *only, crony*; there is evidence of the same shortening in early American pronunciation of: *shone, stone, home,* etc. Sometimes too an original ME long *ō* was restored to pronunciation under the influence of orthography, .as in the case of the proper noun *Rome,* previously pronounced [ru:m].

B. Diphthongs inherited from the late 16th century show little change in the period under discussion. Two separate diphthongs of the 16th

---

[12] In Horn-Lehnert, *Laut und Leben,* I, p. 494 f., the suggestion is made that in this case, and others also where conservative forms of the vowel exist beside normally developed ones, differences in pitch may explain the discrepancies. The word *poor* in particular is supposed to have kept its early ModE *ū* because it was often spoken with affective stress ("gefühlsbetont"), and with high pitch. The explanation is rather speculative, since it can not be applied to all words (e. g., *moor*) in the group. See further Dobson, *op. cit.,* II, pp. 675 ff.

century, [əi] and [ɔi], of similar configuration, tended to merge in
the single diphthong [ai], as can be verified in frequent rimes like *join*:
sign. Since the 18th century the two have once more been separated
and distinguished. The mechanics of this sound change have not
been clearly explained. It would appear that the coalescence was
never complete and universal, even in the age of Pope; that alternate
pronunciations were possible; and that under the influence of orthography, custom favoured the preservation of a distinction. There were
slight divergencies in the development of [iu] / [ju] in both Romance
and Germanic words. After *r*, the result was a simple vowel as in: *rule,
intrude*. After *l*, the *j*-sound was normally lost: *lute, flute*, etc. In some
instances the initial element was lost after having palatalised a preceding sibilant, as in: *sugar, sure*, etc. The pronunciation [ʃuːt] is attested
for *suit*, but ModE has retained the unpalatalised form [sjuːt]; nor has
complete palatalisation occurred in *sue, suet, suicide.*

C. Short accented vowels in the 18th century did not undergo any
striking development except in combination with other sounds.   The
articulation of short *i* and *u* had been lowered, apparently, in prevailing
speech, but they were still sometimes heard in high position, as the rimes
already cited would indicate.[13] In certain positions at least, short *e*
had a higher articulation than in others. It was high, for instance, before
the dental nasal *n* plus a consonant: *frind* is spelled occasionally for
friend, insinscible for *insensible* (noted by Davies). It was also high
before a dental *l*, as in *till* for *tell*. Buchanan's prescription of *i* in
bless and its derivatives may be due to his Northern origin, but to
this very day standard English has the substantive *bliss* beside the verb
bless. (To be sure, the origin of *bless* is in doubt; the two words may be
unconnected). Evidence for the continued high articulation of *u* is found
in occasional spellings like *goons* for *guns, swche* for *such* (Davies), but on
the other hand *gannes* has already been noted for *guns* as early as the
15th century (Wyld). Short *o* was at one time unrounded in fashionable
speech, as is indicated in spellings like *stap* for *stop*, but this was, as we
have seen, ridiculed as an affectation. This pronunciation did not gain

---

[13] The pronunciation of short *u* seems to have veered somewhat
towards *o*, but was not shifted to the mid-tongue position [ʌ] until the
late 18th century, according to Brunner, *Die engl. Sprache*, I, p. 253; but
C. Davies, following Wyld, places the change earlier. See also Dobson,
op. cit., II, pp. 675 ff.

permanent acceptance in England, but it is widely prevalent in America.

Short vowels were, like the long ones, being affected in positions before *r* final or preceding a consonant. The group *-ir, -er, -ur* in such positions levelled the vowel to a central one which was lengthened as the *r* weakened and disappeared. Thus we have [ɜ:] in ModE in words like: *fir, fur, birth, her, heard, hurt*. In the earlier 18th century, schoolmasters' texts indicate differences in quality among these various short vowels before *r*. Buchanan, for instance, attempts to distinguish between *i* and *u* in such position. It is difficult, however, to conclude to what extent his efforts are due to orthography itself, or to temporary vogues among small groups affecting elegant speech, as opposed to broader tendencies prevailing at the time. Standard spellings like *churl* for *cherl* (compare German *Kerl*) indicate the levelling process. Short *e* before *r* often alternated, for historical reasons, with short *a*. In the competition of alternates, 18th century usage still accepted many forms with *a* which today have only the [ɜ:]-form: *larn* for *learn, marcy* for *mercy, varmin* for *vermin*. On the other hand the lower vowel is today standard pronunciation, despite spelling, in: *clerk, Derby, sergeant*. Original *a* (fronted in Shakespeare's time) appears to have had a fluctuating pronunciation before *r* final or followed by a consonant.[14] Original short *o* before *r* had a slack quality; it too lengthened as the *r* disappeared, and thus fell together with the [ɔ:] developed from long *ō* in the same position. The result is the same long vowel in words like *born* and *horn*, which is to be found in *boar* (with original long *ō* from OE long *ā*). The rounding of *a* after *w*, resisted in educated speech in the 17th and earlier 18th centuries, was generally accepted by the middle decades of the latter.

Vowels in unaccented syllables, as was indicated above, were often syncopated, at least in verse, near liquid and nasal consonants: *heav'ns, show'rs*, etc. Syllabic value has been restored in most of these words in modern speech. Monosyllables like: *he, she, it, to*, which then had vowels elided in certain positions, have also had them restored, as have uncontracted forms for: *over, ever, even*, thus giving the modern value in the scansion of verse.

In numerous suffixes which had had short *-e-* in ME, the substitution of a higher vowel spelled *i* or *y* had originally been a sign of the influence of Northern dialects, extending southwards through East

---

[14] Constance Davies deduces a pronunciation [æ:r] when no other consonant follows, but E. Meyer points out that Buchanan wrote *ă* short in words like *bar* as well as *charcoal* and *farther*.

Anglia toward London. In ModE the higher vowel has become the accepted form, for instance in suffixes spelled -es in verbal and nominal inflections, and -ed as sign of the past tense of weak verbs (when this has syllabic value). It also appears in suffixes like: -ness, -less, -edge, etc. In some areas [ə] is heard, or there is fluctuation between [ɪ] and [ə].

As elsewhere, short vowels were affected by a final -r in unaccented syllables. Here the series -er, -ir, -or, -ar levelled to the central vowel [ə] as in: mother, faker, fakir, factor, sugar. Reduction affected unaccented u in French suffixes like -on, -tion, -sion, where today a vocalic consonant is normal, giving [ŋ] in: reason, nation, etc. The rounded French ü [y:] which in accented syllables had normally produced the diphthong [iu], or [ju], was reduced to [ə] in the final syllable of figure; the same pronunciation was to be heard, without palatalisation, in other words like: nature, creature, feature, as well. But today's standard pronunciation of these last words is derived from the alternate form with [ju], causing palatalisation. It presupposes a ME form with accent preserved on the second syllable into the 15th century.

4. LEXICOGRAPHY AND THE DRIVE TO "FIX" THE ENGLISH LANGUAGE

By the middle of the 18th century, knowledge about the immediate origins of English had greatly increased, thanks to the labours of antiquarians, students of history and law, and of lexicographers continuing the work begun in the 17th century (see ch. 4, sec. 3). There was accumulated evidence to show that English, like any other language, is subject to change in pronunciation, vocabulary and grammatical structure. In spite of their augmented knowledge, however, the writers on English for the most part still considered change deplorable. In line with their attitudes on other matters, they tended to assume that a closed-in and finished language conforming to clearly consistent rules was superior to one still in a condition of growth. Their linguistic prejudice was conditioned and strengthened by admiration for two "dead" languages, classical Latin and Greek. Scholars had not yet investigated dialectal forms and medieval continuations of these two tongues, so that it could be assumed that they represented a standard of fixed structures, the more admirable precisely because they seemed to be unchanging.

Under the circumstances, it is not surprising that scholars and men of letters in England should have considered the establishment of an

English Academy to determine, among other things, which words and usages could be considered correct and which ones were to be rejected by persons solicitous for the "purity" of English. The neighbouring example of the Académie Française, which undertook to settle matters of disputed usage and produced a standard dictionary in 1694, contributed a strong stimulus. A committee of the English Royal Society discussed the possibility of founding a similar body with like functions in England (latter 17th century). Jonathan Swift was one of the writers most outspoken in calling for such an institution to "fix" the English language, as the current phrase had it. He set forth his arguments in *A Proposal for Correcting, Improving, and Ascertaining the English Tongue* (1718). Although he admitted that a language might be enlarged by additions, he wished to prevent what was then looked upon as decay and corruption in its vocabulary.

The intellectual climate was at the time auspicious for such a project, and Swift's *Proposal* received a considerable measure of support. But objections were voiced also, and before the end of the 18th century interest in it had died out almost completely.[15] One of the most influential statements in opposition to such a project was made by Samuel Johnson in the Preface to his *Dictionary* (1755). He confessed that he had begun with the flattering idea that he, as lexicographer, could "fix our language, and put a stop to those alterations which time and chance have hitherto been suffered to make in it without opposition." Further study, however, convinced him that any effort at embalming a language is merely derisible. He concluded that legislation on matters linguistic is contrary to the "spirit of English liberty."

The publication of Johnson's *Dictionary* marked a turning point in English lexicography. Yet it was no sudden achievement. Previous to its appearance, in the early decades of the century, solid preparatory work was done in continuation of the pioneering efforts of the 17th century. A *New English Dictionary* had appeared, issued by a certain "J. K." (1701; revised 1713), which was the first to aim at bulk and inclusiveness, giving everyday words as well as difficult and unusual terms.[16] The same anonymous author revised Phillips's *New World of*

---

[15] The authoritative discussion of this problem is H. M. Flasdieck, *Der Gedanke einer englischen Sprachakademie* (Jena, 1928). See Baugh, *History*, pp. 317 ff.

[16] See Starnes and Noyes, *The English Dictionary*, pp. 69 ff.; also the valuable survey by Martin Lehnert, "Das englische Wörterbuch in Vergangenheit und Gegenwart," *Zeitschrift für Anglistik und Amerikanistik*, IV (1956), 265—323.

Words (1706), making of it almost a new book by improvements and additions (for instance, dialect forms and new scientific terms). This J. K. is probably identical with the John Kersey, printer, who published a *Dictionarium Anglo-Britannicum* (1708) containing 35,000 words. The need for a systematic account of origins was filled by Nathan Bailey's *Universal Etymological English Dictionary* (1721) containing 40,000 words, including cant, dialect, and obsolete terms. Still more ambitious was Bailey's *Dictionarium Britannicum* (1730) containing 48,000 words more amply defined than in any preceding work. It was further expanded (1726) to 60,000 words. Among other lexicons of the period may also be mentioned: Thomas Dycke, *A Dictionary of all the Words Commonly us'd in the English Tongue* (1723 and frequently thereafter), the work of a schoolmaster, which offers guidance to correct pronunciation; and Benjamin Martin, *Lingua Britannica Reformata* (1749), an imposing work which improved the ordering of definitions and the distinction of various senses of the same word. Study of synonyms, inspired by French example, was carried forward by others in special works which helped to distinguish shades of meaning, but these sometimes imposed distinctions from without, according to the writers' preconceived ideas.[17]

Johnson's *Dictionary* (1755) was a monument of conscientious labour carried through all but single-handed, with the exception of clerical assistance. It presented the English literary vocabulary much more completely than ever before. While availing himself of the work of outstanding predecessors, Johnson pursued a policy of founding his definitions on the actual usage of English authors. He was an innovator in that he consistently offered references to literary texts as illustration and justification for the meanings given. In fact Johnson himself says in his Preface that where his own definition is inadequate "the sense may easily be collected entire from the examples."

Thus Johnson's method as a lexicographer was in general inductive. To be sure, he undertakes to make decisions in matters of dispute, and here his appeal may be to other tests than general usage. On grounds of etymology, for instance, he decided that the adjectival phrase *averse from* is better than *averse to*, since English *from* echoes the Latin prefix *a(b)*. He shows prejudice, even strong feeling, when he condemns certain widely accepted forms: for instance, he calls *lesser* a barbarous word

---

[17] Gertrude E. Noyes, "The Beginnings of the Study of Synonyms in England," *PMLA*, LXVI (1951), 951—70. The model was *La Justesse de la langue française* by Abbé Gabriel Girard (1718). It was followed closely by John Trusler in his *Difference between Words Esteemed Synonymous in the English Language* (1766).

because it is from the historical point of view a double comparative. It is also true that Johnson has included a number of learned words which can hardly claim naturalisation in English: e. g., *denominable, ataraxy, digladiation, incompossibility,* etc. His etymologies are faulty when information available was incomplete or misleading. The definitions were sometimes needlessly ponderous,[18] and a few were erratic or in-accurate. Nevertheless the *Dictionary* raised lexicography to a new level in England. Although reviewers at the time and later in the century were quick to point out various of the faults just mentioned, and some in particular demanded more service to the ideal of fixing or legislating for the language, the fact is that most authors of the later 18th-century dictionaries used Johnson's work with or without acknowledgment.[19]

Interest in dictionaries became more widespread than ever as the increase in wealth and the expansion of the middle class stimulated an eagerness for literary culture among ever wider sections of the population. It was the age, we must remember, which produced a new type of domestic middle-class drama, the periodical essays and magazines which were precursors of modern journalism, and also that peculiarly middle-class form of fiction, the popular sentimental novel. The enormously successful comic figure of Mrs. Malaprop in Richard Brinsley Sheridan's *The Rivals* (1775) is an index of the interest in the correct use of words. Thomas Sheridan, Dublin-born father of the dramatist, produced a *General Dictionary of the English Language* (1780), including instructions for pronunciation. John Walker, in his *Critical Pronouncing Dictionary,* went farther than Sheridan in attempting to regulate instead of simply recording current speech. For instance, Walker attacked Sheridan for registering reduced or syncopated vowels in unaccented syllables; his own instructions frequently called for "spelling pronunciation" in defiance of accepted usage. His authority caused acceptance of many of these distorted transcriptions as standard. His influence was further increased

---

[18] E. g., two famous ones: *network* was defined as "anything reticulated or decussated [made with the figure X, the sign for Latin *decem* or 10] at equal distances, with interstices between the intersections"; *cough* defined as "a convulsion of the lungs, vellicated [spasmodically convulsed] by some sharp serosity [watery substance]."

[19] Stanley Rypins, "Johnson's Dictionary Reviewed by His Contemporaries," *Philological Quarterly,* IV (1925), 281—86; Gertrude Noyes, "The Critical Reception of Johnson's Dictionary in the Latter Eighteenth Century," *Modern Philology,* LII (1954—55), 175—91; James H. Sledd and G. J. Kolb, *Dr. Johnson's Dictionary: Essays in the Biography of a Book* (University of Chicago Press, 1955).

when he was called upon to add notes on pronunciation to Johnson's dictionary. Both Sheridan and Walker were widely followed in the United States, especially Walker. Here the latter's pedantic prescriptions had great effect, for instance when he demanded full vowel sounds and secondary stresses on normally unaccented syllables. This pedantry of his is the origin of several specific differences between English and American pronunciation today, as in polysyllables like *secretary*, *laboratory* and others.[20]

The words employed in English speech were of course increasing in number during the 150 years before 1800. Italian continued to contribute words connected with the arts, especially with music (*cantato*, *oratorio*, *maestro* and others); French too and Spanish, including Spanish-American. High German yielded a few terms including the names of minerals such as *quartz*, *wolfram*, *nickel* and *meerschaum* (the latter, a metaphorical term literally meaning "sea-foam", was applied to a fine, white, clay-like material mined in Asia Minor). Early contacts with Russia were reflected in terms first recorded in the 18th century: *ukase* (first spelled *oukauze*, 1729), *knout*, *astrakhan* and *suslik* (designating the fur from a small, squirrel-like animal). The expansion of the British Empire in Asia, and the contacts there made with Oriental culture, found reflection in many colourful terms. From Arabic came a group of words associated to this day with the *Thousand and One Nights*: *houri* (through the Persian), *fellah*, *jinnee* or *genie*, *ghoul*, *candy* (1769, ultimately from the Persian *gand* for sugar). Hindustani contributed *na oo*, *guru*, *chintz*, *bungalow* (meaning "of Bengal," 1676) and *juggernaut* in the 17th century; *gunny*, *bandana*, *chit*, *bangle*, *jungle* and *shampoo* in the 18th. The Dravidian languages of Southern India yielded terms such as *pariah*, *teak*, *anaconda* and *mulligatawny* (from *milagu tannir*, "pepper water"). Hebrew words like *shekel*, *sanhedrin*, *cherub*, etc., came through the English translation of the Bible. China, Malaya, Africa and Australia began to lend words to English by the end of the 18th

---

[20] Esther K. Sheldon, "Walker's Influence on the Pronunciation of English", *PMLA*, XLII (1947), 130—46. Walker's attitude is indicated in the comment he makes on the pronunciation of *spirit*, to be found in a Philadelphia (1839) edition of Johnson's Dictionary "as improved by Todd and abridged by Chalmers". Walker says: "The general sound of the first *i* in this word and all its compounds was, till lately, the sound of *e* in *merit*: but a very laudable attention to propriety has nearly returned the *i* to its true sound: and now *spirit*, sounded as if written *sperit*, begins to grow vulgar".

century, thus adding still more to its internal diversification. At the same time modern science began to multiply the words being coined out of Greek elements for new and special uses.

5. Grammar and Syntax

As in questions of pronunciation and in the choice of words, so also in syntax and sentence structure the neo-classical period craved and sought regularity. Gone, after the first decades of the 17th century, was the freedom which had permitted dramatists to be careless with grammatical forms and concords in the writing of idiomatic dialogue. Editors of Shakespeare in the early 18th century like Nicholas Rowe, Alexander Pope and others were careful to correct striking instances of abnormal cases, disagreements between verbs and their subjects, and so forth, so far as this could be done without damage to the rhythm in the verse passages of the plays. Thus Hamlet's question to Polonius (*Hamlet,* II, ii, 193): *Between who?* —though consistently recorded thus in the quartos and First Folio— is corrected to: *Between whom?* in later folios and 18th century editions beginning with Rowe's (1709). In *The Tempest* (V, i, 216) Gonzalo says: here *is* more of us; but Pope corrected this (1723) to read: here *are* more. The shift of case in the line by Ulysses: Praise *him* that got thee, *she* that gave thee suck (*Tr. and Cr.,* II, iii, 245), is emended by both Pope and Johnson (1773) so that we get a formally correct construction, replacing *she* by *her.* A shift of number committed by Duke Orsino: [their]... palate/ That *suffer* surfeit (*Twelfth Night,* II, iv, 134 f.) is set straight by Rowe and others so that the relative pronoun agrees with *palate* (not the distant *their* referring to *women*), and we have: ...that *suffers* surfeit. All this is very indicative of the temper of the age. So is the elimination of double negatives, comparatives and superlatives from general usage. Pleonastic conjunctions like: *the which that, whensoever that, for because that,* etc., were simplified to single words which became the standard forms. Some margin of freedom still existed, as we shall see, in good formal writing, but it was far more restricted than in the Elizabethan age.

Among pronouns the most conspicuous change was the complete elimination of the old second singular forms *thou, thy, thee,* except in Biblical quotations and pulpit oratory. The adoption of a single form, *you,* for both singular and plural meant at the same time the elimination of nuances of semantic distinction for class levels and degrees of formality and intimacy, which still find expression in most continental

languages (very notably in Polish) to this very day. But among the
Quakers, more properly called the Friends —a pacifist democratic sect
originating in the lower middle class (17th century)— the old singular
form was universalised as a linguistic sign of social equality. Nominative
and objective cases were levelled under the single form *thee*, producing
locutions like: Does *thee* think?, *Thee* will come, etc. The pronoun *it*,
now equipped with its own genitive case *its* (as distinct from *his*)
became in this period the only one applied to inanimate things, abstract
qualities, etc., except in cases of definite personification. The relative
pronoun *which*, except in Biblical language and imitations of it, was
also limited to inanimate things, while *who* alone could now refer to
persons. The article *the* was no longer inserted before relatives. A few
minor changes affected indefinite pronouns too: for instance, *other*,
like *one* (in the distributive sense) achieved a plural form: *others, ones*.
Shakespeare had used *other* in the plural both with and without *-s*.
The indefinites *everybody* and *anybody* are referred to by the plural
personal pronoun *they* in some of the best writing of the 18th century:
if he sees anybody nodding,/ [he] sends to *them* (Addison, *Spectator*,
No. 112); everybody else is upon *their* knees (*ibid.*).

Adjectives and adverbs were more strictly handled than in the
16th century. Logic was invoked to fortify the regulations forbidding
double comparatives, superlatives and negatives. Just as the addition
of two negatives gives a positive value in algebra, so two negatives
were said to cancel instead of reinforcing each other in language. The
suffix *-ly* was extended to most adverbs as a regular inflectional ending,
though some uninflected forms still remained admissible which have
since been rejected, as for instance Richard Steele's expression: he
was *extreme* poor (*Spectator*, No. 454), contrasting with: *naturally* jovial
(*ibid.*, No. 2).

Among verbs, treatment of auxiliaries was further standardised. The
usage of *shall* and *will* was subjected to rules. They were not easily
formulated,[21] since many shades of meaning and function had developed
for these words, not all of which could be classified as expressions of
either simple future on the one hand; or of determination and command
on the other. One of the first attempts to reduce the complexity to
ordered rules was contained in a Latin grammar of the English
language, the *Grammatica Linguae Anglicanae* (1653). This text explained that in independent declarative sentences, *shall* in the first
person has the meaning of someone simply foretelling (*simpliciter prae-
dicentis*), and *will*, of someone promising or threatening (*quasi pro-*

---

[21] Discussion by K. Brunner, *Die englische Sprache*, II, 270 ff.

mittentis aut minantis). For the second and third persons, the two senses were declared to be reversed. Other grammarians elaborated this distinction. Nevertheless, actual usage, as revealed in dramas of the period 1560—1700, has always preferred *will* in the first person for simple statements, despite the rules laid down in the text-books.[22]

The auxiliary *do* was generally established in the conventional pattern of today's usage, being limited to the functions of strong emphasis, the introduction of questions and negative statements, and substitution for the notional verb. In the latter 17th century, however, and even somewhat later, the use of *do* as an auxiliary for negation was still not universal. Milton has: though we *mark not*; she *speaks not* (*Areopagitica*), and Dryden still writes: I *say not*; if I *lose not* (Preface to *The Fables*). However, Johnson's I *know not* (*Life of Addison*) is already an archaic stereotype. Only occasionally does the emphatic *do* deviate from modern usage in this period.

The auxiliary *be* was still often used instead of *have*, in archaic Biblical or formal discourse, with intransitive verbs of motion: the children of Israel *were gone* forth..., they *were departed*..., and *were come*..., and *had pitched* [their tents] in the wilderness (Exodus 19: 1—2). In the 18th century, *to be* is to be found only in occasional locutions: time *was come* (Johnson, *Life of Addison*). By the 19th century, *to have* had become the universally used auxiliary for the perfect tenses. At the same time, *to be* became normalised in its function of expressing continuous action, as today.

The subjunctive mood lost ground steadily, as modal auxiliaries —the preterite-present verbs *may, can, shall, will, ought, must*— took over its function of expressing relations of doubt, contingency, possibility and the like. Thus Johnson has: lest it *should be* (*loc. cit.*); and with simple indicative: it may be doubted whether Cato *was* (*ibid.*). Loss of the subjunctive was lamented by Johnson and others. It persisted longest in conditional clauses: if any judgment *be made*, (Johnson, *ibid.*); if your quarrel *be grounded* (Dryden, *Essay of Dramatick Poesy*); if confidence *presage* a victory (*ibid.*); if anything *were wanting* (Burke, *Speech on Conciliation*).

---

[22] According to Charles Carpenter Fries, "The Periphrastic Future with Shall and Will in Modern English," *PMLA*, XL (1925), 963—1024, the preference for *will* in the first person was as high as 90%, as compared with 10% for *shall*, about the year 1680. The shift to the latter form is attributed to the teaching of schoolmasters. The author gives figures indicating fluctuating usage of *shall / will* in all three persons down to the present time.

Among other inflections of verb forms, two developments are important. One is the establishment of -(e)s for the third person singular of the present tense, the only suffix in the entire verbal system to indicate person and number. All other verb forms have what may be called a zero suffix associated with these categories. The endings -est and -eth in the present tense were lost in the 17th century except, once again, for discourse affected by Biblical style. Milton still has the form *he hath*, quite habitually, but after 1700 it was archaic. The second development referred to affected the two systems, strong and weak, of the conjugation of verbs for tense. Strong verbs continued their tendency to shift into the weak conjugational system, so that today only 66 of those originally strong have remained in that group. They may be listed as follows, classified according to the Germanic ablaut series to which they belong by origin.[23]

Class 1: *abide, bite, drive, ride, rise, shine, strike, slide, smite, stride, write*

Class 2: *choose, freeze, cleave* (i. e., to split), *fly*

Class 3: (a) with short vowels: *begin, cling, drink, run, shrink, sing, sink, sling, slink, spin, spring, stink, swim, swing, win, wring*
(b) with lengthened vowels: *bind, find, fight, grind, wind*

Class 4: *bear, break, come, steal, tear*

Class 5: *bid, eat, give, get, lie, see, sit, speak, tread, weave*

Class 6: *draw, forsake, shake, slay, stand, swear, take*

Class 7: *befall, blow, fall, grow, hang, hold, know, throw*

This list is of course restricted to verbs which are historically strong. It omits those which today show internal vowel changes for tense, if they were originally weak: e. g., *bring, catch, hide, sell*. A few verbs also excluded are those which have been attracted wholly or in part to the strong verbal inflection by analogy: *chide, dig, fling, string, strive* (a Romance word) and *thrive*.

During the 18th century there was a tendency of limited scope to level the principal parts of strong verbs to two instead of three. Instances may be found in the works of the best standard writers: a spider *has wove* (Gibbon); let them *be wrote* (Mandeville); by turns *have rose* (Prior); will *have stole* it (Swift); some disaster *has befell* (Gay). But this tendency, like so many others, was checked by prescriptive grammarians and schoolmasters, so that most strong verbs today have three different tense forms.

---

[23] The list is to be found in Charles C. Fries, *American English Grammar* (New York, 1940), p. 61. As given here it is slightly reorganised.

One rather important inflectional novelty was introduced into English in the late 18th century and established by the early 19th. This was the passive voice of the progressive (or continuous) conjugation. Although the progressive active had long since become familiar, as in: I *am attacking*, the corresponding passives like: I *am being attacked*, had not been in use. The nearest approach to them had been a neutral phrase, a verbal noun introduced by the preposition *on* in a weakened form *a-*: the house is *a-burning*; the house is *a-building*. Here, as in gerund constructions like: there is talk *of attacking*, there is no formal indication whether the speaker is in active or passive relation to the attack. Earlier English had, to be sure, made use of something like the passive progressive in absolute constructions such as: this *being known*.... Just before 1800 the finite passive progressive began to appear in expressions such as: the book *is being written*; the treaty *was being discussed*. The construction is still avoided, however, in the future and in all perfect tenses. Instead of: it *will be being discussed*, we have simply: it *will be discussed*.

A few other details were subjected to formal regulation at this time. For instance, use of the nominative forms of pronouns was now required after the finite forms of the verb *to be*. Correctness called for: it is *I*, although popular usage has continued to admit of an objective form (analogous to the French disjunctive nominative in: *c'est moi*) in most persons: it's *me, him, them,* etc. Modern grammar has learned to treat such matters more liberally than did that of the 18th century. Yet in a few details present usage is stricter than the older. Dryden and his contemporaries frequently introduced a dependent relative clause with *and who* or *and which*, though it was not parallel with any preceding clause: great masters in our language, *and who* saw much farther... than those who immediately followed them (Dryden, Preface to *The Fables*). Such non-parallel relative constructions are to be observed in 18th century writers also, but they are avoided today.

6. Levels of Style

In those aspects of sentence structure which are important for the style of formal writing, two strong influences are perceptible: the Hebrew, indirectly conveyed to English through the enormously influential King James version of the Bible, and the Latin, still strongly persistent though less conspicuous than in the Elizabethan age.

In Biblical Hebrew, simple statements follow a word order not far different from that of English. Noun relations are expressed by a fairly simple device in which position is of primary importance; inflection is not much more complicated than in modern English. The verbal system in Hebrew has a certain complexity, but though its categories differ somewhat from the English, they run along similar lines. For these reasons a fairly literal translation of Hebrew gives an acceptable result, stylistically, in English. Even idioms can be rendered with no more violence to the language than a quaint flavour of differentness. The normal relation of a noun dependent on one preceding it may be expressed in English by a phrase introduced by the preposition *of* (the so-called descriptive genitive): Lord *of hosts*, man *of Galilee*. This is closely paralleled by the construct case in Hebrew, making the second of two nouns in sequence dependent on the first. In the more exalted and poetic passages of Hebrew, as in the Psalms and heightened dramatic narratives, rhythmical effect is achieved by a pairing of sentence parts, a repetition of ideas embodied in similar constructions, mostly in paratactical relationship. This type of syntactic balancing is also readily achievable in English. In the 17th century particularly, those writers of the Puritan cause who stood closest to the Bible as a source of inspiration naturally fell into sentence patterns of the same type. This also meant a preference for archaic forms of pronouns and verbs (*thou* and *thee*; verbal endings *-est* and *-eth*; imperatives with pronoun subjects expressed: *go thou*; *mark ye*, etc.). John Bunyan thus built his sentences very often on the Hebrew model at second hand; but he also introduced some absolutes and delaying participles on the model of the Latin.

It was the Latin structure that was still most influential on formal writing, though with diminished flamboyance as compared with the writing of the 16th century. The sermons of Jeremy Taylor (died 1667) contain passages developed in long "Ciceronian" periods, with elaborate suspensions and hypotaxis, complex parallelisms, and mannered sound effects, especially rhythmical conclusions or cadences. A contrasting style known as "curt" was marked by short staccato units of similar length, sometimes unconnected. Both of these styles have antecedents going back to classical antiquity.[24] Milton's prose and his poetry too reflect Latin influence, occasionally in the periodicity of the sentence structure (though the elaborate clauses themselves are sometimes loosely

---

[24] James Roy King, "Certain Aspects of Jeremy Taylor's Prose Style," *English Studies*, XXXVII (1956), 197—210; George Williamson, *The Senecan Amble* (University of Chicago Press, 1951).

strung together),[25] occasionally in the word order, idioms and syntactic constructions which give the impression of someone unconsciously thinking in Latin patterns before expressing himself in the vernacular. The same is true of Sir Thomas Browne in his dignified reflections on life and death, history and archaeology, —reflections which were often adorned by patterns of prose rhythm.

A plain, informal style with loose constructions, uneven units and irregular incidence of accentuation was used by these same writers in their correspondence and casual essays. The Quakers, having begun with a rather decorative style, turned to a plain style as the form of expression best suited to the simplicity of their doctrines and manners.[26]

The height of neo-classicism brought with it a style that combined the advantages of a clear and disciplined order (learned in part from the Latin) with ease and flexibility of expression. John Dryden is one of the first to achieve this happy balance. He may use complex delaying clauses, parallel constructions and Latinate turns of expression; but these are not obtrusive. The sentences of his *Essay of Dramatick Poesy*, in dialogue form, are carefully correct, but they also have a conversational air about them. Unobtrusive devices like ellipsis (e. g., asyndeton) contribute to the flow: I think there is none among us can imagine... (*Essay*). The occasional absolutes, parallel constructions and interrupting clauses and participles are not overdone: the plots of their plays being narrow, and the persons few, one of their acts was written in less compass than one of our well-wrought scenes (*ibid.*); He [Shakespeare] was the man who of all modern, and perhaps ancient poets, had the largest and most comprehensive soul (*ibid.*). A certain looseness in the handling of relative pronouns, already referred to, served to increase the effect of informality: They can produce nothing so courtly writ, *or which* expresses so much the conversation of a gentleman (*ibid.*). A subdued and easy classicism also marks the writing of Addison,

---

[25] Robert Martin Adams, in *Ikon: John Milton and the Modern Critics* (Cornell University Press, 1955), pp. 190 ff., illustrates the extent to which the poet attempted to obtain for English some of the effects of Latin, but he also shows how the effects of the "extended style" differ from classical periodicity. The units, though impressive, are sometimes episodically put together.

[26] Jackson I. Cope, "Seventeenth Century Quaker Style," *PMLA*, LXXI (1956), 725—54. The earliest Quakers, as for instance George Fox in his Journal, permitted themselves the use of metaphors, balanced repetitions, periodic sentence structure and ejaculatory expressions, all later eschewed.

Swift and Steele. Even Johnson, though more ponderous in his stylistic effects, is none the less sure and unlaboured in building up his structures. One's attention is neither strained nor distracted in following the sequence of his periods. Burke himself, though speaking in an oratorical style where extended periods were felt to be eminently appropriate, never sacrificed clarity and ease to intricacy of syntactic form.

In verse sentences, which wei often confined within riming couplets or other short units with end-stopped lines, balanced coordinate elements are frequently found. Symmetry of construction is cultivated. Units in inverted order neatly balance like units in normal order:

> This, only this, the rigid law pursues,   O=OSV
> This, only this, provokes the snarling Muse. S=SVO
> Samuel Johnson, *London*

In verse as in prose, exaggerated periodicity was generally avoided in the 18th century, but there are occasional examples of it, obviously imitative of the classical: for instance, the more elaborate similes translated or paraphrased by Pope from Homer's *Odyssey*.

Conversational style is best represented in the neo-classical period in its comedies, beginning with the Restoration and extending throughout the 18th century. Of course the language is here stylised to a great extent; we may assume that the average cultivated person did not habitually indulge in discourse replete with examples of brilliant antithesis, anticlimax and *double entendre*. Still, the rapid exchanges of dialogue in these plays give us many turns of expression, constructions and idioms then current which did not find their way into more formal prose writing.[27] Relaxed writing, as it has been called, may also be studied in letters and diaries, for instance in the London journal kept by James Boswell, which has recently been the subject of careful linguistic analysis.[28] From this it appears that cultivated persons, moving in the best literary society, were quite capable of violating a number of the rules laid down in the formal grammars of the time. Boswell deviates from prescribed agreement of verb with subject when he writes (with the example of others to support him):

---

[27] H. C. Wyld has studied these in his *History of Modern Colloquial English* (London, rev. ed., 1921), ch. 10.

[28] Esther Sheldon, "Boswell's English in the London Journal," *PMLA*, LXXI (1956), 1067—93. Examples cited are taken from this article. The *Journal* has been edited by Frederick A. Pottle (New York, 1950).

Madam, you said *you was* not a Platonist (*Journal*, p. 101); he yokes a plural demonstrative pronoun with a singular noun in the phrase: *these kind*; he misplaces adverbs: we *only* got a drowsy headache (p. 42, for: *got only a...*); he commits what the grammarians then called "concealed errors" in elliptical expressions where the "proper" form is not carried over but must be supplied: he never has gone, and never will [go]. Even at the height of the age of correctness, then, deviations from the usage prescribed by its grammarians and rhetoricians were not uncommon in certain contexts. As in earlier ages, there were levels of discourse distinguishable within the generally unified system of the accepted national language, and these must be taken into account by any student who tries to form a picture of the conditions of speech in a given era of the past.

CHAPTER VI

MODERN ENGLISH DIALECTS AND THEIR LITERARY USES

1. THE RISING INTEREST IN NON-STANDARD FORMS OF ENGLISH

The cultural attitudes prevailing during the neo-classical age were not auspicious either for the cultivation of original literature in local dialects, or for the scholarly investigation of these and other types of non-standard English. When most authors were looking upon conformity to rules of correctness and decorum as a primary merit, they were not apt to turn their attention to divergent forms of the language or to attempt to embody any of them in their own creative work. Neither would speakers of dialect find a good reception if they tried to gain from polite society a hearing for literature based on their native ways of speaking. The unified national standard, triumphant together with the establishment of a unified political government, was further fortified under 17th-century absolutism, when the royal court set the tone for many aspects of social life. Even after the final defeat of absolutism in 1688, London's world of fashion, still centred on the court, enjoyed a prestige which ensured the universal acceptance of its speech as standard. Whatever interest was occasionally expressed in non-standard English was apt to be intermittent and condescending.

Nevertheless, that interest did appear from time to time. Lexicographers of the 17th and 18th centuries paid some attention to the cant of the underworld and to other special jargons. Their word-lists represent somewhat more systematic investigations that those of their predecessors in the 16th century who had written pamphlets about thieves, beggars and conny-catchers. Elisha Coles listed terms from such jargons in his *English Dictionary* (1670), and Nathaniel Bailey offered more in his *Universal Etymological Dictionary* (1721). An anonymous writer, "B. E., Gent.," produced a separate *Dictionary of the Canting Crew* (ca 1690), which was devoted entirely to the language of the underworld. It included terms already known to the Elizabethans: for instance, *harmans* for stocks, *mort* for a woman, *nip* meaning to steal a purse. In addition, many new terms were given: *briers* for trouble; *glim* for a thief's dark lantern; *jenny* and *betty* (girls' nicknames) for instruments used in robbing; *fork* for a pickpocket; *dead men* for empty pots or bottles at a drinking bout; *mill* (as verb) for to steal. As can be seen from these examples, the origins are various: metaphors, proper names, shortened forms of standard words, and so on.[1] A number of these expressions persisted into the early 19th century. Others, however, had a short life. Shifting terminology is characteristic of the jargon used in illicit occupations, since the purpose behind much of the vocabulary is not only to communicate rapidly and vividly, but also to mystify any representatives of the law who may be within earshot.

A very curious device was worked out, it appears, among coster-mongers of London in the mid-19th century who were on doubtful terms with the police. To evade understanding by outsiders, they roughly approximated a reverse pronunciation, attempting to say the important words backwards: *yenep* for penny; *neves yenep* for seven pence; *say* for *yes*; *dab* for *bad(ly)*; *cool* for look; *namesclop* for policeman *kanurd* for drunk, *top o' reeb* for pot o' beer. The form *on* was used for *no* and also for a negative prefix or a suffix with various meanings. In addition there were some coined expressions for particular situations:

> tumble to your barrikin: understand you
> cool ta the dillo nemo: look at the little woman
> flash it: show it
> a regular trosseno: a regular bad one (bad sort)
> a doogheno or dabheno: is it a good or a bad market?

Henry Mayhew, who recorded these expressions, pointed out that many who used them could neither read nor write. Hence the jargon was not based on spelling but on speech habits as heard from illiterate speakers.[2] It was of course in no sense a rival of the national language; merely a curious aberration in vocabulary conditioned by the special status of a derelict *lumpenproletariat* in the 19th century.

---

[1] Material from B. E.'s *Dictionary of the Canting Crew* and other sources is contained in Eric Partridge's *Dictionary of Slang and Unconventional English* (London 1937). See M. Schlauch, *The Gift of Tongues* (reprinted as *The Gift of Language*, New York, 1955), p. 276 f.

[2] H. Mayhew, *London Labour and the London Poor*, 4 vols., I (London, 1861), p. 23 f.

Slang embraces a broader field than cant or special jargons. It includes temporarily fashionable expressions which are overused by great numbers of people, and rather quickly die out precisely because they have been overused. These aberrations from standard English certainly existed in the 18th century, as we know from Jonathan Swift's indignant protests (ch. 5, sec. 2), and also in part from the lighter literature of the time. Dictionaries of the age give us less information on general slang than on the picturesque special vocabularies current in the 18th century.[3] But scholarly interest in these vocabularies goes back to that period. Today, creative writers manifest a lively interest in slang as linguistic material needed in the realistic imitation of certain types of non-standard speech.

The regional dialects of English had suffered an eclipse of interest since the late Middle Ages. Some characterisation through dialect had persisted —though only in a stylised manner— to supply humour and local colour in Elizabethan drama. But this device later fell into disuse. The country swains of 18th-century pastorals and plays, when they are allowed to appear at all, speak quite classical English. Even John Gay's operettas of the London underworld conceded little to linguistic realism.

It was only with the beginning of that literary movement which we call Romanticism that men of letters, artists and scholars began to turn their attention seriously to the investigation of regional dialects. The reasons for this shift of interest are complex. Partly they have to do with obviously political factors. The forces which were gathering strength for the overthrow of the French absolute monarchy were of course inimical to a dominant courtly style of correctness with respect to art forms and language. Hence they were *a priori* favourable to popular regional speech contrasting with the officially accepted norm. The rising French revolt against courtly classicism naturally had echoes in other countries, including England. As partial manifestation of this revolt we find a new vogue for medieval (as opposed to standard neo-classical) texts; hence, for that very reason, a vogue for texts in various dialects. We find a revulsion away from the periphrases and formalities of conventional diction, and a new enthusiasm for the simple language of ordinary people; of people remote from the courts, living in agricultural communities rather than great cities. Traditional ballads became popular, along with fairy tales and what passed as "primitive" poetry (Ossianic verse) in the late 18th century. The underlying causes of this reaction in literary-

---

[3] Eric Partridge, *Slang To-day and Yesterday* (London, 1933), and also the *Dictionary* cited in n. 1.

linguistic taste are deep and often obscure. From one point of view, the reaction is surely connected with the upsurge of anti-royalist and democratic sentiments. From another, it was connected with less progressive tendencies such as an abnegation of the positive achievements of the Enlightenment, a retreat from reason into irrationalism, an uncritical nostalgia for the Middle Ages, and so on. In short, Romanticism as a general trend is too complex to be classified in a few brief sentences. It showed common features in various spheres of cultural activity, but those were features of style and medium of expression, not pertaining directly to the ideologies expressed.

In English, the manifesto announcing a preference for simple, non-courtly speech was of course the famous Preface written by Wordsworth to the second edition (1800) of the *Lyrical Ballads* composed by himself and Coleridge. Here Wordsworth subjected to sharp attack the traditional language of 18th-century poetry, with its elaborate diction, its periphrases, its frigid personifications and its formal regularities. Students of rural society in the 18th century have many reasons for challenging his idealised picture of peasant life and its speech. Wordsworth's own practice failed to conform to his rather unrealistic demands. But there is no doubt that his manifesto was timely, eloquent, and in accord with a contemporary change in literary taste.

Already in the years before Wordsworth's Preface, the English literary world had been celebrating the resurgence and triumph of one regional dialect as exemplified in the poetry of Robert Burns. Its success was in part explainable by the unique genius of the author, whose originality was easily perceived and appreciated across the dialectal barriers. The success was also in part explainable by the fact that Scottish English had a long history as an independent national language in its own right. Even when the country lost its political independence by the Act of Union (1707), the independent literary tradition was not lost, and the local speech was not replaced by the English of London. Thus Burns had a solid linguistic basis for his creative work, which did not by any means spring up in response to a mere passing literary fad.

The scientific study of dialects is an achievement of modern times. The standard work of reference is still Joseph Wright's *English Dialect Dictionary*, with its associated *English Dialect Grammar*, completed in the first years of the 20th century. Since then further detailed studies have been made on the basis of new information and new techniques in gathering it: interviews, questionnaires, recordings by phonograph, etc. Data thus collected give evidence for the distribution of certain key words and pronunciations which vary from region to region. The lines of demarcation on a map showing where test usage changes are

called isoglosses. With the shifting of population in recent decades, and
the introduction of new forms of aural mass communication (cinema,
radio, television), the old boundaries have become less stable than they
were formerly, and the distinctive traits are tending to disappear as
urban life spreads its influence over the countryside. Nevertheless the
rich and detailed information given by Wright can still be used as a basis
for a general brief description of the surviving English dialects.

2. Literary Scots in Modern Times

For the non-specialist interested in regional forms of ModE, a chief
reason for mastering dialect forms is a desire to become acquainted with
the literature composed in them or making partial use of them. In the
present chapter we shall attempt no more than general guidance as an
aid to the reading knowledge of a representative group of them.

Literary Scots[4] can claim a leading position because of its early
reemergence into eminence as the vehicle used by Robert Burns. An
early aid to the study of the language was offered in John Jamieson's
Etymological Dictionary of the Scottish Language,[5] which affirmed an
attitude like Wordsworth's in its Preface: "The peasantry are the living
depositories of the ancient language of every country"— a statement
which requires explanation, if not essential qualification. While some
prose writers like Walter Scott contented themselves with the use of
regional speech in dialogue passages only, others in the 19th century
began to use it for sustained narrative: for instance, W. Alexander and
John Watson, writing under the pseudonym of Ian Maclaren. There
was a series of minor but very interesting poets who employed the native
language forcefully to express proletarian grievances and aspirations.
They include: David Shaw (1786—1856), who in his "Tammie Treddlefeet" (see Appendix) reflects the plight of unemployed weavers; Edward
L. Sloan (ca 1800—60), who records in "The Weaver's Triumph" the
treatment accorded to an independent worker trying to sell his wares;

---

[4] The situation for all of Scotland is described by Angus McIntosh,
Introduction to a Survey of Scottish Dialects (Edinburgh, 1952), to be
followed by a series of special studies entitled *Linguistic Survey of Scotland.*

[5] First ed. (Edinburgh, 1808); revised and republished (1846 and
1867). The two authoritative modern dictionaries are both in progress
of publication: Sir William Craigie and others, *Dictionary of the Older
Scottish Tongue,* and William Grant and David Murison, *The Scottish
National Dictionary* (Oxford and Edinburgh respectively).

Dorothea Maria Ogilvy of Clova (1823—95), who in "The Weary Spinnin O't" voices the plaint of a woman worker under the same conditions; and Ellen Johnston (1835—75), who in "The Last Sark" vividly describes the plight of a family whose bread-winner is without work.[6] There are other writers of this school during the 19th century.

Today the linguistic situation in Scotland (and elsewhere) is such that there is a divergence between the English officially used and taught in the schools, and the various forms of native speech current among many people. The term commonly applied to the native Lowland English, as opposed to the Gaelic language spoken in the Highlands, is Lallans.[7] The use of Lallans for literary purposes has been vindicated anew by a group of talented modern poets, including Sydney Goodsir Smith, Sir Alexander Gray, Hugh MacDiarmid (C. M. Grieve) and others.[8]

In its outstanding features modern Scots shows a few specific traits of conservatism when compared with the language of the late Middle Ages. Some vowel and consonant sounds have remained close to those prevailing in Old Northern English, though there is variety of treatment under specific conditions.[9] Other sounds have changed as much as in Southern English, but in different directions.

---

[6] All of these poems are contained in the anthology *Scottish Verse 1851—1951*, ed. Douglas Young (London, 1952).

[7] Geoffrey Wagner, "The Use of Lallans for Prose," *Journal of English and Germanic Philology*, LI (1952), 212—25. For bibliographies see David Murison, "Studies in Scots since 1918," *Anglia*, LXIX (1950), 387—97; J. S. Woolley, *Bibliography for Scottish Linguistic Studies* (Edinburgh, 1954).

[8] Linguistic separateness has been used as one argument supporting a movement towards political independence for Scotland, and it is true that literary Scots has a special historical status as compared with other dialects in England. On the other hand, it is doubtful whether the future of Scottish culture could be best served by a political separation which would place an additional barrier between the working people of both countries.

[9] The following remarks refer to literary Scots generally as it is conventionally recorded, and make no effort to indicate the many local variations existing in the spoken language. Details may be found in the section on phonology in Wright's *English Dialect Dictionary* and *Grammar* (Oxford, 1905). The pronunciation of many individual words has been disturbed by the influence of standard English, whereas others have remained unaffected.

Vowels show the following chief traits:

OE ū   has remained essentially unchanged. It is usually written
            oo, as in: *oot, aboot*, etc. In Southern Scots it is sometines
            diphthongised to *eu* ([ɐu] in Wright's notation) when final,
            as in *now*.

OE ō,   having been raised and rounded in MScots, appears as
            [œ:] and [y:], sometimes shortened (Wright, 161 f.). It
            is written *ui, eu* and (by A. Gray) *ü: puir* for *poor, stüde*
            for *stood, leuk* for *look* (Burns).

OE ā   after *w* has been preserved as [a(:)] or shifted to [ɔ:]
            in some parts of Scotland, both sounds being conven-
            tionally written as *a: wha, twa*, etc. But in other parts,
            especially the Southeast, the vowel has been raised to
            long *ē* [e:] (Wright, 120 f.), often represented by *ae:*
            whae, wae, etc. OE *ā* in other positions is also fronted,
            either to this same *ē* or to [i:]. For OE *stān* conventional
            spelling records dialect variants like: *stane, steen, styane*.
            Examples of *ē* are: *hame* for *home, claith* for *cloth, laird*
            for *lord*.[10]

ME ā   lengthened under special conditions from OE short *a*,
            has fallen together with OE *ā: share, shame, bairn*.

ME ē,   open and closed, has not shortened before tongue-tip
            consonants as in a certain group of ModE words. Hence
            we find *deid* for *dead, reid* for *red*.

MScots u,   original and shortened from *ū*, appears as *i* in a number
            of dialect forms: *hinney* for *honey, mither* for *mother*.

MScots i   appears conversely as *u: wull* for *will, fush* for *fish, grup*
            for *grip*.

MScots ī   has been preserved undiphthongised in some dialects
            before -*nd* as in: *find, blind, behind*, etc.

Diphthongs developed before certain consonants. Thus *a* before *l* gave
rise to *au* before another consonant, whether or not the *l* remained:
cald > cauld, hald > haud. Similarly, *o* followed by *l* gave rise to
ou, spelled *ow: folk > fowk; poll > pow*. Before -*ch* (see below) the
diphthong *eu* is found for OE *ō* in: *eneuch* for *enough, pleuch* for
plow, etc.

---

[10] A. McIntosh, *op. cit.*, p. 59 f. On p. 117 there is a map showing
distribution of contemporary forms developed from OE *stān*.

Consonants show a number of points of contrast with Southern dialects.

f and v were lost when final in unaccented words like *of*; they also
disappeared intervocalically in many words: *o'er* for *over*; *hae* for
have; *gie* for *give*.

m and n were lost already in MScots when final in unaccented words
(compare: Old Scandinavian languages): *i'* for *in*, *frae* for *from*,
o' for *on*.

th [θ] final has been lost in the unaccented word *with*.

d final is lost after -*n*: *win'* for *wind*, *frien'* or *freen'* for *friend*.

k and g have been retained unmodified, in contrast to many palatalised
equivalents in cognate Southern words: *kirk* for *church*, *birk* for
birch, *rig* for *ridge*, *mickle* for *much* (compare the family name
Mitchell). These forms often represent loans from OScand.

sk appears as *s* in unaccented words like: *sall* for *shall*, *suld* for *should*,
sanna for *shall not*. Cf. MScots.

ch, representing a single phoneme with variant pronunciations [ç]
and [χ] according to position, is heard in words like: *michty*, *eneuch*,
loch.

l following a back vowel is often lost when final: *fu'* for *full*, *ha'* for
hall; it may also be vocalised before a consonant: *haud* for *hold*.
The combinations *lf* and *lv* are assimilated to *ll* in: *siller* for *silver*,
sel' for *self*.

r is strongly trilled and preserved in all positions. It occasionally shows
metathesis with the neighbouring vowel: *trufs* for *turfs*, *girdle* for
griddle.

The morphology of ModScots recalls the older language in a number
of points. One of them is the occasional use of -*s* with other forms of
the present tense of the verb besides the third singular (but this trait
also appears widely in other dialects today). Another is the use of the
suffix -*it* (compare OScand -*it*, -*ið*) for -*ed* in the past tense and perfect
participle forms of weak verbs: *theekit* for *thatched*, *restit* for *rested*, etc.
The present participle (as in most other contemporary dialects) has been
changed from -*ing* [iŋ] to -*in*; a variant ending -*an* is used by Sydney
Goodsir Smith. Archaic forms of the demonstrative are to be found:
thir and *thae* for *those*. Some nouns have weak plurals unknown to
Southern English, for instance *een* for *eyes*.

The vocabulary of ModScots is varied, colourful, and (to one not
a native) often baffling. The large number of Scandinavian words, the
considerable number of Celtic ones and the scattering of French loans

not current in the South, all reflect the chequered events of Scottish
political history. Here are some examples:

From Celtic:

clachan: a hamlet	gillie: a man-servant
clan: a class or set of people	linn: a pool
coronach: a dirge	strath: a valley
?ingle: a fire or fire-place	tocher: a dowry

Scandinavian:

big: to build < byggja	graith: to prepare < greiða
gar: to cause, to make < görva	roose: to praise < hrósa
	(Mod. Dan. *at rose*)

From French:

bonnie: pretty < bon, bonne	genty: fine, delicate < gentille
braw: brave (cf. also Dan. *brav*)	tenty: careful < attentif, -ive

A few lines from Burns's poem "Guid Ale" will illustrate some of the
above traits:

> O, guid ale comes, and guid ale goes,
>   Guid ale gars me sell my hose,
> Sell my hose, and pawn my shoon;
>   Guid ale keeps my heart aboon....
> Guid ale hauds me bare and busy,
>   Gars me moop wi' the servant hizzy,
> Stand i' the stool when I ha'e done;
>   Guid ale keeps my heart aboon.

Here we have the characteristic preservation of long $\bar{u}$ in *aboon*, the
typical development of long $\bar{o}$ in *guid*, the shift of short *u* to *i* in *hizzy*,
the diphthong *au* from original *al* in *haud*, the loss of -*n* in *i'* and of -*v-*
in *ha'e*. The verb *to gar* is one of the most widely used loan-words from
Scandinavian.[11]

---

[11] See further Erdmut Lehman, *Die französischen Lehn- und Fremd-
wörter in den Werken von Robert Burns* (Breslau, 1933); J. Wilson, *The
Dialect of Robert Burns* (Oxford University Press, 1923); Per Thorson,
*Anglo-Norse Studies: An Inquiry into the Scandinavian Elements in
Modern English Dialects* (Amsterdam, 1936).

3. Northern English Dialects

The dialects in the Northern counties of England proper[12] have had no such literary renaissance in modern times as that enjoyed by the Scottish. The reasons lie of course in the quite different social and political contexts. When a standard national language is established under modern industrial society, with political unity long since realised, the conditions become much less favourable for a separate literary life of the dialects. As spoken, these latter become more and more restricted in currency and tend to die out before the invasion of the standard speech as inculcated in schools and conveyed generally through films, radio and television. The movement of working-class families in search of employment in industry has also contributed to the blurring of dialects and the reduction of their importance.

Nevertheless the regional dialects have remained on English territory, preserved with especial fidelity in rural areas. By the 19th century, normal literary works were no longer composed in such dialects. Vanished and forgotten by most were the days of Richard Rolle, the Yorkshire mystic who in the 14th century wrote highly sophisticated lyrical prose in the dialect of the region. When Wordsworth wrote about peasants of the Cumberland area he did not attempt to employ the local vernacular as part of his delineation. For the most part, dialect writing for the North country, as for other areas, has been limited to conversations interpolated in books otherwise composed in standard English: for instance, some fragmentary Yorkshire passages in *Wuthering Heights* by Emily Brontë. More recently a similar literary use of the Yorkshire dialect has been exemplified in the humorous stories of Eric Knight called *Sam Small Flies Again*.[13] Here once more the dialect is limited to conversations, but Knight devotes an unusually large part of the text to them.

When literary writers of standard English interpolate passages in dialect, they often tend to rely on a few outstanding traits of pronun-

---

[12] This dialect area includes: Northumberland, North Durham, South Durham, most of Cumberland, Westmoreland, Northern Lancashire, the North and East Ridings of Yorkshire and the hilly parts of the West. See W. W. Skeat, *English Dialects* (Cambridge University Press, 1912), p. 108. It must be remembered, however, that some traits of the North Country extend into Northern Midland areas as far as Southern Lancashire.

[13] Reprinted in the United States as *The Flying Yorkshireman* (1942).

ciation, inflection and phraseology which they overwork in order to obtain their effects. For a different reason (that is, limited talent) there may be a similar paucity of effects in the songs written by naive composers using the regional dialects. These products are nevertheless interesting. For Northern English we have a curious body of songs which have come down to us from the mid-19th century, a period of bitter proletarian struggles in the mining and textile industries. These verses reflect the same conditions of misery and extreme exploitation which were eloquently placed before the world in Friedrich Engels's classic description of the *Conditions of the Working Class in Great Britain* (1844). Since then, other scholars have added further detailed information on this aspect of labour history. A collection of songs from the Northern coalfields, some of them written a century and more ago, is now available in a collection entitled *Come All Ye Bold Miners*.[14] A very moving example of verse dealing with the plight of Lancashire weavers is contained in Mrs. Gaskell's novel *Mary Barton* (see Appendix). Tennyson made two experimental efforts adapt the Lancashire dialect to poetic expression in his "Northern Farmer: Old Style" and "Northern Farmer: New Style."

Stylised spelling, often arbitrarily employed, makes these literary efforts difficult for uninitiated readers. However, a few general principles may be cited which will help in the recognition and interpretation of linguistic traits.

Vowels appear as follows:

ME ū, though preserved in some areas of the Northern counties (where it is spelled *oo* as in *hoose* for *house*, East and South Yorkshire and North Lancashire), has elsewhere diphthongised into [au], [aə] and [eə], spelled *eaw* (occasionally also [ɑ:] in other regions; Wright 170 f.)

ME ō has been retained as unshortened [u:] in parts of Yorkshire, Northern Cumberland and parts of Lancashire; it appears as [iu] in parts of Northumbria and in North Durham (Wright, 161 f.). Northwest Yorkshire has [ia] as well, in words like: *bloom, doom, gloom* (Wright, 162). The spelling to be found, for instance in the *Miners' Songs*, is often *yu* or *ew* or *eu*: *tyuk* for *took*, *neun* for *noon*, *lewk* for *look*. The ME *o* lengthened in an open syllable appears as [uə] in Northumbria, Durham, and parts of Yorkshire (Wright, 92 f.).

ME ī, represented by [ai] in standard English, is simplified to [ɑ:], especially when final and before voiced consonants, as

---

[14] Compiled by A. L. Lloyd (London: Lawrence and Wishart, 1952).

in: *my, mine,* etc. This may be observed in many parts of Yorkshire. The conventional spelling is *ah* or *aw*. Other diphthongs representing a continuation of ME long *ī* in Northern and North Midland counties are *ei* and *oi* (Wright, 153 f.). Thus Tennyson writes *toithe* for *tithe*. The result of ME short *i* followed by *ht* is also reflected in the three values [ɑ:] and [ei] and [ɔi]: *raht* is written for *right* (Yorkshire), *moighty* for *mighty* (Lancashire), *neight* and *breight* for *night* and *bright* (North Cumberland and parts of Yorkshire).

ME ẹ̄ and ẹ have generally fallen together under [i:], as in standard English, but the diphthong [ei] also appears (Wright, 130 f., 136 f., 141 f.). Thus words like *feet, heat*; unshortened *ē* has become normal [i:] in *deed* for *dead, breed* for *bread*.

OE ā, instead of being shifted to *ē* as in many parts of Scotland, is represented by a falling diphthong [oə] or [uə] in various parts of the North country; the diphthongs [ia], [ie] and [iə] also appear in a word like *stone* (Wright, 120 f.). The combination *ā + w* remains in some Northern districts as in Scotland: *knaw* for *know*, etc.

ME ā̆ from short *a* lengthened in an open syllable has produced a variety of diphthongs, a number of them falling ones like [eə] and [iə]; simple long vowels are also recorded, e. g. [e:] as in *feyther* for *father*; and the values vary from word to word (Wright, 42 f.). In parts of Yorkshire and Lancashire *oi* [ɔi] appears in words like *lane*. Popular printed texts reflect these values in various ways. The *Miners Songs* have *fyece* for *face, gyet* for *gate*; Tennyson writes *raäte* for *rate, taäke* for *take*.

OE a/o before nasals fluctuates in words like: *many/ mony*.

OE æ has various reflexes, including [æ], [a], [e].

ME u short appears in spellings indicating [ʊ] rather than [ʌ].

ME ei appears as [i:], spelled *ee*, for instance in: *dee, ee* for *die, eye*.

In the treatment of consonants the Northern dialects reveal a number of traits comparable with those of literary Scots. There is the same tendency to drop final consonants in monosyllables not receiving sentence stress: *wi'* for *with, i'* for *in, fro'* for *from, o'* for *on*, etc. There is the same tendency to lose final *-l* after a vowel, giving *fu'* for *full, stoo'* for *stool, foo'* for *fool*, etc. When *l* vocalised after long *ō* from OE *ā*, the result was [ou], written *ow*, as compared with the *aw* of Scots: thus *owd, cowd* for *old, cold*. There are instances of metathesised *r*, as in *gert* for *great*. The unpalatalised equivalents of Southern palatalised consonants are frequently found in the Northern counties: *sic* for *such, pick* for *pitch, skirl* for *shrill,* esc. In some Northern districts the original *sk* appears as *s* in unaccented words: *sall* for *shall,* etc., as in Scots. There are words in which initial [j] has replaced [h]: *yead* for *head.* The semi-vowels [j] and [w] appear as on-glides before initial vowels in *yale* for *ale, woats* for *oats, yence* for *once.*

Special traits of morphology are concentrated chiefly in forms of pronouns and verbs. The old second singular pronoun is preserved in both stressed and unstressed forms: *thoo* and *thee* (both used for both nominative and accusative), *tha,* and the enclitic *-ta* in combinations like *wilta* for *wilt thou.* Very interesting is the survival of ME *hoo* from OE *heo* for the feminine pronoun (Lancashire). A sandhi-form of the article, namely *t'* for *the,* has become generalised in Yorkshire and appears in Lancashire also: *i' t' barn* for "in the barn"; *t' baileys* for "the bailiffs." In verbal inflections, the *-s* ending is often extended to other forms besides the third singular present; strong verbs are made weak or show tense forms differing from the Standard; the plural pre-terite *were* is extended to the singular in place of *was;* the present participle ending is *-in* instead of *-ing.* All of these more general traits mark other regional dialects besides the Northern; the specific differences in the choice of forms, for instance for auxiliaries and for tenses of cer-tain strong verbs, are matters belonging to the detailed investigation of dialects. Characteristic of the North is the use of forms like *maun* (also *mun, 'n*) and *mought* (*mid*) meaning *must, have to, be sure to.*

A few verses from a song commemorating the Durham strike of 1844 will illustrate some of the more obvious linguistic traits of this region. The lines are part of a dialogue, stylised of course by the composer of the text. The speaker is supposed to be a strike leader, Peter Fearless, who is trying to urge another worker to maintain solidarity with his mates.

> Now Dicky, was thoo at the meetin today?
> Aw looked, but aw saw nought o' thoo by the way.
> Aw hope that thoo's not turnin cowardly noo,
> Or yet thinkin o' gannin doon the coal-pit to hew....
>
> So let's keep up oor hearts, Dick, we're sure for to win,
> Our maisters aw knaw before lang will give in,
> Then let us stand fast, never stop by the way,
> And victory we'll shout when we win the day.

Here we find the typical [u:] for Standard [au] in *noo, oor*; the simplified diphthong in *aw* for *I*; the preservation of *a* plus *w* in *knaw,* the variant *lang* for *long*. The second person pronoun *thoo* is used for both nominative and accusative cases. Any other divergences from Standard English are concealed behind the conventional spelling. For more ambitious attempts to reproduce Northern dialects, see the Appendix.

4. SOUTHERN ENGLISH DIALECTS, INCLUDING COCKNEY

A few of the most striking characteristics of Southern Middle English, persisting into the 16th and 17th centuries, were seized upon and stylised by dramatists of that period to represent a kind of generalised rural speech. The most frequently featured details of this generalised Southern were the voicing of *s* and *f* to *z* and *v*, and the use of a few pronoun forms like *(h)un* for *him* (from OE *hine*). Thus Ben Jonson introduces a Southern countryman in *The Tale of a Tub*, who speaks thus:

> Let 'un bring a dog, but to my vace, that can
> Zay, I ha' beat hun, and without a vault;
> Or but a cat, will swear upon a book
> I have as much as zet a-vier her tail,
> And I'll give him or her a crown for 'mends.
> But to give out, and zay, I have robb'd a captain,
> Receive me at the latter day, if I
> Ere thought of any such matter, or could mind it.

Most of this is of course not only correct but even literary speech.

Nineteenth-century writers have attempted to present a wider range of regional traits when making use of the dialects. Here again, however, as in the North, they have for the most part limited themselves to the introduction of short passages of conversation in local dialects, more or less faithfully reported, in the context of long narratives in the standard language. Thomas Hardy (1840—1928) used scraps of local dialect in his stories about the Southwest region he called Wessex, centred in his native Dorsetshire. One of his outstanding heroines, Tess of the D'Urbervilles, is a simple, uneducated girl who is represented as speaking dialect for much of her short life. Yet despite the care lavished on the delineation of her personality and her environment, she is given few speeches —and none of them long— in her native idiom. More recently, other writers have also embodied more or less sustained vernacular conversations in novels otherwise recounted in standard English. An unusually successful combination of the two types of discourse is to be found in the stories of Mary Webb (1885—1927), dealing with the Western area

12

close to the Welsh border. For the rest we have chiefly collections of
short tales, fables, anecdotes and some songs. They are recorded with
varying degrees of fidelity to actual speech.

An exceptionally ambitious attempt to write consistently in a Southern
idiom (that of Dorset) was made by the 19th-century poet William
Barnes (1801—86). His verse is quite serious, unlike much else that is
composed in the modern dialects, but he does not reach the stature of
Burns, partly no doubt because of the limitation of his individual talent,
and partly too because his region offered him no national literary tradition
to be compared with that of Scotland. The enthusiasm of Barnes led
him to write a study of Dorset grammar and vocabulary[15] which, despite
its defects from the scholarly point of view, is a very valuable monument
of first-hand observation. The chief deviations from the vowel sounds
of Standard English, as described by Barnes and compared with Wright's
notation, are these:

ME ę̄   (from West Saxon *ēa* and *ǣ*) usually appears as a diphthong,
        [eə] [iə] (Wright, 130 f. and 182 f.), commonly rendered *eä* in the
        spelling: *cleän, beän*. There are variations in the treatment of
        individual words, both within the Dorset dialect and throughout
        the Southwest area. The [i:] of standard English also appears.
        In some Dorset words, Barnes records a type of open long *ę̄*
        not represented in what he calls "book-English:" for instance,
        in *bead, meat, read*. These he transcribes as: *bêd, mêt, rêd*.

ME e   in closed syllables is frequently raised to *i*, as in: *hidge* for *hedge,*
        min for *men, nit* for *net*. (The same shift of position is to be
        observed, more or less consistently, in other dialects of England
        and the United States.) ME short *e* in an originally open syllable
        was lowered and lengthened (to [æ:] in Dorset; elsewhere, as
        in Wiltshire, it changes to [iə]; (Wright 58 f.): e. g. in *break,*
        breach.

ME a   lengthened in an open syllable, as in words like: *bake, cake,*
        take, etc., is described by Barnes as a diphtong [ia], written
        eä; this corresponds to [iə] in Wright (42 f.), who reports [eə]
        also in the Southwest area. When initial, such a lengthened
        a may appear as [jeə], e. g. in *ache, acorn, acre*. Barnes illustrates
        a number of these diphthongs from ME lengthened *a* in the
        following question: "What have ye a-*meäde* o' the wold *leäme*
        meäre that you wer a leadèn up *leäne* vrom the meäd?" (= What

---

[15] W. Barnes, *A Glossary of the Dorset Dialect with a Grammar of Its*
Word Shapening and Wording (Dorchester, 1886).

have you done with the old lame mare that you were leading up the lane from the meadow?). In special combinations, as before [f], [ð], original *a* develops into [ɛ:] or [ei], spelled *ae* by Barnes: *haef, caef, faether,* for *half, calf, father.*

ME ū has diphthongised to [eu] in the Southwest, with variants such as [eü] and [əu] in East Devon and Dorset (Wright, 170 f.).

ME u has become a rising diphthong, described by Barnes as [əu] in words like: *crust, dust,* etc.

ME ō is either retained as [u:] from early ModE, or diphthongised to [uə] (Wright, 161 f.) in words like: *look, soon, food,* etc.

ME o lengthened in an originally open syllable has diphthongised to [oə] (Wright, 92 f.) in a number of words.

ME oi, of Romance origin, has become *ei* with a preceding on-glide *w*; the combination is written *wei*, thus: *bweile, pweint, cwein,* for *boil, point, coin.* It may be noted here that in various modern dialects there has been a fluctuation in the development of *oi*, the results appearing as both [ai] and [ɔi]. The emergence of [ai] in Norfolk, for instance, was due to a levelling of [ɔi] and [əi] from ME long *ī* in the early ModE period. Traces of that levelling appear elsewhere.

Consonants in Dorset speech show the conspicuous voicing of *s* and *f* already referred to. It is not recorded as universal, however; *sea* alternates with *zea*, etc. In addition, voiceless *th* [θ] becomes *d* before *r*, as in *drow* for *throw*. A voiceless *w* (called a "hard breathed *w*" by Barnes), derived from OE *hw*, contrasts with voiced *w* from OE *w*: thus *whey* is distinct from *way, which* from *witch*, etc. A *w* as on-glide has developed before long *ō* from OE long *ā*, not only initially as in some Northern forms, but also in the interior of words: *woats* for *oats, twoad* for *toad, bwold* for *bold.* In many words, *r* has been lost before a consonant without any subsequent lengthening of the preceding vowel: *hoss* for *horse, cuss* for *curse* (a trait also found in other dialects). There is frequent metathesis of *s* in words like *wapse* for *wasp, haps* for *hasp*; and either metathesis or dissimilation may explain *wordle* for *world*. When two liquids occur in juxtaposition they may be separated by either a dissimilatory consonant or an intrusive vowel: *twirel* or *twirdle* for *twirl, currel* or *curdle* for *curl,* etc.

The morphology of Dorset presents some very curious traits which are also to be found in other parts of the Southwest, for instance in Wiltshire. Among nouns, there is a noticeable extension of the old weak *-en* suffix for the plural: *cheesen, housen, pleäcen, vu'zen* (this last for "furze"). The pronouns preserve traces of OE forms elsewhere replaced by others: the archaic *thou* and *ye* as in Biblical usage, and also *en* (-*m* by assimilation) for the masculine dative-accusative, *em* (never *them*) for the plural of the same case. Personal pronouns are used to refer to inanimate things. Very striking is the use of nominative forms for emphatic accusatives. This is said to be so consistent that it might be more accurate to say that all pronouns have two forms in the accusative: one for emphasis, coinciding with the nominative, and a separate one developed from historical oblique forms, now serving in unemphatic constructions. Barnes illustrates the difference by these expressions: Gi'e *en* the knife; Gi'e *us* the wheat; but: Gi'e the money to *I* (*we*), not *he* (*they*). Among the verbs we find the usual shiftings from strong to weak, the regularising of weak forms, and the levellings already noted elsewhere, such as the extension of -*s* to other forms of the present tense besides the third singular. The infinitive when used absolutely (that is, without an object, and referring to iterative action) has a suffix -*y*; thus: How the dog do *jumpy*; or: Can ye *zewy*? (but not: Can ye *zewy up thëase* zêam?). A prefix *a*- [ə] functions like OE ʒe-, German *ge*-, as sign of the perfect participle: He've *a-broke* the dish.

Examples of Barnes's use of this dialect for creative writing, available in his collected poems, may be compared with the scraps of folkloristic poetry and actual conversation noted down in his *Grammar*. A typical passage of the latter, recorded in his not always consistent orthography, is the following reply he received from a countryman in response to a question about a new waggon he was driving:

> Why, the vust thing I do vine fate wi' is the drats; tha be too crooked: and the tug-irons be a-put in mwore than dree inches too vur back. An' jis' look here, where the rudge-tie and breechen rings be: why, nar a carter in the wordle can't put a hoss into en. I don't call the head and täil a-put out 'o han well. They be a-painted noo-how. Why 'e woon't bear hafe a luoad; tha've a-meäde en o' green stuff a-shook all to pieces. The vust time 'e 's a-haled out in the zun, e'll come all abrode. The strongest thing I do zee about en is the mâin pin; and he is too big by hafe (*Grammar*, p. 95).

Neighbouring Southwest dialects share many traits with Dorset. Passages from the dialect of Wiltshire, given in the Appendix, will offer a basis for typical comparison.

In the Southeast, the dialect which has attracted most attention in literary treatments is that aspect of London speech known as Cockney. According to Wyld,[16] this dialect exists on two levels. As spoken by the educated lower middle classes, it is a regional, urban-centred dialect like

---

[16] H. C. Wyld, *Modern Colloquial English*, pp. 5—7.

many others, contrasting with the official national language spoken side by side with it in the same city. It is marked by some deviations in pronunciation, but few in vocabulary or syntax. As spoken, however, in an impoverished form by the uneducated, it not only deviates noticeably in pronunciation but also in morphology and in the use of a special jargon as part of its vocabulary. This form of Cockney obviously represents a social handicap in competition with speakers of Standard English. G. B. Shaw's play *Pygmalion* clearly portrays the social implications of the contrast in speech. [16a]

As Dickens recorded it somewhat over a century ago in *Pickwick Papers*, Cockney was noteworthy for the interchange of the labial and labio-dental consonants *w* and *v*: *werry* for *very*, *vell* for *well*. This trait was lost by the end of the 19th century. The voiced and voiceless dental spirants [θ] and [ð] are replaced —though not consistently— by [f] and [v] respectively: *fing* for *thing*, *farver* for *father*. This substitution may be found in other dialects; it is not exclusively typical of Cockney. Better known to popular writers of dialect sketches is the interchange of aspirated and non-aspirated initial vowels: *hart* for *art*, *'eart* for *heart*. This too is a trait by no means limited to Cockney (especially the loss of historical *h*-), but it is here unusually conspicuous. The origin of the confusion, it has been suggested, goes back to the period of close contact between Anglo-Norman (with its lightly aspirated initial *h*'s) and Middle English (which inherited a stronger aspiration). The zeal of social inferiors for hypercorrectness may have been a factor in the situation. The glottal stops which appear in certain levels of the London dialect may on the other hand be due to the influence of Northern English dialects.

Another well-known trait of Cockney is the substitution of the diphthong [ai] for standard English [ei] of whatever origin: in *way, day, face, make*, for instance. Though in some cases like *day* it corresponds to an earlier ME *ai*, it is actually a modern development in such words also, not an unbroken continuation of the older sound. This dialectal *ai* is also found in other regions, notably in the Southwest counties (Wright, 48). There are other less striking features in the Cockney treatment of diphthongs, which may also be paralleled in other areas. Vowel length is sometimes indicated by inserting the letter *r*: *abart* for *about*, *orff* for *off*, and so on.

In its morphology and syntax, Cockney again parallels many usages found in other dialects. The *-s* ending is freely extended to other persons

---

[16a] See W. Matthews, *Cockney Past and Present* (London, 1938); J. Franklyn, *A Dictionary of Rhyming Slang* (London, 1960).

besides the third in the present tense of verbs: I *asks* you (often written: I *arsks* yer); you *asks*; we, you, they *asks*. The shift of strong verbs to the weak conjugation, the levelling of articles (*a* for *an* before words beginning with a vowel), the substitution of *-in'* for *-ing* in the present participle, the use of double negatives: all these may be found in regions quite distant from London.

Here are a few lines illustrating Shaw's effort to render Cockney dialect by means of conventional orthography:

> Ahrs is a Free Tride nition. It gows agin us as Hinglishmen to see these bloomin furriners settin up their Castoms Ahses and spheres o hinfluence and sich lawk hall owver Arfricar. Daownt Harfricar belong as much to huz as to them? thets wot we say.

(Captain Brassbound's Conversion, Act I).

In addition to traits already mentioned, we have here examples of the simplification of the diphthong [au] to [ɑ:] in *Ahses* for *Houses,* and of [ai] also to [ɑ:] in *lawk* for *like*; the modification of [ou] to [æu], [aou] in *daownt* for *don't*.

5. THE ENGLISH LANGUAGE IN IRELAND

In the neighbouring island of Ireland, the English language has had a special history. Here the original Celtic speech survived long after the triumph of Anglo-Saxon in England. But beginning with the feudal Middle Ages, the population of Eriu (then still living in a clan society) was subjected to a series of attacks which led eventually to its complete subjection. Ireland was reduced to the status of an English colony. Large tracts of land were acquired by English owners and farmed for them by Irish peasants, who were kept in conditions of extreme poverty. The landlords were usually non-resident or "absentee"; they cared only for the incomes squeezed out of the peasants' labour for them by their managing agents. To political and economic oppression there was added a harsh discrimination against the native Irish (Gaelic) tongue. Only English could be spoken in the schools established in conjunction with the English Church. Children who inadvertently used Irish phrases were, as late as the 19th century, by official regulation subjected to a beating. Education in the native language had to be surreptitious. Ireland is thus a classical example of a situation in which national oppression was related to linguistic discrimination.

Despite all handicaps, the Irish continued to struggle for the preservation of their national culture. Although by 1900 English had become the native first language of a majority of those living in and around Dublin and the Eastern counties, in the Western parts and on the Aran

Islands, Gaelic survived. On the Islands especially it remained the primary language. Towards the end of the 19th century, a vigorous movement for home rule, followed by one for political independence, favoured a conscious revival of Gaelic. A group of literary men and women developed a strong interest in it, and agitated for its use through an organisation called the Gaelic League. They also cultivated the modified form of English spoken in Ireland, an idiom strongly coloured by Gaelic constructions, as a vehicle for literary expression.

Late in the 19th century and early in the 20th, the cultural and political movements received new strength and direction through the participation of organised labour. Sharp struggles in the period of the First World War eventually led to the complete independence of Eriu (as it is officially called), with the exception of Ulster in the North. This province has had a special history of its own. The population has been modified by numerous immigrations from Scotland, and the predominant religion is here (in contrast with the Catholic South) Protestant. Scottish influence on the spoken English is very perceptible, and Southern English influence continues to be marked because of the political connection with England.

The literary activities fostered by the Gaelic League in the South produced some outstanding writers. The poetic resources of the Anglo-Irish dialect were consummately exploited by writers like J. M. Synge, Lady Augusta Gregory, Douglas Hyde and James Stephens. A more realistic style has been developed by the dramatist Sean O'Casey.[17] Meantime Northern Ireland, though still under English rule, and not directly involved in the political struggles of the South, has shared in the impetus of the Celtic revival, and has also produced writers employing the Anglo-Irish idiom of the North in a realistic vein. This dialect, with its distinctive features due to Scotch as well as English immigrations, has been used by the outstanding dramatist St John Ervine.[18] It represents a complex linguistic situation still insufficiently investigated.

---

[17] The first name, also spelled Shawn, is pronounced [ʃɔːn]. In Irish names, O' stands for a contraction of *of*, meaning "son of." It corresponds to *mac*, written *Mac* and *Mc*, in Gaelic names. In the Anglo-Norman used in Ireland during the Middle Ages, the word *fitz* (ultimately from Latin *filius*) was used in the same way: FitzPatrick = son of Patrick. Notice that the Celtic languages, unlike the Germanic, place the element meaning "son of" before the father's name, not after it.

[18] For details on the dialect of Ervine's plays I am indebted to the unpublished master's thesis on the subject by Ewa Suchodolska, University of Warsaw, 1955.

though Wright's *Dialect Dictionary* offers much material on Northern Irish vocabulary and pronunciation.[19]

In the South, the divergences in pronunciation from Standard British English are more clearly due to Gaelic influence than in the North. The influence is manifest first of all in a different intonation and rhythm of speech, and in a less marked contrast between accented and unaccented syllables. As a result, the stress on polysyllables of French origin often varies from that of contemporary English, and may be found to fluctuate from speaker to speaker, in words like: *delegate, duplicity, interrogate,* etc. This condition may also be due in part to the survival of an earlier accentuation in English itself. A number of vowel pronunciations (not universally heard) recall the vocalism of English in the 17th and 18th centuries: the preservation of [e:] in words like *tea, seat, conceit*; the falling together of [ai] and [ɔi] under the former in words like: *join, boy, sign*; the substitution of [a] for [ɔ] in words like: *rod, ford, log.* This last trait is to be found in American English also (see ch. 7, sec. 4). Pronunciations having a limited currency in earlier standard English are also preserved in Ireland today: *sarve* for *serve, arn* for *earn,* etc. A number of Anglo-Irish traits are not only attested in earlier English but are also to be found in other contemporary dialects. Among these is the fronting of short *e* to *i* (especially before nasals) as in *tinnis* for *tennis, timper* for *temper, ivery* for *every.* There are some typical 18th-century contractions, since lost in England, that are still current in Ireland: *'tis, 'twas, 'twill,* etc.

Among the consonants, there is a conspicuous modification in the pronunciation of *t* and *d* before *r* and (original) *-er*. The usual transcription with *-h* seems to indicate dentality rather than aspiration: *wather* for *water, sthrong* for *strong, dhrunk* for *drunk.* It has been attributed to Gaelic influence. On the other hand, Jespersen defines the consonants concerned as interdental stops contrasting with typical English post-dental stops, and recalls in this connection the earlier English fluctuation between *th* and *d* in words like *murder / murther, burden / burthen* etc. [20]

---

[19] See Herbert Huscher, "Das Anglo-Irische und seine Bedeutung als sprachkünstlerisches Ausdrucksmittel," *Max Deutschbein Festschrift* (Leipzig, 1936) for a general description of the Ulster dialect in comparison with Southern Anglo-Irish. J. Hogan, *The English Language in Ireland* (Dublin, 1934), has not been available to me. See also: P. L. Henry, *An Anglo-Irish Dialect of North Roscommon* (Dublin, 1957), and his "Linguistic Survey of Ireland", *Lochlann*, I, 51—208.

[20] Otto Jespersen, *A Modern English Grammar* (Copenhagen, 1947), I, p. 208.

According to him, the articulation may therefore represent an archaic English trait. As for the substitution of *-n* for final unaccented *-[ŋ]*, we have already noted that it is quite general in contemporary English dialects.

It must be remembered that wide discrepancies arise in the concentration and frequency of these traits, depending on speakers' education, social situation, and occasions for contact with Standard English. The same is true of morphological innovations and conservations: for instance, the use of *ye* for *you*, of *them* for *those*, also paralleled in other dialects. Similarly, Anglo-Irish is not alone in its occasional discrepancies in the formal agreement between verb and subject: young girls *is* mighty shy (Synge); the laws of England *is* queer (Gregory). Double negatives are attested in the plays of Ervine, but in those of Synge and Lady Gregory we find rather a linking of *not... hardly*: It *isn't hardly* (Gregory); *won't hardly* be needed (Gregory). Adverbs often appear without the standard *-ly* suffix (cf. *mighty*, above).

The most characteristic and pervasive influence on Anglo-Irish, especially in the South, is derived from the syntax, sentence structure and idiom of Gaelic.[21] As in the Celtic language, the emphatic personal pronoun has a number of uses unknown or at least unusual in standard English. Thus it often appears in non-appositional constructions: It was *yourself* started it (O'Casey). The words *himself* and *herself* (Gaelic *í féin* and *é féin*), standing alone, are often used to refer to a husband and wife when speaking of eachother, or in general reference to the master or mistress of the house: Is *herself* is in it? (meaning: Is my wife there?). In Ulster there are constructions employing the objective case of pronouns where formal standard English calls for the nominative, though colloquial usage may fluctuate: *'Twas me, It's her*, etc. (In the South, *myself* and *herself* would be typical here.) These deviations are not, however, limited to Ireland. Connective words like prepositions and conjunctions, literally translated from the Gaelic, impart a vivid concreteness to abstract relations in Anglo-Irish sentences. For *when, how, as, at*, we find phrases like: *the time that* (Gaelic *an uair*, an early loan from Latin *hora*), *the way that, what way*, etc. In English one says: *When he arrives, let me know so that I can come to see him.* In Anglo-Irish this would be: *The time that* he arrives, let me know, *the way that* I can come to see him. There are special meanings assigned to English conjunctions and prepositions: *till* means *so that*; *without* means *unless*; *against* means *in time for*; and *beside* means *in comparison with*. Many

---

[21] See P. W. Joyce, *English as We Speak It in Ireland* (Dublin, 1910). The thesis by Ewa Suchodolska compares popular syntax in Ervine's plays with that recorded by the Southern writers.

expressions which are expressed subjectively in English, from the point of view of the actor, are expressed objectively in Anglo-Irish, from the observer's point of view: There was great wonder *on me*; I had care *on me* (meaning: I wondered, I worried). Typical idioms are: What is [that] *on you?* (translated from Gaelic: Cad é sin *or-t?*); 'Tis fear for you (Is eagal *du-it-se*), meaning: What is the matter with you? and: You need to be afraid.

A frequently encountered construction in Anglo-Irish is the nominative absolute, with an infinitive or a participle depending on it, used in place of the dependent clauses of standard English. For a noun clause we find: It is no wonder *he to get the job* (meaning: ...that he should get...; Gregory); A great wonder it is *Judas not to have been a woman* (Gregory). For an adverbial clause we find: It would be a queer thing indeed, *I to be satisfied* (meaning: ...if I were...; Gregory); It's little I'll have to do then, *and I to be sitting alone* (meaning: ... when I am sitting...); I saw Michael, *and he mending his nets* (meaning: ...while he was mending...; Synge). Verbal nouns are also used to express what in Standard English is expressed by personal finite verbs. The preposition *at* followed by a verbal noun means action in progress: She is *at the milking of the cow*. Completed action may be similarly expressed with the preposition *after*: She was *after doing it*. A verbal noun construction preceded by *after* is used to express perfect and past perfect tense relationships: I am/was *after finishing my work* (meaning: I have/had just finished my work...).[22]

A traditional pattern of the Gaelic sentence, rendered literally into English, is construed with an impersonal form of the verb *to be* at the beginning, followed by a substantive with a dependent clause modifying it: *It is* myself that is thirsty (for: I am thirsty); *It is thus* Fergus was (for: This is how Fergus was; or: Fergus was in this state). This goes back to a requirement of Old Irish sentence structure that affirmative sentences should begin with a verb, if only a formal [*it*] *is* (*a tá*) followed by a noun, with the essential predication in a relative clause. The pattern

---

[22] There has been some lively debate on the relation of Anglo-Irish nominative absolutes to similar constructions in English, for instance loosely added phrases like: ... *with him lying there*; ... *and him* (*he*) *lying there*. The grammatical question at issue is whether the pronoun is to be regarded as the subject of the following verbal. There are English precedents for the nominative absolute after *and*, independent of Gaelic influence. See G. J. Visser, "Celtic Influence in English," *Neophilologus*, XXXIX (1955), 276—93; Franz H. Link, "And oder With + Participium," *Anglia*, LXXIII (1956), 322—27, both with bibliographies of recent discussions.

has been transferred to the structure of English sentences, giving an effect of emphasis not necessarily associated with the Gaelic construction: *It is soon* he will be coming now, for: He'll soon be coming.

In the use of certain auxiliary verbs there are striking peculiarities of Anglo-Irish, setting it off from standard English. Some of them reflect an earlier stage of English, when the syntax of such forms was more fluid than it is today. Others reflect Gaelic syntax. Among the former is the use of *to be* to form the perfect tenses of intransitive verbs of motion: He *is gone* on; You think me *to be come* (Gregory); What way *is he fled* (Synge). St John Ervine, however, often uses *have* in such constructions. The distribution of *shall* and *will* does not conform to the normal modern English conjugation. The Irish preference is for *will*, not *shall*, to express simple futurity in the first person, even in questions: It is alone *I will* be; *Will we* never have comfort?; *Will* I cut another piece for you? Similarly, the emphatic and continuous conjugations do not conform to the well-defined categories of ModE. The auxiliary *do* appears when there is no linguistic situation involving emphasis or negative statement, and the verb *to be* followed by a present participle appears where there is no situation implying stress on continuity: I *do be thinking* (Synge); It's the tongue that *does be giving out* lies (Gregory). These deviations from ModE appear to be due in part to the influence of Gaelic, in part to that of Tudor English.

There are other traits of Anglo-Irish which might be mentioned here. They include matters of word order such as inversion in indirect questions: I wonder *did she change* her mind (Ervine); ...do you think *can he win* in the race (Gregory). Asyndeton is also frequent in Anglo-Irish. It may possibly be connected with the traditional Gaelic use of contact relative clauses which are signalled as dependent because of special verb forms appearing in them, though they lack a subordinating conjunction. Anglo-Irish examples are: It was *yourself started it* (O'Casey); you'll meet none but Red Linahan, *has a squint in his eye* (Synge). It should be recalled, however, that this type of asyndeton was also well established in Early ModE, quite independently of Gaelic influence.

There are also many details of expression in Anglo-Irish, too numerous to list here, which mark it as a special form of contemporary English. Some of them are idioms like the adverbial phrase *at all at all*, used for emphasis in Ulster as' well as the South; the adverbial phrase *in it* used in the South in place of *there* (it is a translation of Gaelic *ann* from the preposition *in* plus the dative of the pronoun *é*, hence literally meaning *in it*); the adverbial expression *itself* meaning *even* (a translation of *féin*, which means either *even* or *itself* in Gaelic), and many others. All these contribute to that special flavour of Anglo-Irish which has been so

succesfully captured and turned to literary purposes by writers of the
recent decades in Ireland.

The following sentences from the plays of J. M. Synge will illustrate
by way of summary various of the outstanding characteristics of Anglo-
Irish which have just been mentioned.

What way would a woman live in a lonesome place the like of
this place, and she not making a talk with the men passing? (*The
Shadow of the Glen*)

And it's dry I am, surely, with the fear of death you put on me,
and I after driving mountain ewes since the turn of the day (*ibid.*).

It's them that's fat and flabby do be wrinkled young, and that whitish
yellowy hair she has does be soon turning the like of a handful of thin
grass you'd see rotting, where the wet lies, at the north of a sty (*ibid.*).

Let you not put shame on me, Molly, before herself and the smith.
Let you not put shame on me and I after saying fine words to you,
and dreaming... dreams... in the night (*ibid.*).

It's himself was a liar, lying stretched out with an open head on
him, letting on he was dead (*Playboy of the Western World*).

Is it me to go near him, and he the wickedest and worst with
me? (*ibid.*)

Is it rose from the dead? (*ibid.*)

Several of these sentences exemplify the Irish tendency to omit
relative pronouns, and to begin statements with an impersonal *it is*
instead of a direct personal construction. There are also typical absolutes composed of substantive and participle, such as: and *she not
making* a talk, or of substantive with adjective alone: and *he the
wickedest*. Previous action is typically expressed by the preposition *after*
followed by a verbal noun: *after driving, after saying*. Some constructions were at one time admissible in standard English, and others
are paralleled in other contemporary dialects: *it's them; let you not*;
[they] *do be* wrinkled young; is it *rose* (for *risen*). Other constructions
are translated from the Gaelic: *what way* for *how*; *the way* for *so that*;
herself for a woman's name. A number of turns of expression reflect
the characteristic objective organisation of a sentence where English
would present it subjectively: *put shame on* me, the *fear* you *put on* me.
Here problems of linguistics touch on problems of psychology. One of
the most interesting aspects of Anglo-Irish is the evidence that it adopts
a non-English point of view in presenting certain classes of statements
and questions. For this reason Anglo-Irish possesses for the English
reader certain advantages of unexpectedness and vividness, due to the
Celtic linguistic substratum which has shaped the English constructions.

CHAPTER VII

THE ENGLISH LANGUAGE IN THE NEW WORLD

1. THE HISTORICAL BACKGROUND

The expansion of the English language beyond its original boundaries into many parts of the world continued from the age of discovery and exploration (16th and 17th centuries) into the 18th and
19th. There was a diminution of course in the possibilities of obtaining
new possessions in land merely by seizing them from natives living on
a less advanced level of social and economic development, and of
exploiting the labour power in the territories thus preempted. In the
pre-industrial era, lands were simply annexed as colonies, the imperial
power[1] thus claiming them sent governors and a state apparatus of
administration and military control, while the native peoples either
adapted themselves, linguistically and otherwise, to a subservient
position, or retreated into small isolated communities foredoomed to
ethnographic decay if not extinction. The colonisers' linguistic and
general cultural influence varied according to the specific situation.
In the territories of North and South America, annexed by Spanish,
Portuguese and English conquerors, native cultures were in general
destined to submergence and almost complete extinction. The most
striking examples of such loss were the cultures of Mexico and Peru,
where the indigenous peoples had impressive achievements to their credit
in the more peaceful arts and techniques, offsetting the destructive
practices prevalent among some of them (cults of human sacrifice,

---

[1] The term imperialism, if applied to the expansion of European
countries by conquests in the New World, does not of course have the
same meaning as that defined by Lenin in his study of imperialism as
the highest stage of capitalism (1917).

tribal warfare). Nevertheless, the numerical preponderance remained with the native peoples in much of Central and South America, and the languages, though long unrecorded and still insufficiently investigated, have survived with remarkable tenacity under Spanish and Portugese domination.

In the regions lying to the North and East of what was then Mexico, the conquests were carried out with less sensational acts in the beginning, but with a more complete effectiveness in the long run. English fugitives from Stuart absolutism who settled in Massachusetts in the early 17th century, followed by settlers of various social strata along the entire Eastern coast, were alike in the thoroughness with which they sooner or later drove the native Indians off their land and compelled them to move westwards, to the accompaniment of warfare and persecution. This tactic was the easier to carry through effectively because the tribes then occupying the territory of the present-day United States and Canada had not reached an advanced level of material culture. They did not have cities and palaces, walls and temples, nor a social organisation commensurate with these things, as did the Mayas, Aztecs, Incas and others in countries to the South. The Northern tribes were nomadic hunters who still gathered much of their food from uncultivated nature, though they had also, as is well known, developed maize for grain food and also tobacco for smoking (an indulgence previously unknown to Europeans). Extant accounts of wars between colonists and Indian tribes are naturally written from the European point of view. The basic fact is that these, the original inhabitants, were driven westwards and were in the end reduced to a small number of scattered communities, depleted still further by European alcohol and European diseases. No serious effort has been made until recent decades to provide for advanced education and the possibilites for economic betterment, and these remain insufficient.

Few early writers (James Fenimore Cooper was one of them) showed any interest in the native languages or a desire to study them. With the drastic reduction in the Indian population, their languages too were dying out until recent times without any attempt to record them. In the past few decades, however, much serious and effective work has been done by American linguists in order to produce scientific descriptions of the still-spoken Amerindian languages (as they are sometimes called). This work is the more important since some of the communities in question appear to face extinction in the near future.

The cultural contacts between the European settlers and the aborigines were and continued to be negligible. As is usual when a conquering alien culture displaces a native civilisation completely, the loans from the language of the latter into the former have not been numerous. Typically, the borrowed common nouns were restricted to terms unique- ly connected with the autochthonous culture, and to words for flora and fauna peculiar to the new country: *moose, racoon, skunk* and *skunk cabbage*; also the *mocassin flower* and the *water mocassin* (a harmless snake).[2] On the other hand, geographical names, especially names of lakes and rivers, show a hardy resistance to change under these circum- stances. New arrivals in a conquered territory for the most part take them over unchanged. The hydrionomia or terminology for rivers and lakes in the United States still speaks eloquently of vanished Indian cultures in sonorous polysyllabic proper nouns like: Alleghany, Monon- gahela, Susquehanna, Missouri, Mississippi, Michigan and many others.

Many of the words taken into English by the English-speaking settlers were adopted, as has been pointed out, in Spanish forms (see ch. 3, sec. 3). The expansion of English colonists southwards along the Eastern sea-coast, from Massachusetts to Georgia, brought them into contact with other European languages. The Dutch had settled in New York, but this colony was taken over by the English in 1664. Immigration from the Palatinate and other parts of Germany brought German- speaking colonists to Pennsylvania beginning with the latter 17th century. When the population began to move westwards it came into contact with French settlements along the Mississippi valley, as is testified by place names like St. Louis and New Orleans, and by the French ortho- graphy for Indian place names like Michigan and Chicago (the *ch* being here pronounced as [ʃ]), Illinois and Arkansas and Sioux City (final *s* and *x* being unpronounced). The purchase of Louisiana from the French government in 1803 increased the contacts of English with French in the South early in the 19th century. In Canada an important French settlement in Quebec preserved and fostered its language so successfully that it remained the official medium of communication under British dominion rule. In the South, Spanish was encountered in Florida (pur- chased in 1819) and the Southwest. After the war with Mexico (1846—48) the United States was aggrandised by great tracts of territory including California, Arizona, New Mexico and Texas (the latter having been annexed before the outbreak of hostilities). Throughout these regions, though as yet but sparsely settled, Spanish was spoken not only by European settlers but also by such Indians as had had occasion to learn the language from traders, missionaries and others.

---

[2] H. L. Mencken, *The American Language* (New York, 1937 ed.), ch. 3.

These early contacts of North American English with other tongues yielded a number of loan words which differentiated its vocabulary from that used in England. From Dutch came a few terms: *stoop* (meaning verandah), *cookie, cruller, coleslaw, boss, scow*; from French: *prairie, bayou, levee, rapids, crevasse*; from Spanish: *rancho, hacienda, canyon, plaza, patio, mesa* (meaning table-land). Some of the Spanish loan words have been adopted and modified in popular Western speech, as when Spanish *vaquero* became *buckaroo, juzgado* (courthouse and jail) became *hoosegow*, and *vamos* (let us go) became *vamoose* (get out!). French place names have in many instances been transformed by popular etymology, as when *Purgatoire* became *Picketwire* and *Chemin Couvert* became *Smackover* (both in Arkansas). Many place names in the Southwest and West bear evidence to Spanish occupation, especially Spanish missionary activities: San Antonio, Rio Grande, Los Angeles, Palo Alto, and many others.

Finally, a number of native English words were used in new meanings, or combined to make new compounds, as the conditions of frontier life created the need for new terms. Thus *corn*, originally applied to any kind of grain, especially to wheat, became specialized to mean maize or Indian corn. Similarly, *lumber* (derived from Lombard; applied in England to old furniture and household stuff appropriate for second-hand sale) was applied to timber (wood sawed into planks) as the wood industry became a source of wealth when the great forests of the United States and Canadian Northwest were cut down by the labour of much-exploited "lumberers." Special phrases sprung from frontier life also enriched the language with vivid metaphors. From experience of Indian warfare came these expressions:

> to bury the hatchet, meaning to make peace (from a native Indian custom)
> to put on war paint; to go on the war-path
> to scalp; to be after someone's scalp, meaning to attack vengefully
> to walk Indian file (one behind another)

Many expressions persisted long after frontier days and are now current among speakers who do not clearly visualise the circumstances of their origin: *to blaze a trail, to make tracks, to strike pay dirt, to pull up stakes*. Others, connected with farming, were in some cases brought from England and preserved in the popular speech of the new country while they died out or became restricted in the old.

2. ENGLISH PHONOLOGY IN AMERICA: DIALECT AREAS

The foundations of the contemporary regional variations of speech in the United States (as in Canada also[3]) are of course to be found in the variant forms of English spoken by the 17th and 18th century colonists. It is known that the New England colonies of the Northeast were founded by emigrants from the region of London and East Anglia (Essex, Suffolk and Norfolk) with some representation from Southern Yorkshire. Their speech coincided in general with the standard developed in London.[4] These people were however religious and social dissidents; they were craftsmen, small traders, teachers and preachers, but not members of the wealthy and aristocratic classes. They occupied modest farms or carried on the crafts they had learned at home. They did not share in some of the fashionable aberrations of pronunciation which, as we gather from satirists and writers of comedies, were enjoying a vogue in courtly circles of the 17th and 18th centuries. Their way of speaking, transplanted to America, has remained closest to today's standard English of England except for certain deviations now confined to the rural areas.

The class origin of leading colonists in the Southern area was different. Here from Maryland to the Northern border of Florida, men of aristocratic origin received title to large stretches of land granted to them (for a consideration) by the royal authority. The names of the states still bear witness to the monarchs' favour: Maryland and Virginia (the latter named for Queen Elizabeth I), North and South Carolina (from Charles II) and Georgia (from George II).[5] Emigrants to these areas established a quasi-feudal system, in which the labour was perfomed by indentured white workers —debtors, convicts and the like who had forfeited their freedom for a specified period— and later on, to an overwhelming extent, by Negro slaves imported from Africa. By

---

[3] Attention is here concentrated on the United States, where numerous detailed studies of regional dialects have been carried out. Comparably detailed data are still lacking for Canada.

[4] George Philip Krapp, *The English Language in America* (New York, 1925), I; Brunner, *Die engl. Sprache*, I, p. 346 f.

[5] A short account of the situation producing contemporary dialects is given by M. Schlauch, "Początki i Rozwój Narodowego Języka Amerykańskiego," *Z Dziejów Powstania Języków Narodowych i Literackich*, ed. Zdzislaw Stieber (Warsaw, 1956), pp. 121—40.

a curious combination of circumstances, climate and geography served
to strengthen the social differences between New England and the
South already caused by the modes of production. The Northeast, with
its small farms and shipping ports, early introduced the factory system
based on machinery and water power. Here free wage labour was most
desirable and economic from the owners' point of view. In the South,
on the other hand, the production of rice, tobacco and cotton was most
lucrative, and this yielded greatest profits when carried out on large
tracts of land cultivated by slave labour. Hence there developed a sharp
contrast between the two economic systems. The Southern colonies (later
States) required more and more slave labour imported from Africa, while
the ones in the North excluded such labour — though at the same time
readily providing the ships and navigators to import the slaves.

Between New England and the Southern colonies there lies an area
comprising New York, New Jersey and Pennsylvania which had a special
history reflected in its linguistic development. Here there were the minor
linguistic groups previously mentioned: Dutch in New York, German
in Pennsylvania. Emigrants from Scotland and Ireland, especially Ulster,
were added in the 18th century. Many of these pushed westwards and
southwestwards to obtain new lands. About 1750 Benjamin Franklin
estimated that one-third of the population of Pennsylvania was English,
one third Scotch, and one third German. As a result of their westward
migration the Scotch and Irish exercised an influence on the formation
of what is today known as Middle Western speech in the United States,
also in Maryland and areas of the farther South.

When the thirteen original colonies obtained their independence of
Great Britain the newly created state was already diversified in its population, but at the same time proudly self-conscious of its position as
a new nation. The ardent patriotism of the period affected attitudes
to language, among other matters. The recognised spokesman for American
as contrasted with British English was Noah Webster of Connecticut
(1758—1843). As a schoolmaster during the Revolution he produced
books on spelling and grammar; just after it he wrote a book of *Dissertations on the English Language* (1789). Later he compiled *An American
Dictionary of the English Language* (1828). His interest was concentrated
on showing that English had become something especial in the newly
formed United States; that differences in vocabulary and pronunciation
should be recognised, and that standards of preferred speech should
be sought in the actual usage of the States, not in the rules observed
in the mother country. While admitting the basic identity of the language
spoken in the two countries, he took pride in the fact that terms

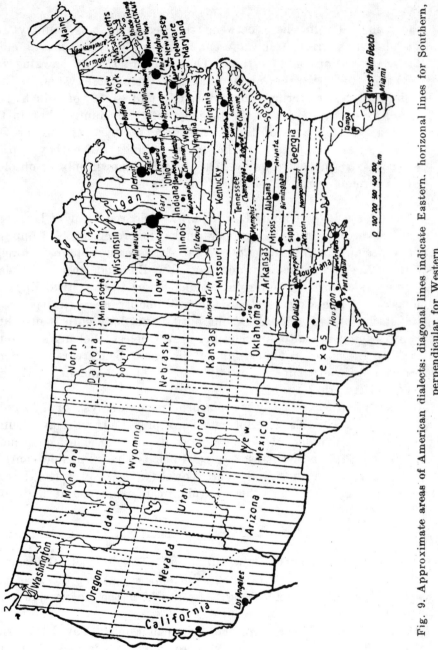

Fig. 9. Approximate areas of American dialects: diagonal lines indicate Eastern. horizonal lines for Southern, perpendicular for Western

connected with feudal society in England were obsolete if not completely forgotten in the United States:

> ...the principal differences between the people of this country and of all others arise from different forms of government, different laws, institutions and customs. Thus the practice of hawking and hunting, the institution of heraldry and the feudal system of England, originated terms which formed, and some of which now form, a necessary part of the language of that country; but in the United States, many of these terms are no part of our present language, and they can not be, for the things which they express do not exist in this country. They can be known only as obsolete or as foreign words (Preface to the 1828 ed.).

Webster looked upon himself as a purifier and regulator of language, a role to which modern lexicographers make no pretension. He opposed himself, especially in the *Dissertations*,[6] to "the corruptions of a foreign court and stage," and he regarded the New England speech of plain countrymen as something purer, something closer to the "true English" of Chaucer and Shakespeare, than the presumably decadent speech of England itself. All of this talk about purity and decadence is of course (in Webster's sense) quite unscientific. Nevertheless Webster's account of the New England pronunciation of his time, being carefully done, offers a point of departure for a study of the development of English phonology in America.

Professor Pilch has recently made a penetrating analysis of the sounds represented by Webster's description.[7] They prevailed, we may assume, in Connecticut and much of New England about 1800. The conspicuous feature of the pattern reconstructed by Pilch is the phonemic contrast still existing between long and short vowels, since vowel length here serves to distinguish words otherwise identical, as indeed it had done in previous centuries.

---

[6] The text has recently been edited by H. R. Warfel (Gainesville, Fla., 1951). The Preface to the 1828 *Dictionary* was reprinted as late as the 1903 ed. (Springfield, Mass.), from which the above quotation has been taken.

[7] Herbert Pilch, "The Rise of the American English Vowel Pattern," *Word*, XI (1955), 57—93. The chart here given is adapted from that on p. 66. For the present situation see J. S. Kenyon, *American Pronunciation* (Ann Arbor, 1940).

feet, fit	i(:)	i⁸ just, truth		u(:) pool, pull
late, let	e(:)	ʌ but	o(:)	hone, home
father, fathom	æ(:)		ɑ(:)	hall, holly
my, joy		ai au		house

Diphthongs were limited, as can be seen, to combinations of *a* with
either a following *i* or *u*; the English levelling of *oi* and *ai* under the
latter diphthong has already been observed in the rimes of Alexander
Pope. Special allophonic variations were noted by Webster, for instance
a simplification of diphthongs on the first element when they occurred
before stops, as in: *fight, rout* (both having [a] alone); also a glide
inserted between a long vowel or a diphthong and a following *r*: e. g.,
bare, mire, parent.

Basically there is no very great difference between the system surmised to be Webster's and the one reconstructed for Shakespeare's
fundamental phonemes.⁹ In both, vowel length still had phonemic significance; in both, allophonic variations of vowels appeared in like
positions (for instance, before *r*) but had not yet attained the status of
fully independent phonemes; in both, the diphthongs corresponding to
today's *oi* and *ai* were similar if not identical.

---

⁸ The character i represents a high central vowel, lax and unrounded,
between [i:] and [u:]. It was appearently limited to New England and
appeared in words like: *cube, just, truth, duty*. See George L. Trager and
Henry Lee Smith, Jr., *An Outline of English Structure* (Norman, Okl.,
1951) = *Studies in Linguistics: Occasional Papers*, No. 3, p. 14, and
vowel chart, p. 11.

⁹ Pilch takes the Kökeritz reconstruction as his historical point of
departure in discussing Webster's system. For certain details this may
be a somewhat dubious procedure, partly because, as Kökeritz himself
points out, Shakespeare's pronunciation may well have preserved provincial traits reflected in his rimes, and partly because no single person's
pronunciation adequately represents the multiplicity of variant accentable
forms current in London at the time. (Perhaps there were comparable
fluctuations in Noah Webster's speech community?) However, the
picture given by Pilch has the advantage of simplicity, and it is accurate
enough for the purpose of establishing the situation from which American
dialects developed.

What has happened in the linguistic territory of the United States since Noah Webster's time has been a disturbance in the pattern of contrasts between long and short vowels. A reduction in contrasts was brought about by the lengthening of originally short vowels before voiced consonants and voiceless aspirants in words like: *led, leg, loss, calf,* etc. The lengthening of the vowel in *led* produced a half-long vowel [le·d] and thus reduced the phonemic distinction between the pairs *led : laid; fed : fade,* etc.[10]; and so with many other pairs of words. The vowel of *sad* [sæ·d] became phonetically almost as long as the one in *sate* [se:t]. But a new trend to diphthongisation now appeared among the originally long vowels. Not only did long *ē* become [ei] and long *ō* become [ou] —a development shared with British English— but long *ī* and *ū* have in general American pronunciation manifested a perceptible interior shift in tongue position, becoming [uu], [ii], and even [uw], [ij] respectively. With the vowel [i] also the original distinction of long versus short quantity has been transformed into one of stability versus shift in pairs like: *just : juice; shut : sure,* etc. The trait which now essentially determines the contrast between *lid* and *lead* (verb) as also between *led* and *laid, god* and *guard,* is the fact that in pronouncing the words with what are traditionally called "short" vowels (here actually half long ones) the tongue remains in a stable position, whereas with the "long" ones it shifts slightly.[11]

The several regional dialects have given rise to many special developments of vowels in particular concrete environments. Some of them have reintroduced or refortified contrasts of length which had been reduced previously. Not all variations of American English, therefore, can be readily described without reference to length as a phonemic feature. The problem of differences in specific details leads to the question of contemporary dialects and their geographical distribution.

3. AMERICAN DIALECTS TODAY: THE NORTHEAST AREA

It has been customary, until recently, to divide the United States into three main dialect areas: Northeast (all of New England and the

---

[10] For a phonetic description of their present status see Harry A. Rositzke, "Vowel-Length in General American Speech," *Language,* XV (1939), 99 ff.; also R.-M. S. Heffer, *ibid.,* XVI (1940), 33—47.

[11] Compare the description of American contemporary pronunciation (Chicago area) given by Leonard Bloomfield, "The Stressed Vowels of American English," *Language,* XI (1935), 97—116. Regional variations of the present-day "shifting" vowels from original long ones are given in strict transcription by Trager and Smith, *op. cit.,* pp. 12—29.

New York area along the Hudson River); Southern (the old slave territory extending on the East of the Mississippi River from Virginia and Kentucky southwards, and on the West of it, into Louisiana and parts of Texas, Arkansas and Missouri); and finally what has been called General American, including the Middle Atlantic area of New York, New Jersey, Pennsylvania and Maryland, and all of the Middle and Far West.[12] This division is however only approximate and needs to be revised in the light of more detailed studies carried out in recent years. First of all, Eastern New England differs from Western. It should be pointed out, too, that there are subdivisions within the Southern area. Louisiana, for instance, contrasts with Virginia or the Southern hill speech of Kentucky or Tennessee. Here are contrasts requiring further study. Moreover, the distinctive character of the midland Eastern area has been neglected in the threefold division. Pennsylvania, which as a colony had a special type of speech due to the mixed character of its population, and also the other Middle Atlantic colonies, contributed greatly to the expansion westwards into Ohio, Indiana and Illinois and thus introduced a distinct central band into the territory which has by some been labelled Midwestern or General American without distinction.[13] Its boundary runs through Pennsylvania and the three states just mentioned. The Far West, an area occupied by many types of settlers, still awaits exhaustive treatment. These subdivisions are however not clearly defined, nor are they clearly reflected in the texts which attempt to make literary use of dialect. Since these will be our primary concern here, as with the regional dialects of England, we shall (pending more detailed information) follow the traditional main divisions of Northeast, Southern and General American, while recognising their very approximate character.

The Northeastern dialect, spoken in New England, and extending into Eastern New York State to a certain extent, is the one which has remained closest to the standard speech of the mother country. This statement is most clearly true of the Eastern sea-board area, among educated speakers. In the 19th century, Boston and the towns

---

[12] This division of dialect areas is given by Krapp, and is also followed by Brunner, *Die engl. Sprache*, II, and Hans Galinsky, *Die Sprache des Amerikaners*, 2 vols. (Heidelberg, 1951—52).

[13] The need for correction of the traditional division has been sharply stated by R. I. McDavid, Jr., in his review of Galinsky's book, *Journal of English and Germanic Philology*, LIV (1955), 167—69. However, as the reviewer admits, the new evidence for dialect divisions is still very largely confined to unpublished and highly special materials.

near it represented a centre of intellectual activity which gave its tone
to cultural life elsewhere in the country. The prestige of the "Boston
dialect," as it may be called, was then higher than it is today, and
its influence extended farther. Yet even at the height of its prestige
the Northeastern dialect was not a unified linguistic phenomenon.
Countrymen in various areas evinced deviations from the speech of
Harvard professors and distinguished writers like Emerson, Longfellow
and Hawthorne. James Russell Lowell, in the *Biglow Papers*, experimented with the writing of New England rural dialect as distinct from
that of Boston. Thus even the most cursory description must distinguish
levels within the general Northeastern area. In the 20th century the
situation has been further complicated by the large-scale immigration
of Irish and Portugese to Massachusetts and adjacent states.

Both urban and rural speakers in the 19th century shared in the
Southern English loss of *r* when not initial or prevocalic; also in the
modification (lengthening and lowering) of the vowel *a* before the
voiceless spirants [s, f, θ] and the combinations -*ns* and -*nt*. Both
changes produced phonetically long vowels, thus: *car, cast; pass, part;
farce, fast*. However, the transformation appears to have been carried
out on the basis of an early phase of British English, when the vowels
in question were still relatively high: [æ] or [a] but not yet [ɑ]—
and for the most part they were not lowered entirely to the [ɑ:] now
prevailing in standard British pronunciation for the words just cited.
Instead we have a higher modern sound *ă*, in which length is no
longer significant (Pilch, *loc. cit.*, p. 79 f.). The result has been a homonymous pronunciation of *pass* and *parse* among many speakers especially
in Eastern New England today. Because of interdialectal influences,
however, this pattern has not become universal. A lowered variety
of *a*, namely [ɑ(:)], also appears in New England before historical -*r*,
and a high [æ] is often heard (as elsewhere in the United States) in
the group *half, pass*, especially in the Western part of the New
England area.[14]

In New England the short *o* of *cot, lot, nod*, and the original ME *au*
of words like *caught, law, launch*, as well as original *o* before *r*, all appear
as [ɔ(:)], with length again a non-distinctive feature.[15] A preceding *w*

---

[14] Map No. 15 of the *Linguistic Atlas of the United States* (New
England) shows the distribution of [a]/[ɑ] versus [æ]. See below,
n. 17. It is reproduced by Galinsky, *op. cit.*, I, p. 54.

[15] Pilch assumes that the sound was universally [ɑ] in *cot, nod*, etc.,
in 17th—18th century London English, and independently returned to
[ɔ] in both England and New England In view of the fluctuations noted

changes *a* to [ɔ] also: in *water, quaff,* etc. The development of Webster's
i varies in specific groups of words. The monophthong *u* is generally
to be heard in: *tube, new, suit*; while *iu/ju* is heard in: *few, cube, music.*
But here again there is variation in the distribution. The simple vowel
is heard more often in the East than in the Western sections.[16]

Rural New England in the 19th century evinced some special traits
distinct from these. Some of them still survive today. Upon examination
it turns out that these dialect features can all be traced back to
variant pronunciations well attested in 18th-century England, most of
them having at least limited currency at that time among standard
speakers. They include: [ai] for today's diphthong [ɔi] (compare Anglo-
Irish) in: *join, boil, roil,* etc.; a reduced vowel [ə] and unpalatalised *t* in
the second syllables of *nature, creature* (compare the standard English
pronunciation of *figure*); *a* for *e* before original *r* plus consonant in:
sartain, varmin(t), etc.; [ʌ] for [ə] from short *u* before the combination
-*rs*, which was assimilated to -*ss* before *r* had elsewhere completely disappeared: *wuss* for *worse, cuss* for *curse,* etc. There was also a reduction
of original long *ō* to *u* in some words, producing homonyms in New
England for pairs of words like: *whole, hull; stone, stun.* Among words
normally having early ModE long *ū* (from ME long *ō*), the New England
dialect has introduced more numerous shortenings than those which
became acceptable in standard speech, for instance: *root, roof, hoof.*
A fronting of short *e* to *i* in words like: *yet, end, friend,* etc., appears in
New England but is by no means limited to it. (Again, compare with
Anglo-Irish also.)

In the period of the Mexican and Civil Wars, James Russell Lowell
experimented with the use of rural New England dialect, sometimes
called Yankee, for political satire in his *Biglow Papers.* For instance,
he makes one of his imaginary characters write as follows to a newspaper
editor:

> Dear Sir,— You wish to know my notions
>   On sartin pints that rile the land;
> There's nothin' thet my natur so shuns
>   Ez bein' mum or underhand;

---

in early ModE, and the choices available to educated speakers, it would
seem more likely that New England simply continued one variety of
pronunciation already current in England. Galinsky, *op. cit.,* I, p. 51,
assumes that both variants were heard in the speech of early New
Englanders.

[16] *Linguistic Atlas* map No. 17; Galinsky, I, p. 138.

> I'm a straight-spoken kind o' creetur
> Thet blurts right out wut's in his head,
> An' ef I've one pecooler feetur,
> It is a nose that wunt be led.

Setting aside some of the minor peculiarities and purely orthographical aberrations, we find here the same kind of speech which James Fenimore Cooper, writing in the earlier 19th century, recorded for the untutored hero of his *Leather Stocking Tales*, originating in upper New York State. The Deerslayer similarly says: *obsarvable* for *observable*, *nat'ral* for *natural*, *creatur'* for *creature*, *ch'ice* for *choice*-- and in addition, *ta'nt* for *taunt*. Cooper merely uses slightly different tricks of spelling to indicate similar marks of dialect. And these same traits, mostly archaisms, are to be found in rural communities of the American South and Southwest as well.

These facts show concretely that the establishment of clear-cut dialect boundaries for any one region in the United States is not easy. What seem at first glance to be marks of regional dialect often turn out to be what Krapp has called (*op. cit.*, I, p. 235 ff.) a general low colloquial type of speech, common to many regions. New England, which alone thus far of American dialect areas has been subjected to an exhaustive linguistic analysis, may have been thought to present a picture of relatively stable archaic traits, but a sociologist's sharp criticism of the methods followed in collecting material for the *Linguistic Atlas*[17] has called in question the validity of the results obtained.[18] New England is, according to this critic, far less removed from other sections of the country than our present linguistic atlas of the area would indicate. The frequency and concentration in the use of regional dialect words[19] is also said to be less marked than the Atlas would lead one to suppose.

---

[17] Hans Kurath and others, *A Linguistic Atlas of the United States* (New England), 3 vols. (Providence, R. I., 1939—43).

[18] Glenna R. Pickford, "American Linguistic Geography, A Sociological Approach," *Word*, XII (1956), 211—33. The author claims that questions to informants were so "slanted" as to emphasise the relatively unimpressive evidence for archaic provincial speech at the expense of evidence for the merging of dialects into a general speech showing levels of culture and education rather than regional distinctions.

[19] Harold Wentworth, *American Dialect Dictionary* (New York, 1944), offers the variant pronunciations of general United States English as well as the words limited to special localities.

189

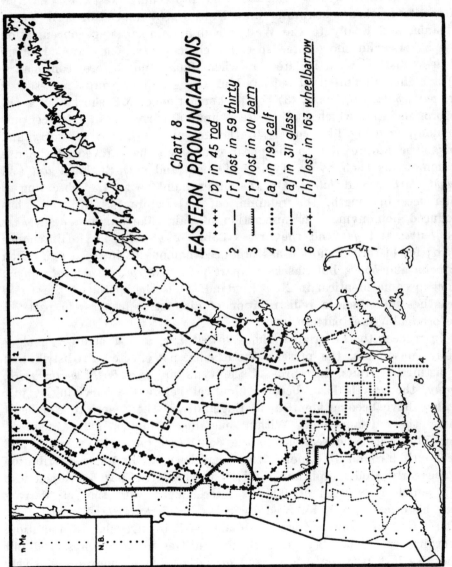

Chart 8
EASTERN PRONUNCIATIONS

1	++++ [ɒ] in 45 rod
2	— — [r] lost in 59 thirty
3	———— [r] lost in 101 barn
4	·········· [a] in 192 calf
5	—··—··— [a] in 311 glass
6	+·+·+· [h] lost in 163 wheelbarrow

Fig. 10. Eastern Pronunciation of key words. The dialect areas of New England

4. MIDDLE ATLANTIC AND MIDDLE WEST;
"GENERAL AMERICAN"

Leaving Eastern New England and proceeding westwards in New York State, then southwards into New Jersey and Northern Pennsylvania, and finally to the West, we find an increasing concentration of speakers who show three special archaic traits. They are: (1) more or less distinctly articulated *r* when final and before consonants; (2) a high articulation of *a* as [æ] in the group of words represented by: *pass, bath, calf, aunt*; (3) the pronunciation of ME short *o* as a [ɑ] (a pronunciation which had at least limited currency in 17th-century London), creating like vowels in the accented syllables of *starry* and *sorry*. The failure of *r* to disappear completely has prevented the rise of homonyms such as are typical of New (and old) England: *tort* and *taught, farther* and *father*. On the other hand, with the obscuring of differences in length, the retaining of [æ] before [s, f, θ], etc. has produced homonymous pronunciation of pairs like *ant* and *aunt; have* and *halve*; and *gas* and the first syllable· of *ghastly*. The maintenance of [ɑ] for historical short *o* has produced homonyms in word pairs such as: *balm* and *bomb*; but has kept apart pairs like *cot, caught; tot,· taught*, which became identical in New England. Thus the speech of these two areas has undergone a redistribution of distinctive features in parts of the original vowel pattern.

In respect to the original short vowels *i, e,* and *u* before *r* final or before consonants, the preservation of *r* has not effected a redistribution of distinctive traits. In words of the type *fir, fur; birth, berth; word, worthy*, the vowels have become identical before the surviving *r*, just as they have become identical in England and the American Northeast where the *r* disappeared. Within one discontinuous area, including New York City and sections to the Southwest (around Nashville) and the South (around Baltimore), there has been an irregular distribution of the early ModE diphthongs [əi]/[ɔi]. The latter has developed into [ʌi], popularly written *oi*. This is interchanged with the [ə:] derived from historical *i, e, u* followed by *r*, as in: *first, further*, spelled *foist, foither* by amateur writers of dialect. This irregular distribution, according to Pilch, may go back to a distinction here preserved but otherwise lost between ME *ui* and *oi*. Others have more speculatively attributed the treatment of these diphthongs to the influence of Jewish or other immigrants (Brunner, *op. cit.*, II, p. 264). When [ə:] is recorded for historical *oi* [ʌi] as in the confusion of *earl* and *oil*, we may have to do with hypercorrect forms arising from the impulse to avoid the discarded diphthong [ai] in such positions (cf. *rile* versus *roil*).

The Middle West, an area having its urban centre in Chicago, represents the core of what is often called General American speech. It is marked by some additional traits besides those previously mentioned: a scattered (not universal) pronunciation of [a] instead of [ɔ] after *w* in *water*, *watch*, etc.; though the Far West in general prefers [ɑ] here as also in words with original short *o*: *cot*, *tot*, *nod*, *log*, etc. (Pilch, *loc. cit.*, p. 79). There is a scattered raising of [a] to an open ę before *r*, creating homonyms of the words *Mary* and *marry* in the Middle and Far West as also in parts of New York and the South. In addition there is a very prevalent tendency to voice intervocalic voiceless consonants, especially -*t*-, when not protected by accent. The result is not a fully voiced consonant but what may be called a half-voiced one transcribed [b̥, d̥, g̥] in words like: *'capital*, *'city*, *'second*, *eco'nomic*, etc.

Under General American it is desirable to mention two very striking deviations from contemporary standard British pronunciation, namely in sentence intonation and rhythm. As between cultivated speakers of both types it is these factors which are most conspicuous and represent the clearest differentiation. Deviations in the pronunciation or usage of individual words often represent, as has just been pointed out, a conservatism in usage rather than an innovation. So far as intonation is concerned, the American pattern is strikingly monotonous. Sentence melody begins on a lower level than the corresponding British melody, and remains close to that level throughout. Galinsky thus represents the difference, for instance, between American and British intonation of questions calling for an answer of *Yes* or *No*:

American	British
Did it all happen yesterday?	Did it all happen yesterday?

(Galinsky, I. p. 15)

The rhythm of general American speech shows characteristics of its own connected with the treatment of unstressed and secondarily stressed syllables. A more even distribution of conspicuous syllables reflects an older pronunciation of many polysyllabic words. This conservatism, possibly connected with the level intonation, was no doubt fortified by schoolmasters who in the 18th and 19th centuries consciously opposed the reduction of accent and slurring of syllables. In this way we obtain the following typical contrasts:

General American	British
'tempor'ary	'temporary or 'temp'rary
'liter'ary	'literary or 'lit'rary
'mili'tary	'military or 'milit'ry
'dormi'tory	'dormit'ry
'restau'rant	'restaurant or 'rest'rant

In nominal Germanic compounds like: *inrush, inroad, output, outgo,* American pronunciation also preserves a more even accentuation. On the other hand, reduced vowels in completely unaccented syllables have been levelled to a greater extent than in British English; [ə] is preferred to [ɪ] (for instance, in the first and last syllables of *entreated*), and there is a greater contrast in clarity between stressed and unstressed syllables. The historically short vowels of sentence-stressed syllables have recently been undergoing a secondary lengthening in the United States which does not affect their phonemic status but may well affect sentence rhythm and distinguish it still further from the English. Galinsky observes such lengthening in the accented vowels of words like: *fit, fed, feet, fade, adopt, together, given, other (op. cit.,* I, p. 28).

A pervasive nasalisation of vowels is also characteristic of General American speech, especially in the Western areas. The habit of nasal articulation goes back to the 17th century in England, where it was particularly marked among the Puritans. Samuel Butler remarks in *Hudibras* (1663), his satirical poem directed against the sect, that its members "blaspheme custard through the nose" and in general speak nasally with a characteristic "bag-pipe drone."[20] The Puritans, then, were probably the immigrants who brought nasalisation to the English of the New World, but it has spread to the West and become even more marked there than in the Northeast.

General American in the broadest sense exists of course on several levels of usage. In its written form it has been exhaustively studied by Charles Carpenter Fries.[21] Three main groups are distinguished by him on the basis of inductive study: Group I, including those who have higher education or its equivalent and are recognised as standard speakers in any community; Group III, made up of those having minimal

---

[20] *Hudibras,* ed. A. R. Waller (Cambridge, 1905), pp. 9 and 16.
[21] Fries, *American English Grammar,* ch. 3.

or no education, who speak low colloquial or "vulgar" English; and a broad intermediate Group II speaking a general colloquial or "common" English. The lowest group habitually uses double negatives (I *don't have no* books); says *he don't* for *he doesn't*, *you was* for *you were*, and *ain't* for *isn't*. It substitutes *them* for *those* as demonstrative plural pronoun (I wrote *them* letters to him) and interchanges nominative and accusative case forms in certain positions: *Him and his brother* came; This is a secret between *you and I* (but never: *Him* came...; ...between *I and you*). There is the to-be-expected shifting of strong verbs to the weak conjugation, and the reduction of three principal parts of strong verbs to two: I *have wrote*; *have stole*; *have gave*; he *run*; he *seen*; he *done*. The dental suffix for past tense is omitted in many verbs of the weak conjugation where the normal inflection would give a phonetically difficult combination of consonants. In this way preterite and present forms are made identical for verbs like: *ask, pick, work, slip*, etc. On the other hand, some weak verbs receive a doubled suffix: *hurted, agreeded, attackted, drownded*.

All of these deviations from the standard have origins or at least analogues in British speech, whether past or present, standard or regional or substandard. We have seen that standard writers of the 18th century employed forms like *has wrote* (ch. 5, sec. 4). Colloquial English, as represented in dialogue passages of 19th century novels, employed both *ain't* and *he don't*. The use of *them* as a demonstrative which is also heard in Anglo-Irish, has been traced back to the 16th century.[22] Southern English dialects like that of Dorset have shifted the cases of pronouns more extensively than has low colloquial American, though not in the same way (see ch. 6, sec. 4).

The general colloquial speech of Fries's middle group is also marked by some usages which are avoided by speakers of the upper group everywhere. These it shares with the lowest group. Among them are: the substitution of *-in* for *-ing* as present participle ending, a wide preference for *will* instead of *shall* in the first person of the future tense, a frequent shift of agreement in expressions beginning with *there is* (*there's many men* left out; *there is six* of them). Here we also find occasional use of *don't* for *doesn't* (not so extensively as in Group III); a preference for *who* instead of *whom* in dative-accusative construction when it stands in head position in a sentence (*Who* did you refer to? *Who* do you want to see?), a choice which may be paralleled in Shakespeare (see ch. 5, sec. 4). In the usage of the two lower groups, as distinct

---

[22] Gerhard Graband, "Neuenglisches them als Demonstrativum," *Zeitschrift für Anglistik und Amerikanistik*, IV (1956), 343—52.

from Group I, subjunctive forms of the verb have practically disappeared, even in non-fact conditions: If *I was* you...; If *he was* with us now..., etc. The common speech avoids passive subjunctives in clauses of indirect command or request by substituting active infinitive constructions: I ask you *to send him*; The officer commanded them *to release him*, etc., instead of the constructions: I ask *that he be sent*; the officer commanded *that he be released*, etc., which are still characteristic of standard writing in America.

It has been observed that the simple past tense is used instead of the present perfect not only among speakers of the middle group but also those of the first (though the latter observe the distinction in writing): I just *came* instead of: I *have* just *come*, etc.[22a]

5. THE SOUTHERN AREA AND ITS DIALECTS

The Southern area, as has already been indicated, is by no means unified linguistically. Geographically, three main types of regional speech have been distinguished:[23] that of tidewater Virginia, the dialect of the hill dwellers, and a widespread lowland type. In addition, the social stratification expressed in linguistic modes is here unusually complex. To begin with, of course, there was the particular nuance —it was little more than that— of English brought to Virginia and later settlements by the class of aristocratic landowners, their domestic servants and other adherents. To these elements were added poor white workers and Negro slaves who carried out the work in plantations and farms; later on, in the incipient industry of the South. After the emancipation of slaves (1864), both Negro and white farmers were to be found cultivating the poorest soil in like conditions of extreme poverty, but the Negro farmers were kept isolated and repressed by many special disabilities connected with discrimination, both social and economic. They found little support in their struggles from white farmers almost as poor as themselves until recent years (beginning in the 1930's). American trade unions were for long unwilling to recognise Negro workers on a basis of equality, or even to admit them into some union organisations. Schooling for Negroes, where it existed, was kept strictly separated from

---

[22a] See Gerard Vanneck in *Word*, XIV (1958), 237—42.

[23] William Cabell Greet, *Culture in the South* (1934), cited by H. L. Mencken, *op. cit.*, p. 364.

institutions for white children. Only in 1955 did an Order of the Supreme Court declare that segregated instruction is unconstitutional; and to this day (1959) some communities of the South are trying by various means to avoid carrying out equal and desegregated schooling.

Traditionally, therefore, the South has developed some complex gradations of speech corresponding to the following groups: white land-owners (including also the white professional class and a limited number of Negroes who have also obtained higher education); semi-literate and illiterate whites and Negroes speaking identical variations of the Southern dialect; and some special instances of Negro or white dialect due to special conditions— for instance, the Gullah dialect or that of Louisiana where French influence is perceptible.

A few phonological traits may be taken as typical for all Southern speech, although even these require further investigation by the precise methods worked out for modern dialect geography. The following traits are among the most general.

The consonant r is lost as also in New England in final position and before a consonant, so that car, cart have [ɑ:] as in standard Southern British. The early ModE long ō has been preserved before r in words like: more [mo:], pork [po:k], lord [lo:d], modified only in recent times to [ou]. The early ModE æ of words like: bath, pass, half, aunt has been generally but not universally preserved in the South, and is also found in: taunt, haunt, while [ɑ] appears for ME short o in: stop, not, log, etc., as in the Middle West. The South has been more faithful than New England in preserving iu/ju in words like: tube, new, duty, while it fluc-tuates in the pronunciation of others in the same group. The half voicing of unaccented consonants (as in Middle Western pronunciation of: city, letter, second) is not characteristic of the South. The ModE diphthong [ai] from ME [i:] has been simplified to [a:] or [ɑ:] in Southern American, especially when final: my, I (compare this with the like simplification in Yorkshire).

Among special developments in the South may be mentioned a pa-latalisation of k and g in words like: car [kʲa:], cow [kʲau] and garden [gʲa:dŋ], to be heard especially in Virginia. (Compare this with the pro-nunciation [hjɑ:] for here, which has however a different origin.) A long vowel, now diphthongised, has been preserved from ME [ɛ:] before dentals in words like: head [heid], death [deiθ]. Final consonants have been dropped in words like: told, old, now pronounced [toul] and [oul], also find, found as [fain], [faun]. (Compare the Scots treatment of -ld.) There are also losses of consonants, not limited to the South, in words like: can'le for candle, allus for always, hoss for horse. The raising of

14

short *e* to *i* in many words, before nasals and elsewhere, is frequent in the South but not limited to it: *tinnis* for *tennis*, *ind* for *end*, *yit* for *yet*. (Compare the Anglo-Irish articulation of *e* in such words.) There is a frequently observed substitution of [j] for initial [h] in: *hear*, *head*, *here*; but not in all words beginning with *h-*.

The general non-standard speech of the South adds to these phonological traits the grammatical simplifications prevalent in General American of the same level. The morphological traits such as extension of *-s* to first and second persons of the present (I *goes*, you *sees*, etc.) are to be found in other dialects as well as the Southern. Only one is peculiar to this region: an agglutinated plural form, *you-all* and *y'all* (the latter from *ye all*), used for the second personal pronoun. This convenient modification of the usual inflection is heard among speakers of all levels. It is used in addressing more than one person, or one person as representative of a group.

Contrary to a widespread popular belief in the United States, there is no "inherent" Negro speech; no linguistic difference between Negro and white speakers on the same levels of illiteracy and semi-literacy. The origin of so-called Negro speech, as of poor white speech, went back to the same type as that of the ruling class, with certain simplifications common to the uneducated of both sections in the community. The African slaves, derived from many different native tribes, were suddenly cut off from their original speech communities and thrown upon an alien culture where they were not helped or encouraged to achieve the linguistic level of their owners. The white owners themselves contributed to the shaping of the kind of substandard English which became a social mark of slave status. As Krapp says:

> The English speech which the whites probably used in addressing their savage slave captives was the much simplified, infantile English which superiors sometimes assume in addressing inferiors, or which with repetition and vociferation is used in trying to communicate with people who do not know the language (*op. cit.*, I, p. 252).

For most Negroes, the acquisition of anything like standard English has remained not only difficult but even dangerous, since educated speech when coming from a Negro was looked upon by white racists as a sign of unwarranted arrogance. On the present situation in the countryside, Mencken has this to say:

> Put a Negro and a white man, both from the same part of rural Georgia and both on the same economic level, behind a screen and bid

them speak the same words, and it will be difficult if not impossible to distinguish one from the other.[24]

One of the first serious attempts to make literary use of continuous utterances by an uneducated Negro was realised by Joel Chandler Harris in his collection of *Uncle Remus Stories* (1880). They record Georgian plantation folklore in the shape of animal stories, partly it would seem preserved from African sources and partly adapted in the New World. Though distorted by the author's dependence on conventional orthography and his lack of linguistic training, and also by a certain condescending attitude to both material and informant, these stories have a distinct interest for students of both linguistics and oral literature. An extract of a few sentences will exemplify the nature of the dialect as Harris wrote it down:

...Brer Fox wanter hurt Brer Rabbit bad ez he kin, so he cotch 'im by de behime legs en slung 'im in de middle er de briar-patch. Dar wuz a considerabul flutter whar Brer Rabbit struck the bushes, en Brer Fox sorter hang 'roun' fer to see w'at wuz gwineter happen. Bimeby he hear somebody call 'im, en way up de hill he see Brer Rabbit settin' cross-legged on a chinkapin log komin' de pitch outen his her wid a chip. Den Brer Fox know dat he bin swop off mighty bad. Brer Rabbit wuz bleedzed fer ter fling back some er his sass, 'en he holler out: "Bred en' bawn in a briar-patch, Brer Fox, bred en' bawn in a briar-patch!" en wid dat he skip out des ez lively ez a cricket in de embers.

A special case of dialect among Negro Southerners is to be found in Gullah, where the simplified English learned from early masters (what Krapp has called the "Pan-African English" of the slave coast) has

---

[24] Mencken, *op. cit.*, p. 364. G. P. Krapp refutes the popular view that Negro habits of speech "have corrupted" English in the South, *op. cit.*, I, p. 226. Charles Dickens, in his *American Notes* (1842), was one of the first to suggest that white Southerners, especially women, were affected by Negro speech because they had black nurses when they were children. Brunner also refers to this possible influence, *op. cit.*, II, p. 365. Actually, all traits of general Southern pronunciation, whether educated or low colloquial, may be traced back to earlier English tendencies, sometimes exaggerated. See for example Cleanth Brooks, "The Relation of the Alabama-Georgia Dialect to the Provincial Dialects of Great Britain," *Louisiana State University Studies,* XX (1935).

been the point of departure for a unique development. This dialect is native to the rice fields of South Carolina and Georgia. It has been used with some effort at fidelity by Ambrose Gonzales in his *Gullah Stories of the Carolina Coast* (1922), and by DuBose Heyward in his *Porgy* tales on which both play and opera were based. In isolated communities, for instance on islands off the Carolina coast, it has carried farther than most dialects the innovations going back to the days of slavery. Evidence has been produced to indicate that Gullah vocabulary contains words and expressions surviving from native African languages.[25] It is conceivable that the same linguistic background may have affected the grammatical structure of the dialect spoken today, but on this problem no special study has as yet been made. In any event, the basis of Gullah morphology as of its phonology is the somewhat slurred English of white settlers in the 17th and 18th centuries, with final consonants weakly articulated, *r*'s already lost as in today's Birtish standard, [ð] weakened in unaccented words to [ð̥] or [d̥] (written *d* by Harris in his *Uncle Remus*), and so on.

The levelling of grammatical forms in Gullah has gone so far as to obliterate a number of the distinctions still surviving in conventional English. Among them is the special sign for an inflected genitive case, producing locutions like: *a ho'n owl eye, de dog foot, dat woman hat,* for: *a horn owl's eye, the dog's foot, that woman's hat.* Here, therefore, word order or position alone indicates the syntactic relationship — a grammatical device for the genitive which is to be found paralleled in other languages, including some outside of the Indo-European family. Loss of inflectional endings has also levelled the distinction between singular and plural nouns, though sometimes a demonstrative or other adjectival pronoun gives the clue: *summuch dog* for *so many dogs; dem Nyankee* for *those Yankees* (or possibly: *damned Yankees?*). Among the pronouns, traditional objective forms serve as subjects and nominative forms as objects and even possessive modifiers, though the pattern is not strict. Perhaps it would be more accurate to say that a wider choice of forms is possible in these various constructions than in standard English. Dialect writers report constructions like the following: *'e foot,* for *his foot; 'e book* layin' dere, for *his (her) book* is lying there; *him an' me* come in bimeby, for *he and I* came in by and by; *dem car* break down, for

---

[25] Alonso Turner, *Africanisms in the Gullah Dialect* (University of Chicago Press, 1949). The author probably overstates his case, since he compares words and epithets of Gullah with African terms having quite different meanings. Nevertheless some of the evidence adduced is impressive.

their car broke down; *her an' de boy* wants some mo', for *she and the boy* want some more. Verbal inflections have for the most part been reduced to a single form showing neither ablaut nor external suffixes as marker of change in tense. Thus: *cross, jump, look, see,* for *crossed, jumped, looked, saw* (in the Appendix selection of Gullah, p. 275).

In compensation for this reduction in morphology, a new device has been developed to indicate distinctions of time in action expressed by verbs. This is the insertion of an indeclinable particle *done,* from the verb *to do,* placed before the main verb to indicate past time in any of its aspects: I *done give,* he *done see,* etc. But even this particle does not appear consistently; *done* and *see* alone may mean *did* and *saw,* according to context. Omission of all forms of the copula is common: de gyaden big, for the garden *is* big; dey dey, for they *are* there. Forms of *to be* may have been lost as a consequence of either gradual phonetic weakening or the deliberate distortion of speech practised by whites in addressing slaves, or both. In any event the result offers a curious parallel with other languages —for instance, Russian and Hebrew— which omit the copula under similar conditions.

From the point of view of the linguist, a regional dialect like Gullah presents an interesting case study exemplifying what may happen to a language having a long literary tradition, when it is isolated socially and geographically, and confined to speakers cut off from that tradition. To teachers and social reformers it presents many problems which are not our primary concern here. However, it may be remarked that, as Professor Fries has said of American "vulgar" English in general, the solution of such problems depends not so much on the inculcation of rules of "correct" speech by exercises in the schools, as in enriching a language equipment which is at the present time impoverished. The main emphasis on a corrective language program should be less on drill and more on the providing of "a language experience that is directed toward acquaintance with and practice in the rich and varied resources of the language,"[26] using direct observation as the most important tool of instruction. So far as the speakers of Gullah and other substandard dialects are concerned, this obviously implies a significant change in society, including equality of opportunities for both Negroes and whites to share in the literary culture of English. When these are realised the consequences will no doubt be reflected in all Southern dialects, and will become a subject of study for future historians of the English language in the United States.

---

[26] Fries, *op. cit.,* p. 288.

6. AMERICAN LINGUISTIC TRAITS COMPARED
WITH STANDARD BRITISH

The phenomena of differentiation separating British from American
English, and the signs of influence exercised by the latter on the former,
have been the subject of considerable discussion in recent years. Attention
has been called to the problem by the achievements of American novelists
and playwrights who abundantly make use of vernacular idiom for literary
expression. The discussion has become lively, and at times even acri-
monious, in proportion as technical advances in communication (besides
military and economic relations) have fortified the American impact
on contemporary culture in other English-speaking countries.

Differences in standard vocabulary are among the most obvious
elements of contrast.[27] They are also the most readily studied and explained. Visitors in England and America find themselves obliged to
substitute back and forth between word pairs such as the following:

British	American	British	American
biscuit	cracker	lorry	truck
book (as verb)	reserve, order	perambulator, pram	baby carriage
braces	suspenders	public house, pub	saloon
chemist's shop	drugstore	reel of cotton	spool of thread
drawing-pin	thumb-tack	spanner	monkey-wrench
goods waggon	freight car	sweets	candy
ironmongery	hardware	tin (container)	can

However, though these distinctions[28] may assume crucial importance
in a given practical situation, they are hardly significant enough to
support the claim, advanced by H. L. Mencken, that a quite new language
has been developed in the United States. Nor are the strictly morphological differences very great between English and American, when
viewed on the level of standard usage. Certain strong and weak verbs
do show somewhat different forms, with the American fairly often though
not always the more conservative: U. S. *gotten* versus English *got*; *proven*

---

[27] The reference dictionary of standard American English is Sir William
Craigie and James R. Hulbert, *A Dictionary of American English on
Historical Principles*, 4 vols. (University of Chicago Press, 1938—44).
See also M. M. Mathews, *Dictionary of Americanisms* (Chicago, 1951).

[28] A classified list of such Anglo-American synonyms is given by
Galinsky, *op. cit.*, II, pp. 7—44. Mencken also provided a list in his
American Language.

versus *proved*; *wakened* versus *woke*; *swelled* versus *swollen*; *sheared* versus *shorn*, etc. These and other such deviations are conspicuous because they have to do with some of the few surviving inflections in the English language.

Perhaps it may be said that linguistic differences between the two communities are to be noticed primarily in the ways in which they make use of the common linguistic heritage, both in word formation and in certain patterns of syntactic usage. Even here, of course, many of the distinctions tend to be obliterated with time. American neologisms are quickly conveyed to England and become familiar to readers, theatre-goers and film enthusiasts. In some cases they are finally adopted. Others die out on both sides of the Atlantic. Neologisms are frequent in both domains, and it is interesting to observe how they arise.

In both countries, new terms arise from the native stock by a method of compounding an uninflected verbal root with an adverbial particle, either preceding or following it. The former method produces words like: *income, inset, inlay, outlay, overpass, output, underwrite(r)*. These are current on both sides of the Atlantic. But insofar as new formations are created with postpositional particles, the greater activity appears to be carried on in the United States. The coinages may not be far more numerous, but their use appears to be more prevalent. Nouns formed in this way have a strong stress on the verbal element but none on the particle, as distinguished from the similarly constituted verbs which have more evenly distributed stress on the two elements. Thus among the nouns we have: *set-up* (a term with many meanings), *run-around, check-off, check-up, run-in, feed-back, feed-in, fall-out* (applied to radio-active substances), *knock-out, sit-down, lock-out, pay-off, show-down, build-up, walk-away* (easy victory), *brush-off, work-out*, and many others. These are sometimes found inflected for plural number by adding -(*e*)*s* to the attached particle: *set-backs, check-offs, flare-ups*, etc. The verbs formed from these same elements are given a more even accentuation, being treated as a complex of two stressed elements: to *'check 'off* (as opposed to *'check-off*); to *'set 'back* (as opposed to *'set-back*), etc.

American usage not only inclines to the somewhat wider use of such newly minted (or re-minted) terms, but also displays a greater freedom —shall we say license?— in the use of them, as compared with contemporary British English. By placement before another noun these become adjectival in function, for instance: *a knock-down, drag-out fight*; *a try-out performance*; *a sit-down strike*; *a walk-away success*. A stylistic change is effected when these nouns derived from verbs are used to convey the notion of activity which in conventional sentences would be conveyed by the verb itself, while the verb is reduced to something colourless like *is, have, give*, etc. Thus an American speaker will say: They *gave him the run-around* or *the brush-off*, instead of: They *evaded him* or *thrust him aside*; His press-agent *gave him a build-up*, instead of: *praised him* and his accomplishments for commercial purposes; They *had a show-down*, instead of: *settled the matter finally*; There *was a try-out performance*, instead of: The actors *performed* the play as a test; Let's *have a check-up*, instead of: Let's *verify* our results. If the tendency here noted were to prevail, the predicate would cease to be the part of a sentence conveying a message of activity, while this function would be discharged by a noun object. It is still too early, however, to decide whether such a shift is occurring in American English. The probability is that the tendency will be held in check by competing tendencies in the linguistic system.

American English takes certain freedoms with grammatical categories which are avoided or infrequently used in British English. Nouns appear as verbs in expressions like: to *chair* a meeting (to act as chairman), to *author* a book (to write it), to *pressure* (exert pressure upon) someone; to *vacation* (spend one's holidays), to *radio* a message, to *captain* a team. Conversely, verbs appear as nouns: a big *push*; a good *buy*; an *assist*; an athletic *meet*. There are adjectives freely employed as nouns, sometimes with the nominal inflection for plural number added; young *hopefuls*, *comics, funnies, empties* (empty bottles), *Reds* (loosely applied to Communists and other militant progressives), *flimsies* (thin sheets of paper used for making carbon copies), *uppers* and *lowers* (berths in a train or ship). Adjectival participles may even be inflected like nouns: *marked-downs* (merchandise reduced in price). Whole phrases appear from time to time in adjectival position before the nouns modified: *portal-to-portal* pay; an *on-the-spot* conference; an *off-the-record* speech; an *out-of-town* district; *down-the-line* support; a *round-the-clock* watch. Another conspicuous nominal construction is what has been called the block compound by a recent commentator.[29] This type arises by the placement of two or more nouns in series so that each one modifies the meaning of the following one and serves in place of a prepositional phrase. The simpler type is represented by sets like: *pupil activities* (in place of a subjective genitive), *child guidance* (in place of an objective genitive),

---

[29] Gustav Kirchner, "Recent American Influence on Standard English: The Syntactical Sphere," *Zeitschrift für Anglistik*, V (1957), 29–42. On general usage see Margaret Nicholson, *A Dictionary of American-English Usage* (Oxford, 1957); and especially B. and C. Evans, *A Dictionary of Contemporary American Usage* (New York, 1957).

and *sex appeal* or *eye appeal* (in place of a modifying phrase). More complicated types are represented by: *Natural Resources Committee Report* (i. e., report of the committee concerned with natural resources); *election reform law* (law for the reform of elections); *price control board* (board dealing with the control of prices). Similar in its effect of concentration is the combination of a noun followed by an adjective or perfect passive participle, when the noun stands in place of a modifying phrase: *space-minded* (thinking in terms of space); *fashion-conscious*; *union-interlocked finances* (finances interlocked with those of a union); *land-hungry* peasants (those hungry for land), etc.

Journalistic writing in the United States has fostered such linguistic creations in great numbers. They do not, to be sure, represent a complete innovation. Older compounds were made on the same pattern: *bed-ridden*, *care-free*, *war-weary*, etc. But such forms are especially favoured in journalism because they, like the block compounds, permit the shifting of a concrete image from a postponed dependent position to the leading position in a phrase. The same impulse to placement in head position leads, in journalistic writing, to the use of inflected genitives where normal usage calls for *of*-phrases. The total effect is of a crowding of information into the limited space available before the subject of a sentence: *North Carolina's* Democratic Senator Sam Erwin (*Newsweek*, 6 May 1957), *Chicago's* week-long centenary celebration (*ibid.*). Besides being challenging in a strident sort of way, this type of construction also saves words. The drive for economy of space, especially in headlines, has led to the choice of less usual short words in place of ordinary long ones: *probe* for *investigation*, *wed* for *married*. Yet these special devices of journalism, consciously thought out for specific stylistic purposes, do not appear in normal American discourse, whether oral or written.

Nor is space-saving the only motive of journalistic abbreviations. Some of them result from linguistic playfulness and the desire to attract attention. Portmanteau words launched by newspaper writers, a few of which gain a limited currency, are primarily designed for entertainment. Thus a luminary of the social world is called a *socialite* (a term fairly often found in "gossip columns" of the press); a matron who has just received a divorce in the capital city of Nevada is said to be *Renovated*; slang is referred to as *slanguage*, and elocution as *yellocution*.

American slang[30] is of course very striking in respect to the number and range of its creations. Because of the wide prevalence today of

---

[30] Maurice H. Weseen, *A Dictionary of American Slang* (New York, 1934); Berrey and van den Bark, *American Thesaurus of Slang* (New York, 1942 and 1947).

American films and light fiction, this esoteric vocabulary has become familiar far beyond the borders of the United States. It is baffling to outsiders, not only because of the special circumstances of its origin, but also because of its rapid changes. When Krapp wrote his book on American English, he mentioned the following words as typical of slang in the 1920's: *oodles, flabbergasted, mollycoddle, blooey, foozle, frazzle, woozy, dotty.* Most of them are now out of date if not completely dropped. Among those now current, many are expressions substituting a concrete image for the more abstract or colourless expressions of ordinary speech:

Term	Meaning:	Term	Meaning:
bone orchard	— cemetery	lift the elbow	— take a drink
brass tacks	— essentials	pound the sidewalk	— walk
coffin-nail	— cigarette	put the finger on	— betray
cut a melon	— divide profits	scare the pants off	— terrify
flatfoot	— policeman	squeal on someone	— inform to the police
flat tire	— boring person	stick-in-the-mud	— a conservative
gum shoe	— detective	wooden overcoat	— a coffin

Many such terms combine vivid imagery with sound effects such as alliteration, assonance and rime: *face lace* for whiskers, *hot squat* for electric chair, *rock 'n' roll, city slicker, hush money, live wire, slow poke, slush fund* (money used for corrupt political practices). Humorous prolixity gives rise to metaphors like: *ball and chain* for wife; *yesterday, today and forever* for hash; *bats in the belfry* for insane. But abbreviations also gain currency: *D. A.* for District Attorney, *M. C.* for master of ceremonies, *pen* for penitentiary, and so on. Many single standard words substitute for others in slang parlance. Among the terms for a girl or woman are: *baby, dame, doll, femme, fluff, frail, frill, jane, mouse, skirt, tomato.* There is an imposing list of terms also to designate a condition of intoxication: *blotto, canned, cock-eyed, corned, flooey, fried, pickled, plastered, stewed, stiff.* — It will be noticed that metaphors from cooking are well represented here.

Despite its vividness and gamesomeness, however, the terminology of slang is seldom adopted in serious writing, save in passages of realistic dialogue, and seldom achieves a long life, whether in England or America.

Another problem connected with the American vocabulary is its infiltration with foreign loan words of recent date, due to the influx of immigrants from various European countries in the late 19th and early 20th century.[31] Of permanent loan-words into English there are relatively few, and these are restricted to a narrow field, notably that of the kitchen: *sauerkraut, leberwurst, ravioli, smörgaas, egg foo young, matzoh, barsch, chile con carne*. The influence of alien grammatical constructions on American English is negligible, and when apparent is frequently humorous in intention, for instance in the unidiomatic inversions: *food* I have to cook for him; *dresses* he says I can buy, etc. Here the intonation also undertakes to imitate a foreign model, thus emphasising the humorous tone.[32]

It would be hazardous to attempt any prophecy now concerning the future relations of British and American English. The fate of the language as a whole is of course bound up with factors lying outside of the sphere of pure linguistics. In general it may be said that despite the persistence of regional dialects in both countries, the tendency in both is towards a single national language. This condition is in turn dependent for both on the extension of advanced education to the utmost possible and the abolishment of class barriers. Notwithstanding the divergencies manifest between American and British speech on certain levels, the language of cultured communication still resists any marked separation of the two; notwithstanding the attachment to native linguistic conservatism in both England and America (probably more conscious in England than in America), modern technology in communication may be counted on to bring closer these two important parts of the English-speaking world and to level out the differences between them. There was a time when American patriots deplored the servile imitation of British models; there is a time now when British purists deplore the influx of Yankee phraseology. It is possible that the roles may be reversed once more, and then ultimately the reasons for deploring one way or the other may disappear as peoples draw closer together in a cultural exchange where spatial separation means very little. But these are purely speculative matters for the present. We can do no more at the moment than indicate their existence and record the situation as we see it now.[33]

---

[31] On the contacts of English with these other languages in America, H. L. Mencken has collected much material, both in his original book and the Supplements to it. There are also a number of special studies in this field.

[32] On standard American intonation see Kenneth Pike, *Intonation of American English* (University of Michigan Press, 1946).

[33] In addition to authorities already cited, the student should consult W. N. Francis and R. I. McDavid, Jr., *The Structure of American English* (New York, 1958).

CHAPTER VIII

THE ENGLISH LANGUAGE TODAY

1. GEOGRAPHICAL EXPANSION AND INNER CHANGES

The expansion of the English language over the earth's surface by no means ceased with the end of the earlier period of discovery and exploration. British military power having defeated the previous French efforts to obtain control of India, that huge country was subjected to a century and a half of English rule, with the inevitable introduction of the conquerors' language for purposes of trade, finance, administration and government. Here, however, the many native languages continued to be used while English was employed as a tongue supplementing rather than displacing others. Though the present Indian Parliament continues to conduct its debates in English, a project is being considered to have Hindustani recognised as the official medium for such purposes. Linguistic history developed otherwise in Australia and New Zealand, heavily colonised during the 19th century, where the native populations retreated before the white settlers and dwindled into small communities exercising but a negligible influence on the triumphant Anglo-Saxon culture.[1] In South Africa, English rule replaced that of Dutch colonists as a result of the Boer War (1899—1901), and the English language became associated with Afrikaans (the form of Netherlandish spoken there) and the native African languages, which still survive. It was at this time, too, that the United States obtained hegemony over the Hawaiian

---

[1] As an example of the extinction of a native language under white domination, Joshua Whatmough cites the Aranta of central Australia, who numbered about two million inhabitants in 1900, but only 300 in 1930. See his *Language: A Modern Synthesis* (London, 1956), p. 47.

Islands in the Pacific Ocean (organised as a territory in 1900), and, as a result of the Spanish-American War, over the Phillipines (which obtained political if not economic independence in 1946).

Among other areas attached to the British Empire in recent times are Kenya, Uganda and the Gold Coast (now independent as Ghana) in Africa, and British Guiana in South America and British Honduras in Central America. In these regions too the English language has been introduced for governmental administration, missionary activities and commercial enterprise. But its influence is also to be felt, to a great extent though less directly and obviously, in those parts of the world which have been penetrated and controlled by English or American business without complete loss of national independence: in Burma and Malaya and countries of the Near East where British capital has traditionally played a decisive role (now contested, to be sure, by American) and in the Latin American countries (where American capital has expanded rapidly, though contested by British). In China, as is well known, both British and American commercial interests exercised a strong control and maintained a privileged position until the final victory of the Chinese national revolution in 1948. The total effect of all these developments has been to make English, by one means or another, into a language of first-rate importance in all parts of the world.

In those situations where imperialist control has been exercised behind a front of national independence for the country exploited, the linguistic influences by English and on English have been less obvious, of course, than in the cases of outright annexation. One curious mutation of the language has arisen in the Far East (China, the islands of the Pacific and elsewhere) as a means of communication between natives and English-speaking traders. This is called Pidgin English (*pidgin* being a corruption of the word *business*)— a *lingua franca* popularly supposed to result from the putting together of uninflected English words as they would appear in the sequence of a Chinese sentence structure. Actually this distortion of English is in part due to the same attitude of contemptuous superiority which led to the formation of the Negro Gullah dialect among American slaves of African origin (see ch. 7, sec. 5). The foreign traders perpetuated a system of garbled speech which may have been appropriate to the first years to intercommunication, but could easily have been replaced by standard English if the social and economic situation had been different. As it is, Pidgin English has developed and become established in a structure peculiar to itself, so that persons wishing to use it in any part of the Orient must learn the pattern there current like that of a foreign language, in order to be understood.[2]

The wide dissemination of English over the surface of the globe by means peaceful and warlike, commercial and cultural, has left its mark on innumerable other languages encountered on the way. In each situation, the English loan words give an index of the most important contacts: in politics and sport, business and technology. These borrowings are not however of primary concern here. More germane to the history of English is the influx of loan words from the alien languages into it (see sec. 2 below).

As contacts multiplied with outside languages and cultures, the learned world of Europe found enormous new fields for linguistic study. The naive first reports of explorers and missionaries were followed by more abundant and accurate descriptive accounts from the four extra-European continents. In India, an 18th-century English judge, Sir William Jones, studied Sanscrit in order to investigate the history of native law. When he brought this ancient Indo-European language to the attention of European scholars (1796), they were quick to realise that it must be closely allied with the classical Mediterranean languages already well known. Before long the field of comparative investigation was widened, and the kinship of other outstanding members of the Indo-European family —Germanic and Celtic, Baltic and Slavonic, as well as Italic, Hellenic and Indo-Iranian— was demonstrated by a group of pioneer linguists including Franz Bopp, Rasmus Rask, Jacob Grimm, August Leskien and others.[3] The historical-comparative method here employed was extended to other major families of languages, such as Semitic, Hamitic, Bantu, Dravidian and Malay-Polynesian. So illuminating were the researches into linguistic origins that the historical approach may be said to have become the predominant one in 19th century linguistics. Certainly there was a marked preoccupation at the time with what we should now call diachronic descriptions of language.

Studies of English shared somewhat belatedly in the general preoccupation with historical grammar. Joseph Wright's grammars of Old

---

[2] A linguistic description of one type of Pidgin has been made by R. A. Hall, Jr., for the American Linguistic Society: *Melanesian Pidgin Phrase-Book and Vocabulary* (1942); *Melanesian Pidgin English: Grammar, Texts, Vocabulary* (1943).

[3] A general survey is given by Holger Pedersen, *Linguistic Science in the Nineteenth Century*, translated by John Spargo (Harvard University Press, 1931).

and Middle English, taken in conjunction with his Gothic and comparative Greek grammars, placed the earlier history of English on a firm foundation and also showed its relation to other members of the Indo-European family. Ellis's early studies on historical phonology were climaxed by Henry Sweet's epoch-making history of English sounds.[4] The Old English grammar of Eduard Sievers,[5] translated into English, was for several generations a standard textbook used along with Wright's, and general histories of English, as well as special articles, have continued since the turn of the century to enrich our understanding of its development in all periods.[6]

General linguistic studies have served to illuminate many general tendencies in the history of English sounds. The work in phonetics initiated by Alexander Bell, Ellis and Sweet, has been continued in recent times by Daniel Jones and others who, with the aid of modern laboratory equipment, have been able to give extremely precise descriptions of contemporary pronunciation, and even to observe tendencies towards further changes in the pattern of essential sounds within recent decades.

To envisage trends in the present situation, let us first revert to the one existing at the end of the 18th century. At that time long open $\bar{e}$ [ɛ:] had followed closed $\bar{e}$ in becoming [i:], and the short vowels i and u had been generally lowered long since to their present positions [ɪ] and [ʌ] respectively. We may note briefly the following additional changes and recent tendencies. In the first place, the midtongue vowels, long $\bar{e}$ and $\bar{o}$, have diphthongised in British as well as American speech. In England the new diphthong [ou] from long $\bar{o}$ has recently shown a further tendency to change, the first element being shifted to a fronted open

---

[4] Joseph and Mary Wright, *An Old English Grammar* (Oxford, 1908); A. J. Ellis, *Early English Pronunciation*, 5 vols. (Chaucer Society Publication, 1869—89); Henry Sweet, *History of English Sounds* (Oxford, 1888).

[5] E. Sievers, *Angelsächsische Grammatik*, 3rd ed. (Halle, 1898).

[6] Among outstanding historical studies of the language may be mentioned: Friedrich Kluge, *Geschichte der englischen Sprache* (Strassburg, 1890); Max Kaluza, *Historische Grammatik der englischen Sprache* (Berlin, 1907); Karl Luick, *Hist. Gram. der englischen Sprache* (incomplete; Leipzig 1914 and 1929); Henry Cecil Wyld, *A Short History of English* (London, 1914; 3rd ed. 1937); Otto Jespersen, *Growth and Structure of the English Language* (Leipzig, 1919; revised and republished, 9th ed., Oxford 1938); René Huchon, *Histoire de la langue anglaise* (incomplete; Paris, 1923—30); Karl Brunner, *Die englische Sprache* (Halle, 1950—51).

position [ɜ], giving a combination [ɜʊ] in words like *know, goal,* etc.[7] There is also, as in America, a shifting of position towards a breaking in long *ī* and *ū.* Though transcribed as [i:] and [u:] by Daniel Jones for standard speech, the phonetic value is actually recorded as [ij] and [uw] according to recent observations.[8] English speech shares with American the tendency to replace the traditional contrast between all sets of long and short vowels with a different sort of contrast, namely that between stable and unstable ones. The qualitative results of the common tendency are, however, somewhat different. Recent experiments conducted with speakers of standard London English have indicated that here too the essential contrast is one of quality (high versus low position, tight versus relaxed articulation), rather than duration in time. Apparently it is this qualitative difference which chiefly enables listeners to discriminate between word pairs like: *sit* and *seat, soot* and *suit,* etc.[9] Shortening without change of quality —hence without phonemic significance in the present situation— has been observed in the case of the long back vowels [u:] and [ɔ:], as in: *room, spoon, often, cross, loss.*[10] The short *u,* having been lowered to [ʌ], has recently shown a trend to further lowering and open articulation as [a] or [ɑ].[11] Modern short *e* is also low in comparison with the corresponding sound in French and other

---

[7] Wiktor Jassem, *Fonetyka Języka Angielskiego* (Warsaw, 1954), p. 75. The second element of the diphthong, written [w] by Jassem, is transcribed by others as [u]. Trager and Smith, *Outline,* p. 17. ascribe this pronunciation to "class-dialects, mostly British." The first element is that of the vowel in *bird, word,* etc., written [ə:] by others.

[8] In the preface to his *English Pronouncing Dictionary* Daniel Jones remarks that [i:] tends towards and is often replaced by a diphthong consisting of an opener *i* followed by a closer one; similarly [u:] by an opener *u* followed by a closer one, (9th ed., London, 1948), p. xix. Jassem and others transcribe these as [ij], [uw].

[9] A. C. Gimson, "The Phonemic/ Chronemic Grouping of English Vowels," *Acta Linguistica,* V (1945—49), 94—100.

[10] Simeon Potter, "Trends in Current English", *Moderna Språk: Tidskrift för Språkundervisning* (1956), 255—67. This shortening may be compared with that noted in the New England dialect of America (ch. 7, sec. 3).

[11] See Gimson, *loc. cit.* This trend is clearly indicated by the fact that when [ɑ:] was experimentally shortened before a voiceless consonant as in the word *part,* the result was mistaken for [ʌ] by 90 per cent of the listeners under observation.

continental languages; hence probably low in comparison with the ME equivalent. Thus the entire list of early ModE short vowels has now a lowered position as a common phonetic trait.

2. Vocabulary, Lexicography and Problems of Semantics

With the continued spread of the British Empire into Africa and Asia, the influx of exotic borrowed words continued also, not only because of the direct practical contacts of government and business with native cultures, but also because journalists, travellers and writers of fiction like Kipling, Conrad and E. M. Forster helped to familiarise the reading public with these civilisations by indirect knowledge of them. Reporters of the Boer War began the borrowing of words from Dutch as spoken in South Africa (Afrikaans), for instance: *trek, voortrekker, spoor, veld, kraal* (this last ultimately from Portugese *corral*). Some native African words are: *gnu, impi, tse-tse, assagai* and *voodoo*. In India, Burma, Indonesia and Malaya the colonisers and traders have picked up such words as: *chit, durwan, betel, anaconda, chutney, ourang-outang, amok, tuan, sari, ingyi* and *khaki*. Some words referring directly to imperialist domination and the political struggle against it are: *raj* (connected ultimately with Latin *reg-ere*), *swaraj* (the first element being ultimately connected with Latin *suus*, Polish *swój*), *kowtow, pukka sahib, babu, chokra, coolie*. Place names appear but slightly transformed as names for merchandise in: *madras, calico, shantung, nankeen*. The story of these words, as given in any unabridged modern dictionary, is eloquent of the wide geographical contacts established by the English language in modern times.

Knowledge of the origins and connections of English words has of course been greatly extended since the time of Samuel Johnson. Scientific etymology, like all other aspects of linguistic study, was put on a firm basis in the light of the comparative researches already mentioned. A distinct advance for its time was represented by the etymological dictionary published by Skeat in 1882. This is now outdated and should be used with caution even in the most recent editions.[12] Skeat drew on a still limited field for his cognate forms, and he made

---

[12] W. W. Skeat, *A Concise Etymological Dictionary* (Oxford University Press) appeared in 1882; since then it was revised twice (1901 and 1911), the latter edition having benefited from the advance in knowledge of comparative Indo-European, notably from the *Lateinisches etymologisches Wörterbuch* of A. Walde (Heidelberg, 1906 ed.).

his reconstructions of prehistoric roots before the recovery of Hittite had revolutionised our conceptions of the parent Indo-European language.[13] Nevertheless Skeat's work is still of use for initial orientation. Today all complete dictionaries such as Webster's *Unabridged Dictionary* in America, or the *Universal Dictionary of the English Language* edited by H. C. Wyld in England, give information on the immediate origins of English words, though they do not attempt to propose reconstructions of prehistoric forms. For the history of English words since the late Middle Ages we have the ten volumes of the *New English* (also called *Oxford English*) *Dictionary*,[14] which not only gives immediate etymologies and detailed definitions, but also dated quotations from writers through the centuries to illustrate the various nuances of meaning for every word entered. The examples constitute in fact the body of evidence upon which the definitions are inductively based.

Another type of reference book called the thesaurus was developed in the 19th century as an aid in the study of English lexical resources for practical purposes. Here words and phrases are grouped together according to the areas of meaning with which they are associated. Human experience is subdivided into topics like: abstract relations, space, matter, intellect, volition and affections; the first of these (for instance) is subdivided into topics like: existence, relation, and causation; the subtopic of change, into simple and complex types with antithetical subdivisions like: change and permanence; cessation and continuance; revolution and substitution. Under the single heading of *revolution*, to take but one example, there are clustered numerous terms drawn from the fields of psychology, politics, biology, sociology, etc. (e. g.: *transilience, revulsion, overthrow, upset, bouleversement, breakup, mutiny, uprising*). Indices enable the reader to locate any term under all of the several headings where it is listed. Such a work is, in short, a vocabulary builder for the practising writer. Peter Mark Roget (1779—1869) projected the first one early in the 19th century (1805); his book, first published in 1852, was repeatedly reissued and expanded, both by himself and his son John Lewis Roget. There have been many popular reprints and editions, down to the present time.

---

[13] For exhaustive information on the Indo-European cognates of English words one should now consult A. Walde and J. Pokorny, *Vergleichendes Wörterbuch der indogermanischen Sprachen* (Berlin, 1928—30) revised ed. in progress.

[14] Edited by James Murray and others as *A New English Dictionary on Historical Principles* (Oxford, 1884—1928); reissued as the *Oxford English Dictionary* (1933).

In the area of scientific discourse ModE has, like many related languages, turned to Greek and Latin (especially the former) for the creation of special terminologies. Here the prefixes, suffixes and roots of words familiar to students of classical philology proliferate a steadily increasing swarm of neologisms. Medicine, chemistry and physics abound in them. Their origins often give immediate clues to their present meanings. Thus it is with: *thermodynamics, entropy, neutron, nuclear fission, psychosomatic, leucocyte* and many others. In some cases, however, interesting historical shifts of meaning are involved. *Toxic, toxin* and *antitoxin* are connected with the Greek word τόξον meaning — not poison, but a bow, because the derivative word, τοξικόν, was applied to a special poison smeared upon arrows used in warfare. Similarly, the word *thyroid* is adapted (with suffix) from Greek θυρεός, meaning a shield, because the gland in question resembles one. The Latin term *vermiform appendix* conceals another similitude based on appearance. A number of prefixes and suffixes from the classical languages function today as morphemes entering into the formation of new words, not always in their original sense and not always in combination with roots from the same language. In this way hybrids are formed. Thus the Greek prefix *hyper-* is combined with a word of Latin origin in *hypertension*; so also in *auto-suggestion*. The Greek prefix *para* meaning *beside* has been modified to a sense of ancillary or accessory in neologisms like: *paramilitary, parasymptomatic*. A homonymous prefix from the Latin (and also Italian) *parare* appears in *parachute* and has become active in creating words like: *parabomb, paramarine, paratrooper* (here meaning equipped with parachute). Other classical prefixes now active are: *crypto-, neo-, proto-, pseudo-*; *de-, extra-, semi-*. Among the most active of classical suffixes are: *-ate, -ite, -ism, -ize (-ise)*.[15] A peculiarity of classical formations in English, especially those from the Greek, is the movable accent which appears in families of derivatives from the same source:

'antiphon but *an'tiphonal*	*'reticule* but *re'ticulated*
'climate but *cli'matic*	*'spectroscope* but *spectro'scopic*
'pseudonym but *pseu'donymous*	*'theme* but *the'matic*

Foreign loans and adaptations account, however, for only a part of the recent vocabulary. The internal resources of English are also being

---

[15] For information on the living affixes in English today, and the degree to which they are active, see F. W. Harwood and Alison M. Wright, "Statistical Study of English Word Formation," *Language*, XXXII (1956), 260—73.

exploited constantly to create new combinations. Pairs of simple words are quite freely compounded into fresh units, with the two parts standing in various types of syntactic relations to each other. The dividing line between two separate words, on the one hand, which are merely frequently associated (like: a *black market*, a *strong hold*), and those actually compounded, on the other (*blackbird, stronghold*) is not easily defined in English, the more so as spelling and punctation or spacing offer no safe guide. There are however some objective tests which may be applied in order to identify a genuine compound as such: that is, a new single word, as opposed to a locution of two or more words, no matter how often used together. One test is connected with accent and intonation,[16] for the compound will usually be found to have only one element strongly stressed, whereas the two independent words characteristically have two stresses. A compound is also contrasted with a non-compounded syntactic group of words by the limitations on the morphological changes it may undergo.[17] The word *stronghold* meaning *fortress* may be inflected in the plural as *strongholds*; but the inflected form **strongerholds* can not substitute for the expression *stronger fortresses*. On the other hand, the non-compounded parallel expression in the sentence: He gripped it with a *'strong .'hold* is capable of morphological modification affecting the

---

[16] The whole problem of distinguishing words as irreducible units is closely bound up with the problem of stress, as has been pointed out by W. Jassem, "Stress in Modern English," *Biuletyn Polskiego Towarzystwa Językoznawczego*, XI (1952), 21—49.

[17] Hans Marchand, "Notes on Nominal Compounds in Present-Day English," *Word*, XI (1955), 216—27. Marchand's definition is this: "When two or more words are combined into a morphological unit, we speak of a compound" (p. 216). The test is thus formulated: "the compound must be morphologically isolated from a parallel syntactic group" (p. 220). See now Marchand's book *The Categories and Types of Present-Day English Word Formation* (Wiesbaden, 1960). Leonard Bloomfield in his book *Language* (New York, 1933), p. 228, appealed to the test of accentuation alone. Other writers have either failed to distinguish between words frequently used in close association and genuine compounds, or have referred unspecifically to the degree of psychological unity achieved in the concept underlying the compound, with some consideration for intonation. Thus H. Koziol, *Handbuch der englischen Wortbildungslehre* (Heidelberg, 1927), p. 46 f.; Jespersen in his *Modern English Grammar*, VI (Morphology), 8: 12, refers to unity of concept alone. This psychological aspect is no doubt important, but we are concerned here with external linguistic signs of it.

first element: ...a *'stronger 'hold*. Similarly with compounds like: *'childbearing age* (but not **childrenbearing*), *'waste-paper basket* (but not **wastedpaper basket*), etc.[18] Moreover, the semantic relations of genuinely compounded elements differ from those existing between like elements which are merely juxtaposed. A *'frying pan* (compound noun) means a pan for frying, whereas *'frying 'food* (a syntactic group) means food that is frying; and so likewise with many other pairs.

Among the most numerous of the newly compounded substantives are those formed on the analogy of verbs followed by adverbial (prepositional) particles, but treated accentually as single units. We have noted that the type *frame-up, get-away, show-down*, etc., has become very productive in America, and the same is true in England, though not to the same extent or with the same results.[19] In England, for instance, the term *lead-up* is used for an introduction, whereas *build-up* is favoured in America. In neither country is there a comparable activity in producing nominal compounds with the adverbial particle preceding another element instead of following it, as in: *outflow, underpass*, etc.[20]

So much for the noun compounds. As for the verbal expressions composed of two words, a verb proper and an adverbial particle, these are maintaining their currency at least as successfully as the single-word synonyms (mostly of Romance origin) which compete with them. They are also adapted for new meanings. Thus to *take off* is used for *depart* (of an airplane), to *call up* for to *telephone*, to *set up* for *establish*, and many others. In the verbal use, it will be noticed, the two elements are not stressed as a single unit: The machines *'break 'down* contrasts with: They had a *'break-down*. Preference for the native verb with particle over the single Romance word is especially marked in spoken English. It has been suggested that this may be due to the ability of the separated particle in end position to carry an emphatic stress and intonation curve: *Throw* that hat *a'way*, versus *Dis'card* that old hat.[21]

Since the beginning of the 20th century, linguists have devoted increasing attention to problems of semantics in connection with vocabulary.

---

[18] There are a few exceptions to this principle noted by Marchand, for instance *father-in-law* with its plural *fathers-in-law*.

[19] New formations of this type were studied by U. Lindelöf, *English Verb-Adverb Groups Converted into Nouns* (Helsinki, 1937), but the number has increased markedly since then.

[20] Hans Marchand, "Compounds with Locative Particles as First Elements in Present-Day English," *Word*, XII (1956), 391—98.

[21] Dwight L. Bollinger, "Intersections of Stress and Intonation," *Word*, XI (1955), 195—203.

This means that they have extended their researches beyond definitions, etymologies and the mechanisms of word formation, in order to inquire into the nature of the shifts and gradations of meaning which have marked the history of individual words and groups of words in a given language. A study of semantic changes —the types represented and the reasons for them— must necessarily draw upon extra-linguistic disciplines for aid: upon history, for instance, and psychology and sociology. The history of words like: *knave, hussy, bigot, puny, scab* (applied to persons), and many others, represents pejorative change which is closely bound up with the social history of England. Knowledge of this domain helps to illuminate the transitions in meaning from one age to another. There are other tendencies, such as expansion and contraction of meanings, differentiations and substitutions, modifications due to psychological associations and the influence of homonymous morphemes. When a single English term achieves a wide range of meanings, some of them may be distinguished from the rest by a difference in orthography, though the pronunciation is unaffected. Hence arise what may be called pseudo-homonyms, and a lexicographer may find himself puzzled as to whether they should be treated as one word or more than one. Thus ModE *plane* meaning "flat" and *plain* meaning "unadorned" both come ultimately from Latin *planus* through French *plain*. The areas of meaning overlap, and yet the modern writer of English, unaware of their etymology, treats them as distinct units. The two spellings *phantasy* and *fantasy*, though identical in sound and origin, have acquired a differentiation in the meanings respectively associated with them.[22]

Such are some of the problems called to linguists' attention by the first essays in semantics by Bréal and others, beginning fifty or sixty years ago.[23] Studies devoted to English semantics have ranged from essays in popular vein (by Weekley and Kittredge) to technical ones written for specialists by authorities like Stern and Ullmann.[24] An instructive type of investigation, undertaken recently by German linguists

[22] See H. W. Fowler on these two words in *A Dictionary of Modern English Usage* (Oxford University Press, 1937).

[23] Michel Bréal, *Essai de sémantique* (Paris, 1897), translated as *Semantics: Studies in the Science of Meaning* (London, 1900).

[24] Gustaf Stern, *Meaning and Change of Meaning with Special Reference to the English Language* (Göteberg, 1931); Stephen Ullmann, *Principles of Semantics* (University of Glasgow, 1957), preceded by special articles such as: "Range and Mechanism of Changes of Meaning," *Journal of English and Germanic Philology*, XLI (1942), 46—52; "Word-Form and Word-Meaning," *Archivum Linguisticum*, I (1949), 126—39.

especially, is devoted to specific fields of meaning (*Bedeutungsfelder*): for instance, words associated with some one aspect of human experience historically considered. A pursuit of the ramifications of usage and etymology for terms clustering around such chosen fields will often lead to a new understanding of social attitudes and also of the psychological activities involved in linguistic creation.[25] It is a curious fact, for instance, that verbs meaning "to come" and "to go" readily give rise to terms of moral judgment (for instance: English *unbecoming* behaviour; French *inconvenable*).

It should be perhaps mentioned here that the general topic of semantics in a not strictly linguistic sense has become a matter of widespread interest among popular writers on social problems, both in England and America. They have performed a certain service in emphasising the obscurities and ambiguities surrounding the basic terminology of the social sciences, and in calling for stricter definitions of disputed terms. But the popularisers, especially in America, have helped to foster the illusion that fundamental conflicts of interest in society (for instance, issues of the class struggle) can be amicably solved by reference to the dictionary on the part of the disputants.[26] Quite different is the use of the term semantics by a school of philosophers who insist on a logical system in which the meanings of statements are tested for consistency and developed within the system itself without reference to the world outside of it.[27]

---

[25] A leading example of special field studies in semantics is Jost Trier's *Der deutsche Wortschatz im Sinnbezirk des Verstandes* (Heidelberg, 1931). The method here defined and exemplified led to a whole school of special studies. They are surveyed by Otto Springer, "Probleme der Bedeutungslehre," *Germanic Review*, XIII (1938), 159—74. On the methodology see further Suzanne Öhman, "Theories of the Linguistic Field," *Word*, IX (1953), 123—34. For a popular discussion of semantics see M. Schlauch, *The Gift of Language*, ch. 5.

[26] E. K. Ogden and I. A. Richards called attention to the difficulties connected with the problem of definition in *The Meaning of Meaning* (London, 1923), calling for a sharp differentiation of word-signs from both the objects referred to and also the referents or subjective experiences associated with these word-signs by both listeners and speakers (readers and writers). Later the cult of semantics as a substitute for social action was developed by Stuart Chase, *The Tyranny of Words* (New York, 1938), and others.

[27] Thus for instance Rudolph Carnap, *Introduction to Semantics* (Harvard University Press, 1942).

Neither of these applications of the term *semantics* is of immediate concern here. Nevertheless the purely linguistic discipline of semantics (like other aspects of linguistic science) sooner or later confronts the investigator with questions of philosophical significance. One very fundamental question which vexes linguists of various schools is (to put it very simply) this: Can any unit of language which has meaning, whether a word, a part of a word (for instance a bound morpheme) or a group of words, be explained exclusively in terms of the internal structure of a language, or must recourse be made at some point or other to the objective world of phenomena outside of language? Those who take the former position believe that the meaning of a morpheme, whether bound or independent, is in effect the sum total of the environments in which it may appear in connected discourse. That is to say, no reference is made by them to factors outside of the structure of the language itself (hence the term structuralist linguistics). Those who take the latter position believe on the other hand that the definition of meaning on any level requires an appeal to the external objects and relationships about which language speaks. Marxist writers on linguistics adhere decisively to the second group. They do not regard language as a closed, self-explanatory system, whether it is viewed as a structure divorced from human consciousness (the mechanist view) or confined to the private consciousness of individual speakers (the subjective idealist view).

These are very complex problems, and we can do no more than mention them here in passing. They present themselves to any advanced student, not only in connection with separate units of a language like words and compounds, but also in connection with groups of such units as organised syntactically in sentences and sentence equivalents.

3. DESCRIPTION OF MODERN ENGLISH STRUCTURE

Syntax, it is usually said, is that branch of linguistics which describes the use of words, whether inflected or not, in sentences. Actually the domains of morphology and syntax, as usually taught, will be found to overlap to a certain extent, for the descriptions designating the modified forms of various classes of words already imply at least a partial knowledge of their uses in sentences (for instance, comparative degrees of adjectives, conditional forms of verbs, genitive cases of nouns). One of the most ambitious attempts to define the scope of syntax in general, that made over 60 years ago by

J. Ries,[28] proposed that this domain should be limited to the relations of groups of words, not single words, to a sentence as a whole. Thus in the sentence: He saw *me* do it, the functioning of *me* as subject of the infinitive would be regarded as an aspect of morphology, contributing to our understanding of what the accusative (objective) case means in English.[29] On the other hand, the construction of the whole infinitive phrase *me do it* would be a matter of syntax. Most writers, however, include under syntax an account of the functioning of single words as parts of speech (to use the traditional term) according to their uses in sentences.

The study of English syntax in the early 19th century was still, as in the ages preceding, very largely under the influence of Latin grammar, from which so much of our traditional terminology is derived. To take but two examples, the existence of datives of indirect object and accusatives of extent of time in Latin affected the interpretation of such English sentences as: He taught *the boy* geometry, and He taught *all day*. With the rise of historical grammar as a recognised discipline, a change in attitude set in. Writers on English syntax having a knowledge of Germanic philology in general and of Old and Middle English in particular began to insist that the modern language should be interpreted in terms of its own origins. Thus Henry Sweet, in discussing modern English syntax, appealed to the earlier history of grammatical constructions in order to explain their present status.[30] Leon Kellner and Eugen Einenkel devoted particular attention to the historical development of constructions into modern English.[31] Even those authors who based their descriptions of the contemporary language on inductive observation of modern literary works have frequently relied on earlier usage to "explain" present-day usage. For instance, in discussing expressions like: *two miles* distant, *no way* different, etc., Wendt classified them as

---

[28] John Ries, *Was ist Syntax?* (Prague, 1894; 2nd ed. 1927). The definition of Ries is explicitly rejected by Max Deutschbein (see below, n. 34), p. 5 n., as too narrow.

[29] Throughout, Ries insists that there are two aspects of morphology: what he calls *Formenlehre* and *Bedeutungslehre*. Under the one is to be classified the repertory of inflected forms which a given word may assume; under the other, the study of functions associated with these forms (i. e., their grammatical "meanings").

[30] Henry Sweet, *A New English Grammar, Logical and Historical*, II: *Syntax* (Oxford, 1898).

[31] Kellner, *op. cit.* (ch. 1, n. 24); Eugen Einenkel, *Geschichte der englischen Sprache*, II: *Historische Syntax* (3rd ed., Strassburg, 1916).

object constructions,[32] apparently on the analogy of both Latin and Old English, where they are accusatives. In other words, an appeal was now made in such cases to earlier English usage instead of, or at most along with, Latin syntax.

Meantime, the terminology of Latin grammar was retained by grammarians like Onions and Curme.[33] It was not only retained but actually further elaborated by Deutschbein[34]. For instance, in discussing the moods of verbs —a problem which, like others, the author approached from a point of view of mentalist psychology— he proposed no less than four categories of mood, depending on the relation of the speaker's consciousness to the action or state expressed in the verb in question: cogitative, optative, voluntative and expectative. These four could each appear in any one of four grades according to the speaker's expressed or implied attitude to the realisation of the action. The expectative mood, for example, could be simple, unreal (*irrealis*), dubitative or heightened. Similarly, in the discussion of aspects of verbs (p. 67 ff.) Deutschbein introduced Latin terms like iterative, frequentative, incohative and causative. But on examination of his definitions and examples it turns out that most of these terms refer— not to categories and distinctions of either morphology or syntax, but purely and simply to the lexical meanings of the words chosen. He illustrates inchoative aspect by citing the verbs *become, grow, get*; but there is nothing about either the form or inflection of these words (as there is in Latin incohatives like *crescere, rubescere, tumescere*) which indicates entrance into a state of being or action. Similarly, there is nothing about the form or construction of: I *used to go*, as compared with: I *wanted to go*, to indicate that the former verb is what Deutschbein called frequentative (as there is in Latin *jactare*, a true frequentative, as compared with *jacere*).

In recent decades a reaction has set in against the explanation of modern English either by Latin analogies or Germanic (Old English) origins. The point of view has shifted away from the diachronic to the synchronic, which means simply a preference for describing the language as a contemporary structure without reference to early stages. Such

---

[32] G. Wendt, *Syntax des heutigen English*, II: *Die Satzlehre* (Heidelberg, 1914), p. 90.

[33] C. T. Onions, *An Advanced English Syntax* (London, 1905); George Curme, volumes on *Accidence* and *Syntax* in the *Grammar of the English Language* (Boston, 1935); Curme, *Principles and Practice of English Grammar* (New York, 1947).

[34] Max Deutschbein, *System der neuenglischen Syntax*, 4th ed. unrevised (Leipzig, 1931), p. 113 ff.

a description would take a construction like: *I was given* a book, entirely
as it stands today, and not on the basis of the older type: *Me was given*
a book, which has been superseded by it. Grammarians have recognised
more and more clearly that since word order has become the device
for indicating most English syntactic relations, rather than inflection
and concord,[35] analyses of the contemporary language should cease to
confine it within categories no longer relevant to its present status.

A great advance toward the synchronic description of English was
made by those scholars who tried to construct their analyses inductively
from detailed evidence drawn from modern creative writers, essayists and
superior journalists.[36] Otto Jespersen was one of the first to make a decisive
break with the old-fashioned categories and attempt a fresh approach.[37]
His division of sentence elements into ranks called primaries, secondaries
and tertiaries is well known. In this system a leading term, for instance
a noun subject, is a primary; its direct modifier (e. g., an adjective) is
a secondary; and the modifier of a modifier (e. g., an adverb) is a tertiary.
And so on. The verb itself is, in relation to its subject, a secondary.
The advantage of this neutral terminology is that it does not invite

---

[35] In the terminology proposed by Leonard Bloomfield in his book
Language, taxemes of order have come to prevail over taxemes of selection
in the great majority of cases. A taxeme is defined as "a simple feature
of grammatical arrangement," p. 166. For an account of the change,
see Charles C. Fries, "On the Development of the Structural Use of Word-
Order in Modern English," *Language*, XVI (1940), 199—208. His conclusion is that the historical trend in English grammar has been largely
"a movement away from the type of grammatical structure ·in which
taxemes of selection (inflections or word forms) express both the essential
and the dispensable grammatical concepts, toward a type of structure
in which taxemes of order form the essential or unavoidable relationships."
On the two types of relational concepts, unavoidable and dispensable,
see E. Sapir, *Language* (New York, 1921), p. 99.

[36] Two such grammars have been done by Dutch scholars: H.
Poutsma, *A Grammar of Late Modern English* (Groningen, 1914—28),
and E. Kruisinga, *Handbook of Present Day English* (Utrecht, 1925).
A short synchronic description has recently been made by R. W. Zand-
voort in his *Handbook of English Grammar* (London, 1957).

[37] O. Jespersen, *A Modern English Grammar on Historical Principles*,
especially VII: *Syntax* (Copenhagen and London, 1949). Very useful
is the shorter work of Harold E. Palmer, *A Grammar of Spoken English
on a Strictly Phonetic Basis* (Cambridge, 1924). This text has the advantage
of including intonation patterns, which often have syntactic relevance.

a premature classification of forms apart from their usage. How one
and the same word may be used in all three ranks may be illustrated by
the following:

As primary: *Home* is a good place to return to.
As secondary: He works in the *Home* Office; I worked in
               the *home* fields.
As tertiary: He has just come *home*.

In his discussion of "word classes," however, Jespersen follows in the
main the traditional doctrine of parts of speech, and throughout the
grammar he makes at least brief reference to historical causes for modern
constructions. To this extent, therefore, he still makes use of a diachronic
approach.

In a separate work Jespersen did attempt to evolve a symbolic representation of English structure which would be completely synchronic
and also break away from traditional formulations.[38] In this system,
the parts of sentences are represented by capital and small letters: S for
subject, V for verb, v for auxiliary verb, O for object, P for predicative,
p for preposition, etc. Following each item, if it represents more than
one word, there is written in parentheses a further detailed analysis of
it expressed in numerals standing for primaries, secondaries and tertiaries. Thus the sentence: Very good students will enter among the
first, would be transcribed as S (321) v V p 1. The result is a concise
notation which may serve usefully as a kind of shorthand for sentence
analysis. But the system is not entirely consistent as Jespersen himself
handles it. For instance, in one and the same sentence analysed as an
example, a preposition followed by its object is first represented as p 1,
and then by p O.[39] Moreover, Jespersen has introduced among the symbols for structural relations some which actually refer to other than
syntactic matters. For instance, it is difficult to see why he offers to
designate some types of nouns by special letters according to their
meanings rather than their functions in the sentences. He proposes the

---

[38] O. Jespersen, *Analytic Syntax* (Copenhagen, 1937).

[39] *Ibid.*, p. 92, in the analysis of the sentence from Samuel Johnson.
Another example of needless duplication: when a subject is implicit
but not expressed in the verb form, as in Latin *amo*, Jespersen on one
occasion proposes the transcription S⁰ V (with the superscript zero indicating absence of expressed subject); but he also uses brackets {S V}
to indicate that one form expresses both subject and verb. See p. 17.

symbol X for what he calls "nexus substantives"[40] (i. e., abstract nouns such as *pride* or *kindness*), and Y for agent substantives (e. g., *admirer*) as well as participle forms (*admiring, admired*). Here again lexicography appears to intrude on the syntactic realm, for there seems to be no reason for designating these particular substantives by a special label when they behave like many other types within the framework of sentences.

The most consistent efforts to get away from all considerations of meaning and to offer purely formal analysis of sentences have been made by certain American linguists, in studies dealing not only with English but also with other languages. Scholars investigating the native languages of the American continents (many of which have lacked alphabets until the recent past) were perforce limited to synchronic descriptions in the absence of historical materials. For such situations linguists have worked out a technique of eliciting information from native speakers in such a way as to discover the structure of a given unwritten language without trying to impose on it alien categories of any kind, Indo-European or other. That technique identifies phonemes and morphemes, words and constructions by isolating them as repeated units in the stream of utterance; it then establishes their functions by studying the environments in which they occur and the extent to which one form may be substituted for another without protest from the native informant. Within a relatively short time very imposing results in linguistic analysis have been gained by this method.

Since the method relies so greatly on discovering the positions which language units may occupy, it has given rise to a theory, held by some, that complete linguistic descriptions are possible on the basis of position alone, without reference to meaning. This attitude has already been mentioned in connection with the problem of defining single words. (See the preceding section.) It has been most forcefully expressed by two writers, Smith and Trager,[41] who have attempted to outline the structure of English, including its syntax, purely by means of substitution techniques. As they say: "It is emphasised that all this [analysis] is done without the use of 'meaning': it is formal analysis of formal units" (p. 68). The authors concede that meaning itself may be subjected to the same sort of structural analysis— but only after the

---

[40] So called by Jespersen because such substantives imply predication: *pride = being proud; kindness = being kind*, etc. See his *Essentials of English Grammar* (London, 1933), p. 317.

[41] Trager and Smith, *Outline* as cited in ch. 7, n. 8. For critique see James Sledd, *Language*, XXXI (1955), 312—45.

establishment of an "objective syntax," quite independent of it[42]. In other words, the procedure of syntactic analysis presents anew the same methodological and philosophical problem encountered in connection with the study of individual words.

The most ambitious attempt to describe English in exclusively structural terms, abandoning the traditional terminology for parts of speech and sentence elements, has been made by Fries.[43] His thesis is: "In order to know the structural meanings signalled by the formal arrangements of our sentences one need not know the lexical meanings of the words but he must know[44] the form-classes to which the words belong." Fries rejects the traditional classifications of "parts of speech" as depending too much on the lexical meanings known in advance. Instead he proposes a classification with a neutral terminology of numbers and letters. According to the positions that they may occupy in sentences, Fries deduces that there are four major form-classes, identified by substitutions of the following type:

Class 3	Class 1	Class 2	Class 4
good	students	remember	clearly
(the) good	student	remembers	perfectly
bright	students	remembered	well
(the)	boys	wrote	seldom

---

[42] Eugene A. Nida proposes terminology for the study of grammatical meaning in his "A System for the Description of Semantic Elements," *Word*, VII (1951), 1—14. It should be mentioned that L. Bloomfield, in his book *Language* which has served as a fundamental text for the American structuralists, did not abjure the concept of meaning, but he interpreted it behaviouristically. See also Charles C. Fries, "Meaning and Linguistic Analysis," *Language*, XXX (1954), 57—68. Fries concludes that social and cultural meanings do not seem "to form any part of the frame in which to test either lexical forms or structural forms," p. 68.

[43] Charles C. Fries, *The Structure of English: An Introduction to the Structure of English Sentences* (New York, 1952). For a general theoretical exposition, using English examples, see Zellig Harris, *Methods of Structural Linguistics* (University of Chicago Press, 1951).

[44] In a footnote to this sentence, p. 64, Fries explains "know" as meaning "respond to": a definition according with behaviouristic terminology.

and so on. These four classes recall but do not coincide with Jespersen's
primaries (class 1) secondaries (classes 2 and 3) and tertiaries (class 4).
They likewise have a correspondence which is only very proximate
with the traditional categories of nouns, verbs, adjectives and adverbs.
In addition to them, Fries identified 15 groups of function words (all
of which he designates collectively by the symbol f):

Group A, determiners, e. g. *the,*   Group F, "prepositions," defined
    a, any (also designated   positionally with refe-
    as *D*)   rence to words of

B, "auxiliary verbs"   classes 1, 2 and 3

C, the word *not*   G, the verb *do*

D, words pre-posed before   H, the particle *there*
    words of class 3 and 4,   I, "interrogative
    e. g., *very*   adverbs"

E, "conjunctions"   J, "conjunctions" in
                            3 possible positions

K—N, various types of sentence-introductory words

By the use of superscripts, subscripts and other symbols, Fries further
indicates categories of number (minus sign for singular, plus sign for
plural, $\pm$ where number is not indicated), gender (indicated by the
substitute pronoun written below the designation of class 1), a series
of identical references such as appositions, repetitions, substitutions
(indicated by identical superscript letters). In the analysis of sentences
Fries also links words in phrasal units which are likewise delimited by
the technique of substitution. Such groups of words belonging together
structurally are called "immediate constituents," sometimes referred to
by the abbreviation IC's.[45] Arrows linking words indicate concord.
Here is the scheme of a sentence analysed by Fries as an example (p. 268):

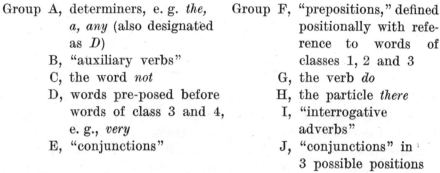

This particular social event of the season usually claims the full
$\quad D \qquad 3 \qquad\qquad 3 \quad 1^a \quad f \quad D \quad 1^b \qquad 4 \qquad 2 \quad D \quad 3$

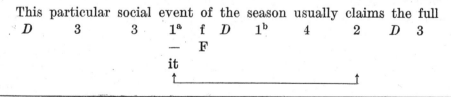

---

[45] On the identification of these grouped elements see Kenneth
L. Pike, "Taxemes and Immediate Constituents," *Language,* XIX (1943),
65—82; further Richard S. Pittman, "Nuclear Structures in Linguistics,"
ibid., XXIV (1948), 287—92, and Seymour Chatman, "Immediate
Constituents and Expansion Analysis," *Word,* XI (1955), 377—85.

attention of the students who stay in town

1ᶜ	f	D	1ᵈ	f	2	f	1ᵉ
it	F		+	J	+	F	−
			he	he			it

The modified subject, regarded as an immediate constituent, is subdivided thus:

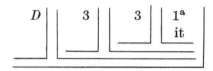

On close examination of the system proposed by Fries, it will be found that despite his avowed efforts to exclude all but quite formal tests and definitions, meaning is nevertheless appealed to in more than one instance. On the one hand, the subject of a sentence is defined, purely formally, as a particular construction for a class 1 word; "it is not a matter of the meaning of the word with reference to a real situation" (p. 176). On the other hand, a subject is said (p. 179) to signal "that which is identified" when it is bound with any one of a list of verbs (*to be* and the like) followed by a class 1 word having the same "referent" as the class 1 word which is the subject: e. g., *John* is my *brother*. But the statement of identity of referents implies a knowledge of the extra-linguistic situation, or is posited on a lexical meaning of the verb. In the end Fries himself advocates the admission of "total meaning" in structural analysis (p. 293), and even goes so far as to say: "One cannot determine whether one item is substitutable for another in any frame without in some way knowing whether the result is 'same' or 'different'" (*ibid.*). This is indeed the crux of the matter.[46]

In contrast to the total or partial rejection of meaning by the American structural linguists just cited, Soviet grammarians refer to it as a pertinent standard. In the most recent study of English syntax to appear

---

[46] See the reviews of Fries by James Sledd, *loc. cit.* above, n. 41, and also in *Modern Philology*, L (1952—53), 140 f. For a general dissent from the structuralist approach to meaning in language see Joshua Whatmough, *Language* (London, 1956), chs. 5 and 7. Whatmough's own definitions of meaning are however based on that "goal-directed activity" which he finds not only in animals and humans but also in machines. He looks to a future application of statistical methods, already used by communications engineers in solving other problems, to throw light on the problem of semantics; *op. cit.*, p. 73.

in Russian,[47] the authors employ three types of tests to identify parts of speech: morphological, semantic (смисловый) and syntactic tests. Under the headings of substantives and verbs, lists are given of those suffixes (bound morphemes) which are associated with the one part of speech or the other: -dom, -ism, -ness, etc. for noun substantives, and -ize (-ise), -ify, etc. for verbs. Although relatively few nouns or verbs in English —unlike Russian, the analogy of which is often cited— can be identified by such a morphemic test, there appears to be no reason for rejecting it in those cases where it does apply. The appeals to meaning do not all have an equal persuasiveness. The authors offer a non-functional, non-positional definition of a noun,[48] depending on its meaning with reference to external phenomena (p. 19), and this leads them to classify day as a noun in the sentence: Next day we left. The conclusion is debatable at least. Here the systems proposed by Jespersen and Fries would appear to be preferable, since they do not in advance commit a given form like day to a single syntactic usage, no matter what its reference may be to the world of non-linguistic reality. English is notoriously capable of shifting its grammatical categories: a fact that the Soviet scholars recognise (loc. cit.) but explain by recourse to a concept of grammatical homonyms. On the other hand, when there is a common lexical feature shared by a certain class of words syntactically related (e. g., certain transitive verbs incapable of being changed from active to passive voice because of their meaning, see p. 129), that feature is with reason said to have syntactic relevance. A structuralist, on the contrary, would presumably exclude such a factor of common meaning from his description.

These are but typical instances of questions which may be raised in connection with various efforts made —and some of them have been original as well as ambitious— to portray the syntactic structure of the English language. It may be deduced that a completely satisfying description has still to be written. Meanwhile the number of special studies on special problems multiplies from day to day, and the work already done has cleared the way for an eventual synthesis which may supersede all those previously undertaken.

---

[47] В. И. Жигадло, И. П. Иванова, Л. Л. Иофик, *Современний Английский Язык* (Moscow, 1956). In their critical comments the authors have passed over in silence the analyses proposed by Nida, Fries, Smith and Trager and other structuralists.

[48] "A noun substantive is a part of speech referring to a concept objectively, regardless of whether the phenomenon underlying the given concept exists as a separate and concrete object or not," p. 19.

4. Modern English Style and Stylistics

The present period of English is marked by an enormous variety in the styles of expression used by writers and speakers for various purposes: by journalists, political commentators, scientists, essayists, orators, advertisers, and the authors of poetry and fiction. By many of these the language is handled quite consciously as a medium freely subjected to planned innovation, rather than as a formal structure based on strictly established rules. Hence the neologisms, the liberties taken with traditional grammar, the unconventional handling of sentence structure, that can be observed in both American and English popular writers, especially journalists and advertisers. Hence too the stimulating but also frequently baffling treatments of the language by the creative experimenters in prose and verse.

In spite of the variety of styles presented by contemporary writing and speaking, English stylistics (that is, the study of style) has not yet been discussed on the same scale as, for instance, French, German and Russian.[49] Definitions of the scope and content of stylistics vary. For some, this discipline would include all characteristics of a language which reveal how it may be adapted to a given end, whether ordinary or exalted; for others, it includes only the adaptations of language resources to specifically artistic ends. Those who confine their attention to literary expression alone conceive of style as a deviation from normal usage, even a violence imposed on it for aesthetic purposes.[50] Most

---

[49] For French, the work of Charles Bally, *Traité de stylistique française*, 2 vols. (Heidelberg, 1902) was an epoch-making achievement, useful also for students of English. See also Leo Spitzer, *Stilstudien*, 2 vols. (Munich, 1928). A bibliography of recent studies will be found in two articles: P. Guiraud, "Stilistiques," *Neophilologus*, XXXVIII (1954), 1—11, and J. A. Verschoor, "Parole, langue, et les deux stylistiques," *ibid.*, XXXIX (1955), 184-91. A study of German has recently been done by E. Riesel, *Abriss der deutschen Stilistik* (Moscow, 1954).

[50] Guiraud, *loc. cit.*, citing Valéry, speaks of style as hingeing on an *écart*, a deformation or aberration from normal structure. The formalist critics in Russia and other Slavic countries in the period before and after World War I also stressed a deliberate deformation as a means of vivifying the linguistic medium and making it seem both new and strange. See William E. Harkins, "Slavic Formalist Theories in Literary Scholarship," *Word*, VII (1951), 177—85; also V. Erlich, *Russian Formalism: History and Doctrine* (The Hague, 1955).

writers are agreed at least that style involves choice, whether broadly or narrowly conceived. Those limiting their attention to literary styles alone are concerned exclusively with the question: How can the linguistic resources of the standard language be adapted to a concrete aesthetic purpose? Those extending their interests beyond literature ask further: How can the resources of all variations of the language (non-standard as well as standard) be adapted to all sorts of purposes, not merely aesthetic? Finally there are studies which undertake to define the immanent stylistic advantages and limitations of English as a whole as compared with other languages. These last assume the point of view that there is a style-in-general inherent in the structure of the language, quite apart from creative innovations or deformations of it introduced by professional writers for immediate purposes of effective expression.

Such is the point of view of Aronstein,[51] who undertook as his main task to delineate the "general style" of English in specific contrast with that of German. At the same time he admits that there are also styles of individuals, groups and historical epochs. The well-known fact that English is an analytical language stripped of most of its original inflections, while German is still notably synthetic, means that English has automatically, as it were, developed a general style of its own contrasting with those of the more conservative tongues. Besides its obvious freedom in handling the parts of speech, Aronstein notes its greater preference for coordinate constructions in loose series, as opposed to the tighter, more complex German patterns of subordination. In general he finds a trend to brevity, clarity and emphasis in English; the same qualities which led Jespersen to speak of the language metaphorically as "masculine."[52]

More complicated, perhaps, is the task of distinguishing specific styles within the general national language. As Deutschbein has remarked,[53] and as this survey has had occasion to point out more than once, there are levels of style corresponding to certain types of social environment and to differing occasions in the same environment; there are temporal phases also (an archaic style like that of William Morris contrasting, let us say, with one replete with neologisms today), and there are special spheres corresponding with individual values and purposes. Vocabulary (slang, scientific terminology, metaphors, etc.) is an obvious reflector of such distinctions, but so are syntactic constructions. The vigorous expressiveness of English is seen by Deutsch-

---

[51] Philipp Aronstein, *Englische Stilistik* (Leipzig—Berlin 1924).

[52] Jespersen, *Growth and Structure*, 9th ed. (Oxford, 1938), p. 2.

[53] Max Deutschbein, *Neuenglische Stilistik* (Leipzig, 1932), p. 12.

bein to reside in such syntactic traits as the predominance of transitive verbs, the shift of intransitive ones into transitive, (e. g., to *fly* a kite), the preference for personal over impersonal constructions (ModE *I like* as compared with German *es gefällt mir* and older English *it likes me*), and the replacement of simple verbs by phrases made up of colourless words like *have, make, give, take* followed by a noun or infinitive: *have a wash, take a walk, give a lecture.* This last device is seen as part of the tendency to favour concatenated structure, especially in nominal constructions: e. g., a book *now procurable* (for: one *that can be procured*), his *daily teachers* (for: *those who taught him every day*); also ellipses like: *when a child, though strongly urged,* etc. (We have noted all of these trends in American English.) In the handling of sentence elements there are, according to Deutschbein, several possibilities. He contrasts especially the predicative sentence, which may be complicated but is apprehended as an organic whole (as in Ciceronian Latin), and the attributive sentence which adds a succession of elements in series— a summation which may be loosely organised in an impressionistic manner (p. 152 ff.). The attributive sentence is said to favour appositions, parentheses, parallel constructions and appended comments. A simple example illustrating the two types is the pair of sentences: The band is playing in the park (predicative; the activity seen as a whole), and There is a band playing in the park (attributive; information imparted in segments). Modern literature in English offers many sentences of the additive impressionistic type. Many typical examples will be found in Virginia Woolf's *The Waves*, where a series of coordinate images often ends in a reprise construction or an apposition subsuming the whole series. The influence of Proust's similar impressionistic style in French —additive and also complex— is visible among his imitators in English, as for instance in this sentence by Jean Stafford:

> Thus we may say of people who were once in love that they cannot "recapture" their joy and the words "I was in love with that person" are an historical statement which may be attended by illustrations: a café visited by the lovers when they were in love, a railway carriage where they sat with arms entwined, a shop where they met one day by chance. (*Boston Adventure* [New York: Harcourt, Brace and Co., 1944], p. 337; quoted by permission of the publishers.)

The proclivity for parentheses and interruptions may be illustrated by the following sentence from William Faulkner:

> He told it —of the next eight or nine or ten days, he did not remember which, while the four of them —himself and the woman

and baby and the little wiry man with rotting teeth and soft wild bright eyes like a rat or a chip munk, whose language neither of them could understand— lived in the room and a half. (*The Old Man* [New York: Random House, 1939] from ch. 4; quoted by permission of the publishers.)

The relation of the two stylistic types of sentence to grammatical predication and attribution is not made entirely clear by Deutschbein. But the contrast of two stylistic types, the tight and the loose, may with justification be connected with an historical trend in English writing. The highly organised predicative type was conspicuous, as we have noticed, in the periods when Latin influence was strong, whereas the attributive is conspicuous today among impressionistic writers who present material to the imagination as a chain of images rather than a single organised whole. Not only prose writers but also poets exemplify the contemporary trend, which in verse became marked with the pioneer writings of Walt Whitman. The frequent use of verbless presentations belongs in the same style.[54] Perhaps the trend towards loose attribution is connected with broader tendencies in the representational arts such as cinema and painting, but this is a question for comparative aesthetics to solve. In any event, if such a trend exists in modern writing generally, it may be said that the less inflected languages like English, French and Dutch can be said to fall in with it more easily than can the more highly inflected ones like Icelandic, German, and the Slavic languages, whose very structure requires extensive concordance and subordination.

The leading suggestions made by Deutschbein, though stimulating, remain incompletely worked out and leave a large territory for further investigation. Even within the limitations of normal English word order, with all its restrictions, there is a range of choice for the disposition of parts in which changing factors of rhythm, balance, focus of attention, cumulation and climax play a part. The possibilities may be studied on a small scale by comparing the effects of the following variations on a sentence by Dylan Thomas at the end of *The Portrait of the Artist as a Young Dog*:

All around him the disturbed inhabitants of the house were falling back into sleep;

---

[54] See M. Schlauch, *Modern English and American Poetry: Techniques and Ideologies* (London, 1956), ch. 3.

The disturbed inhabitants of the house were falling back into sleep all around him;

Back into sleep were falling the disturbed inhabitants of the house, all around him;

All around him the disturbed inhabitants of the house were falling asleep again;

—and so on. The varieties increase, of course, when the sentence is hypotactic. We still await an exhaustive analysis of these devices in modern English from the stylistic point of view.

Experimental writing today is attempting many kinds of deviation from normal sentence structure as well as normal phraseology. The segmentation may be rendered as not only dislocated but also fragmentary. Such treatment of sentence parts is frequently encountered in the writing of fiction which follows the stream of consciousness technique, for instance in certain passages of the *Ulysses* of James Joyce. At the other extreme of stylistic usage is the naive type of discourse which suffers from ill organised and incomplete structure, with frequent lapses into anacoluthon and artless aposiopesis. Modern fiction of the realistic school pays more attention now than previously to the imitation of these traits within passages of reported conversation. That is to say, there is an effort to reflect the simpler styles of discourse with greater phonographic exactitude than was attempted some decades ago. The change becomes clear if we compare the stylised colloquies of Joseph Conrad's uneducated characters (sailors and the like) with those put down by writers like Steinbeck, Hemingway and others today. Conrad's people speak in sentences which maintain a classical syntactic structure whether they are standard or dialectal, long or short; while contemporary realists are at pains to reflect the structural irregularities of colloquial English speech very scrupulously. Its characteristics have yet to be analysed with the careful attention which has been devoted to the analogous level of French discourse.[55]

In conclusion a word may be said about the most esoteric of all writing today, which depends on recondite allusions, double and triple polyglot puns, as well as sound effects, rare words and striking deviations from normal sentence structure. The most baffling example of composition in this style is Joyce's *Finnegans Wake,* which has elicited a vast amount of commentary and explication. Other works are being composed on

---

[55] Henri Frei, *La Grammaire des fautes* (Paris, 1929).

a less ambitious scale but with a similarly difficult technique, both in prose and in verse. The permanent value of many of these creations is open to question, but they belong to the multiple stream of literary creation in the English language today, and future research in the development of English style will need to take account of them, if only to determine how much or how little they will have affected the shaping of the literary language for the generations to come.

1. Chaucer's use of regional dialect. Two university students from
the North visit a miller near Cambridge, whom they suspect of
cheating when he grinds their corn. The passage occurs in the
Reeve's Tale, A 4020 ff.

> John knew the wey,— hem nedede no gyde,—
> And at the mille the sak adoun he layth.
> Aleyn spak first, "Al hayl, Symond, y-fayth!
> How fares thy faire doghter and thy wyf?"
> 5   "Aleyn, welcome," quod Symkyn, "by my lyf!
> And John also, how now, what do ye heer?"
> "Symond," quod John, "by God, nede has na peer.
> Hym boes serve hymself that has na swayn,
> Or elles he is a fool, as clerkes sayn.
> 10 Oure manciple, I hope he wil be deed,
> Swa werkes ay the wanges in his heed;
> And forthy is I come, and eek Alayn,
> To grynde oure corn and carie it ham agayn;
> I pray yow spede us heythen that ye may."
> 15 "It shal be doon," quod Symkyn, "by my fay!
> What wol ye doon whil that it is in hande?"
> "By God, right by the hopur wil I stande,"
> Quod John, "and se howgates the corn gas in.
> Yet saugh I nevere, by my fader kyn,
> 20 How that the hopur wagges til and fra."
> Aleyn answerde, "John, and wiltow swa?
> Thanne wil I be bynethe, by my croun,
> And se how that the mele falles doun
> Into the trough; that sal be my disport.
> 25 For John, y-faith, I may been of youre sort;
> I is as ille a millere as ar ye."

> This millere smyled of hir nycetee,
> And thoghte, "Al this nys doon but for a wyle.
> They wene that no man may hem bigyle,
> 30   But by my thrift, yet shal I blere hir ye,
> For al the sleighte in hir philosophye.
> The moore queynte crekes that they make,
> The moore wol I stele whan I take...."

> From Chaucer's *Works* as edited by
> F. N. Robinson, (Boston, 1957). Other
> Chaucer excerpts from the same edition.

2. Prose sentences from Chaucer:

Hastow foryeten thilke ryght oolde lawe of thi citee, in the whiche cite it es ordeyned and establysschid, that what wyght that hath levere founden therin his sete or his hous than elleswhere, he may nat ben exiled by no ryght fro that place? For whoso that is contened in-with the palys and the clos of thilke cite, there nys no drede that he mai deserve to ben exiled; but who that leteth the wil for to enhabyten there, he forleteth also to deserve to ben citezen of thilke cite. (Boethius translation, I, prose 5)

For certes swich is the condicioun of alle mankynde, that oonly whan it hath knowynge of itself, thanne passeth it in noblesse alle othere thynges; and whan it forletith the knowynge of itself thanne it is brought bynethen alle beestes. (*Ibid.*, II, prose 5)

For every thing that may naturely usen resoun, it hath doom by which it discernith and demeth every thing; thanne knoweth it by itself thinges that ben to fleen and thinges that ben to desiren. And thilke thing that any wight demeth to ben desired, that axeth or desireth he; and fleeth thilke thing that he troweth be to fleen. Wherfore in alle thingis that resoun is, in hem also is liberte of willynge and of nillynge. (*Ibid.*, V, prose 2)

But now, if so be that dignytees and poweris ben yyven to gode men, the whiche thyng is ful selde, what aggreable thynges is ther in tho dignytees or powers but oonly the goodnesse of folk that usen hem? (*Ibid.*, II, prose 6)

3. Informal conversation among courtly people:

> Quod Pandarus, "Thus fallen is this cas — "
> "Why, uncle myn," quod she, "who tolde hym this?
> Why doth my deere herte thus, allas?"
> "Ye woot, ye, nece myn," quod he, "what is.
> 5   I hope al shal be wel that is amys;
> For ye may quenche al this, if that yow leste.
> And doth right so, for I holde it the beste."
>
> "So shal I do to-morwe, ywys," quod she,
> "And God toforn, so that it shal suffise."
> 10 "To-morwe? allas, that were a fair!" quod he.
> "Nay, nay, it may nat stonden in this wise,
> For, nece myn, thus writen clerkes wise,
> That peril is with drecchyng in ydrawe;
> Nay, swiche abodes ben nought worth an hawe....
>
> 15   "And nece myn — ne take it naught agrief —
> If that ye suffre hym al nyght in this wo,
> God help me so, ye hadde hym nevere lief, —
> That dar I seyn, now ther is but we two.
> But wel I woot that ye wol nat do so;
> 20 Ye ben to wys to doon so gret folie,
> To putte his lif al nyght in jupertie."
>
>   *Troilus and Criseyde*, III. 841 ff.

4. Complex formal sentences in Chaucer's verse:

> And at the laste hire love thanne hath she founde,
> Betynge with his heles on the grounde,
> Al blody, and therwithal a-bak she sterte,
> And lik the wawes quappe gan hire herte,
> 5 And pale as box she was, and in a throwe
> Avisede hire, and gan hym wel to knowe,
> That it was Piramus, hire herte deere.
> Who coude wryte which a dedly cheere
> Hath Thisbe now, and how hire heer she rente,
> 10 And how she gan hireselve to turmente,
> And how she lyth and swouneth on the grounde,
> And how she wep of teres ful his wounde;

How medeleth she his blod with hire compleynte;
How with his blod hirselve gan she peynte;
15 How clyppeth she the deede cors, allas!
How doth this woful Tisbe in this cas!
How kysseth she his frosty mouth so cold!
"Who hath don this, and who hath been so bold
To sle my leef? O spek, my Piramus!
20 I am thy Tisbe, that the calleth thus."
And therwithal she lifteth up his hed.

Legend of Good Women, 862 ff.

"For som men seyn, if God seth al biforn,
Ne God may nat deceyved ben, parde,
Than moot it fallen, theigh men hadde it sworn,
That purveiance hath seyn before to be.
5 Wherfore I sey, that from eterne if he
Hath wist byforn oure thought ek as oure dede,
We han no fre chois, as thise clerkes rede.

"For other thought, nor dede also,
Myghte nevere ben, but swich as purveyaunce,
10 Which may nat ben deceyved nevere mo,
Hath feled byforn, withouten ignoraunce.
For yf ther myghte ben a variaunce
To writhen out fro Goddis purveyinge,
Ther nere no prescience of thyng comynge,

15 "But it were rather an opynyoun
Uncerteyn, and no stedfast forseynge.
And certes, that were an abusioun,
That God sholde han no parfit cler wytynge
More than we men that han doutous wenynge.
20 But swich an errour upon God to gesse
Were fals and foul, and wikked corsednesse...."

Troilus and Criseyde, IV, 974 ff.

5. From the *Paston Letters,* written by a Norfolk family of the 15th century.
No. 713, from Richard Calle to Margery Paston (1469).

Myn owne lady and mastres, and be for God very trewe wyff, I with herte full sorowefull recomaunde me unto you, as he that can not be mery, nor nought shalbe tyll it be othewise [*sic*] with us then it is yet,

for thys lyf that we lede nough [= now] is nowther plesur to Godde
nor to the worlde, consederyng the gret bonde of matrymonye that is
made be twix us, and also the greete love that hath be, and as I truste
yet is be twix us, and as on my parte never gretter; wherfor I beseche
Almyghty Godde, comfort us as sone as it plesyth Hym, for we that
ought of very ryght to be moost to gether ar moost asondre; me semyth
it is a mll [thousand] yere a goo son that I speke with you. I had lever
thenne all the goode in the worlde I myght be with you. Alas, alas!
goode lady, full litell remembre they what they doo that kepe us thus
asunder; iiij. tymes in the yere ar they a cursid that lette matrymonye;
it causith many men to deme in hem they have large consyence in other
maters as wel as herin. But what lady suffre as ye have do; and make
you as mery as ye can, for I wys, lady, at the longe wey Godde woll
of Hys ryghtwysnes helpe Hys servants that meane truly, and wolde
leve accordyng to Hes lawys, &c.

I understende, lady, ye have hadde asmoche sorwe for me as any
gentelwoman hath hadde in the worlde, aswolde Godd all that sorwe that
ye have hadde had rested upon me, so that ye hadde be discharged of it,
for I wis, lady, it is to me a deethe to her that ye be entreted other
wise thene ye ought to be. This is a peyneful lyfe that we lede. I can
not leve thus withoute it be a gret displesure to Godde.

Also like you to wete that I had sent you a letter be my ladde
from London, and he tolde me he myght not speeke with you, ther
was made so gret awayte upon hym and upon you boothe. He told
me John Threscher come to hym in your name, and seide that ye
sent hym to my ladde for a letter or a token, weche I shulde have
sent you, but he truste hym not; he wold not delyver hym noon. After
that he brought hym a rynge, seyng that ye sent it hym, comaundyng
hym that he schulde delyver the letter or token to hym, weche I con-
ceyve sethen be my ladde it was not be your sendyng, it was be my
mastres and Sir Jamys [a priest's] a vys. Alas, what meane they? I suppose they deeme we be not ensuryd to gether, and if they so doo
I merveyll, for thene they ar not wele avised, remembryng the pleynes
that I breke to my mastres at the begynnyng, and I suppose be you
bothe, and ye dede as ye ought to do of very ryght; and if ye have
do the contrare, as I have be enformed ye have do, ye dede nouther
concyensly nor to the plesure of Godde, withoute ye dede it for feere,
and for the tyme to please suche as were at that tyme a boute you;
and if ye so dede it for this service it was a resonable cause, consederyng the grete and importable callyng upon that ye hadde, and
many an on trewe tale was made to you of me, weche God knowt I
was never gylty of.

My ladde tolde me that my mastres your modre axyd hym if he hadde brought any letter to you, and many other thyngs she bare hym on hande, and a monge all other at the last she seide to hym that I wolde not make her prevy to the begynnyng, but she supposyd I wolde at the endyng; and as to that, God knowt sche knewe furst of me and non other. I wott not what her mastreschip meneth, for be my trowthe ther is no gentylwoman on lyve that my herte tendreth more then it dothe her, nor is lother to displese, savyng only your person, weche of very ryght I ought to tendre and love beste, for I am bounde therto be the lawe of Godde, and so wol do whyle that I leve, what so ever falle of it. I supose, and ye telle hem sadly the trouthe, they wold not dampne ther soules for us; though I telle hem the trouthe they woll not be leve me as weele as they woll do you; and ther for, goode lady, at the reverence of Godde be pleyne to hem and telle the trouthe, and if they woll in no wise agree therto, betwix God, the Deelf, and them be it, and that perell that we schuld be in, I beseche Godde it may lye upon them and not upon us. I am hevy and sory to remembre ther disposicion, God sende them grace to gyde all thyngs weele, as wele I wolde they dede; Godde be ther gide, and sende them peas and reste, &c.

I mervell moche that they schulde take this mater so heedely as I undrestonde they doo, remembryng it is in suche case as it can not be remedyed, and my desert upon every halfe it is for to be thought ther shulde be non obstacle a yenst it; and also the worchipfull that is in them, is not in your mariage, it is in ther owne mariage, weche I beseche Godde sende hem suche as may be to ther worschip and plesur to Godde, and to ther herts ease, for ell[es] were it gret pety. Mastres, I am aferde to write to you, for I undrestonde ye have schewyd my letters that I have sent you be for this tyme; but I prey you lete no creatur se this letter. As sone as ye have redde it lete it be brent, for I wolde no man schulde se it in no wise; ye had no wrytyng from me this ij. yere, nor I wolle not sende you no mor, therfor I remytte all this matre to your wysdom. Almyghty Jesu preserve, kepe, and [give] you your hertys desire, weche I wotte weele schulde be to Goods plesur, &c.

Thys letter was wreten with as greete peyne as ever wrote I thynge in my lyfe, for in goode feyth I have be ryght seke, and yet am not veryly weele at ease, God amend it, &c.

The Paston Letters, ed. James Gairdner (London, 1904), V, pp. 25—28. Note: This letter appears with divergent readings in the selection from the *Paston Letters* by Norman Davis (Oxford, 1958).

6. From the Chester Play of Noah's Ark and the Flood. Played by "the Watter Leaders and Drawers of Dee."

Noye: Wiffe, come in: why standes thou their?
   Thou arte ever frowarde, I dare well sweare;
   Come in, one Godes halfe! tyme yt were,
   For feare leste that we drowne.
5 *Noyes Wiffe:* Yea, sir, sette up youer saile,
   And rowe fourth with evill haile,
   For withouten [anye] fayle
     I will not oute of this towne;
   But I have my gossipes everyechone,
10   One foote further I will not gone:
   The shall not drowne, by Sante John!
     And I may save ther life.
   The loven me full well, by Christe!
   But thou lett them into thy cheiste,
15   Elles rowe nowe wher thee leiste,
     And gette thee a newe wiffe.
Noye: Seme, sonne, loe! thy mother is wrawe:
   Forsooth, such another I doe not knowe.
Sem: Father, I shall fetch her in, I trowe,
20   Withouten anye fayle. —
   Mother, my father after thee sende,
   And byddes thee into yeinder shippe wende.
   Loke up and see the wynde,
     For we bene readye to sayle.
25 *Noyes Wiffe:* Seme, goe againe to hym, I saie;
   I wil not come theirin to daye.
Noye: Come in, wiffe, in twentye devilles waye!
     Or elles stand there without.
Cam: Shall we all fecche her in?
30 *Noye:* Yea, sonnes, in Christe blessinges and myne!
   I woulde you hied you be-tyme,
     For of this flude I am in doubte....
Jeffatte: Mother, we praye you all together,
   For we are heare, youer owne childer,
35   Come into the shippe for feare of the weither,
     For his love that you boughte!
Noyes Wiffe: That will not I, for all youer call,
   But I have my gossippes all.

Sem: In faith, mother, yett you shalle,
40   Wheither thou wylte or [nought].
Noye: Welcome, wiffe, into this botte.
Noyes Wiffe: Have thou that for thy note!
Noye: Ha, ha! marye, this is hotte!
    It is good for to be still.
45   Ha! children, me thinkes my botte remeves,
    Our taryinge heare highlye me greves,
    Over the land the watter spreades;
        God doe as he will.

Edited by Alfred W. Pollard, English Mi-
racle Plays, Moralities and Interludes
(Oxford, 1914), pp. 14—16

7. Complex sentences in a description of Troy by **John Lydgate**:

    And of this toun the stretis large and wyde
    Wer by crafte so prudently provided,
    And by workemen sette so and devided,
    That holsom eyr amyddis myght enspire
5   Erly on morwe to hem that it desyre;
    And Zephirus, that is so comfortable
    For to norysche thinges vegetable,
    In tyme of yere, thorugh-oute every strete,
    With sugred flavour, so lusty and so swete,
10   Most pleasantly in the eyr gan smyte,
    The cyteyeyns only to delyte;
    And with his brethe hem to recomfort,
    Whan thei list walke hem silven to disport.
    And thorugh the toun, by crafty purviaunce,
15   By gret avys and discret ordynaunce,
    By compas cast, and squared out by squires,
    Or pulsched marbil up-on strong pilleris,
    Devised wern, longe, large, and wyde,
    In the frountel of every stretis syde,
20   Fresche alures with lusty highe pynacles,
    And moustryng outward riche tabernacles,
    Vowted above like reclinatories,
    That called werne deambulatories,
    Men to walke to-gydre tweine and tweyne,

²⁵ To kepe hem drie whan it dide reyne,
    Or hem to save from tempest, wynde, or thonder,
    Yf that hem list schrowde hem silve therunder.

From the *Troy Book*, as reprinted in
W. A. Neilson and K. G. T. Webster, *Chief
British Poets of the Fourteenth and Fifteenth
Centuries* (Boston, 1916), p. 218 f.

8. Caxton's original prose: from the Preface to the *Eneydos*.

After dyverse werkes made, translated, and achieved, havyng noo
werke in hande, I, sittyng in my studye where as laye many dyverse
paunflettis and bookys, happened that to my hande came a lytyl booke
in frenshe, whiche late was translated oute of latyn by some noble clerke
of fraunce, whiche booke is named Eneydos... And whan I had advysed
me in this sayd boke, I delybered and concluded to translate it into
englysshe, and forthwyth toke a penne & ynke, and wrote a leef or
tweyne, whyche I oversawe agayn to corecte it. And whan I sawe the
fayr & straunge termes therin I doubted that it sholde not please some
gentylmen whiche late blamed me, sayeng that in my translacyons I had
over curyous termes whiche coude not be understande of comyn peple,
and desired me to use olde and homely termes in my translacyons. And
fayn wolde I satysfye every man, and so to doo, toke an olde boke
and redde therin; and certaynly the englysshe was so rude and brood
that I coude not wele understande it ...

And certaynly our langage now used varyeth ferre from that whiche
was used and spoken whan I was borne. For we englysshe men ben
borne under the domynacyon of the mone, whiche is never stedfaste,
but ever waverynge, wexynge one season, and waneth & dyscreaseth
another season. And that comyn englysshe that is spoken in one shyre
varyeth from a nother. In so moche that in my dayes happened that
certayn marchauntes were in a shippe in tamyse, for to have sayled
over the see into zelande, and for lacke of wynde, thei taryed atte
forlond, and wente to lande for to refreshe them. And one of theym
named Sheffelde, a mercer, cam in-to an hows and axed for mete; and
specyally he axyd after eggys. And the goode wyf answerde, that she
coude speke no frenshe. And the marchaunt was angry, for he also coude
speke no frenshe, but wolde have hadde egges, and she understode hym
not. And thenne at laste a nother sayd that he wolde have eyren. Then
the good wyf sayd that she understod hym wel. Loo, what sholde a man

in thyse dayes now wryte, egges or eyren? Certaynly it is harde to
playse every man by cause of dyversite & chaunge of langage.

Preface to the *Eneydos*, ed. M. T. Culley
and F. J. Furnivall, EETS, ES, No. 57
(1890)

9. A Scottish pastoral by Robert Henryson:

> Robene sat on gud grene hill,
>   Kepand a flok of fe;
> Mirry Makyne said him till,
>   "Robene, thow rew on me;
> 5   I haif the luvit lowd and still,
>   Thir yeiris two or thre;
> My dule in dern bot gif thow dill,
>   Doutless but dreid I de."
>
> Robene answerit, "Be the rude,
> 10   Nathing of lufe I knaw,
> Bot keipis my scheip undir yone wid,
>   Lo quhair thay raik on raw:
> Quhat hes marrit the in thy mude,
>   Makyne, to me thow schaw;
> 15 Or quhat is lufe, or to be lude?
>   Fane wald I leir that law...."
>
> "Robene, tak tent unto my taill,
>   And wirk all as I reid,
> And thow sall haif my hairt all haill,
> 20   Eik and my maidenheid.
> Sen God sendis bute for baill
>   And for murnyng remeid,
> In dern with the, bot gif I daill,
>   Dowtles I am bot deid....
>
> 25 "Robene, thow reivis me roif and rest;
>   I luve bot the allane."
> "Makyne, adew, the sone gois west,
>   The day is neir hand gane."
> "Robene, in dule I am so drest,
> 30   That lufe wil be my bane."

"Ga lufe, Makyne, quhair evir thow list,
 For lemman I lue nane."...

Mawkyne went hame withowttin faill,
 Full wery eftir cowth weip.
35 Than Robene in a ful fair daill
 Assemblit all his scheip.
Be that sum pairte of Mawkynis aill
 Outthrow his hairt cowd creip;
He fallowit hir fast thair till assaill,
40 And till hir tuke gude keip.

"Abyd, abyd, thow fair Makyne,
 A word for ony thing;
For all my luve it sal be thyne,
 Withowttin depairting.
45 All haill thy harte for till haif myne
 Is all my cuvating;
My scheip to morne quhill houris nyne
 Will neid of no keping."

"Robene, thow hes hard soung and say,
50 In gestis and storeis auld,
The man that will nocht quhen he may
 Sall haif nocht quhen he wald.
I pray to Jesu every day
 Mot eik thair cairis cauld,
55 That first preissis with the to play,
 Be firth, forrest, or fauld."...

Malkyne went hame blyth annewche,
 Attour the holttis hair;
Robene murnit, and Makyne lewche;
60 Scho sang, he sichit sair;
And so left him, bayth wo and wrewche,
 In dolour and in cair,
Kepand his hird under a huche,
 Amangis the holtis hair.

Abbreviated from Neilson and Webster,
op. cit., p. 383 f.

10. Two aureate stanzas by William Dunbar:

> Ryght as the stern of day begouth to schyne,
> Quhen gone to bed war Vesper and Lucyne,
>   I raise, and by a rosere did me rest;
> Up sprang the goldyn candill matutyne,
> ⁵ With clere depurit bemes cristallyne,
>   Glading the mery foulis in thair nest;
>   Or Phebus was in purpur kaip revest
> Up raise the lark, the hevyns menstrale fyne,
>   In May, in till a morow myrthfullest.
>
> ¹⁰ The cristall air, the sapher firmament,
> The ruby skyes of the orient,
>   Kest beriall bemes on emerant bewis grene;
> The rosy garth depaynt and redolent,
> With purpur, azure, gold, and goulis gent
> ¹⁵   Arayed was, by dame Fflora the quene,
>   So nobily, that joy was for to sene;
> The roch agayn the ryvir resplendent
>   As low enlumynit all the leves schene.

From "The Golden Targe," Neilson and
Webster, op. cit., p. 386, Stanzas 1 and 5

11. Spenser's archaic speech, from the *Shepherd's Calendar*. A dialogue between two shepherds, Thomalin and Morrell.

> *Thom.* Is not thilke same a goteheard prowde,
>   that sittes on yonder bancke,
>   Whose straying heard them selfe doth shrowde
>   emong the bushes rancke?
> ⁵ *Mor.* What ho, thou iollye shepheards swayne,
>   come vp the hyll to me:
>   Better is, then the lowly playne,
>   als for thy flocke, and thee.
> *Thom.* Ah God shield, man, that I should clime,
> ¹⁰   and learne to looke alofte,
>   This reede is ryfe, that oftentime
>   great clymbers fall vnsoft.
>   In humble dales is footing fast,
>   the trode is not so tickle:

15   And though one fall through heedlesse hast,
         yet is his misse not mickle.
      And now the Sonne hath reared vp
         his fyriefooted teme,
      Making his way betweene the Cuppe,
20   and golden Diademe:
      The rampant Lyon hunts he fast,
         with Dogge of noysome breath,
      Whose balefull barking bringes in hast
         pyne, plagues, and dreery death.
25   Agaynst his cruell scortching heate
         where hast thou couerture?
      The wastefull hylls vnto his threate
         is a playne ouerture.
      But if thee lust, to holden chat
30   with seely shepherds swayne,
      Come downe, and learne the little what,
         that Thomalin can sayne.
 Mor. Syker, thous but a laesie loord,
         and rekes much of thy swinck,
35   That with fond termes, and weetlesse words
         to blere myne eyes doest thinke.
      In euill houre thou hentest in hond
         thus holy hylles to blame,
      For sacred vnto saints they stond,
40   and of them han theyr name.
      S. Michels mount who does not know,
         that wardes the Westerne coste?
      And of S. Brigets bowre I trow,
         all Kent can rightly boaste:
45   And they that con of Muses skill,
         sayne most what, that they dwell
      (As goteheards wont) vpon a hill,
         beside a learned well.
      And wonned not the great God Pan,
50   vpon mount Oliuet:
      Feeding the blessed flocke of Dan,
         which dyd himselfe beget?
 Thom. O blessed sheepe, O shepheard great,
         that bought his flocke so deare,
55   And them did saue with bloudy sweat
         from Wolues, that would them teare.

12. From Spenser's notes to the above Eclogue:

line 1 A Goteheard: By Gotes in scrypture be represented the wicked and reprobate, whose pastour also must needes be such.

1. 2 Banck: is the seate of honor.

1. 3 Straying heard: which wander out of the waye of truth.

1. 8 Als: for also

1. 12 Great clymbers: according to Seneca his verse, Decidunt celsa grauiore lapsu. Clymbe: spoken of Ambition.

1. 16 Mickle: much.

1. 19 f. The Cupp and Diademe: Be two signes in the Firmament, through which the sonne maketh his course in the moneth of Iuly.

1. 21 Lion: Thys is Poetically spoken, as if the Sunne did hunt a Lion with one Dogge. The meaning whereof is, that in Iuly the sonne is in Leo....

1. 28 Ouerture: an open place. The word is borrowed of the French, and used in good writers.

1. 29 To holden chatt: to talk and prate.

1. 33 A loorde: was wont among the old Britons to signifie a Lorde. And therefore the Danes, that long time vsurped theyr Tyrannie here in Brytanie, were called for more dread then dignitie, Lurdanes s. Lord Danes....

1. 34 Recks much of thy swinck: counts much of thy paynes.

1. 35 Weetelesse: not vnderstoode.

1. 41 S. Michels mount: is a promontorie in the West part of England.

1. 47 A hill: Parnassus afforesayd.

1. 49 Pan: Christ.

1. 51 Dan: One trybe is put for the whole nation per Synecdochen.

Spenser, *The Shepheardes Calender:* July. Ed. Ernest de Sélincourt in Spenser's *Minor Poems* (Oxford: Clarendon Press, 1910)

13. A canting song in two versions, illustrative of underwold vocabulary. From Thomas Dekker, *Lanthorne and Candle-light* (1609).

> The Ruffin cly the nab of the Harman beck,
> If we mawn'd Pannam, lap or Ruff-peck,
> Or poplars of yarum: he cuts, bing to the Ruffmans,
> Or els he sweares by the light-mans,
> 5   To put our stamps in the Harmans.

The ruffian cly the ghost of the Harman beck
If we heaue a booth we cly the Ierke.
If we niggle, or mill a bowsing Ken
Or nip a boung that has but a win
10 Or dup the giger of a Gentry cofe's ken,
To the quier cuffing we bing,
And then to the quier Ken, to scowre the Cramp ring,
And then to the Trin'de on the chates, in the lightmans
The Bube and Ruffian cly the Harman beck and harmans.

Thus Englished:

The Diuell take the Constable's head,
If we beg Bacon, Butter-milke, or bread,
Or pottage, to the hedge he bids vs hie
Or sweares (by this light) i' th' stocks we shall lie.
5 The Deuill haunt the Constable's ghoast
If we rob but a Booth, or are whip'd at a poast.
If an° ale-house we rob, or be tane with a whore
Or cut a purse that has inst a penny, and no more,
Or come but stealing in at a Gentleman's dore,
10 To the Iustice straight we goe,
And then to the Iayle to be shakled: And so
To be hang'd on the gallowes i' th' day time: the pox
And the Deuill take the Constable and his stocks.

Reprinted by Furnivall in his edition of
A w d e l e y, *Fraternitye of Vacabondes*, p. xx f.

14. An anecdote about two knaves who come to a country inn.
They pretend to be the long-lost nephews of the local priest,
and thus gather information about him in order to rob him.

Then they, fayninge that they had an vncle a priest, and that he
should dwel in these parts, which by all presumptions it should be he,
and that they came of purpose to speake with hym..., and began to
inquier of his name....

So when it was about xii. of the clocke, they came to the house and
lurked nere vnto his chamber wyndowe; the dog of the house barked
a good, that with the noise, this priest waketh out of his sleepe, and
began to cough and hem; then one of these roges stepes forth nerer the
window and maketh a ruful and pityful noise, requiring for Christ sake

some reliefe, that was both hongry and thirstye, and was like to ly with
out the dores all nighte and starue for colde, vnles he were releued by
him with some small pece of money. "Where dwellest thou?" quoth
this parson. "Alas! sir," saithe this roge, "I haue smal dwelling, and
haue com out of my way; and I should now," saith he, "go to any towne
nowe at this time of night, they woulde set me in the stockes and punishe
me." "Well," quoth this pitifull parson, "away from my house, either
lye in some of my out houses vntyll the morning, and holde, here is
a couple of pence for thee." "A god rewarde you," quoth this roge;
"and in heauen may you finde it." The parson openeth his wyndowe,
and thrusteth out his arme to geue his almes to this Roge that came
whining to receiue it, and quickly taketh holde of his hand, and calleth
his fellowe to him, which was redye at hande with the horse locke, and
clappeth the same about the wrest of his arm, that the mullions standing
so close together for strength, that for his life he could not plucke his
arme againe, and made him beleue, vnles he would at the least geue
them. iii. li., they woulde smite of his arme from the body.

Thomas Harman, *Caueat*, Furnivall ed.,
pp. 38—41

15. Shakespeare's Mrs. Quickly reminds Sir John Falstaff of
a promise to marry her.

Thou didst swear to me upon a parcel-gilt goblet, sitting in my Dolphin-
chamber, at the round table, by a sea-coal fire, upon Wednesday in
Wheeson week, when the prince broke thy head for liking his father
to a singing-man of Windsor, thou didst swear to me then, as I was
washing thy wound, to marry me and make me my lady thy wife. Canst
thou deny it? Did not goodwife Keech, the butcher's wife, come in then
and call me gossip Quickly? coming in to borrow a mess of vinegar,
telling us she had a good dish of prawns; whereby thou didst desire to
eat some, whereby I told thee they were ill for a green wound? And
didst thou not, when she was gone down stairs, desire me to be no more
so familiarity with such poor people; saying that ere long they should
call me madam? And didst thou not kiss me and bid me fetch thee
thirty shillings? I put thee now to thy book-oath: deny it if thou canst.

Henry IV, Part 2, II, i

Mrs. Quickly warns Sir John that she will have no swaggerers in her inn.

Pray you, pacify yourself, Sir John: there comes no swaggerers here....
Tillyfally, Sir John, never tell me: your ancient swaggerer comes not

in my doors. I was before Master Tisick, the deputy, t'other day; and,
as he said to me, — 'twas no longer ago than Wednesday last, — 'Neighbour Quickly,' says he; — Master Dumbe, our minister, was by then; —
'Neighbour Quickly', says he, 'receive those that are civil, for,' said he,
'you are in an ill name;' now, a' said so, I can tell whereupon; 'for,'
says he, 'you are an honest woman, and well thought on; therefore
take heed what guests you receive: receive,' says he, 'no swaggering
companions.' There comes none here: — you would bless you to hear
what he said. No, I'll no swaggerers.

Ibid., II, iv

16. Shakespeare introduces an amiable type of cheating rogue as
peddler: Autolycus speaks in *The Winter's Tale*:

I understand the business; I hear it. To have an open ear, a quick
eye, and a nimble hand, is necessary for a cut-purse: a good nose is
requisite also, to smell out work for the other senses. I see this is the
time that the unjust man doth thrive. What an exchange had this been
without boot! what a boot is here with this exchange! Sure, the gods
do this year connive at us, and we may do anything extempore. The
prince himself is about a piece of iniquity; stealing away from his father
with his clog at his heels. If I thought it were a piece of honesty to
acquaint the king withal, I would not do 't: I hold it the more knavery
to conceal it, and therein am I constant to my profession. Aside,
aside; here is more matter for a hot brain. Every lane's end, every
shop, church, session, hanging, yields a careful man work

(IV, iii)

17. Sir Thomas Elyot on the need for ranks in a class society.
From *The Boke named the Gouernour*, Bk. i, ch. 1. (Elyot is
discussing the meaning of the Latin word *plebs*, which "is in
englishe communaltie: and Plebeii be communers.")

For as moche as *Plebs* in latin, and comminers in englisshe, be wordes
only made for the discrepance of degrees, wherof procedeth ordre:
whiche in thinges as wel naturall as supernaturall hath euer had suche
a preeminence, that therby the incomprehensible maiestie of god, as
it were by a bright leme of a torche or candel, is declared to the blynde
inhabitantes of this worlde. More ouer take away ordre from all thynges
what shulde than remayne? Certes nothynge finally, except some man

wolde imagine eftsones *Chaos*: whiche of some is expounde a confuse mixture. Also where there is any lacke of ordre nedes must be perpetuall conflicte: and in thynges subiecte to Nature nothynge of hym selfe onely may be norisshed, but whan he hath distroyed that where with he dothe participate by the ordre of his creation, he hym selfe of necessite muste than perisshe, wherof ensuethe uniuersall dissolution.

But nowe to proue, by example of those thynges that be within the compasse of mannes knowlege, of what estimation ordre is, nat onely amonge men but also with god, all be it his wisedome, bounte, and magnificence can be with no tonge or penne sufficiently expressed. Hath nat he set degrees and astates in all his glorious warkes? [Gradations in ranks of natural creatures are cited.]

Nowe to retourne to the astate of man kynde, for whose use all the sayd creatures were ordayned of god, and also excelleth them all by prerogatife of knowledge and wisedome, hit semeth that in hym shulde be no lasse prouidence of god declared than in the inferiour creatures; but rather with a more perfecte ordre and dissposition. And therfore hit appereth that god gyueth nat to euery man like gyftes of grace, or of nature, but to some more, some lesse, as it liketh his diuine maiestie.

Ne they be nat in commune, (as fantasticall foles wolde haue all thynges), nor one man hath nat al vertues and good qualities.

Ed. Foster Watson (London, 1907), p. 3 f.

18. Shakespeare's Ulysses discourses on the same subject:

> The heavens themselves, the planets, and this centre
> Observe degree, priority, and place,
> Insisture, course, proportion, season, form,
> Office, and custom, in all line of order:
> 5 And therefore is the glorious planet Sol
> In noble eminence enthron'd and spher'd
> Amidst the other; whose med'cinable eye
> Corrects the ill aspects of planets evil,
> And posts, like the commandment of a king,
> 10 Sans check, to good and bad: but when the planets
> In evil mixture to disorder wander,
> What plagues, and what portents, what mutiny,
> What raging of the sea, shaking of earth,
> Commotion in the winds, frights, changes, horrors,
> 15 Divert and crack, rend and deracinate
> The unity and married calm of states

Quite from their fixture! O! when degree is shak'd,
Which is the ladder to all high designs,
The enterprise is sick. How could communities,
20 Degrees in schools, and brotherhoods in cities,
Peaceful commerce from dividable shores,
The primogenitive and due of birth,
Prerogative of age, crowns, sceptres, laurels,
But by degree, stand in authentic place?
25 Take but degree away, untune that string,
And, hark! what discord follows; each thing meets
In mere oppugnancy: the bounded waters
Should lift their bosoms higher than the shores,
And make a sop of all this solid globe:
30 Strength should be lord of imbecility,
And the rude son should strike his father dead:
Force should be right; or rather, right and wrong—
Between whose endless jar justice resides—
Should lose their names, and so should justice too.
35 Then every thing includes itself in power,
Power into will, will into appetite;
And appetite, a universal wolf,
So doubly seconded with will and power,
Must make perforce a universal prey,
40 And last eat up himself....

Troilus and Cressida, I, iii

19. A complex sentence under the influence of classical syntax, from a prose romance.

But then, Demagoras assuring himselfe, that now Parthenia was her owne, she would never be his, and receiving as much by her owne determinate answere, not more desiring his owne happines, then envying Argalus, whom he saw with narrow eyes, even ready to enjoy the perfection of his desires; strengthening his conceite with all the mischievous counsels which disdayned love, and envious pride could geve unto him; the wicked wretch (taking a time that Argalus was gone to his countrie, to fetch some of his principall frendes to honour the mariage, which Parthenia had most joyfully consented unto,) the wicked Demagoras (I say) desiring to speake with her, with unmercifull force, (her weake armes in vaine resisting) rubd all over her face a most horrible poyson: the effect whereof was such, that never leaper lookt more ugly then she did: which done, having his men & horses ready, departed away in spite of her servants, as redy to revenge as they could be, in such an unexpected mischiefe.

Sir Philip Sidney, *The Countesse of
Pembrokes Arcadia,* I, 6, ed. Albrecht
Feuillerat (Cambridge, 1939), p. 34.

20. Hamlet discusses with Horatio the drinking of wassail at Danish banquets. They are awaiting the second appearance of the ghost of Hamlet's father.

Hor.	Is it a custom?
Ham.	Ay, marry, is't:

But to my mind,— though I am native here
And to the manner born,— it is a custom
More honour'd in the breach than the observance.
5   This heavy-headed revel east and west
Makes us traduc'd and tax'd of other nations;
They clepe us drunkards, and with swinish phrase
Soil our addition; and indeed it takes
From our achievements, though perform'd at height,
10 The pith and marrow of our attribute.
So, oft it chances in particular men,
That for some vicious mole of nature in them,
As, at their birth,— wherein they are not guilty,
Since nature cannot choose his origin,—
15 By the o'ergrowth of some complexion,
Oft breaking down the pales and forts of reason,
Or by some habit that too much o'er-leavens
The form of plausive manners; that these men,
Carrying, I say, the stamp of one defect,
20 Being nature's livery, or fortune's star,
Their virtues else, be they as pure as grace,
As infinite as man may undergo,
Shall in the general censure take corruption
From that particular fault: the dram of eale
25 Doth all the noble substance of a doubt,
To his own scandal—[1]

Hor.	Look, my lord, it comes.
Ham.	Angels and ministers of grace defend us!

Hamlet, I, iv

---

[1] The Oxford ed. places a full stop after: To his own scandal; some others regard the sentence (as here) as unfinished, according to the function assigned to *doth.*

21. Macbeth receives tidings that "The queen, my lord, is dead."

> *Macb.* She should have died hereafter;
> There would have been a time for such a word.
> Tomorrow, and tomorrow, and tomorrow,
> Creeps in this petty pace from day to day,
> 5　To the last syllable of recorded time;
> And all our yesterdays have lighted fools
> The way to dusty death. Out, out, brief candle!
> Life's but a walking shadow, a poor player
> That struts and frets his hour upon the stage,
> 10　And then is heard no more; it is a tale
> Told by an idiot, full of sound and fury,
> Signifying nothing.
>
> *Macbeth*, V, v

22. Sir Thomas Browne (1605—82) on the early English language, from the *Discourse of Languages*.

The Saxons settling over all England, maintained an uniform language, onely diversified in dialect, idioms, and minor differences, according to their different nations which came in to the common conquest, which may yet be a cause of the variation in the speech and words of several parts of England, where different nations most abode or settled, and having expelled the Britanes, their wars were chiefly among themselves, with little action with foreign nations untill the union of the Heptarchy under Egbert; after which time although the Danes infested this land and scarce left any part free, yet their incursions made more havock in buildings, churches and cities, than in the language of the country, because their language was in effect the same, and such as whereby they might easily understand one another.

And if the Normans, which came into Neustria or Normandy with Rollo the Dane, had preserved their language in their new acquists, the succeding conquest of England, by Duke William of his race, had not begot among us such notable alterations; but having lost their language in their abode in Normandy before they adventured upon England, they confounded the English with their French, and made the grand mutation, which was successively encreased by our possessions in Normandy, Guien and Aquitain, by our long wars in France, by frequent resort of the French, who to the number of some thousands came over with Isabel Queen to Edward the Second, and the several matches of England with the daughters of France before and since that time.

But this commixture, though sufficient to confuse, proved not of ability to abolish the Saxon words; for from the French we have borrowed many substantives, adjectives and some verbs, but the great body of numerals, auxiliary verbs, articles, pronouns, adverbs, conjunctions and prepositions, which are the distinguishing and lasting part of a language, remain with us from the Saxon, which, having suffered no great alteration for many hundred years, may probably still remain, though the English swell with the inmates of Italian, French and Latin. An example whereof may be observ'd in this following:

English I

The first and foremost step to all good works is the dread and fear of the Lord of Heaven and Earth, which thorough the Holy Ghost enlighteneth the blindness of our sinfull hearts to treat the ways of wisedom, and then leads our feet into the land of blessing.

Saxon I

The erst and fyrmost stæp to eal gode weorka is the dræd and feurt of the lauord of heofan and eorth, whilc thurh the Heilig Gast onlihtneth the blindnesse of ure sinfull heorte to træd to the wæg of wisdome, and thone læd ure fet into the land of blessung.....

English VI

Thus are we far beneath and also worse than the rest of God's works; for the sun and moon, the king and queen of stars, snow, ice, rain, frost, dew, mist, wind, fourfooted and creeping things, fishes and feathered birds, and fowls either of sea or land do all hold the law of his will.

Saxon VI

Thus eare we far beneoth and ealso wyrse thone the rest of Gods weorka; for the sun and mone, the cyng and cquen of stearran, snaw, ise, ren, frost, deaw, miste, wind, feower fet and crypend thinga, fix and gefetherod brid, and fælan auther in sæ or land do eal heold the lag of his willan.

Thus have you seen in few words how near the Saxon and English meet.

From: *The Miscellaneous Writings* of Sir Thomas Browne, edited by Geoffrey Keynes (London 1931), pp. 89—91 and 94. (Capitalisation modernised.)

23. Biblical narrative in English:

And David sat between the two gates: and the watchman went up to the roof over the gate unto the wall, and lifted up his eyes, and looked, and behold a man running alone.

And the watchman cried, and told the king. And the king said, If he be alone, there is tidings in his mouth. And he came apace, and drew near.

And the watchman saw another man running: and the watchman called unto the porter, and said, Behold another man running alone. And the king said, He also bringeth tidings.

And the watchman said, Methinketh the running of the foremost is like the running of Ahimaaz the son of Zadok. And the king said, He is a good man, and cometh with good tidings.

And Ahimaaz called, and said unto the king, All is well. And he fell down to the earth upon his face before the king, and said, Blessed be the Lord thy God, which hath delivered up the men that lifted up their hand against my lord the king.

And the king said, Is the young man Absalom safe? And Ahimaaz answered, When Joab sent the king's servant, and me thy servant, I saw a great tumult, but I knew not what it was.

And the king said unto him, Turn aside, and stand here. And he turned aside, and stood still.

And, behold, Cushi came; and Cushi said, Tidings, my lord the king: for the Lord hath avenged thee this day of all them that rose up against thee.

And the king said unto Cushi, Is the young man Absalom safe? And Cushi answered, The enemies of my lord the king, and all that rise against thee to do thee hurt, be as that young man is.

And the king was much moved, and went up to the chamber over the gate, and wept: and as he went, thus he said, O my son Absalom! my son, my son Absalom! would God I had died for thee, O Absalom, my son, my son!

2 Samuel 18: 24—33 King James Version

24. From Christian's adventures in *Pilgrim's Progress*:

Then said Evangelist, "If this be thy condition, why standest thou still?" He answered, "Because I know not whither to go." Then he gave him a parchment roll, and there was written within "Flee from the wrath to come!" The man, therefore, read it, and looking upon Evangelist very carefully, said, "Whither must I flee?" Then said Evangelist, pointing with his finger over a very wide field, "Do you see yonder wicket-gate?" The man said, "No." Then said the other, "Do you see yonder shining light?" He said "I think I do." Then said Evangelist, "Keep that light in your eye, and go up directly thereto; so shalt thou see the gate, at which, when thou knockest, it shall be told thee what thou shalt do." So I saw in my dream that the man began to run....

[Christian and his companion are captured and put in a cage at Vanity Fair:]

There, therefore, they lay for some time, and were made the objects of any man's sport, or malice, or revenge, the great one of the fair laughing still at all that befell them. But the men being patient, and not rendering railing for railing, but contrariwise, blessing and giving good words for bad, and kindness for injuries done, some men in the fair, that were more observing and less prejudiced than the rest, began to check and blame the baser sort for their continual abuses done by them to the men. They, therefore, in angry manner let fly at them again, counting them as bad as the men in the cage, and telling them that they seemed confederates, and should be made partakers of their misfortunes.

John Bunyan, *Pilgrim's Progress*, Part I, chs. 1 and 13

25. Scientific prose in English:

The *vis inertiae* is a passive principle by which bodies persist in their motion or rest, receive motion in proportion to the force impressing it, and resist as much as they are resisted. By this principle alone there never could have been any motion in the world. Some other principle was necessary for putting bodies into motion; and now they are in motion, some other principle is necessary for conserving the motion. For from the various composition of two motions, 'tis very certain that there is not always the same quantity of motion in the world. For if two globes joined by a slender rod, revolve about their common center of gravity with an uniform motion, while that center moves on uniformly in a right line drawn in the plane of their circular motion; the sum of the motions of the two globes, as often as the globes are in the right line described by their common center of gravity, will be bigger than the sum of their motions, when they are in a line perpendicular to that right line. By this instance it appears that motion may be got or lost. But by reason of the tenacity of fluids, and attrition of their parts, and the weakness of elasticity in solids, motion is much

more apt to be lost than got, and is always in decay. For bodies which
are either absolutely hard, or so soft as to be void of elasticity, will
not rebound from one another. Impenetrability makes them only stop.
If two equal bodies meet directly *in vacuo*, they will by the laws of
motion stop where they meet, and lose all their motion, and remain in
rest, unless they be elastick, and receive new motion from their spring.
If they have so much elasticity as suffices to make them re-bound with
a quarter, or half, or three quarters of the force with which they come
together, they will lose three quarters, or half, or a quarter of their
motion. And this may be try'd, by letting two equal pendulums fall
against one another from equal heights. If the pendulums be of lead
or soft clay, they will lose all or almost all their motions: if of elastick
bodies they will lose all but what they recover from their elasticity...

> Sir Isaac Newton, *Opticks*, Book III,
> Part 1 (1704; capitalising normalised)

26. A periodic sentence in heroic couplets:

In such a night, when every louder wind
Is to its distant cavern safe confin'd;
And only gentle zephyr fans his wings,
And lonely philomel, still waking, sings;
5 Or from some tree, fam'd for the owl's delight,
She, hollowing clear, directs the wand'rer right;
In such a night, when passing clouds give place,
Or thinly vail the heav'n's mysterious face;
When in some river, overhung with green,
10 The waving moon and trembling leaves are seen;
When freshen'd grass now bears itself upright,
And makes cool banks to pleasing rest invite,
Whence springs the woodbind, and the bramble-rose,
And where the sleepy cowslip shelter'd grows;
15 Whilst now a paler hue the foxglove takes,
Yet checquers still with red the dusky brakes;
When scatter'd glow-worms, but in twilight fine,
Shew trivial beauties watch their hour to shine;
Whilst Salisb'ry stands the test of every light,
20 In perfect charms, and perfect virtue bright:
When odours, which declin'd repelling day,
Thro' temp'rate air uninterrupted stray;
When darken'd groves their softest shadows wear,

And falling waters we distinctly hear;
25 When thro' the gloom more venerable shows
Some ancient fabrick, awful in repose,
While sunburnt hills their swarthy looks conceal,
And swelling haycocks thicken up the vale:
When the loos'd horse now, as his pasture leads
30 Comes slowly grazing thro' th'adjoining meads,
Whose stealing pace, and lengthen'd shade we fear,
Till torn-up forage in his teeth we hear:
When nibbling sheep at large pursue their food,
And unmolested kine rechew the cud;
35 When curlews cry beneath the village-walls,
And to her straggling brood the partridge calls;
Their short-liv'd jubilee the creatures keep,
Which but endures, whilst tyrant-man do's sleep:
When a sedate content the spirit feels,
40 And no fierce light disturbs, whilst it reveals;
But silent musings urge the mind to seek
Something, too high for syllable to speak;
Till the free soul to a compos'dness charm'd,
Finding th' elements of rage disarm'd,
45 O'er all below a solemn quiet grown,
Joys in th' inferiour world, and thinks it like her own:
In such a night let me abroad remain,
Till morning breaks, and all's confus'd again;
Our cares, our toils, our clamours are renew'd,
50 Or pleasures, seldom reach'd, again pursu'd.

"A Noctural Reverie," by Anne Finch,
Lady Winchelsea. Reprinted by Kathleen
W. Campbell, *Poems on Several Occasions
written in the Eighteenth Century* (Oxford
1926), p. 22 f. (Capitalisation modernised)

27. Classical prose with rhetorical questions:

Is not the house built by the labour of the carpenter and the brick-layer? Is it not built for the profit of the architect and the use of the inhabitant, who could not easily have placed one brick upon another? Is not the cloth or the silk wrought into its form and variegated with all the beauty of colours by those who are forced to content themselves with the coarsest and vilest part of their work, while the profit and enjoyment of their labours fall to the share of others? Cast your eye

18

abroad, and see who is it lives in the most magnificent buildings, feasts his palate with the most luxurious dainties, his eyes with the most beautiful sculptures and delicate paintings, and clothes himself in the finest and richest apparel; and tell me if all these do not fall to his lot who had not any the least share in producing all these conveniences, nor the least ability to do so.

Henry Fielding, Jonathan Wild, ch. 8

28. A comic dialogue:

Mrs. Malaprop: There's a little intricate hussy for you!

Sir Anthony Absolute: It is not to be wondered at, ma'am; all this is the natural consequence of teaching girls to read. Had I a thousand daughters, by heaven! I'd as soon have them taught the black art as the alphabet!

Mrs. Mal.: Nay, nay, Sir Anthony, you are an absolute misanthropy.

Sir Anth.: In my way hither, Mrs. Malaprop, I observed your niece's maid coming forth from a circulating library!.... From that moment I guessed how full of duty I should see her mistress!

Mrs. Mal.: Those are vile places, indeed!

Sir Anth.: Madam, a circulating library in a town is as an evergreen tree of diabolic knowledge! It blossoms through the year! And depend upon it, Mrs. Malaprop, that they who are so fond of handling the leaves, will long for the fruit at last.

Mrs. Mal.: Fie, fie, Sir Anthony, you surely speak laconically.

Sir Anth.: Why, Mrs. Malaprop, in moderation, now, what would you have a woman know?

Mrs. Mal.: Observe me, Sir Anthony. I would by no means wish a daughter of mine to become a progeny of learning; I don't think so much learning becomes a young woman; for instance, I would never let her meddle with Greek, or Hebrew, or Algebra, or Simony, or Fluxions, or Paradoxes, or such inflammatory branches of learning; neither would it be necessary for her to handle any of your mathematical, astronomical, diabolic instruments. But, Sir Anthony, I would send her, at nine years old, to a boarding school, in order to learn a little ingenuity and artifice. Then, sir, she should have a supercilious knowledge in accounts; and as she grew up, I would have her instructed in geometry, that she might know something of the contagious countries; but above all, Sir Anthony, she should be mistress of orthodoxy, that she might not mis-spell, and mis-pronounce words so shamefully as girls usually do; and likewise that she might reprehend the true meaning of what

she is saying. This, Sir Anthony, is what I would have a woman know;
and I don't think there is a superstitious article in it.

Richard Brinsley Sheridan, The Rivals, I, ii

29. A 19th-century Scots poem on the plight of unemployed weavers,
by David Shaw (1786—1856).

Tammie Treddlefeet

My name is Tammie Treddlefeet,
  I live in Shuttle Ha';
And I hae been a weaver lad
  This twenty year and twa;
5 Wi waft and warp, and shears sae sharp,
  My rubbin bare, my reed and heddles,
Sae nimbly as my shuttle flees,
  While up and doon I tramp my treddles.

We weaver lads were merry blades
10   When Osnaburgs sellt weel,
And when the price o ilka piece
  Did pay a bow o meal,
The fowk got sale for beef and veal,
  For cash was rife wi everybody;
15 And ilka ale-hoose had the smell
  O roas'en pies and reekin toddy.

But fegs, sic sport was unco short,
  Thae times hae crept awa,
And left us noo wi scarce a shoe
20   Or any hose ava.
And troth I fear when meal's sae dear
  There's some fowk heardly get their sairin,
And gin the price agin sud rise
  We'd a' be stairved as deid's a herrin.

25 Gin times wad come like times that's gane
  We sud be merry a';
We'll jump and prance and lowp and dance
  Till we be like to fa',

And syne you see we'll happy be,
30　　And ilka wab we'll hae a drink on;
We'll lauch and sing "God save the King,"
And a' the songs that we can think on.

From *Scottish Verse, 1851—1951*, ed. Douglas
Young (London: Nelson, 1952), p. 2 f.

30. An experiment in translating German verse into Lallans, by Sir
Alexander Gray (contemporary). The original is Heine's "Still
ist die Nacht, es ruhen die Gassen," from *Das Buch der Lieder*.

The nicht's deid still; there's no a soon'.
In this hoose dwalt the lass I lo'ed.
It's lang, lang sin' she quat the toon,
But aye the hoose stands whaur it stude.

5　A callant stands and gowps abune;
He seems to dree the rage o' Hell.
It gars me grue when by the mune
I see nane ither than mysel'.

You ill-daein' wraith, gae hod your face.
10　What gars you geck at a' the pein
That ance I tholed upon this place
Sae mony a nicht in auld lang syne?

Alexander Gray, *Selected Poems*, (Glasgow:
William MacLellan), p. **31**. Reprinted with
the author's permission.

31. Two Scottish poems by Sydney Goodsir Smith (contemporary).

Sweet Womankind

Ma hert is deid wantan thee,
Wantan thee I dwine,
O whaur in God's ain warld wald I be
Gin thee I eer should tine?...

⁵   And truth it is, ma dearest lass,
         Tho fou I be the nicht,
      Wantan thee I'm a tuim glass
         And black is the braw munelicht.

Sydney Goodsir Smith, *The Devil's
Waltz* (Glasgow: William MacLellan, 1946)
p. 24. Reprinted with the author's permission.

A Bairn Sick

O wae the wind weaves wae
Its wearie wey it wanders throu the autumn nicht
Frae far, thort continents and seas its traivellin
   Laden wi a generation's greit.
⁵   (The 3rd Plenarie Convene o U N O
       Has skaillit for the autumn recess.)

Greitan Aie! Aie!
It greits i the winnock's peerie neuks
Throu the thin streets, the cauld treen
¹⁰ Like a wraith seekan rest. Sleep and rest.
   And sleep.
       (The 4th Plenarie Convene for Control
       O' the Atom Boomb has been postposuit
       Due til an epidemic, amang the delegates
¹⁵   O' thrush.)

But rest there's nane...
Na will be or my wean
Is grown til womanheid
And then...?
²⁰   Sleep, sleep my seick Katrine
     Your mither's newlie opened bud
     Her flouer and her fruct.
     Sleep, my lassie. Sleep.
       Until she's grown til woman. — Till....
²⁵   (The 5th Plenarie Convene o God-kens-what
       Has nou been summoned or dissolvit
       Or suicedit or forgot.)

—I canna keep up wi the news thae days.
Like a wraith the wae wind owre the sleepan toun
30 Its coronach o gray October croons
Wearie wearie weavan its wearie wey
　　Until at length
It croodles doun til sleep at last
By the white bedside o my ailan wean.
35　　　(The 6th etc., etc., etc.)
Wae the wind wae it maens
Luloo... Lullay
　　We canna sleep.

S. G. Smith, printed in *The New Statesman and Nation*, Vol. XLVI, No. 1174 (Sept. 5, 1953); reprinted with the author's permission.

32. From Hugh MacDairmid's "Second Hymn to Lenin."

Oh, it's nonsense, nonsense, nonsense
Nonsense at this time o' day
That breid-and-butter problems
S'ud be in ony man's way.

5　They s'ud be like the tails we tint
On leavin' the monkey stage;
A' maist folk fash aboot's alike
Primaeval to oor age.

We're grown-up that haena yet
10　Put bairnly things aside
　—A' that's material and moral—
And oor new state described.

Sport, love and parentage,
Trade, politics, and law
15　S'ud be nae mair to us than braith
We hardly ken we draw.

Freein' oor poo'ers for greater things,
And feg's there's plenty o' them,
Tho' wha's still trammelt in alow
20　Canna be tenty o' them—.

Reprinted with the author's permission

33. A poem in the Lancashire dialect sprung from the labour struggles
of the 19th century.

The Oldham Weaver

Oi'm a poor cotton-weyver, as mony a one knoowas,
Oi've nowt for t' yeat, and oi've worn eawt my clooas,
Yo'ad hardly gi' tuppence for aw as oi've on,
My clogs are both brosten, an' stuckings oi've none,
5   Yo'd think it wur hard,
       To be browt into th' warld,
To be clemmed, an' do th' best as yo con.

Owd Dicky o' Billy's kept telling me lung,
Wee s'd ha' better toimes if I'd but howd my tung,
10 Oi've howden my tung, till oi've near stopped my breath,
Oi think i' my heeart oi'se soon clem to deeath,
       Owd Dicky's weel crammed,
       He never wur clemmed,
An he ne'er picked ower i' his loife.

15 We tow'rt on six week— thinking aich day wur th' last,
We shifted, an' shifted, till neaw we're quoite fast;
We lived upo' nettles, whoile nettles wur good,
An' Waterloo porridge the best o' eawr food,
       Oi'm tellin' yo' true,
20   Oi can find folk enow,
As wur livin' na better nor me.

Owd Billy o' Dans sent th' baileys one day,
Fur a shop deebt oi eawed him, as oi could na pay,
But he wur too lat, fur owd Billy o' th' rent
25 Had sowd th' an' cart, and ta'en goods for th' rent,
       We'd neawt left bo' th' owd stoo',
       That wur seeats fur two,
An' on it ceawred Margret an' me.

Then t' baileys leuked reawned as sloy as a meawse,
30 When they seed as aw t' goods were ta'en eawt o' t' heawse,
Says one chap to th' tother, "Aws gone, theaw may see;"
Says oi, "Ne'er freet, mon, yeaur welcome ta' me."
       They made no moor ado,
       But whopped up th' eawd stoo',
35 An' we booath leet, whack— upo' t' flags!

Then oi said to eawr Margret, as we lay upo' t' floor,
"We's never be lower i' this warld, oi' m sure,
If ever things awtern, oi'm sure they mun mend,
For oi think i' my heart we're booath at t' far eend;
40   For meeat we ha' none,
        Nor looms t' weyve on,—
Edad! they're as good lost as fund."

Eawr Margret declares, had hoo cloo'as to put on,
Hoo'd goo up to Lunnon an' talk to th' greet mon;
45 An' if things were na awtered when there hoo had been,
Hoo's fully resolved t' sew up meawth an' eend;
        Hoo's neawt to say again t' king,
        But hoo loikes a fair thing,
An' hoo says hoo can tell when hoo's hurt.

                          Mrs. Gaskell, *Mary Barton* (1848), ch. 4

34. A text in Southeast Lancashire dialect by **Edwin Waugh** (1870)

Owd Pinder

Owd Pinder were a rackless foo,
    An' spent his days i' spreein';
At th' end ov every drinkin-do,
    ` He're sure to crack o deein';
5 "Go, sell my rags, an' sell my shoon,
    Aw's never live to trail 'em;
My ballis-pipes are eawt o' tune
    An' th' wynt begins to fail 'em!

"Eawr Matty's very fresh an yung;—
10   'T would any mon bewilder;—
Hoo'll wed again afore it's lung,
    For th' lass is fond o' childer;
My bit o' brass 'll fly—yo'n see—
    When th' coffin-lid has screen'd me—
15 It gwos again my pluck to dee,
    An' lev her wick beheend me:

"Come, Matty, oome, an' cool my yed;
    Aw'm finish'd, to my thinkin';"

Hoo happed him nicely up, an' said,
20   "Thae'st brought it on wi' drinkin'."—
"Nay, nay," said he, "my fuddle's done,
    We're partin' tone fro tother;
So promise me that, when aw'm gwon,
    Thea'll never wed another!"

25 "Th' owd tale," said hoo, an' laft her stoo;
    "It's rayly past believin';
Thee think o' th' world thea'rt goin' to,
    An' lev this world to th' livin';
What use to me can deeod folk be?
30   Thae's kilt thisel' wi' spreein';
An' iv that's o' thae wants wi' me.
    Get forrud wi' thi deein'!"

Reprinted by Skeat, English Dialects,
p. 119 f.

35. Conversation with a Wiltshire countryman, as reported by A. G.
Street.

Just as my train pulled out of Waterloo the other day,... a man
blundered in [to my carriage] rather out of breath. He... sat down,...
put one hand on each widespread knee, beamed at me, and said, "Jist
in time, but I damned near missed her, zno."...

"That's the best way to catch trains," I said, "waiting about a railway
station is a poor job."

"Ay, 'tis you," he replied, "An' this un's a good train, zno. Me
cousin, 'ee 'm an engine driver on the line, 'ee told I to ketch this
un. 'Thee ketch the dree o'clock, Tom,' 'ee says, 'an she'll git 'ee
down to Zalisbury, in a hour an' a 'alf.' Be you gwaine to Zalisbury, zur?"

"Yes," I said, "and I rather think that we come from the same
county."

"Wilsher, guvner, an' you cain't bate it. This yer Lunnon now,
a poorish sort o' place. Volk do seem as 'ow they be drove all the time.
'Urryin' an bustlin' about. 'Twouldin' do fer I.

"Ay, we shall git to Zalisbury at 'alf atter vower, an' then I shall
ketch the vive back to —." Here he named his village.

"Don't you use the buses?" I asked.

"No, guvner! They buses be no good to I. You zee, I be situated
favourable fer trains. I got a lil' 'ouse right on the station. I kin be

a-weedin' me onions, zee the train come in, put on me cwoat, an' stroll awer an' ketch un comfortable. You'll live in Zalisbury, I 'low?"

"No," I said, "just outside"...

"You'll be a varmer, guvner?" I nodded.

"Ay, I knows thic estate you be on. Poorish zart o' do now like all tother-me. Thee's know wot I mane. Estates be gone back. Tidn' like wot twer years ago. The gentry be done like. Tidn' their vault, zno, 'tis their misvortune, as you mid say, but varmin' do suffer zmartish droo it.... Ah!... I be lucky, zno. I zeed it comin'. Zmelled it as you mid zay. I bin a groom, an' I bin a keeper. Then I 'its me 'ack in the war. Poorish job that, jist waste o' time. When I come back 'ome I looks about fer a job. 'Course I could a 'ad me old keeperin' job, but it didn' zim good enough zumhow. I looks aroun', an' I thinks it all awver, an I decides agen it. 'Tom,' I zays to meself, 'the gentry's done. You 'm best out o' that.' "

"And then?" I queried.

"Well, vust I 'ops about a bit. 'Ad a smack at all sorts like, and then, as I wur sayin', I wur lucky. I gits the ziliry postman's job, a part-timer. Thee's know. Brings in jist enough to carry on, an' laves I free to pick up a bit yer and ther as I be minded. I tell 'ee I be fitted up proper."...

A black cloud was coming over. "Getting dark," I said, "we're going to get a storm. Well, we can do with it." ·

"You mid be able to," said my companion, "but I don't want none fer a bit. I got vower days gardenin' to do.... I mid be a trifle behin', but 'taint me own vault, guvner. I bin messin' about up in Kent fer dree days buryin' a cousin. You know 'ow 'tis. Volk do be born, do marry, an' do die, an' when any o' that do 'appen, zumbody in the vamily got to zee to it. Theaze time the lot vell on I, an' there 'twer. 'Owsomever, we've a-planted 'im all right, an' I'd a zight zooner bin plantin' spuds. Buryin's a poor sort o' job. But you be like all they farmers. You do want rain, an' you don't care a mossel about nobody else.... I do know a main bit about farmers. Not but what I didn't git on all right wie 'em, when I wur a keeper. You cain't run a keeperin' beat an' be quarrelin' wie the farmers. But look 'ow they do worry on about rabbits, an' never nother a bit about ketchin' their rats."

"Rabbits do a lot more harm to a farmer," I protested.

"They does 'arm, granted, and so do rats. But you can't tell I. I knows all about it. A rabbit do vetch a vew aypence, an' a rat do vetch nothin'. But I wur allus death on rats. One on 'em bit I when I wur a nipper, an' I ant never fergied 'em. I 'ates em. I 'low I killed a dam zight more rats than Germans when I wur in the war. An' when I wur keeperin' I wur death on 'em. Wuss 'an pizen I wur, an' I be now. If I wur a toff an' 'ad a 'state, I should make all me farmers keep their rats down, er know the reason why.... Ah, you mid laff, but I 'low I should run a 'state as well as the main o' thease 'alf skim agent vellers from Lunnon, wot do run the main o' the estates nowadays, fer as I telled 'ee, the gentry be done like, an' in a girt many ways 'tis a pity.

"Well, yers Zalisbury, guvner, an' we mus' part. But I've enjoyed comin' down wie 'ee. Jist about. Most volk in trains do zit up mum, zno, as though if they did speak they'd be givin' zummat precious away. But you've zpoke I vair all the way along, an' you've telled I a lot. Good day to 'ee."

From "The Art of Conversation," in *Harvest by Lamplight*, a selection from the works of A. G. Street (London: Faber and Faber, 1941), pp. 57—64. Reprinted with the permission of the publishers.

36. A fable in Wiltshire verse by J. Yonge Akermann (1853).

The Harnet and the Bittle

A harnet zet in a hollur tree—
A proper spiteful twoad was he;
And a merrily zung while he did zet
His stinge as shearp as a bagganet;
5   Oh, who so vine and bowld as I?
I vears not bee, nor wapse, nor vly!

A bittle up thuck tree did clim,
And scarnvully did look at him;
Zays he, "Zur harnet, who giv thee
10 A right to zet in thuck there tree?
Vor ael you zengs so nation vine,
I tell 'e 'tis a house o' mine!"

The harnet's conscience velt a twinge,
But grawin' bwold wi' his long stinge,
15 Zays he, "Possession's the best laaw;
Zo here th' sha'sn't put a claaw!
Be off, and leave the tree to me,
The mixen's good enough for thee!"

Just then a yuckel, passin' by,
20 Was axed by them the cause to try;
"Ha! ha! I zee how 'tis!" zays he,
"They'll make a vamous munch vor me!"
His bill was shearp, his stomach lear,
Zo up a snapped the caddlin' pair!

Reprinted by Skeat, English Dialects,
p. 128 f.

37. Cockney dialect as recorded late in the 19th century. The speaker is a child living in a former slum district of London called the Jago, now rebuilt.

"I don't s'pose father's 'avin' a sleep outside, eh?... No, I ain't seen 'im: I just looked in the court. I 'ope 'e's done a click... copped somethink, o' course. Nicked somethink. You know.... W'en 'e brought 'ome that there yuller prop— the necktie pin— w'y, where did 'e git that? 'E ain't 'ad a job for munse and munse: where's the yannups come from wot's bin for to pay the rent, an git the toke, an' milk for Looey? Think I dunno? I ain't a kid. I know.... Straight people's fools, *I* reckon. Kiddo Cook says that, an' 'e's as wide as Broad Street. W'en I grow up I'm goin' to git toffs' clo'es an' be in the 'igh mob. They does big clicks.... It's the mugs wot git took.... An' quoddin' ain't so bad.... S'pose father'll be smugged some day, eh, mother?"

Arthur Morrison, A Child of the Jago
(Penguin Books reprint of 1946), p. 15 f.;
first published 1896.

A dialogue adapted from the same source. The child's father is approached by a colleague Bill in reference to a projected robbery.

Bill: Are you on for a job?
Josh: Wot sort o' job's this?
Bill: Wy, a bust— unless we can screw it.
Josh: Awright. Depends, o' course.
Bill: O, it's a good 'un. It's a good un— you can take yer davy o' that. I bin a thinkin' about it for a fortnight, but it wants two. Damme, it's a nobby! Wotjer think... wotjer think o' screwin' a fence?
Josh: Wot fence?
Bill: Wy, ole Weech! 'Ow's that strike ye, ole cock? It'll be a fair cop for 'im. 'E's treated us all pretty mean, one time or other. Wy, I bet

'e *owes* us fifty quid atween us, wot with all the times 'e's squeeged us for a bit. It'll on'ly be goin' to bring away our own stuff!

Josh: G-r-r-r-! ...it was 'im as put me away for my laggin'. Bleedin' swine!

Bill: Wot— im? Ole Weech narked ye? 'Owjer know that?....

Josh: I'm on. It's one way o' payin' 'im, an' it'll bring a bit in. On'y 'e better not show 'isself w'ile I'm abaat! *'E* wouldn't git auf with a punch on the chin, like the bloke at 'Ighbury!

Bill: Blimy! an' so it was 'im, was it? I often wondered 'oo you meant. Well, flimpin' 'im's the best way. Won't 'e sing a bleedin' 'ymn w'en 'e finds 'is stuff weeded! But there,— let's lay it out.

Ibid., p. 166 f.

38. Anglo-Irish used for literary purposes. The monologue is spoken by an old woman wandering along the roads and muttering to herself about her past life and present state. (The rows of dots appear as given in the original; they do not indicate omissions.)

"Ah, God be with me," said she, "an old woman on a stick, that hasn't a place in the wide world to go or a neighbour itself.... I wish I could get a cup of tea, so I do. I wish to God I could get a cup of tea.... Me sitting down in my own little house, with the white tablecloth on the table, and the butter in the dish, and the strong, red tea in the teacup; and me pouring cream into it, maybe, and telling the children not to be wasting the sugar, the things! and himself saying he'd got to mow the big field today, or that the red cow was going to calve, the poor thing!— and that if the boys went to school, who was going to weed the turnips— and me sitting drinking my strong cup of tea, and telling him where the old trapesing hen was laying.... Ah, God be with me! an old creature hobbling along the roads on a stick. I wish I was a young girl again, so I do, and himself coming courting me, and him saying that I was a real nice little girl surely, and that nothing would make him happy or easy at all but me to be loving him.— Ah, the kind man that he was, to be sure, the kind decent man.... And Sorca Reilly to be trying to get him from me, and Kate Finnegan with her bold eyes looking after him in the Chapel; and him to be saying that along with me they were only a pair of old nanny goats.... And then me to be getting married and going home to my own little house with my man— ah, God be with me! and him kissing me, and laughing, and frightening me with his goings-on. Ah, the kind man, with his soft eyes, and his nice voice, and his jokes and laughing, and him thinking the world and all of me — ay indeed.... And the neighbours to be coming in and sitting round the fire in the night time, putting the world through each other, and talking about France and Russia and them other queer places, and him holding up the discourse like a learned man, and them all listening to him and nodding their heads at each other, and wondering at his education and all: or, maybe, the neighbours to be singing, or him making me sing the Coulin, and him to be proud of me.... and then him to be killed on me with a cold in his chest.... Ah, then, God be with me, a lone, old creature on a stick, and the sun shining into her eyes and she thirsty — I wish I had a cup of tea, so I do. I wish to God I had a cup of tea and a bit of meat... or, maybe, an egg. A nice fresh egg laid by the speckledy hen that used to be giving me all the trouble, the thing! Sixteen hens I had, and they were the ones for laying, surely.... It's the queer world, so it is, the queer world — and all the things that do happen for no reason at all.... Ah, God be with me! I wish there weren't stones in my boots, so I do, and I wish to God I had a cup of tea and a fresh egg. Ah, glory be, my old legs are getting tireder every day, so they are. Wisha, one time — when himself was in it — I could go about the house all day long, cleaning the place, and feeding the pigs, and the hens and all, and then dance half the night, so I could: and himself proud of me....

James Stephens, *The Crock of Gold*
(first ed. London: Macmillan Co., 1912);
excerpt from ch. 11. Reprinted with the
permission of Mrs. Stephens and the
publishers.

39. New England dialect of the 19th century as recorded by James Russell Lowell; from a poem satirising efforts to recruit soldiers for the Mexican War (1846).

> Them that rule us, them slave-traders,
>   Haint they cut a thunderin' swarth
> (Helped by Yankee renegaders),
>   Thru the vartu o' the North!
> 5 We begin to think it's nater
>   To take sarse an' not be riled; —
> Who'd expect to see a tater
>   All on eend at bein' biled?

Ez fer war, I call it murder,—
10   There you hev it plain an' flat;
I don't want to go no furder
        Than my Testyment fer that;
God hez sed so plump an' fairly,
        It's ez long ez it is broad,
15 An' you've gut to git up airly
        Ef you want to take in God.

'Taint your eppylettes an' feathers
        Make the thing a grain more right;
'Taint a-follerin' your bell-wethers
20   Will excuse ye in His sight;
Ef you take a sword an' dror it,
        An' go stick a feller thru,
Guv'ment aint to answer for it,
        God'll send the bill to you.

25 Wut's the use o' meeting-goin'
        Every Sabbath, wet or dry,
Ef it's right to go a-mowin'
        Feller-men like oats an' rye?
I dunno but wut it's pooty
30   Trainin' round in bobtail coats,—
But it's cur'us Christian dooty
        This 'ere cuttin' folks's throats.

They may talk o' Freedom's airy
        Tell they're pupple in the face,—
35 It's a grand gret cemetary
        Fer the barthrights of our race;
They jest want this Californy
        So's to lug new slave-states in
To abuse ye, an' to scorn ye,
40   An' to plunder ye like sin.

Aint it cute to see a Yankee
        Take sech everlastin' pains,
All to git the Devil's thankee
        Helpin' on 'em weld their chains?
45 Wy, it's jest ez clear ez figgers,
        Clear ez one an' one make two,

Chaps thet make black slaves o' niggers
 Want to make wite slaves o' you....

Hain't they sold your coloured sea-men?
50   Hain't they made your env'ys wiz?
Wut'll make ye act like freemen?
 Wut'll git your dander riz?
Come, I'll tell ye wut I'm thinkin'
 Is our dooty in this fix,
55 They'd ha' done't ez quick ez winkin'
 In the days o' seventy-six.

Clang the bells in every steeple,
 Call all true men to disown
The tradoocers of our people,
60   The enslavers o' their own;
Let our dear old Bay State proudly
 Put the trumpet to her mouth,
Let her ring this messidge loudly
 In the ears of all the South:—

65 "I'll return ye good fer evil
 Much ez we frail mortils can,
But I wun't go help the Devil
 Makin' man the cus o' man;
Call me coward, call me traiter,
70   Jest ez suits your mean idees,—
Here I stand a tyrant-hater,
 An' the friend o' God an' Peace!"

Ef I'd *my* way I hed ruther
 We should go to work an' part,
75 We take one away, they take t'other,
 Guess it wouldn't break my heart;
Man had ough' to put asunder
 Them thet God has nowys jined;
An' I shouldn't gretly wonder
80   Ef there's thousands o' my mind.

J. R. Lowell, *The Biglow Papers*, No. 1
(1846)

40. Joel Chandler Harris as a recorder of general Southern dialect in Georgia. In this passage, a poor white woman named Mrs. Bivins is maintaining the right of her son to have married into a distinguished family of the neighbourhood. Her speech is on the level of low colloquial.

Deely [i. e., Delia] Wornum married my son, an' Henry Clay Bivins made 'er a good husbun', if I do have to give it out myse'f. Yes, 'ndeed! An' yit if you'd 'a' heern the rippit them Wornums kicked up, you'd 'a' thought the pore chile'd done took 'n' run off 'long of a whole passel er high pirates frum somewheres er 'nother. In about that time the ole Jedge, he got sorter fibbled up, some say in his feet, an' some say in his head; but his wife, that Em'ly Wornum, she taken on awful. I never seen her a-gwine on myse'f; not that they was any hidin' out 'mongst the Bivinses er the Sanderses, — bless you, no! bekaze here's one what wa'n't afeared er all the Wornums in the continental State er Georgy, not if they'd 'a' mustered out under the head er ole Nick hisse'f, which I have my doubts if he wa'n't somewheres aroun'. I never seen 'er, but I heern tell er how she was a-cuttin' up.

Joel Chandler Harris, *Mingo and Other Sketches in Black and White* (Boston, 1884), p. 15.

41. An example of Gullah dialect recorded in the 20th century:

Maussuh, uh binnuh stan' een Willtown road close to Mas' Edwu'd Baa'nwell' Clifton place, w'en uh yeddy de dog duh comin' fuh me, an' uh stop fuh liss'n. Bimeby, uh see de mukkle duh shake, en', fus' t'ing uh know, de deer jump out de t'icket en' light een de big road en' look 'puntop me! 'E foot fall saaf'ly 'pun de groun' same lukkuh cat duh sneak 'puntop 'uh bu'd. 'E tu'n 'e head en' look 'puntop me lukkuh somebody, 'cep'n suh 'e yeye big lukkuh hawn owl' eye. 'E look at me so positubble, uh t'ink mus' be 'e duh haant, en' uh dat 'f'aid 'e gwine t'row one spell 'puntop me, uh tu'n 'way me head. W'en uh look roun' 'gen, 'e gone! Yuh come de dog'! Uh nebbuh see summuch dog! Dem full' de road, en dem woice' roll 'tell you nebbuh yeddey shishuh music. Dem cross' de road, en' dem gone! Attuh leetle w'ile, uh yeddy 'um duh giv dem toung een de gyaa'd'n uh ole Maussuh' Clifton house wuh dem Nyankee bu'n down eenjurin' de wah. De gyaa'd'n big ez uh cawnfiel', en' 'e full' uh high rose bush duh climb up 'pun de tree, en' all kind'uh briah en' t'icket dey dey. Uh yeddy de dog' mek uh sukkle roun' de gyaa'd'n, den dem stop. Bimeby, yuh come de ole buck duh run puhzackly 'pun 'e back track, en' w'en 'e git to de big

road weh him lef' me duh stan' up, uh t'awt at de fus' 'e bin gwine
jump 'puntop me, but 'e tu'n shaa'p roun' en' light down de road
gwine Paa'kuh' Ferry Cross-Road'.... Da' duh de las' uh shum, en'
uh nebbuh yeddy 'um no mo' attuh 'e done gone.

Ambrose E. Gonzales, *The Black Bor-
der: Gullah Stories of the Caroline Coast*
(Columbus, S. C., 1922), quoted by George
Philip Krapp, *The English Language in
America.* I (1925), p. 251 f.

42. An example of simple colloquial Southern English as spoken
   by a Negro, Mrs. Isiah Nixon, whose husband was shot by
   illegally organised white racists because he voted in the primary
   elections of 1948 in Georgia. Mrs. Nixon's account of what happened was recorded directly on tape by the Progressive Party
   and used during the election campaign.

Isaiah Nixon was my husband. He was a good husband.

It was on September the eighth he got shot, on votin' day.

Isaiah went to the poll. He voted, and after he got through he came
on back to the house and set down and listened to the radio. He
played with the baby for a while, and then he got up and he went
in the kitchen, and he had his supper. He had peas and bread, biscuits
and meat, and sweet potatoes for supper.

And I went on the porch and I saw a car coming, and the car drove
up, and they asked was he at home, and I told them yes, and they
asked him had he saw Evan Johnson, and he told them no, sir, he
hadn't saw him that day, and he said, "Well, stop down a minute,"
and he went to the fence where he was, and he throwed the gun —the
pistol— on him, and come back toward the house, and the white boy,
he—. And they just shot him down. That's all I can tell you.

I don't know why they'd shoot him no less'n it was 'cause he
voted. 'Cause he had a rights to vote. He hadn't done anything to
them. He hadn't had no words that I know of.

I sit and think of him when night come.

I have six children. I don't hardly know how to take care of them
by myself. I needs help with them.

I wish I could explain just why and know just why we have such
a hard time in this part of the country.

Quoted by Barrows Dunham, *Giant in
Chains* (Boston: Little, Brown & Co., 1953),
p. 34. Reprinted by permission of author
and publishers.

43. A literary portrayal of the language situation among Spanish-speaking workers of Mexican origin in the Southwest. A barely literate sheriff interviews an old man, a Mexican-American worker who has been left in charge of the village children during a struggle involving violence, provocations and arrests. The sheriff speaks:

"You José Amadda Contreras?"

The old fellow nodded. "Jou go' 'rest me?" he whispered.

Burns was inclined to whisper, too, but it seemed somehow beneath him, and he asked aloud, pointing to the other man:

"Who's that?"

"Este? mi amigo. Se llama Juan Dombraski."

Dombrowski. That was the one, all right. "He spik English, savvy?"

"Inglés, no. Nada, nada— *not!*" he emphasized.

"How about you? You spik English—"

"Leetla beet, no muncho [sic]."

"Listen. I'm standing out in the street. I hear a man say in English, 'Don't shoot, that's my son.' And something about a bad foot. It wasn't you?"

"Me? No, no. Me slip." He pantomimed sleep. "Him slip too." He made a snoring noise. "Puede ser otra casa," he suggested hopefully.

"No, it wasn't no other casa. It come right from here. You sure him no spik English. Never?"

"No, nunca, nunca. No sabe hablar, el."

Somebody's a goddam liar, Burns thought. He suspected the old Cossack. Who ever heard of a man who couldn't speak *some* language? To hell with it. This old devil was more important.

"You was in that delegation to Sheriff McKelway yesterday, wasn't you?"

"Yo? En una delegacion—? Ah! la comité del Concilio de los Sin-empleados!"

"The committee, yeah— unemployed, that's right. You on that committee?"

"Como no?"

"What I thought. You in the Plaza this morning?"

"En la Plaza? Hoy en la mañana?" The old geezer didn't like that one so well. "Pues..." Couldn't decide how much to admit. "Tal vez... sí. Allá, sí, estaba. Pero en el callejón, no! No fuí en el alley [where the sheriff had been shot under cover of tear gas thrown by the police]."

Not in the alley, like all the rest of 'em. To listen to them you'd think there hadn't been anybody in shat son-of-a-bitchin' alley. No use to ask 'em any more.

"Okay, vamoose," he said. "Poco questiones in my oficina."

"Jou lukin' for Ramón Arce, qué no? Ramón no here. Aw gone — psht!" He laughed with glee, skidding one palm off the other, to suggest how fast Arsy had skipped. "No ketch. Ramón go psht."

Lars Lawrence, *Morning Noon and Night*, (New York: Putnam, 1954), p. 249 f. Reprinted with the author's permission.

44. An example of general low colloquial American with slang. A base-ball player writes to his friend Al about his adventures.

I had a run in with Kelly last night and it looked like I would have to take a wallop at him but the other boys separated us. He is a bush outfielder from the New England League. We was playing poker. You know the boys plays poker a good deal but this was the first time I got in. I was having pretty good luck and was about four bucks to the good and I was thinking of quitting because I was tired and sleepy. Then Kelly opened the pot for fifty cents and I stayed. I had three sevens. No one else stayed. Kelly stood pat and I drawed two cards. And I catched my fourth seven. He bet fifty cents but I felt pretty safe even if he did have a pat hand. So I called him. I took the money and told them I was through.

Lord and some of the boys laughed but Kelly got nasty and begun to pan me for quitting and for the way I played. I says Well I won the pot didn't I? He says Yes and he called me something. I says I got a notion to take a punch at you.

He says Oh you have have you? And I come back at him. I says Yes I have have I? I would of busted his jaw if they hadn't stopped me. You know me Al.

I worked here two times once against Los Angeles and once against Venice. I went the full nine innings both times and Venice beat me four to two. I could of beat them easy with any kind of support. I walked a couple of guys in the forth and Chase drops a throw and Collins lets a fly ball get away from him. At that I would of shut them out if I had wanted to cut loose. After the game Callahan says You didn't look so good in there to-day. I says I didn't cut loose. He says Well you been working pretty near three weeks now and you ought to be in shape to cut loose. I says Oh I am in shape all right.

He says Well don't work no harder than you have to or you might get hurt and then the league would blow up. I don't know if he was kidding me or not but I guess he thinks pretty well of me because he works me lots oftener than Walsh or Scott or Benz.

From Ring Lardner, *You Know Me Al.*
(first ed. and copyright New York: Charles
Scribner's Sons, 1916; copyright 1944 by
Ellis A. Lardner). Reprinted by permission
of the publishers.

45. Presentative sentences in Dickens:

Fog everywhere. Fog up the river, where it flows among great aits and meadows; fog down the river, where it rolls defiled among the tiers of shipping, and the water-side pollutions of a great (and dirty) city. Fog on the Essex marshes, fog on the Kentish heights.... Fog in the eyes and throats of ancient Greenwich pensioners, wheezing by the fireside of their wards; fog in the stem and bowl of the afternoon pipe of the wrathful skipper, down in his close cabin; fog cruelly pinching the toes and fingers of his shivering little 'prentice boy on deck. Chance people on the bridges peeping over the parapets into a nether sky of fog, with fog all round them, as if they were up in a balloon and hanging in the misty clouds.

Gas looming through the fog in divers places in the streets, much as the sun may, from the spongey fields, be seen to loom by the husbandmen and plowboy. Most of the shops lighted two hours before their time— as the gas seems to know, for it has a haggard and unwilling look....

In Lincoln's Inn Hall at the very heart of the fog, sits the Lord High Chancellor in his High Court of Chancery....

Charles Dickens, *Bleak House* ch. 1.
(1853).

46. An experiment in writing archaic English. William Morris imagines John Ball (leader in the uprising of 1381) addressing the rebellious men of Kent:

Forsooth, too many rich men there are in this realm; and yet if there were but one, there would be one too many, for all should be his thralls. Hearken, then, ye men of Kent. For overlong belike have

I held you with words; but the love of you constrained me, and the joy that a man hath to babble to his friends and his fellows whom he hath not seen for a long season.

Now, hearken, I bid you: To the rich men that eat up a realm there cometh a time when they whom they eat up, that is the poor, seem poorer than of wont, and their complaint goeth up louder to the heavens; yet it is no riddle to say that oft at such times the fellowship of the poor is waxing stronger, else would no man have heard his cry. Also at such times is the rich man become fearful, and so waxeth in cruelty, and of that cruelty do people misdeem that it is power and might waxing. Forsooth, ye are stronger than your fathers, because ye are more grieved than they, and ye should have been less grieved than they had ye been horses and swine; and then, forsooth, would ye have been stronger to bear; but ye, ye are not strong to bear, but to do.

And wot ye why we are come to you this fair eve of holiday? and wot ye why I have been telling of fellowship to you? Yea, forsooth, I deem ye wot well, that it is for this cause, that ye might bethink you of your fellowship with the men of Essex....

Men of Kent, I wot well that ye are not so hard bestead as those of other shires, by the token of the day when behind the screen of leafy boughs ye met Duke William with bill and bow as he wended Londonward from the woeful field of Senlac; but I have told of fellowship and ye have hearkened and understood what the Holy Church is, whereby ye know that ye are fellows of the saints in heaven and the poor men of Essex; and as one day the saints shall call you to the heavenly feast, so now do the poor men call you to the battle,....

William Morris, *A Dream of John Ball*, ch. 4 (1888)

47. Rhetorical prose by a Romantic poet (Shelley):

Poetry is the record of the best and happiest moments of the happiest and best minds. We are aware of evanescent visitations of thought and feeling sometimes associated with place or person, sometimes regarding our own mind alone, and always arising unforeseen and departing unbidden, but elevating and delightful beyond all expression: so that even in the desire and regret they leave, there cannot but be pleasure, participating as it does in the nature of its object. It is as it were the interpenetration of a diviner nature through our own; but its footsteps are like those of a wind over the sea, which the coming calm erases, and whose traces remain only, as on the wrinkled sand which paves it. These and corresponding conditions of being are experienced principally by those of the most delicate sensibility and the most enlarged imagination; and the state of mind produced by them is at war with every base desire. The enthusiasm of virtue, love, patriotism, and friendship, is essentially linked with such emotions; and whilst they last, self appears as what it is, an atom to a universe. Poets are not only subject to these experiences as spirits of the most refined organization, but they can colour all that they combine with the evanescent hues of this ethereal world; a word, a trait in the representation of a scene or a passion, will touch the enchanted chord, and reanimate, in those who have ever experienced these emotions, the sleeping, the cold, the buried image of the past. Poetry thus makes immortal all that is best and most beautiful in the world; it arrests the vanishing apparitions which haunt the interlunations of life, and veiling them, or in language or in form, sends them forth among mankind, bearing sweet news of kindred joy to those with whom their sisters abide — abide, because there is no portal of expression from the caverns of the spirit which they inhabit into the universe of things. Poetry redeems from decay the visitations of the divinity in man.

Percy Bysshe Shelley, Defence of Poetry
(1821) ed. John Shawcross in Shelley's
Literary and Philosophical Criticism (Lon-
don, 1909).

48. A descriptive passage by a pioneer in impressionistic writing:

In these then, the favourite incidents of Giorgione's school, music or the musical intervals in our existence, life itself is conceived as a sort of listening — listening to music, to the reading of Bandello's novels, to the sound of water, to time as it flies. Often such moments are really our moments of play, and we are surprised at the unexpected blessedness of what may seem our least important part of time; not merely because play is in many instances that to which people really apply their own best powers, but also because at such times, the stress of our servile, everyday attentiveness being relaxed, the happier powers in things without are permitted free passage, and have their way with us. And so, from music, Giorgione passes often to the play which is like music; to those masques in which men avowedly do but play at real life, like children "dressing up," disguised in the strange old Italian dresses, parti-coloured, or fantastic with embroidery and furs, of which the master was so curious a designer, and which, above all the spotless white linen at wrist and throat, he painted so dexterously.

But when people are happy in this thirsty land water will not be far off; and in the school of Giorgione, the presence of water —the well, or marble-rimmed pool, the drawing or pouring of water, as the woman pours it from a pitcher with her jewelled hand in the Fête Champêtre, listening, perhaps, to the cool sound as it falls, blent with the music of the pipes— is as characteristic, and almost as suggestive, as that of music itself. And the landscape feels, and is glad of it also — a landscape full of clearness, of the effects of water, of fresh rain newly passed through the air, and collected into the grassy channels. The air, moreover, in the school of Giorgione, seems as vivid as the people who breathe it, and literally empyrean, all impurities being burnt out of it, and no taint, no floating particle of anything but its own proper elements allowed to subsist within it.

Walter Pater, *The Renaissance* (1873)

49. Conversation and stream of consciousness:

The mourners moved away slowly, without aim, by devious paths, staying awhile to read a name on a tomb.

—Let us go round by the chief's grave, Hynes said. We have time.

—Let us, Mr Power said.

They turned to the right, following their slow thoughts. With awe Mr Power's blank voice spoke:

—Some say he is not in that grave at all. That the coffin was filled with stones. That one day he will come again.

Hynes shook his head.

—Parnell will never come again, he said. He's there, all that was mortal of him. Peace to his ashes.

Mr Bloom walked unheeded along his grove by saddened angels, crosses, broken pillars, family vaults, stone hopes praying with upcast eyes, old Ireland's hearts and hands. More sensible to spend the money on some charity for the living. Pray for the repose of the soul of. Does anybody really? Plant him and have done with him. Like down a coalshoot. Then lump them together to save time. All souls' day. Twentyseventh I'll be at his grave. Ten shillings for the gardener. He keeps it free of weeds. Old man himself. Bent down double with his shears for clipping. Near death's door. Who passed away. Who departed this life. As if they did it of their own accord. Got the shove,

all of them. Who kicked the bucket. More interesting if they told
you what they were. So and so, wheelwright. I travelled for cork lino.
I paid five shillings in the pound. Or a woman's with her saucepan.
I cooked good Irish stew. Eulogy in a country churchyard it ought
to be that poem of whose is it Wordsworth or Thomas Campbell.
Entered into rest the protestants put it. Old Dr Murren's. The great
physician called him home. Well it's God's acre for them. Nice country
residence. Newly plastered and painted. Ideal spot to have a quiet
smoke and read the *Church Times*. Marriage ads they never try to
beautify. Rusty wreaths hung on knobs, garlands of bronze-foil. Better
value for the money. Still, the flowers are more poetical. The other gets
rather tiresome, never withering. Expresses nothing. Immortelles.

James Joyce, *Ulysses* (London: Bodley
Head ed.), p. 104, Reprinted with the
publisher's permission.

50. Puns and sound effects in Joyce (stream of the subconscious):

I pity your oldself I was used to. Now a younger's there. Try not
to part. Be happy, dear ones! May I be wrong! For she'll be sweet
for you as I was sweet when I came down out of me mother. My
great blue bedroom, the air so quiet, scarce a cloud. In peace and
silence. I could have stayed up there for always only. It's something
fails us. First we feel. Then we fall. And let her rain now if she likes.
Gently or strongly as she likes. Anyway let her rain for my time is come.
I done me best while I was let. Thinking always if I go all goes.
A hundred cares, a tithe of troubles and is there one who understands
me? One in a thousand of years of the nights? All me life I have been
lived among them but now they are becoming lothed to me. And I am
lothing their little warm tricks. And lothing their mean cosy turns. And
all the greedy gushes out through their small souls. And all the lazy
leaks down over their brash bodies. How small it's all! And me letting
on to meself always. And lilting on all the time. I thought you were all
glittering with the noblest of carriage. You're only a bumpkin. I thought
you the great in all things, in guilt and in glory. You're but a puny.
Home! My people were not their sort out beyond there as far as I can....

Finnegans Wake (London: Faber & Faber,
1939), p. 627. Reprinted by permission of
the administrators of Joyce's estate (Monro,
Pennefather and Co., London).

GLOSSARY

Note: Forms which differ from Standard English merely in details of orthography are not included: e. g., *abyde* for *abide* in ME. When no specific modern dialect is indicated, the form in question is to be found in more than one. ME forms agreeing with the London dialect are not specifically designated.

A

a (dial.): have
a' (Sh.): he
a' (Sc. dial.): all
a vys = avys: advice, counsel
abaat (Cock. dial.): about
a-bak: backward
abart (Cock. dial.): about
aboon (Sc. dial.): above, aloft
aboot (Sc. dial.): about
abrode (Dor. dial.): broken
abune: *see* aboon
abusioun: abuse, wrong
'ack (dial.): blow, strike, hack
'ad = had
addition (Sh.): title, mark of reputation
adew: adieu
ael: *see* vor ael
again, agayn: against
agen, agin (dial.): again, against
a-grief: heavily, amiss
a-gwine (US Sth colloq.): going
ah (dial.): I
ahr (Cock. dial.): our
aich (dial.): each
aill: ailment, illness
ain (Sc. dial.): own
airly (dial.): early
allane: alone
allus (dial.): always

along with (colloq.): compared to
alow (Sc. dial.): ablaze; (naut.): below
als: as, also
alures: covered passages
amang (Sc. dial.): among
ance (Sc. dial.): once
and: if
annewche (MScots): enough
'appen (dial.): happen
Arfricar (Cock. dial.): Africa
'arm (dial.): harm
arn (dial.): earn
as (dial.): who
asmoche = as much
ataraxy: imperturbability, mental calm
atter (dial.): after
attour: over, around
attuh (Gul. dial.): after
atween (dial.): between
auctorite: authority
auf (vulg.): off
auld (MScots): old
autem (sl.): church
ava (Sc. dial.): at all
'ave = have
a-vier (Sth dial.): afire
avisen: deliberate, consider
aw (dial.): all
aw (dial.): I
awa' (Sc. dial.): away

awayte: watching, spying, observing
awer (dial.): over
awm (Cock. dial.): harm
awright (vulg.): all right
awter(n) (Nth dial.): alter
ax, axen: ask
ay: always, ever
aypence = halfpenny

B

baby (US sl.): girl
bagganet (dial.): bayonet
bailey (dial.): bailiff
baill (MScots): bale, sorrow
bairn (Sc. dial.): child
bairnly (Sc. dial.): childish
ball and chain (US sl.): wife
ballis (Nth dial.): bellows
bane (arch.): death
barrikin (sl.): meaning
barthrights (dial.): birthrights
bate (dial.): beat, excel
bats in the belfry (US sl.): insane
bayth (MScots): both
be: by
be leve = believe
beck (sl.): constable
beet (dial.): bit
begouth (MScots): begins
bekaze (US dial.): because
belike (arch.): perhaps
bene (sl.): good; benshyp: very good
beren on hande: accuse, assert
beriall: of beryl
bestead (arch.): hard pressed
bethink oneself (arch.): reflect on
betty (sl.): tool used for robbery
bewis (MScots): boughs
bewpere (sl.): companion, accomplice
big (Sc. dial.): build
bigyle: beguile
bile (US dial.): boil
bill (arch.): staff with blade attached
bimeby (vulg. pron.): by and by
bin = been
bin, binnuh (Gul. dial.): was, been
bing (sl.): go, hasten
birk (Sc. dial.): birch
bit (sl.): a small coin; a four-penny piece

bittle (dial.): beetle
biword: parable
bleedin' (sl.): damned; *euph. for* bloody
blere: deceive, blear
blimy (sl.): blind me (a mild oath)
bloke (sl.): person, fellow
blooey (US sl.): awry, out of order
blotto (US sl.): drunk
blud, bluid (Nth dial.) blood
boen (impers. vb.): behoove, befit
bone orchard (US sl.): cemetary
bong, boung (sl.): purse
bonnie (Sc. dial.): fine, pretty
boot: profit
bot: *see* but
botte: boat
boung: *see* bong
bow' (Sc. dial.): bowl
bowse, booze (sl.): to drink (alcoholic beverages)
bowsing ken (sl.): inn
box = box tree
braith (Sc. dial.): breath
brass (US sl.): money
brass tacks (US sl.): essentials
braw (Sc. dial.): brave, fine
breechen (Dor. dial.): breaches
breed (Nth dial.): bread
breid (Sc. dial.): bread
breight (Nth dial.): bright
breke = break; divulge, reveal
brennen: burn
briah = brier
briers (sl.): trouble
brood = broad
brosten (dial.): broken
browt (dial.): brought
bube (sl.): pox, plague
buck (US sl.): dollar
buckaroo (US sl. < Sp. vaquero): cowboy
bu'd = bird
bu'n = burn
bush (US sl.): belonging to a small organisation or "bush league"
bust (sl.): to break in (for robbery); to smash
but: unless; without
bute (MScots): remedy, relief
bweile (Dor. dial.): boil
bwold (Dor. dial.): bold

byforn: before, in advance, beforehand
bynethen: beneath, lower than

C

caddlin' (dial.): quarrelsome
caef (dial.): calf
cair (MScots): care
cald, cauld (Sc. dial.): cold
call: in playing poker, to demand a show of cards
callant (Sc. dial.): young man
callyng upon: requirement, duty, need
canned (US sl.): drunk
cant(e): to speak
carriage: *punned with* courage *by Joyce*
cas, case: situation, condition, case
Castoms Ahses (Cock. dial.): Customs Houses
'cause (dial. and colloq.): because
cawnfiel' (US Sth): cornfield
ceawr (Nth dial.): cower
certes: certainly
chare (Sth dial.): care
chates (sl.): gallows
cheere: aspect, appearance, cheer
chile (US Sth): child
circumcision: *malapropism for* circumference
city slicker (US sl.): sly, clever person from the city
claith (Sc. dial.): cloth
clem (dial.): oppress, abuse, starve
click (sl.): robbery
clim (dial.): climb
clippen, clyppen: embrace
clog: wooden shoe
clooas, cloo'es = clothes
clos: enclosure
cly (sl.): take, grab, steal
cock (sl.): fellow
cockeyed (US sl.): drunk; crazy
cofe: *see* cove
coffin-nail (US sl.): cigarette
comyn: common
con: study, learn to know
concyensly: conscientiously, in accord with conscience
contagious: *malapropism* for contiguous
cool (sl.): look
cop (sl.): to grab, steal; a theft

corned (US sl.): drunk
coronach (Gael.): dirge
corry favell = curry favour
corsedness: wickedness, cursedness
cove (sl.): man, person
cowd (Nth dial.): cold
cowd, cowth: could, was able
cquen ⇌ quen (Sir Thomas Browne)
cram: stuff, supply abundantly
cramp ring (sl.): iron fetters
creke: wile, trick
croodle (Sc. dial.): cower
croun: head
cuffing (sl.): man, person
curdle, currel (Dor. dial.): curl
cur'us (dial.): curious
cus, cuss (dial.): curse
cut (sl.): say, command
cut: in baseball, to strike a ball so as to deflect it
cut a melon (US sl.): to divide profits
cuttle-boung (sl.): a knife used in cutting the strings of a purse
cuvating = coveting
cwein (Dor. dial.): coin
cwoat (Sth dial.): coat

D

D. A. (US): District Attorney
da' (dial.): that
dab (sl.): bad(ly)
dabheno (sl.): not bad
daill (MScots): dally, deal with
daill (MScots): dale, valley
dame (US sl.): woman
dampnation: *malapropism for* domination
dampnen: to damn
dander (dial.): anger
daownt (Cock. dial.): don't
darkmans (sl.): night time
davy (sl.): oath, affidavit
de (dial.): the
dead men (sl.): empty bottles
de (Nth dial.): die
deambulatories: covered places for walking
decussate: to design by means of the figure X, the Roman numeral for 10
dee (Nth dial.): die
deed, deeod (dial.): dead

Deelf: devil
deide (Sc. dial.): dead
dem (Gul. dial.): they, their, them, those
demen: to judge, deem
denominable: capable of being named
depairting (MScots): division, separation
depaynt: painted
depurit (MScots): cleansed, made pure
dern: secret; secrecy
devulgate: divulge, make known
dey (dial.): they; there
dhrunk (Ir. dial.): drunk
digladiation: fighting with swords; strife
dill: to reduce, dull
dillo (sl.): little
do (colloq.): activity, undertaking
doctryne: instruction
doll (US sl.): woman
doogheno (sl.): not good
doom: judgment; faculty of reason
dooty = duty
dotty (US sl.): silly
doubte: fear
doutless, dowtles = doubtless
doutous: doubtful
dradde: dreaded
drats (Sth dial.): shafts of a cart
drecching: delaying
drede, dreide: fear
dree (Sc. dial.): endure
dree (Sth dial.): three
drest: arranged, fixed, dressed
dror (dial. pron.): draw
drow (Dor. dial.): throw
dueties = duties
duh (Gul. dial.): do
dule (MScots): dole, grief
dunno (vulg. pron.): don't know
dup (sl.): open, do up
dwalt (Sc. dial.): dwelt
dwerch: dwarf
dwine (Sc. dial.): fade away

E

'e, 'ee (dial.): he
'e (Gul. dial.): his, it, its
eale (Sh.): *a doubtful word in* Haml.,
  variously emended; possibly evil
eaw (Nth dial.): owe
eawd (Nth dial.): old

eawr (Nth dial.): our
eawt (Nth dial.): out
'ee (dial. and colloq.): he; ye, you
ee, *pl.* een (dial.): eye
eek (arch.): also
een (Gul. dial.): in
eenjurin' (Gul. dial.): during
eik (MScots): also
'em (dial. and colloq.): them
emerant: emerald
emong = among
en (Sth dial.): him, it
eneuch (Sc. dial.): enough
enhabyten: to inhabit
enlumyne: illuminate
ennewed: renewed
enny = any
enow (arch.): enough
ensuren: make sure, secure
enterprise (vb.): undertake
entrete(n): to treat
env'y (dial.): envoy
eppylettes (dial.): epaulettes
er (colloq.): of; or
ey: island
eyr: air
eyren (dial.): eggs
ez = as

F

fa' (Sc. dial.): fall
face lace (US sl.): whiskers
faether (dial.): father
'f'aid (Gul. dial.): afraid
fait: deed
fallow (MScots): follow
familiarity: *malapropism for* familiar
fane = fain
farver (Cock. dial.): father
fate (Sth dial.): fault
fauld (MScots): fold, sheepfold
faute: fault
fay, fey: faith
fe: cattle
fegs (Sc. dial.): faith, indeed
felen: to perceive, experience
femme (US sl. < Fr.): woman
fence (sl.): receiver of stolen goods
fene = fain
feng (sl.): steal, grab

fergied (dial.): forgiven
feyne = feign
feyther (Nth dial.): father
fibbled up (US Sth dial.): ailing
fille: fell
fine: limit, boundary
fine(d): refine(d)
fing (Cock. dial.): thing
flabbergasted (US sl.): astounded
flash (sl.): show
flatfoot (US sl.): policeman
flat tire (US sl.): boring person
fleen: flee from
flimp (sl.): steal
flooey (US sl.): drunk
flude, fluide (Nth dial.): flood
fluxions: *malapropism for* fractions
fly ball: a ball batted in the air
foller (US dial.): follow
foin (sl.): pickpocket
fond: foolish
foo' (Sc. and Nth dial.): fool
foon: foes
foozle (US sl.): bungle
forbeare: forego
foren = foreign
fork (sl.): pickpocket
forland: land covered by tidal waters
forleten: abandon, leave
forrud (dial.): forward
forthi, forthy: therefore
forthwith, forthwyth: at once
foryeten: forgotten
ɪou' (Sc. dial.): full, drunk
fowk (Sc. dial.): folk
frae (Sc. dial.): from
fro (Nth dial.): from
frail (US sl.): woman
frazzle (US sl.): to exhaust, wear out
freet (Nth dial.): fret
fried (US sl.): drunk
frill (US sl.): woman
fro-sent: apostle
frountel: front part, façade
frowarde: disobedient, obstinate
frowards: misshapen forms
fructuous: fruitful
frydge (sl.): beg, ask, wander about
fu' (Nth dial.): full
fuddle (dial.): drinking-bout

fuh (US Sth): for
furder (dial.): further
furriner (dial.): foreigner
fus' (dial.): first
fush (Sc. dial.): fish
fust: see fus'
fyece (Nth dial.): face

G

gae (Sc. dial.): go
ga(n) (Nth dial.): to go; *3rd sg.* gas;
    perf. part. gane
gan: began
gan (sl.): mouth
gar (Sc. dial.): to do, cause, make
garth: yard, garden
geck (Sc. dial.): mock at
geezer (sl.): person
'gen (dial.): again
gent: noble, fine
genty (Sc. dial.): gentle, delicate
gert (dial.): great
gessen: guess
gestis: tales
gide: guide
gi'e (dial.): give
gif (Sc. dial.): if
giger (sl.): door
gillie (Sc. dial.): man-servant
gin, gi'en (Sc. dial.): if
girdle (Sc. dial.): griddle
girt (Sth dial.): great
git (dial. and colloq.): get
give out: announce, proclaim
glim (sl.): thief's dark lantern
godsib: gossip, companion
gois (MScots): goes
goteheard: goat-herd
goulis: gules; red colour used in heraldry
gowp (Sc. dial.): gape, stare foolishly
graith (Sc. dial.): prepare
grawin' (dial.): growing
green winckard (sl.): tattered vagabond
greet, greit (Sc. dial.): weep; weeping
gret (dial.): great
grette: greeted
groun' (dial.): ground
grue (Sc. dial.): shudder
grup (Sc. dial.): grip
gud, guid (Sc. dial.): good

gum shoe (US sl.): detective
guvner (colloq.): governor, sir
guy (sl.): person
gwain (Sth dial.): going
gwine (US Sth dial.): going
gwo (Nth dial.): go
gyaa'd'n (US Sth dial.): garden
gyde: guide
gyet (Nth dial.): gate
gyger (sl.): door

H

ha, hae (Sc. dial.): have
ha' (Sc. dial.): hall
haant (US dial.): haunt
haef (dial.): half
hafe (dial.): half
haif (MScots): have
haile (Nth dial.): health, success
haill (MScots): whole
hair (MScots): hoar, old, gray
hald, haud (Sc. dial.): hold
halfe: side, sake; half
halidome: sanctuary, holy object
hall (Cock. dial.): all
ham, hame (Nth dial.): home
han = haven: have
hap (dial.): to cover
happe: to happen, chance
haps (Dor. dial.): hasp
hard = heard
Harfricar (Cock. dial.): see Arfricar
harmans (sl.): stocks
harnet (dial.): hornet
haud (Sc. dial.): hold
hawe: hawthorn berry
hawn owl (US Sth): horn owl
heard = herd
heardly: with difficulty
heaue, heave (sl.): rob
heawse (Nth dial.): house
heddle: cord or wire used in sets to guide the warp threads in a loom
heedely: with heed, carefully
heern (US dial.): heard
hente: take
hes = his
heyff: hythe, an inlet or bay in a river
heythen: hence
hidge = hedge

him (Gul. dial.): he, his, it, him
hinfluence (Cock. dial.): influence
Hinglishmen (Cock. dial.): Englishmen
hinney (Sc. dial.): honey
hisself (dial.): himself
hizzy (Sc. dial.): hussy
hòd (Sc. dial.): hide
hollur (dial.): hollow
holt: forest, wooded hill
hoo (Nth dial.): she
hoose, hous (Nth dial.): house
hoosegow (US sl. < Sp. juzgado): gaol
hopen: expect
hopur: hopper
hoss (dial.): horse
hot squat (US sl.): electric chair
howgates: in what way
howd (Nth dial.): hold
huche: cliff
hundreder: centurion
hush money (US sl.): blackmail payment
huz (Cock. dial.): us

I

i': in
I wys: see ywis
ich (Sth dial.): I
ierke, jerk (sl.): whip, whipping
'igh (Cock. dial.): high
'Ighbury (Cock. dial.): Highbury
ilka (Sc. dial.): each, every
ilke: same
ill-daein' (Sc. dial.): ill doing
'im (dial. and colloq.): him
importable: unbearable
incompossibility: incompatibilit⁻
ine = inn
infortune: misfortune
ingle (Sc. dial.): fire, fire-place
ingrame: *malapropism for* ingrate, un-grateful
inkhorn(e): pertaining to the ink-well or study; artificial
inning: part of a baseball game during which one side has a turn at the bat
insisture: persistency, constancy
inst (in Dekker's poem): *error for* in't?
intricate: *malapropism for* intriguing
in-with: within
'it (dial.): hit

ither (Ir. dial.): other
ivery (dial.): every

J

jane (US sl.): woman
jenny (sl.): tool used for robbery
jest (dial.): just
jigger (sl.): door
jine (dial.): join
jis' (dial.): just
jou (dial.): do you, are you
jupartie: jeopardy

K

kaip (MScots): cape
kanurd (sl.): drunk
keeperin' job: job as keeper
keip (MScots): to keep, pay attention
    to; attention
ken (Sc. dial.): to know
ken (sl.): house
kest (dial.) = cast
ketch (dial.): cast
kick the bucket (US sl.): to die
kick up (colloq.): make or cause an out-
    break, quarrel, etc.
kid (sl.): to joke, jest
kin (dial.): can, be able
kirk (Sc. dial.): church
knawen (Nth dial.): know

L

lach (Sc. dial.): laugh
laconically: *malapropism for* symbolic-
    ally?
laesie: lazy
laft (dial.): left
lag (sl.): to serve a term in prison
lauhte: laughed
laird (Sc. dial.): lord
lang (Nth dial.): long
lap (sl.): butter-milk
las' (dial. and colloq.): last
lat (dial.): late
late: recently
lave (dial.): leave
lawk (Cock. dial.): like
leäme (Dor. dial.): lame
leäne (Dor. dial.): lane

leaper: leper
lear (dial.): empty
lẹẹf: dear
lẹẹf: leaf
leet (Nth dial.): alighted
leetla, leetle (dial.): little
lef' (dial. and colloq.): left
leir: learn
leiste: *see* list
leme: beam
lemman: lover
lest(e): *see* list
leten: leave, give up
let, lette: hinder, prevent
lettrure: written sources, texts
leuk (Nth dial.): look
lev (dial.): leave
leve(n): live
levere: preferably, rather
lewche (MScots): laughed
lief: dear, pleasing
lift (Sc. dial.): sky
lift the elbow (US sl.): take a drink
light (colloq.): alight, descend
lightmans (sl.): light time, day time
like: compare, liken
like (dial.): in a way, in a manner of
    speaking
linn (Sc. dial.): pool
lino (sl.): linoleum
list: to be pleasing; to please
live wire (US sl.): a vigorous person
loch (Sc. dial.): lake
lo'e (Sc. dial.): love
loife (dial.): life
loike (dial.): like
'long of (US dial.): with, along with
lothed: *pun by Joyce on* loathed *and*
    lost
lother: loather, more unwilling
low: flame
'low (dial.): allow, affirm
lowp (Sc. dial.): leap
lude (Sc. dial.): loved
lue: (Sc. dial.): love
lufe (Sc. dial.): love
lukkah (Gul. dial.): like, as
lung (dial.): long
luoad (Dor. dial.): load
lust (impers. vb.): be pleasing to

M

ma (dial.): my
maen (Sc. dial.): moan
main (dial.): great, great part
mair (Sc. dial.): more
mane (dial.): mean (vb.)
-mans (sl. suffix): one who, that which
marchaunt = merchant
marrit (MScots): marred
mas', maussuh (Gul. dial.): master
mastres: mistress
maun, mun, 'n (Nth dial.): may, must, ought to, have to, be sure to; *pret.* mot, mought, mid
maussuh: *see* mas'
mawn (sl.): beg for
M. C. (US slang): master of ceremonies
me (dial.): my
meäd (Dor. dial.): meadow
meäde (Dor. dial.): made
meäre (Dor. dial.): mare
meawse (Nth dial.): mouse
meawth (Nth dial.): mouth
medelen: to mix
mek (dial.): to make
mele: meal (of grain)
menstrale: minstrel
mervell, merveyll: marvel, wonder
michty (Sc. dial.): strong, mighty
mickle (Nth dial.): much, great
mid: *see* maun
mill (sl.): rob
min (dial.): men
misanthropy: *malapropism for* misanthropist *or* misogynist
misdeem (arch.): suppose mistakenly
mither (Sc. dial.): mother
mixen (dial.): dung-heap, midden
mo: more
moighty (dial.): mighty
mollycoddle (US sl.): to treast with excessive care; one who is so treated
monstryng: showing
moop (Sc. dial.): associate with
moot: must
mort, morte (sl.): girl, woman
—glimmering morte: a beggar woman who enters a house on the pretext of asking for a light
mossel (dial.): morsel, bit

mot, mought: *see* maun
mouse (US sl.): woman
mude (Sc. dial.): mood
mug (sl.): dupe, fool
mukkle (Gul. dial.): myrtle
mun: *see* maun
munch (dial.): meal
mune (Sc. dial.): moon
munelicht (Sc. dial.): moonlight
munse (dial.): months
murning = mourning
mwore (Dor. dial.): more
mycher (sl.): a petty thief; one who lurks
mysel' (dial.): myself

N

na (Nth dial.): no, not (also as enclitic)
nab (sl.): head
nadde = ne hadde
nae: *see* na
nane (Nth dial.): none
naow (Cock. dial.): no
nar, nary (dial.): never, not one
nark (sl.): inform to the police
nater (dial.): nature
'nation (sl. and dial.): damnation; damned, very
naught: *see* nought
neaw (Nth dial.): now
neawt (Nth dial.): nought
nebbuh (Gul. dial.): never
neden (impers. vb.): to need, require
neid (MScots): need
neight (Nth dial.): night
neir hand (MScots): almost
nemo (sl.): woman
nere: were not
neuk (Sc. dial.): nook
neun (Nth dial.): noon
neves (sl.): seven
nicht (Sc. dial.): night
nick (sl.): steal
Nick, old (colloq.): the devil
niggle (sl.): to have sexual relations
nillynge = not willing
nip (sl.): steal a purse
nipper (sl.): young boy
nit = net
no less'n (US dial.): unless

nobby (sl.): fine, stylish
nocht (Nth dial.): not
noo (Nth dial.): now
nor (dial.): than
note: benefit
nother < an other
nough: now
nought: not, not at all
nowt (dial.): nothing
nowther: neither
nunquam (sl.): a lazy errand boy
Nyankee (Gul. dial.): Yankee
nycetee: shyness, scrupulousness
nys: is not

O

'o (dial. and colloq.): of, on
o' (dial.): all
o'er-leaven (Sh.): leaven too much, corrupt
of (dial. and colloq.): have
Oi (dial.): I
ol', ole (dial): old
'ome (dial.): home
on (sl.): no, un-
on'y (dial.): only
'oo (Cock. dial.): who
oodles (US sl.): very much
oor (Nth dial.): our
oot (Sc. dial.): out
'op (dial.): hop
'ope (Cock. dial.): hope
or: before
orff (Cock. dial.): off
orthodoxy: *malapropism for* orthography
'ouse (dial.): house
outfielder: one who plays in the outer
  part of a baseball field
outthrow: throughout
'ow (dial.): how
owd (Nth dial.): old
ower (dial.): over
'owjer (dial.): how did you
'owsomever (dial.): however, howsoever

P

palys: paling, enclosure
pan (US sl.): criticise severely
pannam (sl.): bacon
paradoxes: *malapropism for* paradigms?

parcel-gilt: partly gilt; made of gold
parfit: perfect
passel (dial.): parcel
pat: fit, opportune
paunflettis: pamphlets
peerie (Sc. dial.): very small
pein (Sc. dial.): pain
pen (US sl.): penitentiary
perell: peril
persed: pierced
pety: pity.
phizz (sl.): face, physiognomy
pick (Nth dial.): pitch
pick over: to throw a shuttle
pickled (US sl.): drunk
pileris: pillars
pizen (dial.): poison
plastered (US sl.): drunk
plausive: pleasing, plausible; specious
playse: please
pleäce (Dor. dial.): place
pleuch (Sc. dial.): plow
plew (Nth dial.): plow
pleynes: plans
plump: blunt, bluntly
poo'ers (Sc. dial.): powers
pooty (dial.): pretty
poplars (sl.): pottage, porridge
pore (US Sth dial.): poor
positubble (Gul. dial.): strange, strangely
pot (colloq.): total number of bets on
  a game
pound the sidewalk (US sl.): walk
pow (Sc. dial.): poll, head
pozz (sl.): positively
preissis (MScots): presses
prevy: privy, having private information
progeny: *malapropism for* prodigy
prop (sl.): a tie-pin
prosperitee: good fortune
psaume, saume: psalm
puhzackly (Gul. dial.): exactly
puir (Sc. dial.): poor
pulsched: polished
'pun, 'puntop (Gul. dial.): upon, on top of
pupple (dial.): purple
purveiance: providence, foresight
purveyinge: foreseeing
put the finger on (US sl.): betray
pweint (Dor. dial.): point

Q

qu-: *see* wh-

quat (Sc. dial.): *pret. of* quit

quappe: quiver, shake

quier (sl.): wrong; having to do with crime

quier cuffing (sl.): magistrate

quier ken (sl.): gaol

queynte: clever, artful

quhair (Sc. dial.): where

quhat (Sc. dial.): what

quid (sl.): a pound sterling

quod: quoth, said

quod (sl.): prison; to be in prison

quoite (dial.): quite

R

raäte (Nth dial.): rate, tax

rackless (dial.): reckless

raik (vb.): range, stretch out

rain: *punned with* reign *by Joyce*

raise (MScots vb.): rose, arose (pret.)

rakel: rash, hasty

raw (MScots): row

rayly (dial.): really

reawnd (Nth dial.): round, around

reclinatories: couches, places for reclining; confessionals

recomfort: comfort

reden: to read, interpret

redoughted: redoubted, feared

reeb (sl.): beer

reed: part of a loom through which yarns are drawn

reede: saying, advice

reial: royal

reid (MScots): advice, advise

reid (Sc. dial.): red

reive (MScots): reave, rob, deprive of

reke: count, reckon

remeid (MScots): remedy

remeve(n): move

remytte: transfer, confide, remit

Renovated (US sl.): divorced

rep (sl.): reputation

reprehend: *malapropism for* apprehend

'rest (low colloq.): arrest

reticulated: made like a net

revest: clothed

rew: rue, have pity

rig (Sc. dial.): ridge, back

rile (US dial.): roil, disturb

rippit (US dial.): fuss

riz (dial.): risen

roas'en (Sc. dial.): roasted

roch: rock

roge = rogue

roger (sl.): a begging rogue

roif (MScots): quiet

Rome (sl.): fine, superior

roose (Sc. dial.): praise

rosere: rose bush or bower

rouch: rough

roun' (dial.): round

rubbin = robbin, a piece of yarn

rude (MScots): rood

rudge (Sth dial.): ridge, back

ruff = rough

ruffian, ruffin (sl.): devil; ruffian

ruffmans (sl.): hedge

ruff-peck (sl.): bread

run in (US sl.): fight

runnegate: vagabond

ruther (dial.): rather

rutter (sl.): one who provokes a quarrel

ryfe: current, rife

ryghtwysnes: righteousness

S

saaf'ly (Gul. dial.): softly

sadly: seriously

sae (Sc. dial.): so

sair (MScots): sore, sorely

sairin (Sc. dial.): sufficiency

sall (Sc. dial.): shall

sanna (Sc. dial.): shall not

sans (< Fr.): without

sapher: sapphire

sapyent (sl.): a quack

sarce (US dial.): impudence, sauciness

sarve = serve

sauh, saugh: *pret. of* to see

say (sl.): yes

sayne: to say

scare the pants off (US sl.): to terrify

scarnvully (Sth. dial.): scornfully

schaw, schew: show

scheip (MScots): sheep

schene: fine, beautiful

schtowde: cover, protect

sçowre = scour

screw (sl.): to obtain by sharp practice or extortion

sech (dial.): such

seed (dial.): *pret. of* to see

seely: poor, weak, simple

seke: sick

sel' (Nth dial.): self

selde: seldom, rare

sentence: opinion, view, sentence

serosity: watery substance

set (dial.): sat

sethen: afterwards

seyn: say

shaa'p = sharp

sha'sn't (dial.): shalt not

shells (sl.): money

shishuh (Gul. dial.): such a

shoon: shoes

shrowde = shroud, covering

shum (Gul. dial.): see him

sic, sik (Nth dial.): such

sich (dial.): such

sich(e): sigh

siller (Sc. dial.): silver

silven: self, selves

simony: *malapropism for* sums?

skaill (Sc. dial.): separate, disperse

skill: knowledge

skim (dial.): skimmed, finished

skirl (Nth dial.): shrill

skirt (US sl.): woman

slanguage (US sl.): language of slang

sle, sleen: slay

sleighte: art, artifice

slip = sleep

slow poke (US sl.): a slow-moving person

sloy (dial.): sly

slush fund (US sl.): money used for bribery

smoke (sl.): to spy out a victim

smug (sl.): arrest

socialite (US sl.): social light, socially eminent

sodeyne: sudden

son: soon

sone: sun

soon' (Sc. dial.): sound

sowd (Nth dial.): sold

speken, *pret.* spak: speak

spik = speak

spuds (dial.): potatoes

squeal (US sl.): inform to the police

squeege: squeeze

squires: squares

stairve: starve

stamps (sl.): legs

stan' (dial.): stand

stane (Sc. dial.): stone

'state: estate

steen (Sc. dial.): stone

steik = steak

stered: stirred

stern: star

sterte: started

stewed (US sl.): drunk

sthrong (Ir. dial.): strong

stick-in-the-mud (US sl.): conservative

stiff (US sl.): drunk; a corpse

stoo' (Nth dial.): stool

strath (Sc. dial.): valley

stretis: streets

stuckings (dial.): stockings

stude (Sc. dial.): stood

styane (Sc. dial.): stone

sud (Sc. dial.): should

suh (Gul. dial.): so; that

sukkle (Gul. dial.): sniffing sound

suld (Sc. dial.): should

summuch (Gul. dial.): so much

supercilious: *malapropism for* superficial

superstitious; *malapropism for* superfluous

swa (Nth dial.): so

swarth = swath

swich: such

swinck: toil, work

swounen: swoon, faint

syker: certain(ly)

syne (Sc. dial.): since, then

T

t' (Nth dial.): the

taäke (Nth dial.): take

tacquite = to acquit

taill (MScots): tale

take on (US colloq.): make a fus

Tamyse: Thames River

tane: taken

tater (US dial.): potato

t'awt (Gul. dial.): thought

'tell (dial.): until
teme = team
tendren: treat with love or pity
tent (MScots): heed, attention
tenty (Sc. dial.): careful
th', -tha, -ta: thou
tha (Dor. dial.): they
thaccompt: the account
thae (Sc. dial.): those
thaest (dial.): thou hast
that: so that
the: they
thea, thee (dial.): thou
theäse, theaze (Sth dial.): this
theaw (Nth dial.): thou
theek (Sc. dial.): thatch
theigh: though
their: there
then, thene, thenne: than
there as: where
thets (Cock. dial.): that's
they (dial.): there
they (dial.): those
thic, thilk, thuck (dial.): that, that same
this (Sc. dial.): these, those
thole (Sc. dial.): suffer, endure
thort (Sc. dial.): across
thous: thou is, for thou art
thrift: good fortune, welfare
throwe: short period of time
thrush: infection of the mouth
thuck: see thic
t'icket (dial.): thicket
tickle: unsteady
tidn' (dial.): it isn't
till (MScots): to, in order to
tine (Sc. dial.): lose
t'ing (dial.): thing
t'ink (dial.): think
tinnis (dial.): tennis
timper (dial.): temper
tit: nag
tocher (Sc. dial.): dowry
toff (sl.): fine person
toforn: before
toke (sl.): food, bread
tomato (US sl.): woman
tong, toung: tongue
toon (Nth dial.): town
top (sl.): pot

tone, tother: the one, the other
tother-me: other ones
tow'rt (dial.): toward, going on
tradoocer = traducer
trapes (colloq.): wander about
travell: labour, care
tride (Cock. dial.): trade
trine (sl.): to hang
trode (n.): tread
trosseno (sl.): bad sort
t'row (dial.): throw
trowen: believe, trust
truf (Sc. dial.): turf
tuke (MScots): took
tuim (Sc. dial.): empty
tumble to (colloq.): understand
tumbling cast (sl.): act of being hanged
tu'n = turn
tung: see tong
twa (Sc. dial.). two
twer (dial.): it were for it was
tweyne: two
twirdle (Dor. dial.): twirl
twoad (Sth dial.): toad

U

uh (Gul. dial.): I
'um (dial.): them; him
un (dial.): one
un (Sth dial.): him, it
unco (Sc. dial.): very, uncommon(ly)
'urry (dial.): hurry

V

vacabones: vagabonds
vacation: malapropism for vagabond?
vace (Sth dial.): face
vair (Sth dial.): fair
vamily (Sth dial.): family
vamoose (US sl. < Sp. vamos): get out!
vamous (Sth dial.): famous, fine
variaunce: variation, difference
varmer (Sth dial.): farmer
vartu (dial.): virtue
vault (Sth dial.): fault
vear (Sth dial.): fear
vell (Cock. dial.): well
vell (Sth dial.): fell
veller (Sth dial.): fellow
vellicate: convulse spasmotically

velt (Sth dial.): felt

verser (sl.): one who lures a prospective victim

vetch (Sth dial.): fetch

vew (Sth dial.): few

vine (Sth dial.): find

vine (Sth dial.): fine, well

vive (Sth dial.): five

vly (Sth dial.): fly

volk (Sth dial.): folk

vor (Sth dial.): for; vor ael: for all, although

vower (Sth dial.): four

vowted: vaulted

vrom (Sth dial.): from

vulgar tunge: the vernacular

vur (Dor. dial.): far

vust (Sth dial.): first

vu'zen (Dor. dial.): furze trees

vys: *see* a vys

W

wab (Sc. dial.): web

wad (Nth dial.): would

wae (Sc. dial.): woe

wah (dial.): war

wald (Sc. dial.): would

walk: in baseball, to give a base on balls to someone

wang: molar tooth

wapse (dial.): wasp

war: aware, on guard against

warld (Nth dial.): world

wasteful: full of wastes

wather (Ir. dial.): water

wax (arch.): increase

'way (colloq.): away

wean (Sc. dial.): child

weche = which

weed (sl.): to steal

weel (Sc. dial.): well

weetlesse: witless

weh = where

weither (Nth dial.): weather

weip (Sc. dial.): weep

w'en = when

wenen: think, suppose

wepen, *pret.* wep: weep

werken: to cause pain, to hurt

werry (Cock. dial.): very

weyve, weyver (dial.): weave, weaver

wha, whae (Sc. dial.): who

whaur (Sc. dial.): where

Wheeson: Whitsun

whoile (dial.): while

whop (Nth dial.): move or grasp quickly

wi', wie' (Sc. and Sth dial.): with

wick (dial.): quick, living

wid (MScots): wood

wide (sl.): clever, bright

w'ile = while

winnock (Sc. dial.): window

wiltow = wilt thou

win (sl.): penny, small coin

wirk (Nth dial.): work, do

wit: knowledge, skill

withoute: unless, without

wiz = whizz

woats (dial.): oats

woice (Gul. dial.): voice

wol(l), wolde: will, would

wonen, wonnen: dwell

wooden overcoat (US sl.): coffin

woozy (US sl.): dizzy, mentally defective

worchipfull: worthy of respect

wordle (Sth dial.): world

worth: become, befall

wot = what

wot, wotte: knows, knew

wotjer (vulg. pron.): what do you

wrawe: angry, hostile

wrewche: wretched(ness)

writhen: to twist, turn

wull (Sc. dial.): will

wunt (dial.): won't

wur (dial.): were, was

wuss (dial.): worse

wut (dial.): what

w'y = why

wyght: person, wight

wys (Cock. dial.): ways

wytynge: knowledge

Y

yale (Nth dial.): ale

yannup (sl.): *see* yenep

yarum (sl.): milk

yate: gate

y-drawe: drawn

ye: *orthog. for* the

ye: eye(s)
ye, yea: yes, indeed
yead (dial.): head
yeat (dial.): eat
yed: *see* yead
yeddy (Gul. dial.): heard
yeinder: yonder
yellocution (US sl.): elocution
yence (Nth dial.): once
yenep (sl.): penny
yenst < ayenst: against
yer (dial.): here
yers (dial.): here is
yeye (Gul. dial.): eye
yiven, yaf, yiven (yyven): to give
'ymn (dial.): hymn
yuh (Gul. dial.): here
ynt (Cock. dial.): ai'nt
yuckel (dial.): woodpecker
yuller (dial.): yellow, golden
ywis, ywys: certainly

Z

Zalisbury (Sth dial.): Salisbury
zart (Sth dial.): sort

zay (Sth dial.): say
zea (Sth dial.): sea
zeam (Sth dial.): seam
zee (Sth dial.): see
Zelande = Zeeland (Holland)
zeng (Sth dial.): *see* zing
zet (Sth dial.): sat
zewy (Dor. dial.): to sew
zight (Sth dial.): sight
ziliry (Sth dial.): salary
zim (Sth dial.): seem
zing, zeng (Sth dial.): sing; *pret.* zung
zit (Sth dial.): sit
zmartish (Sth dial.): smartly, sharply
zmell (Sth dial.): smell
zno (Sth dial.): indeed, you know
zo (Sth dial.): so
zooner (Sth dial.): sooner
zpoke (Sth dial.): spoken
zumbody (Sth dial.):somebody
zumhow (Sth dial.): somehow
zummat (Sth dial.): somewhat, something
zun (Sth dial.): sun
zung: *see* zing
zur (Sth dial.): sir

SPANISH EXPRESSIONS
from Appendix No 43

allá: went
casa: house
como no: why not? indeed yes
en la Plaza: in the Square
en una delegación: in a delegation
estaba: was
este: that one
hoy en la mañana: this morning
inglés: English
la comité del Concilio de los Sinempleados: the committee of the Council of Un-employed Workers
mi amigo: my friend
muncho *for* mucho: much
nada: nothing, not at all
no sabe hablar, el: he doesn't know how to talk

no fuí en el alley: I wasn't in the alley
nunca: never
oficina: office
pero en el callejón, no!: but in the alley— no!
poco questiones: a few questions
puede ser otra casa: it might be another house
pues: then
qué no?: isn't it so?
savvy (US sl. < Sp. saber): you know; do you know?
se llama Juan Dombraski: his name is Jan Dombrowski
sí: yes
tal vez: in that case; well then
yo: I

INDEX

Numbers refer to pages. For bibliographical information about books and articles,
consult the first foot-note entry under which each item appears.

Smith, Henry Lee, Jr.: see Trager, George

Smith, Sydney Goodsir 157. 262—64

soriasmus 81

South Africa 209, 211

Southern English dialects 17, 24, 26, 27, 48, 49, 54, 84, 101, 155, 157, 161, 163—68, 169, 267—71

Southworth, J. G., on Chaucer's final -e 8 n.7

Spanish loan words 77, 78, 140, 177, 178

Spanish in America 140, 177, 178, 277—78

Spargo, John: see Pedersen, Holger

Spectator, The 142

spelling pronunciation 81, 134, 139, 160

Spenser, Edmund 41, 50, 71, 106, 245—47

Spingarn, J. E., ed. *Critical Essays of the Seventeenth Century* 118

Spitzer, Leo, *Stilstudien* 228 n.49

Springer, Otto, "Probleme der Bedeutungslehre" 217 n.25

Stafford, Jean, *Boston Adventure* 230

Stafford, Lady, Correspondence 127 n.5

standard English 71, 72, 73, 84, 129, 134, 135, 150, 152, 155, 159, 162, 163, 164, 167, 170, 171, 172, 173, 174, 179, 229

— and American usage 175—205, 178, 179 n.4, 187, 191, 193, 196, 200—05

Starnes, DeWitt T., "Richard Huloet's *Abecedarium*" 107 n.20

— and Noyes, Gertrude, *The English Dictionary* 107 n.21, 137 n.16

statistical methods in linguistic studies 226, n.46

Steele, Richard 142, 148

Steinbeck, John 232

Stephanus, *Dictionnaire françoise-latin* 107

Stephens, James 169

— *Crock of Gold, The* 271—72

Stepney, *Spanish Schoolemaster* 107

Stern, Gustaf, *Meaning and Change of Meaning* 216 n.24

Stieber, Zdzisław, ed. *Z Dziejów Powstania Języków Narodowych* 179 n.5

stream of consciousness 232, 282—83

Street, A. G. "Art of Conversation" 267—69

stress: see accentuation

structuralist linguistics 218, 223—227

style 36, 56—61, 62, 75, 111—17, 117—21, 123, 124, 145—49, 152, 192—93, 228—33

— colloquial 58, 74, 102, 103, 113, 116, 117, 126, 138, 141, 148, 166—68, 193, 232

— curt 146

— extended 147, n.25

— formal 36—37, 61, 117—21, 145, 148

— impressionistic 230, 284—85

— levels of 36, 111, 149, 152—53, 229

stylistics, modern 228—33

subjective idealism 218

subjects omitted 33

subjunctive mood 54, 55, 105, 106, 143, 194

successive word order 113, 114

Suchodolska, Ewa 169 n.18, 171 n.21

suffixes 12, 47, 48, 49, 50, 52, 53, 63, 89, 92, 100, 101, 106, 128, 135—36, 142, 144, 151, 165, 166, 171, 193

Summersgill, Travis L., on Nashe and the Marprelate tracts 120 n.27

superlatives, double 53, 142

suprasegmental morphemes 34 n.25

Surrey, Henry Howard Earl of 64

Sweet, Henry, *History of English Sounds* 209 n.4

— *New English Grammar* 219 n.30

Sweeting, Elizabeth J., *Early Tudor Criticism* 66 n.5, 68 n.10

Swift, Jonathan 126, 137 n.15, 148, 152

synchronic descriptions of language 220, 221, 222

synchysis 78

syncope of vowels 50, 126, 135, 139

Synge, J. M. 169, 171, 172, 173, 174

synonyms 61, 138 n.17

syntax, early ME 50—56

— late ME 95, 96

— ModE 117, 141—45, 167, 173, 218—27

synthetic language 229